Alain Locke, in his famous 1925 anthology *The New Negro*, declared that "the pulse of the Negro world has begun to beat in Harlem." Often called the father of the Harlem Renaissance, Locke had his finger directly on that pulse, promoting, influencing, and sparring with such figures as Langston Hughes, Zora Neale Hurston, Jacob Lawrence, Richmond Barthé, William Grant Still, Booker T. Washington, W. E. B. Du Bois, Ralph Bunche, and John Dewey. The long-awaited first biography of this extraordinarily gifted philosopher and writer, *Alain L. Locke* narrates the untold story of his profound impact on twentieth-century America's cultural and intellectual life.

Leonard Harris and Charles Molesworth trace this story through Locke's Philadelphia upbringing, his undergraduate years at Harvard—where William James helped spark his influential engagement with pragmatism—and his tenure as the first African American Rhodes Scholar. The heart of their narrative illuminates Locke's heady years in 1920s New York City and his forty-year career at Howard University, where he helped spearhead the adult education movement of the 1930s and wrote on topics ranging from the philosophy of value to the theory of democracy.

continued on back flap

Alain L. Locke

Aaron Douglas, Locke's personal bookplate, circa 1925.

Alain L. Locke

BIOGRAPHY OF A PHILOSOPHER

Leonard Harris *&* Charles Molesworth

The University of Chicago Press   CHICAGO *&* LONDON

LEONARD HARRIS is professor of philosophy at
Purdue University.

CHARLES MOLESWORTH is professor of English at Queens
College, City University of New York.

The University of Chicago Press, Chicago 60637
The University of Chicago Press, Ltd., London
© 2008 by Leonard Harris and Charles Molesworth
All rights reserved. Published 2008
Printed in the United States of America

17 16 15 14 13 12 11 10 09   2 3 4 5

ISBN-13: 978-0-226-31776-2 (cloth)
ISBN-10: 0-226-31776-5 (cloth)

Library of Congress Cataloging-in-Publication Data

Harris, Leonard, 1948–
     Alain L. Locke : bibliography of a philosopher / Leonard
Harris and Charles Molesworth.
          p.   cm.
     Includes bibliographical references and index.
     ISBN-13: 978-0-226-31776-2 (cloth : alk. paper)
     ISBN-10: 0-226-31776-5 (cloth : alk. paper)
     1. Locke, Alain LeRoy, 1886–1954. 2. African American
philosophers—Biography. 3. African American intellectuals—
Biography. I. Molesworth, Charles, 1941– II. Title.
E185.97.L79H37 2009
191—dc22

                                        2008028664

♾ The paper used in this publication meets the minimum
requirements of the American National Standard for Information
Sciences—Permanence of Paper for Printed Library Materials,
ANSI Z39.48-1992.

In memory of

JAMILA R. HARRIS-GRANT

CONTENTS

ILLUSTRATIONS

ACKNOWLEDGMENTS

Charles Molesworth wishes to thank several people and institutions, especially the American Academy in Berlin, where much of the narrative was written. The generosity of the academy's director, Gary Smith, along with the attentive Marie Unger and her courteous staff, made such work exceptionally pleasurable and efficient. Special gratitude must go to Yolande Korb, whose ability to find American material in German libraries is breathtaking. While at the academy, I was helped by Claudia Koontz, and also by Paul Rahe, who offered sound advice and an important suggestion about Locke's Rhodes Fellowship. For *The Berlin Journal*, published by the academy, editor Miranda Robbins and her assistant Deirdre Foley-Mendelssohn accepted and skillfully edited my essay on Locke's role in the production of *Sahdji*. Also in Berlin, Christa Schwartz met with me and later provided important material; Rosanna Warren introduced me to Marc-Oliver Schach, a most admirable translator. Sabine Broeck and Paola Boi kindly published an early article of mine on Locke, which was first presented at a symposium sponsored by the Conference on African American Research (CAAR) in Sardinia in 2001.

Also, I enjoyed two PSC/CUNY grants, the first in 1994 when beginning my research at the Moorland-Spingarn, and then several years later when I made two more extended visits there. Esme Bhan and Helen Rutt were exceptionally generous in the first instance, and later Joellen El Bashir continued in the same vein. In 1990 several participants in my NEH Summer Seminar for College Teachers urged me to explore the Harlem Renaissance in the context of modernist poetry. A number of friends—especially Fred Kaplan, Jonathan Buchsbaum, Barbara Bowen, and Tony O'Brien—gave helpful support and advice over a good number of years. My wife Carol was remarkably and indispensably steady throughout a decade and a half of various situations, now happily concluded.

Leonard Harris acknowledges the steadfast support received from the Department of Philosophy at Howard University. The department has supported my research on Locke's philosophy and life ever since 1982, when I first entered the second-floor offices of the department in Alain Locke Hall. A special thanks goes to Segun Gbadegesin and Patrick Goodin for hosting my lectures over the years at the Alain Locke Symposiums, allowing me to receive feedback on my research, publications, and analysis of Locke's ideas; and thanks to Denise Spriggs, Administrative Secretary, for digging through the departments files year after year to help me uncover Locke's history. The meetings of the Society for the Study of Africana Philosophy, hosted by Al Prettyman in his New York apartment for a quarter of a century, were occasions for lively debates on the merits of Locke's philosophy that have enriched my appreciation of Locke's genius. I am indebted to the Philosophy Born of Struggle Association, especially Everet Green, Zay Green, and James Williams for supporting lectures and discussions of Locke's philosophy since the association's first conference 1993.

As a fellow of the Robert R. Moton Center for Independent Study in Philadelphia, I was free to work on the history of African American philosophers, such as William T. Fontaine, while also researching Locke's place in the history of African American philosophy. The Oxford Centre for African Studies summer institute in 1990 allowed me to walk in Locke's footsteps at Oxford and conduct research. The Departments of Philosophy at the University of Addis Ababa, Ethiopia, and Makerere University, Uganda, in 1998 and 1999 as a Fulbright Scholar provided me with a wonderful experience where, lecturing on Locke's philosophy of cosmopolitanism, I was challenged to show its relevance for contemporary African societies. I am appreciative of the W. E. B. Du Bois Center for African American Studies at Harvard for allowing me to be a nonresident fellow for the year of 2001–2002 and thereby gain access to Harvard's library. And thanks to the Yale University Beinecke Rare Book and Manuscript Library for helping me uncover William Grant Still's original score with his revisions of *Sahdji* as well as Locke's account of *Sahdji's* history.

The welcome I received from the Department of Philosophy, University of South Africa in 2005 and 2006, to research the life of Pixley Seme and present talks on my research is deeply appreciated. The American offices of the Rhodes Trust, particularly the African American Rhodes Scholars' committee, for their networking me with scholars they employed to research Locke during his years in Oxford, will be forever cherished.

Joellen ElBashir, Esme Bhan, and Ida Jones of the Moorland-Spingarn Research Center have been pillars upon whose shoulders I have stood for years. I am especially indebted to Joellen for her encouragement. Darryl Scriven, Jacoby Carter, and Eze Chielozona have provided invaluable discussions and interpretations of Locke's conception of value. Jamila Grant, Jarrard Harris, and Leonard N. Harris, my children, provided personal encouragement and steadfast belief that I could finish a project long in the making.

Both authors contributed to the writing, archival research, and interpretation contained in the biography. Leonard Harris concentrated on the philosophy and its intersection with Locke's literary concerns. Charles Molesworth composed the bulk of the narrative.

ABBREVIATIONS

ALPHU   Papers of Alain Leroy Locke, Moorland-Spingarn Research Center, Howard University.
Quotations from correspondence and manuscripts (of published and unpublished items) in the Locke archive are given by reference to series, box, and folder numbers; e.g. ALPHU 164-32/15.

PAL   *The Philosophy of Alain Locke.* Edited by Leonard Harris. Philadelphia: Temple University Press, 1989.

NMNA   *The Negro and His Music* and *Negro Art: Past and Present.* New York: Arno Press and the New York Times, 1969.

NN   *The New Negro: Voices of the Harlem Renaissance.* Edited by Alain Locke, introduction by Arnold Rampersad. New York: Atheneum, 1962.

CTAL   *The Critical Temper of Alain Locke: Collection of His Writings on Art and Culture.* Edited by Jeffrey Stewart. New York: Garland Publishing, 1963.

RCIR   *Race Contacts and Interracial Relations.* Edited by Jeffrey Stewart. Washington, D.C.: Howard University Press, 1992.

In 1948, near the end of his teaching career—and near the end of his life—Alain Locke was asked to teach at the New School in New York City. Given virtual carte blanche, Locke offered three courses directly connected to his life's work: "The Philosophy of Value," "Race Relations," and "The Philosophy of Aesthetic Experience." Virtually everything Locke had written revolved around these three subjects, which together form a thread connecting the activities and accomplishments that made Locke the most influential African American intellectual born between W. E. B. Du Bois and Martin Luther King Jr.

Locke's accomplishments were numerous: he was the first African American to win a Rhodes Scholarship to Oxford (where he wrote on the philosophy of value), he was a leader in the New Negro movement, and he produced a formative commentary on African American literature and the arts. He championed African art as a source of aesthetic inspiration, and his philosophical papers on cultural pluralism, democracy, and value theory influenced readers in diverse fields. He offered personal advice and support to dozens of writers, painters, singers, and others with artistic gifts and ambitions. In addition, he taught for four decades at Howard University in Washington, D.C., where he headed the philosophy department, founded the literary magazine and the theater company, and gathered the collection of African art that forms the core of the university's holding in this field.

The three subjects of race, culture, and value are the organizing principles of Locke's intellectual life. The unity these three subjects offer is best pursued by thinking of them less as academic courses—though Locke understood the need to turn them into such—and more as the special combination of his burdens and possibilities. They were what his own education and his role as an educator had taught him mattered most.

Locke once said, with a wry twist on biblical idiom, that "verily paradox has followed me all my days." A man of considerable intellectual energy, he was educated to a level experienced by only the smallest fraction of his generation. As far as the "talented tenth" was concerned, Locke was exponentially more elite and educated. Becoming educated, to someone born before the full flowering of the modern liberal welfare state, was not something Locke felt he automatically had a right to, but it was something he owed himself, and something that made him owe others. Locke saw education as both private and a set of laws unto itself—in other words, a possibility that had the weight of a privilege.

But he also saw education as a potential burden, because, unless put to proper use, it separated the individual from the group. Education entailed a self-consciousness that was bound up with its tangle of obligations, and that self-consciousness stood in the way of solidarity with others.

Locke was a special student of the philosophy of value, or value theory as it was often called in his time. Since he lived at a time when increasing numbers of people felt it more and more imperative to accept the relativity of their knowledge and their values, a strong emphasis on values might seem a throwback to a more rigid culture. Locke, however, did not see values as a covert form of discipline, though he personally had a propensity for authoritative judgments. He spent a great deal of time making judgments and expressing his feelings, and he clearly wanted them to be correct. As a critic of art and as a spokesperson on racial matters he was very often convinced he was right. This attitude was sometimes seen by his friends and opponents as elitist or simply snobbish. He earned for himself the nickname "The Proust of Lenox Avenue" not only for his fastidious sense of style and dress, and very likely for his sexual orientation, but also because many felt there was a refined egotism at the heart of his endeavors.[1]

However, Locke's main philosophical commitment, and the core of his project as an educator, was the belief that everyone's value system had to be subject to scrutiny and critical judgment. He placed values at the heart of his philosophical work as part of his effort to classify and analyze them. For himself, Locke's central values derived in large measure from his being an African American: his sense of justice, and his commitment to full social and economic equality for all African Americans. This fullness could only be achieved in and through an equitable distribution of rights and opportunities for all Americans and eventually all people everywhere. In a sense, Locke took a simple but difficult stance toward the issue of racism: he felt America should deliver on what it promised, and until it did so for everyone, the value of its gifts for any one of its citizens was not fully redeemed. Fighting the insidious ugliness of racial supremacy in the first half of the twentieth century meant Locke often shifted course, from attacking imperialism to resorting to electoral politics, from reconsidering the problems of leadership to imagining new ways to educate large numbers of people. In all this he was like many others joined together in the same struggle. Like most of the educated African Americans of his time, Locke made common cause with others of his race, though, also like others, his allegiances changed depending on his judgment of the historical moment.

Locke was constantly engaged with artistic and cultural activity. By the end of the nineteenth century the main value of art was justified by analogy with the logical or natural processes of individuation. Art was good insofar as it made clear that the singular artist was expressing something at once universal and individual, and insofar as it helped the reader (or listener or observer) understand that individuating expression was a symbolic invitation to, and justification of, the reader's freedom. The esthetic experience, however, is always in some ways communal and shared, and so creates its force as both an individual expression and a group record or testament. Art addressed these group identities and experiences even if it sometimes looked as if it might best flourish by ignoring group concerns and expressing only individual views. Locke was at the center of the main artistic controversies that occupied African Americans in the modern period. In an important sense a modernist, he thought and argued about such modernist issues as the relation between creativity and criticism, and the relation between tradition and the individual talent, as T. S. Eliot's famous essay phrased it. (Locke wrote on this latter subject while a student at Harvard, shortly before Eliot started his education there.) He appreciated the paradox in modern thought that conjoined and disjoined the values of singular genius and communal wisdom.

Locke more recently has become best known as one of the founders of what we today know as multiculturalism, though his phrase for it was cultural pluralism. Cultural pluralism—and to use one of Locke's more technical terms for it, intercultural reciprocity—served as the common ground for his three concerns of race relations, value theory, and esthetic experience. The story of Locke's life shows that cultural pluralism is the governing idea behind all that Locke produced. The life itself has genuine drama and interest, we believe, from his well-known academic and literary accomplishments to lesser known "worldly" events, such as his attending the opening of King Tut's tomb, his sociological writings on Harlem in 1935, or his special meeting with Ras Tafari. But what his life can show us, or make generally available as exemplifying various burdens and possibilities, can best be seen in his writings—or to put it another way, his meaning is in the complex intersections of his life and his work. It is in those intersections where paradox thrives, and where we hope that what follows can be most clarifying.

CHAPTER ONE

The Lockes of Philadelphia

Alain Leroy Locke was born in Philadelphia on September 3, 1885. His parents had not decided upon a name beforehand. Pliny Locke, his father, wanted any name but Pliny. He had lived with this Roman distinction, and perhaps he felt enough was enough. Mary Hawkins Locke, the boy's mother, could not decide at first, though she clearly wanted something impressive. Fill out the birth certificate with "Arthur" or "any old thing," she told the doctor. Dr. Smedley, who had just delivered the child, felt that he could not name such a nice child "Roy," as that was the name of his horse. So, for the time being it was "Arthur Locke" who entered the world. But within days, after he was officially named, Mary Locke would provide a different name for use by the family. She had a notion that her first child's initials should spell something. So she picked "Allen" and "Leroy" in order to end with the acronym "ALL." That his middle name meant "the king" and his initials spelt out a synonym for the universal probably made his limitlessly doting parents very happy. He made himself happier still when some years later he changed "Allan" to "Alain," but by then he had already begun to develop his own sense of style.[1]

Pliny Locke, a man of some note, displayed accomplishments that were the result of hard work and native talent. His family background connected him to Liberia, the colony founded in 1822 by black Americans to serve as the home for freed slaves. Acting as missionaries there, Pliny's parents participated in the training and education of the indigenous black population before the country's independence in 1847.

Pliny's father, Ishmael Locke (1814–52), a freeborn black person, began teaching in 1843 at the first African American school in Salem, New Jersey, organized by the Coloured School Association of Friends. Family tradition had it that he had attended Cambridge University, although there is no evidence of his matriculation. After starting his career as a teacher in Salem, and after a brief stay in England, he went to Liberia, where he spent four years setting up schools for the native population. Upon his return to America he became the head of a school in Rhode Island and later assumed the job of principal at the Institute for Colored Youth in Philadelphia, which was also supported by the Society of Friends. Among its well-known graduates were Henry Ossawa Tanner, perhaps the finest black painter of his day, and Richard T. Greener, who would be the first black admitted to Harvard. It was when Ishmael Locke was in Africa that he met his future wife, Mathilda Saunders, herself involved in increasing educational opportunities for Africans. Mathilda Saunders, who was born in Liberia of a black mother and a white father of German origin, was fair skinned, with blue-grey eyes and straight brown hair. In a genealogy he would draw up later, Locke also noted that his paternal grandmother was "uneducated but not illiterate." This same genealogy listed Ishmael's features as "broad but very aquiline" and described Pliny as having the same. Ishmael died in 1852.[2]

Committed from an early age to the advantages of education, Pliny graduated from the Institute for Colored Youth in Philadelphia and intended to teach mathematics. However, he also volunteered to teach in a Reconstruction school in North Carolina, and after returning from that job, decided to enter Howard University Law School, from which he graduated in 1874 at the top of his class. There he studied with the man after whom the university was named, General Oliver O. Howard, and for a time acted as his private secretary. His law school graduation day speech was on "Equity," and in it he discussed the millennial possibility of a reign of justice and reason, themes that he would pass down to his son. Because he refused to give up smoking, Pliny's services were no longer accepted by General Howard, and furthermore he was told by his fiancée that she would not accept living in Washington, D.C. Locke later joked that if it were not for these two circumstances, he would have been born on the Howard campus. Pliny joined the civil service in 1876, and taught school for a few years, eventually becoming principal of a school in Chester, Pennsylvania. As a result of a competitive examination in 1883, he was appointed by the Republican administration as a supervisor in the Philadelphia Post Office at an annual salary of six hundred dollars. He was the first black to hold the position. In this same year he finally married Mary Hawkins, after a lengthy engagement. He diligently worked his way up to inspector in the Civil Service Commission, but by 1890 he was again a schoolteacher. His career, oscillating as it did between a restricted range of civil service jobs and the "profession" of public schoolteacher, epitomizes the economic and social opportunities available to African Americans in this relatively liberal Northern city.[3]

On his maternal side, Locke also descended from educators. His maternal grandmother, Sarah Shorter Hawkins, was, like Ishmael Locke, involved in setting up schools in Liberia. Her daughter, Mary Hawkins, a dedicated teacher, greatly valued the teacherly riches of both the paternal and maternal lineages that she and her son unceasingly took pride in, and she stressed that with such riches came the need for constant education and self-betterment. This esteem for education permeated the atmosphere in the Lockes' Philadelphia home. In addition to their vocation as teachers, Locke's parents took pride in being freeborn blacks as opposed to freed slaves. This pride was transmitted to their son as a sense of privilege, or at least a feeling that race and skin color were ultimately irrelevant, or should be, when set against one's ability to learn and teach any manner of subject. Mary Hawkins Locke exercised a pious attitude toward the biblical truths she lived by, but she also would become devoted to the work of Felix Adler and his Ethical Culture movement, which virtually made a religion of education. Her son would turn the religious commitment into a life's work.[4]

Locke's ethical sense and his notions of personal propriety were also shaped by the city into which he was born. Philadelphia was in 1900 one of the world's ten most populous cities, with a population of approximately 1.3 million people; the 1890 census recorded 39,371 blacks, or about 6 percent of the total. The city was known as a center not only of Unionist sentiment but also of Abolitionist activity. As such, it offered its black population relatively better treatment that many other cities in the northeast. But all was not peaceful; there had been antiblack rioting in 1865, and a resultant Jim Crow law forbade blacks to ride in horsecars, though this ordinance was overturned in the 1870s. When W. E. B. Du Bois prepared his impressive and standard-setting study of the city, *The Philadelphia Negro,* in 1896–97, he used statistical sociology in a pathbreaking way. Working out of house-to-house canvasses, Du Bois left a detailed picture of life in the Seventh Ward. There were poverty and repression, especially built on the restricted access to jobs that applied to almost all Negroes, even those who had labored to educate themselves. Du Bois also briefly recorded the history of the Institute for Colored Youth, where Pliny Locke studied; it was founded in 1832 with a bequest from a West Indian ex-slaveholder. Its stated purpose was to instruct "the descendants of the African race in school learning . . . in order to prepare, fit and qualify them to act as teachers." Though Du Bois's tables show that this school and others like it produced graduates who worked in a variety of professions, most of them were teachers, and so their economic prospects were limited, even as their sense of social duty was reaffirmed. Du Bois also tartly observed that Philadelphia had been plagued by "the slow advance, if not 'actual retrogression,' of the Negro since the Civil War."[5]

Pliny almost certainly met his wife in Philadelphia, where Mary Hawkins was working as a teacher. She was born in 1853, a "member of an old Philadelphia family," as her obituary in the *Crisis* put it seventy years later. She spent thirty-six years in the schools of Camden, New Jersey (just across the river from Philadelphia) and Camden County in the same state. For a brief while, according to a card printed with her maiden name, she worked as a hairdresser at an "emporium" in Cape May, New Jersey. Before that, she too had graduated from the Institute for Colored Youth in Philadelphia, and she may have met her future husband while a student there. By 1880 she had earned a teaching certificate in Delaware County, Pennsylvania, and taught the first four grades at the Catto School in Camden for several years beginning in 1883. She took two years off after she started teaching, when she bore her only child, for she lists herself as a housekeeper for the years 1884–86. She received her teacher's certificate in New Jersey in 1901, and by 1904 she had transferred to the Mt. Vernon Grammar School in Camden, where she taught the first grade boys' class. Her entire life was devoted to education, and she took justifiable pride in the intellectual growth she induced in others, but in no instance more than in that of her talented son. The Institute for Colored Youth thought to send her a congratulatory letter when her son won a Rhodes Scholarship in 1907; it was written on a letterhead that listed both John Dewey and Booker T. Washington as members of the "Advisory Educational Committee." She finally retired from teaching in 1915.[6]

This dedication to education of the highest possible order was something that both of Locke's parents not only urged but embodied to the full. Pliny Locke knew mathematics and Latin, and he was also trained in classical oratory, at least to the extent that this formed the model of written composition in the late nineteenth century. Skill at oratorical exposition was fully in evidence in his long essay on the twentieth anniversary celebration of the Emancipation Proclamation, which appeared in a newspaper, presumably in 1883. A yellowed, undated copy, pasted to a piece of stiff paper, was apparently preserved by either Pliny or Mary and kept by their son until the end of his life. In many ways it sounds the themes of Locke's concerns as a leader of his

FIG. 1.1. Mary Hawkins Locke. Always a model of decorum, she taught school for most of her life and traveled with Locke to Europe in the years just after his stay in Oxford. Moorland-Spingarn Research Center.

FIG. 1.2. Pliny Locke. This is dated on the reverse, September 10, 1875, a decade before Locke's birth. Moorland-Spingarn Research Center.

race, and even conveys some of the tone, and range of references, that Locke was to use many years later in discussing the traditions of African American history and culture. Ancestry was animated by language and thought.[7]

The essay begins by talking quite bluntly about slavery, choosing not to gloss over or sidestep the brutality of this degrading system. Pliny rehearses the history of Negroes up to the Emancipation Proclamation, talks about Frederick Douglass and other figures, and then moves on to the Reconstruction era, while also mentioning such "extraterritorial" events as the Haitian revolution and the founding of Liberia. He acknowledges the role of the Republican Party, but in a significant turn also says that on this occasion politics should be set aside, a possible reference to the ending of Reconstruction and the eventual diminution of the Negroes' reliance on the Republicans. The overall structure of the argument is strengthened by its historical framework and clarity of presentation. But the tone of the "oration" might best be conveyed by this sentence:

> For years we have furnished the muscle, let us now add to it brains, and we shall soon assume among the nations of the earth that rank and station to which we are entitled. (ALPHU 164-5/28)

The first person plural pronoun here reverberates with a striking ambiguity, since it could be read as referring either to African Americans or to all citizens of the Republic. Separatism based on nationalist sentiment did not arise strongly until later, with Marcus Garvey and others. Yet the "we" of the first half of the sentence ostensibly means only those to whom the Proclamation applied; if that "we" is extended consistently through the sentence, then Pliny is suggesting something like nationhood for African Americans. This suggestion, however, remains undeveloped throughout the rest of the oration, which remains fairly traditional in its invocation of American patriotism. But such ambiguity will echo in Locke's own writing about the place of African Americans in the "larger" national identity of America.

Contemporary records of Locke's earliest years are very scarce, almost nonexistent. Documents of his school days exist for his high school years, but otherwise the only glimpses are erratic, and some of them come from his later reminiscences. One particularly intriguing example is in an undated letter he wrote to his mother while he was at Oxford, presumably in 1909. As part of his gentlemanly image in those days, Locke had taken up riding, an activity he pursued with considerable gusto despite having a heart condition brought on by rheumatic fever at an early age. He was returning to the stable one day and went to see the groom to ask him to repair a stirrup. As he did, there flashed into his mind an early scene from his Philadelphia childhood; he was walking along Fifth Street and a man—or as he put it "some body or other"—insulted him by asking him to hold a horse's head. Obviously Locke did not appreciate being treated like a stable boy, and, even though he had "quite forgotten the incident," it "came up so vividly and funnily" years later and three thousand miles away. Locke later was known by his contemporaries as someone who did not suffer fools gladly, but he was even more unwilling to suffer condescension from anyone.[8]

Another early reminiscence involves a visit to the Apprentices' Library at Fifth and Arch Streets in Philadelphia to do genealogical research. This may have been for a school project, or it may have been an exercise of family pride—an exploration of the earlier days of Philadelphia's educated black community. He remembered the activity fondly, and the resultant sense of ancestral history would always play a part in his sense of racial justice and respect. Obviously he was applying to the group's collective sense of worth the lessons he had learned for and about himself as an individual. He supplemented this memory with a 1927 essay about his home town, called "Hail Philadelphia." It contains a resonant detail: he was especially conscious of the portraits of black predecessors, many of them freeborn blacks, who looked down on him from the walls of the library. Years later, writing about himself in the third person, he told a friend: "Even when he couldn't recognize anything, each day he was taken out of the Negro slums into Rittenhouse Square in order that he might grow up a pure little gentleman." What later developed into a strong sense of elitism was for Locke firmly rooted in his family pride.[9]

Locke related another childhood memory to his mother in the spring of 1906, when he was twenty. According to him, he always had a very good sense of people and could estimate their reliability with great accuracy. This skill he remembers having become aware of even by the time of his fifteenth birthday. It was one of the things that contributed to his self-confidence, which his mother often had to counsel him to control. He recalled being reassured when he was able to figure out a certain individual:

> Whenever I'm not quite sure that I can understand human nature, I recall the like and grow conceited again—which for all that it is my own eyes—but I soon get myself back on my pedestal in my little niche and feel at home again. (ALPHU 164-51/14)

More than a bit of humorous self-deprecation is here, but also considerable pride, as he rather peremptorily joins his ancestors in the estheticized frame of an elevated niche. Locke would often act as mediator between various of his friends, and he later took pains to record how he had been completely aware of various machinations on the part of his opponents. He could admit readily to being dismayed by people's behavior, but never surprised by it.

The elevated status of the pampered only child would add immeasurably to Locke's self-confidence, an attribute reflected often in his relations with others throughout his adult life.

Locke's self-awareness is one of his most striking features. As far as family and hometown reminiscences go, however, Locke did not indulge in them publicly very often; an exception is the autobiographical portraits he wrote for the Harvard Class reports (which do not reach back into his childhood) and the "author's note" he submitted to various publications. These offer brief glimpses into general attitudes more than specific incidents. For example, in one self-description that appeared in 1942, he writes of how he was born to "native Philadelphians and schoolteachers; and thus into smug gentility." In the same brief essay, he says that "a professional career was mandatory, all the more so because of the frantic respectability of the free, educated Negro tradition, their bulwark against proscription and prejudice." This sense of defensiveness woven into self-respect and pride, even if it sometimes took on a "frantic" cast, was evident in the letters between Locke and his mother that began when he went away to college.[10]

One incident, though it occurred when Locke was already in his twenties, reveals this "frantic respectability." A black newspaper in Camden ran a gossip column featuring very local items about its readers. Mary Locke evidently attended some function, dressed more smartly than the norm. The newspaper reported this, describing her dress in detail. She was upset by the notoriety she felt attached to such public notice and mentioned the incident to her son. Locke responded with a rather surprising level of measured fury. Not only did he resort to crude epithets in describing the editor to his mother, he wrote a letter to the newspaper that was stern to the point of threatening. "I meant to head off his nigger tendency of talking back in his columns," he boasted, attempting to find recompense for his mother's wounded pride. Respectability for Locke meant knowing when not to claim too much or call undue attention to one's public identity, but also to know when social barriers were breached.[11]

Although his feelings about many things, not least of all his family background, ran deep, the claims of respectability often led Locke to be self-protective, with the result that many saw him as remote, cold, and unfeeling. Nonetheless, in the late 1920s he began making notes for an autobiography, which he mentioned to Charlotte Osgood Mason, his patron and confidante. (Since public display was always a vexed issue for Locke, we can only speculate on why he did not finish this project.) As the notes for the autobiography are undated, and often written on similar note cards, it is hard to place them in terms of Locke's thinking, except to say that he apparently thought about the project at some length.

In addition to these notes there is an autobiographical sketch that sheds considerable light on Locke's childhood. A little over two pages long, typed double-spaced and undated, the sketch reads in part like a psychoanalytic session, focusing on the family circle. Here Locke clearly analyzed the affective patterns and telling incidents that shaped his later psychological development.[12] The sketch begins with a paragraph headed "Father." He mentions that he, Locke, was born "six years after a relatively late marriage," and that his parents had been "engaged for some sixteen years before marriage." (Locke's recollections may be faulty: his parents married two years before his birth, and, if the sixteen-year engagement is true, they would have had to become engaged when they were fifteen and students at the Institute of Colored Youth.) The parents had agreed that, if their first child were a male, they would have only one. All this contributed to his being "idolized" by both parents. Indeed, "early childhood life was unusually close with my father, who changed his position from day to night shift in the post-office to be able to take care of me":

> This included bathing and all intimate care since father was distrustful of the old-fashioned ways of both grandmothers. He became my constant companion and playmate, though forced to resume daytime work when I was four. He died when I was six.

This father-son bond, though strong, proved to be the source of some difficulty, as Locke goes on to relate that the question of the child's discipline became the occasion for a power struggle that altered the family dynamics:

> . . . when during one of mother's absences he [Pliny] chastised me with the only whipping I remember ever having had; my grandmothers were strictly forbidden to discipline me (and I knew that, much to their chagrin). [I]t was then decided (when I was somewhere between four and five) that mother was to have final authority in discipline. I either remember or was told this was one of the few serious quarrels of their married life, and that it had been settled that way on mother's ultimatum.

One could speculate here about how the change of discipline led Locke, in social and political matters, to value the role of "indirect" improvements, based on cultural rather than direct agitational means or physical discipline. In any case, the "serious quarrel" about the correct application of discipline and exercise of authority was something that Locke struggled with, both as teacher and a critic, throughout his long career.

As for his mother's role in his upbringing, Locke reported that even before the death of his father she was a full partner in the parental "fixation on their one and only." The doctor ordered prolonged lactation by special diet, so that Locke was

> nursed at the breast until the age of three, and after weaning had to be fed milk by the spoonful. I would take it in no other way and it had to be whipped into bubbles; presumably because of being used to the aeration in breast feeding.

Locke describes himself as being "indulgently but intelligently treated" and puts this down to the fact that, since both parents were "breadwinners," they were "extremely strong-willed personalities and knew not to cross one another."

The father planned for Locke to go to military school for his early training, and in anticipation of this each night would see to it that the boy's clothes were inspected and arranged on a chair beside his bed. All part of a nightly ritual, this routine no doubt reflected a very orderly household routine during other parts of the day. The mother indulged in very little kissing, and no "frightening talk or games." In fact, Pliny dismissed one housekeeper who terrified the boy with tales of "the Boogy-man." And "though a relatively poor family, household etiquette was extreme." Locke recalls that, except when he was being bathed, he was never in the bathroom with anyone. All of this led to a strong sense of self-discipline in terms of grooming and personal appearance. Most of the photographic images we have of Locke show him dressed fashionably, and, later in life, he always stressed to his students the important relation between morals and manners. Locke would be referred to by many as "dicty" during most of his adult life, and in the 1920s he even earned the sobriquet "The Proust of Lenox Avenue." This obviously glanced at his sexual orientation as well as his devotion to high European culture and personal fastidiousness.

His father's death in 1892 threw Locke, who was then not quite six years old, "into the closest companionship" with Mary Locke. "As a child I stopped play promptly and waited for her return every school day, and the only childhood terror I vividly remember, was about accidents that might have happened to her, if by chance she was late." The security offered by the mother, along with the atmosphere in the house, added up to an unshakable sense of self-possession:

> I was a self-centered, rather selfish and extremely poised child, mature enough even before my father's death to be indifferent to others and what they did or thought. I would not accept money or gifts from other people, no matter how tempting. Was trained to be extremely polite but standoffish with others. I was unusually obedient, but never had any unreasonable conditions to put up with, since most things were explained to me beforehand.

The picture here compares in some respects to the therapeutic standards of a later time, and the emphasis on reasonable explanations—derived in part by Mary Locke from her commitment to Adler's Ethical Culture—can be seen as contributing to many aspects of Locke's career and character: his teacher-liness, his trust in critical standards to account for esthetic effects, his willingness to serve in a leadership role if it is defined chiefly as making things clear to those who are being led. In many ways Locke's upbringing was what one might expect for those who have educators as parents, but with him the effects of the dynamic seemed especially thorough.

Nevertheless, the enlightened approach to the training of children always has to contend with questions of balance and inward disposition. Too much control, even if administered with the kindest of intentions, can turn the enlightened child into one not quite ready to face the world. Here is the concluding passage of Locke's self-description:

> Relations with mother, though deeply affectionate, were unemotional in outward expression. I would, for example, hug her waist on meeting her, but rarely remember kissing until we got home and she had taken off her hat, coat and washed. It was a household where we washed interminably, and except to keep from open offense to others, I was taught to avoid kissing or being kissed by outsiders. If it happened, I would as soon as possible without being observed, find an excuse for using my handkerchief, often spitting surreptitiously into it if kissed too openly.

The recurrence here of the images of openness (and the cognates, observed, outward, and outsider) are germane to Locke's preoccupation with the tension between individual integrity and group identity. The inwardness that attaches to a certain understanding of individualism was not necessarily that of a radical subjectivity—in which only the inward is true—but rather is seen by Locke as a term in a dialectic relation with how and under what conditions one should make oneself available or visible to others. The social aspects and values in human experience are inescapably there but are likely to be more than occasionally a source of pollution, even though this very threat, as the surreptitiousness suggests, is to be mediated in socially acceptable ways.

One modern historian of Philadelphia has described the city's culture as being a mixture of the patrician and the provincial, a combination that set it off from other cities of similar size such as Boston and New York:

> Patrician, because of the close relationship of families composing its principal social and financial institutions; indifferent, rather than hostile to the rising new rich, even when the latter were ready to make their public contributions. . . . This had something to do with the long-standing Philadelphian tradition of privacy. Interior life was what counted in Philadelphia, including interior decorousness and the interior decoration of lives.[13]

These generalizations might not apply directly to the African American community, of course, but they would set a standard of social values of which even the Lockes would be aware. And since Locke uses a vocabulary of family life that reflects some of these principles, it is apparent, in an important sense, that he was a true Philadelphian.

Locke's relationship with his mother grew and deepened and solidified over the years. She came to represent all the ideals that he felt were worth striving for, and when he began to outstrip her cultural learning he saw to it that her reading was widened and her cultural activities maintained or even increased. He was able in his later years to comprehend the relationship in something like a three-dimensional context. One of his autobiographical notes sums it up with striking clarity and honesty:

> My wise and loving Mother dipped me as a very young child in the magic waters of cold cynicism and haughty distrust and disdain of public opinion and died with satisfaction of an almost hurt-proof child. However the all too vulnerable Achilles heel of homosexuality—which she may have suspected was there, both for her sake and my own

safety—I kept in an armored shoe of reserve and haughty caution. I realize that to bask in the sunshine of public favor I would have to bathe in the dangerous pool of publicity. (ALPHU 164-143/5)

What vulnerability Locke here gives up to public view he partially redeems, as it were, with the play of the heroic trope of Achillean strength and weakness.

Another of his autobiographical notes gives a picture of how the Locke household was self-aware, to a marked extent, of its own social mediations. These were, needless to say, revolving around issues of race, or even if not about such issues directly, the strategy of mediation often derived from a racial consciousness. This note talks about the question of humor:

Laughter was barred in our house—and the smile substituted not in a sour but in a debonair way—This was the antidote of being Negro—the distinguished protest of the 2nd & 3rd generation away from slavery. My father & mother could laugh—but rarely did—Father took it out in whistling. (ALPHU 164-143/5)

Locke accepts the debonair smile and the whistling as "the antidote of being Negro"—the only treatment available in the absence of a cure for racism. The process of social awareness and compensation, however, never completely obliterates the fact that something—in this case, unchecked laughter—is being denied. This sense of things contributed to the sublimations that Locke associated with education, since he often talked about it as a "gift," but a gift obtained at a considerable cost, even though the final result was a decided improvement over the "natural state of affairs."

In 1931 Locke revealed some more of the details of his family life in a letter to Charlotte Mason. His maternal grandmother, who probably lived with the Lockes or close by, warned the young boy to stay out of the sun because "You're black enough already." Somewhat ironically, this letter to Mason was written when Locke was an adult seeking treatment at a spa in Germany, and he had been urged to take sun-lamp treatments to improve his vigor. This advice prompted the following memory and judgment of his grandmother:

Really I think that dear old misguided soul had much more influence on me than I had realized—and she, rather than mother, is to blame for some of the false notions that until recently have been cramping [my] wings. (ALPHU 164-69/7)

Written at least partly in the tone of an analysis, the letter came at the time when Locke seemed to have been engaged in a self-analysis, prompted in part by his relation with Mason. Though he does not specify the "false notions," they probably involved his thinking that he needed to prove his cultural standing to a white audience. At this time Mason, for her part, was full of ideas that equated the so-called primitivism of colored peoples with an energy that would revitalize a decadent Western civilization, and she felt Locke was too cautious and repressed in announcing his own excellence. Locke may have been responding to her when he proposed a self-description that stressed the need to break down certain forms of control. He goes on to reminisce about the family's sense of propriety:

> The family was always honest with itself behind closed doors—But how those doors were barricaded! Even the family wash had to go out on the line as early as possible—before the neighbors were up. (ALPHU 164-143/5)

Again the theme of open and closed appears, and the notion of pollution is replaced with that of warfare, as the family barricades separate the world of utter honesty and the world of social appearance, where a certain amount of deception is not only tolerated but necessary—as if the family wash could make its appearance all by itself.

The sense of socialization as a process grounded in control and denial is not especially original, obviously, nor is it striking to suggest that a sense of recompense or sublimation helps to make such a process more palatable. But with Locke the economy of costs and gains extends beyond the issue of race and the family circle to include his sense of himself. In another note, this being one of the few that is dated—October 1, 1949—he writes:

> Three minorities—Had I been born in ancient Greece I would have escaped the first; In Europe I would have been spared the second; In Japan I would have been above rather than below average. (ALPHU 164-143/5)

With the mention of three minorities, Locke refers to his homosexuality, his race, and his short stature (he was just over five feet tall, in part as a result of the rheumatic fever that left him with an enlarged heart and a susceptibility to other afflictions). The implicit suggestion, that the status of each of these "minorities" is equivalent to the other, and that they are all in some way escapable, results from considering racial and cultural identities as malleable and, at least to some extent, shaped by human choice. But Locke comes to this view only in the course of a long reflection about such identities. Clearly his own membership in certain groups was data that was ready at hand to help him understand the larger issues.

——•——

For the primary grades, Locke attended the Charles Close School, at Seventh and Dickinson Streets in Philadelphia. Mary Locke taught at this school before, during, and after Locke was a student there, from 1886 to 1903, then joining Mt. Vernon. It combined primary and grammar schools, with a total of about seven hundred students, all boys. Some of his records from this school survive and show that Locke was an excellent student. In the eighth grade, for example, he got a score of 98 on his language test. A small, undated newspaper clipping states: "In one of the divisions of the tenth grade the smallest and youngest boy, LeRoy Locke, is said to be doing the most satisfactory work and is leading his class. Locke is doing specially good work in mathematics." Many years later, Locke mentioned the dislike most children have for the bright students, who are too often used as a yardstick to measure their accomplishments. The difficulty was vividly felt when Locke's academic excellence carried him into a class where the average age of the other students was two years beyond his: "leading to the cycle—more frustration—more study." A rare early letter to his mother (who has apparently taken a trip somewhere), dated June 23, 1893, supports this sense of competition, for he tells her that he is "Getting along nicely in school and the boys are growing jealous." Any extraordinary individual had to contend with the group's insistence on its own norms.[14]

Though sheltered and perhaps even unduly favored in grammar school, Locke would quickly show that his impressive academic results were not dependent solely on his mother being his teacher. He began his secondary education at Philadelphia's Central High School in the fall of 1898, when he was just thirteen years old. His first year notebook gives some idea of the range of subjects he was expected to study: notes on history from Philip of Macedonia to Unitarianism and William Ellery Channing, and geography notes on Africa and the Free Congo State, these latter to play an important part in his work. He also studied several languages, including Greek and Latin.

Elocution, literature, astronomy, and architectural drawing complete one of his schedule cards. A copy of a geometry exercise in 1898 shows that he had already begun to spell his name "Alain." One of his teachers, struck by a sense of the boy's ironic disdain, wrote on his French translation: "Be fresh but not flip." Later in life Locke would also be fairly notorious for his conversational wordplay and indulgence in puns. His study habits were more than impressive, and they compensated for his physical weakness, about which he never seems to have complained.[15]

Some of his grade reports from Central High survive, and they show in his freshman year that he received all "Ex's," for Excellent, except for a "G" (Good) in drawing; his sophomore records show all "Ex's" except for a "G" in Latin. To excel at Central High was to do well in a very competitive and advanced academic environment, much of it shaped by an emphasis on European cultural traditions. The first high school to be established by a special law of the Commonwealth of Pennsylvania, it had been founded in 1836. Its original building was on Juniper Street, south of Market, in the city's commercial center. Within twenty years it had outgrown this site, and a new building opened in 1853 at Broad and Green Streets. The cornerstone for the third building was laid in 1894, and classes began there in 1900, at the start of Locke's junior year. At its 1902 dedication ceremonies President Theodore Roosevelt was the honored speaker, attesting to the school's high reputation. Locke later celebrated the occasion with an essay that praised the president's "versatility and genuineness of character." The building featured a 137 foot tower and cost $1.5 million, a very considerable sum for those days; the building would last until 1939, and by 1909 had well over two thousand students. Among a long roster of famous alumni was Thomas Eakins, a member of the thirty-eighth graduating class.

A noteworthy feature of Central High was *The Mirror*, a monthly student publication that appeared during the school year, supported in part by advertisements and the Associated Alumni, and featuring not only club news but also various features written by the students. One of the issues, from February 1900, contained a short story, called "The Curse of Kinship," about two men who meet on a train. One of them tells his story to the other. He had gone to Africa, married a black girl and was hunted by her brother. The narrator later tells of reading how the man was found dead, slain by a poisoned African dart. Devoid of any explicit moral, the ending is deeply ambiguous. It's an odd story and deserves mention in part because Locke may have read it and imitated it to some extent with a story, called "Rain," that he would

FIG. 1.3.   Locke at his Central High School. Locke is in the second row of standees, eleventh from the left. Moorland-Spingarn Research Center.

later write while at Harvard. *The Mirror* also gives some flavor of the college preparatory atmosphere that prevailed at Central; even the names of the clubs—Le Bum Bum, The Yahoos, and The Merriate—some of which would change from year to year, convey a sensibility that was at once frivolous and sophisticated.

The only time that Locke's name appeared in *The Mirror* during the four years that he attended Central was in the April 1902 issue, just months before his graduation. In this issue Locke displayed what is probably his first published work, a three-page essay called "The Alhambra; its Historical Position and Influence." Though it seems to have originated as a class assignment, the sophisticated essay somewhat surprisingly deals with what would become in later life one of Locke's major themes: race contacts. The Alhambra, a Muslim building of great beauty and significance, set as it is inside Spain, often serves as a symbol of cultural and historical "crossings." And this is how Locke treats it. He presents his subject in suitably exalted terms: "In no other country can we find the historical and the poetical so indescribably intertwined as in this land of legend and tradition, of song and of ballad, of romance and chivalry." The moral of the piece, however, is a bit more shaded. One can only wonder if Locke, even as a seventeen year old, knew the sorts of ambiguities he was releasing when he presented the building as a symbol of Moorish culture, whose "highest" significance was that it led to organized Christian resistance to the invaders from North Africa:

> This was the mission of the brightest bloom Mohammedism ever pro-
> duced, Europe was ablaze with the marvelous light which they had
> kindled, even their antipathy was beneficial, for it resulted in the ener-
> gizing and unification of the Christian world. (ALPHU 164-150/2)

The idea that antipathy can be beneficial stands as the sort of paradox that would become typical of Locke's thought. For good measure Locke concluded by referring to Christian culture as the "Providence-chosen bearer of learning." No one would readily expect a high school student in such a context openly to challenge the received pieties of his teachers, despite his own experiences of racial prejudice. Nevertheless, such prejudice was all too apparent in the racism of one of the club notes in *The Mirror* that alludes to a popular song of the day: "Every Nation Has a Flag but the Coon." Still, by the time Locke developed his theory, forty years later, of the complex way races and cultures meet and interpret one another, his sense of who carries the blaze and who carries the bloom would be more complex.

In 1902 Locke finished his high school training at one of the country's better public institutions. But contrary to what might have been the expectations of many, including himself, Locke did not immediately enter a four-year college. He took the entrance examination for nearby Haverford College, and while he passed Latin, despite his earlier good marks in mathematics, he missed the mark in algebra and plane geometry, thereby failing to be admitted. Instead of Haverford, however, Locke entered the School of Pedagogy and Practice. This was an extension of Central High School; today it would be called a teachers' college. Organized to devote one year to the practical aspects of teaching and another to the theory and principles of instruction, it eventually provided Locke with the avenue to considerably more education than even Haverford would have offered.

It was here that Locke met Dr. Francis Brandt, a Harvard graduate, who was to exercise considerable influence over his development as a scholar and teacher. At Harvard, Brandt had studied with Josiah Royce and others, and he later was able to provide Locke with helpful letters of reference as well as encourage him to read the works of his, Brandt's, former teachers. For several years beyond his time at the School of Pedagogy, Locke corresponded with Brandt, who increasingly approved of his student's skills and success. As for the school itself, it had a policy of admitting Central High graduates without an examination. Organized in 1891, it became a graduate department of Central High five years later; eventually it added its own grammar school, where the practical aspects of teaching were implemented, but this began only after Locke had completed his time there. By 1904, after fewer than fifteen years of operation, the school had produced 107 graduates, eighty of whom were teaching in the public schools and twenty of whom were principals. After two years there, Locke graduated number one among the small class of only eight boys; he had established an average grade of 92.6, despite doing rather poorly in mathematics.

Two important things happened to Locke at the School of Pedagogy. First, he developed a genuine interest in the vocation and techniques of teaching. He was later to put this interest to use in several areas, perhaps chiefly the Adult Education movement in which he was a forerunner. Second, by the completion of a heavy schedule of written assignments, Locke greatly increased his skills as a writer. This facility remained apparent throughout his life, and it is especially impressive when one considers how well he did in meeting deadlines and in writing clearly and expressively for a variety of audiences and in a range of subjects, often at the same time. Many of the exercises Locke wrote as his "Daily Theme" at the School of Pedagogy have survived. These give a very clear sense of Locke's compositional skills, for they are always literate and well organized, with a coherent point of view, even though some may have been composed extemporaneously. They also shed light on Locke's opinions and temperament at this time, though occasionally the thoughts in them seem a bit stilted and taken up only in order to complete the assignment. However, some pieces display real sophistication, containing ideas and views that Locke would later develop. Among these papers are early versions of essays that Locke rewrote and used as submissions for the writing awards he would win at Harvard. By their mixture of topics, from "classical" subjects to current events, they offer a glimpse into Locke's concerns and habits of thought during a period when there is little else of him on record.[16]

Locke took a class with Dr. Brandt in Psychology and Pedagogy, and also a class on education in industrial society. There were also classes in Logic and in German, with other teachers. But the daily themes were often done for Locke's class in English Literature, presumably the subject he was considering teaching at the high school level, as he prepared himself along with his classmates for the public school system's growing need for instructors. Consequently many of the themes read like a quite advanced course in literary criticism or esthetics. He writes about George Saintsbury's two-volume *History of Criticism*, suggesting that the English critic will become known as a new Sainte-Beuve. An essay on the relative merits of Art for Art's Sake and Art for Humanity's Sake dispassionately concludes that, though the "methods are different, the results are approximately the same." The struggle between a purely esthetic sense and the use of art and cultural expression for social and political advancement would be one of the dominant tensions in his life. In the fall of 1903 he offers a strong opinion in pointing to "the much heralded fact that current literature is being carried away in the whirlpool of commercialism." (In the late 1920s Locke chose a similar term for the whirlpool that threatened literature: exhibitionism.)

In the spring of 1903 Locke argues: "In all the range of poetic literature, the nearest approaches to true poetry . . . [of] faultless melodious singing I believe to have been attained by Keats's last five odes and the five lyrics of Tennyson's Princess." Though in some ways a received opinion, Locke's high estimation of Keats shows his sensibility was open to Romantic expressiveness. Other literary topics covered are Shelley's "Prometheus Unbound" and the Prometheus myth itself, an important motif that recurs in his writing at Harvard, perhaps suggestive of Locke's view of himself. There is also a review of Josiah Royce's *The World and the Individual,* the two volumes of which had appeared in 1900–1901; Locke would soon be a pupil of this post-Kantian idealist, and Royce would help enhance Locke's study of value, which was to be one of his chief philosophical concerns. Such diligent compositional labors afforded Locke—in terms of form and content—a rich literary and cultural background that he added to continuously. The very range of the subjects of the essays complemented his growing agility as a writer and introduced him to the broad interests that form part of his polymath identity.

Not all the topics were literary or philosophical. Locke also wrote about "The Alien Invasion," the then hotly debated issue of immigration and the theories of nativism, which claimed that the indigenous and traditional culture of America was under threat of dilution or worse by the large number of newcomers. Locke, however, intelligently demurred, sensing that such "theories" as nativism were just barely veiled expressions of racism. Instead he wrote: "I do not think that history furnishes grounds for our fear in the infusion of new blood." He went on to suggest that America and its culture could use help from all resources, and his use of a long historical perspective to counteract unthinking prejudice formed a cornerstone of his later work. An essay on "Business Ideals" contended that most businessmen had moral ideals below those of the rest of the country. A composition with the somewhat flamboyant title, "J. Pierpont Morgan as a Typical Money God," allowed the young man to opine that the robber baron had no virtues worth heroicizing. As for ideals, the essay called "Pride of Lineage" finds Locke expostulating on what was already for him a closely held value, and one that had definite social consequences:

> The person who has a father and a grandfather to be proud of will . . . have greater care of his personal conduct than he who has no such ancestry. . . . [T]he extreme of such pride is a haughty overbearing air but this is less harmful to both individual and society than one which is laxly democratic. (ALPHU 164-152/9)

Soon the word "ancestry" will return in Locke's personal lexicon, and this passage reveals how he was able to write about himself while at the same time pretending to objectivity.

Not all of Locke's work at the School of Pedagogy was to remain unpublished. In 1904, after he had already started classes at Harvard, Locke published an article in the April issue of the *Teacher.* After what might be called the in-house publication of the essay on the Alhambra, this is Locke's first appearance in print. But it, too, is probably the result of Locke's connection with one of his teachers, for presumably Brandt or one of the other instructors at the School of Pedagogy helped the essay into the light of publicity. Though an apprentice piece, designed in part for a restricted audience of other teachers, the polished essay nevertheless raises an issue in the field of education that is almost always controversial: is school the place for moral training? As is the case with much of Locke's writing, this argument draws on a number of sources and intertwines a number of his abiding concerns.[17]

Locke launches into his topic by defining a code of ethics as "a more universal standard of right and wrong action, that is . . . the common property of the organic whole." The whole is here meant to be society itself as well as the educational process that serves its needs. Quoting Felix Adler, whose educational theories were important to Mary Locke, he suggests that education is moral or it is nothing: "There is no school where the moral influence is wanting." Since school inevitably influences conduct and standards of right and wrong, teachers are better advised to proceed with self-awareness on this score and arrive at a consciously shaped set of decisions about ethical questions. These ideas anticipate some of the work of John Dewey, whose educational theories were inflected with a critical sense of ethical development. This means, among other things, that favorable conditions for promoting and discussing ethics should supplement the instinct for moral education. Locke, with a startling sort of prescience about his own later concerns, says that this calls for the establishment of "a definite subject matter for moral training; and that is the classification and study of the moral qualities." Fifteen years later, at Harvard, he would complete his Ph.D. thesis on the classification of values.

Locke does not, however, simply suggest a scientific or logical approach by his call for a classification of moral qualities. He supplements this by urging that teachers see the place of moral education in the teaching of many subjects, perhaps most of all in literature. It is through the reading of literature that people imagine alternative, and more expansive, models for themselves. He supports this point by paraphrasing Emerson on Shakespeare: "All that Shakespeare says of the king the boy feels to be true of himself." Here he anticipates the optative role that he sees for culture in his later work in The New Negro movement. He further indicates his first interest in pragmatism when he explicitly quotes John Dewey's inductive formula for educational growth, "I see, I like, I wish I were, I will be." Locke approves of this continuum between observation, desire, and self-definition, as opposed to the deductive belief that the enunciation of moral truth will automatically produce morally acceptable behavior, an approach summed up by the formula, "To know is to do." Actually, Locke says that both the deductive and inductive approaches produce failures and successes, and each is therefore needed to supplement the other. He ends by announcing one more of his themes when he defines morality as "the connecting bond between the social and the individual life." Though still a student, Locke had already defined and raised standards and philosophical reflections for himself as a teacher, and they would influence all of his public activities over the next several decades. The coherence, as well as the breadth of his thought, was coming into view.

Locke took his A.B. degree from the School of Pedagogy, the equivalent of a collegiate certificate. In a sense he had already completed the equivalent of two years of college work, and now it was time, and he was fully ready, to pursue yet higher educational achievements. In an undated letter, Brandt wrote to Locke that he was "glad to know the way is clear for your admission to Harvard as a special anyhow [Locke had provisional or "special" status, and still needed to satisfy certain course requirements], but we shall hope for still better things."[18] The years at the School of Pedagogy, combined with the special attention of Dr. Brandt, were able to do for Locke what Central High, with all its elite traditions, could not quite manage: launch him into a college career. He was, however, just that more thoroughly prepared for the next level of his education. At the first annual banquet for the school in June of 1904, Locke was asked to give the toast to the faculty. This may have been a result of his valedictorian status, or it may have been because all his teachers there saw that he was well on his way to a life of scholarship, learning, and public service—that, in effect, he was to replicate all their values.

Only a month or two after Locke arrived in Cambridge in the fall of 1904 to start at Harvard, he would write home: "If I could get a nice bunk up here Phila[delphia] would never see me again"; he added that he had dispelled for himself any idea of a New England coldness of character.[19] He was not only optimistic about his future, he had begun to associate greater intellectual horizons with new social environments. The verve with which Locke frequently took on the next step in his life is evident here. In such ebullience his character showed through again and again, for with all the repressed and guarded awareness that he had acquired, he remained remarkably self-possessed and confident about his ability. His own cultural crossing was waiting to unfold, and he would seem at times almost blasé about it.

CHAPTER TWO

Harvard

Alain Locke arrived at Harvard with considerable ambition, after two years at the School of Pedagogy. But even he did not foresee that in his senior year, as the first African American winner of a Rhodes Scholarship, he would become the object of national attention. Harvard aided in the intensity of that attention. In the opening decade of the twentieth century the college could be seen as one of the birthplaces of modern culture, considering the influence of figures such as Oliver Wendell Holmes, William James, George Santayana, and T. S. Eliot. For Locke to make his mark in such sterling company he would have to transform his outlook, but it was a task he set himself without flinching. His letters home are almost completely free of anxiety; indeed, he seems to the manor born in the way he was able to take full advantage of the literary and cultural life that the college abundantly supplied. At the same time, however, he was to discover new facets of his racial identity and to set in motion ideas and concerns that would lead him in a direction quite distinct from the vast majority of his classmates.

Locke, who became one of the most distinguished students to graduate in 1907, was not, however, the first African American to receive a degree from Harvard. That honor belongs to Richard Greener, of the class of 1870. While Locke claimed many more honors at America's oldest college than did Greener, his experience there nevertheless owed something to his predecessor. For it is through Greener's career as a student, and even more so as a graduate of Harvard, that a horizon of expectations was created for Locke. Between 1870 and 1907 there also occurred the early career of another Harvard student, W. E. B. Du Bois (who was the first African American to earn a doctorate at Harvard), and it was his formulation of the notion of the "talented tenth" that articulated the experience of both Greener and Locke. This phrase, and its many expectations, worked its way into Locke's conscious and unconscious images of himself, not only as a gifted student but as a would-be leader of his race. Greener went on to become a member of the bar and a diplomat and thereby one of the representative educated African Americans of his day. He also taught law at Howard University and was active in the Niagara Movement headed by Du Bois just at the time Locke was attending Harvard. Eventually, however, his career ended in disappointment and bitterness because the arena of his public service was circumscribed by historical factors, not the least of which was the racial attitudes of post-Reconstruction America.[1]

Although Locke never joined the diplomatic corps or the Niagara Movement, he would eventually come to think of himself as dedicated to public service as well as a dutiful member of the "talented tenth." For Locke the word "talented" had special meaning in a way that did not apply to Greener. At Harvard, although dedication to service was constantly in the background and often enough in the foreground, Locke was also strongly drawn toward a life of esthetic contemplation and self-fulfillment. Mentioning that he was outgrowing some of his Philadelphia friends, Locke told his mother that he addressed a class devotional meeting on the topic, "Self Culture versus Service in University Life." These tense alternatives would extend far beyond the university's boundaries, as tension between public service and personal fulfillment in Locke's Harvard career became a template for his entire life.[2]

However much Locke's time at Harvard shared in the larger patterns of his life, it had distinctive features as well. Not only was it the first time Locke spent considerable time away from home, it was also the first opportunity he had to test his self-regard—indeed his own elitist sense of himself—against a wide variety of people, many of whom were as elitist as he. It was also the first time that he was able to work with teachers who could show him the way into the world of the dominant class's cultural ideas and values. "I am going to be choice [*sic*] and pick my company," he told his mother, announcing a determination that continued to grow. He never lacked for ambition, no matter how much his desire to be prominent and respected was mediated through a commitment to education and service. Though Locke came with strong recommendations from Dr. Brandt, his teacher and mentor at the School of Pedagogy, now he was to meet the teachers who had taught—and inspired and measured—the man who had taught him.

Cambridge was not all completely new territory for him. There existed at Harvard a network of graduates not only from the School of Pedagogy but also from Central High School. Some of these young men would become life-long friends of Locke. Indeed, he knew some of them well even while still at Central—especially David A. Pfaff, known as Dap, and C. Henry Dicker-man, both from Philadelphia. At one point Locke remarked to a friend, re-ferring to the influence Brandt had on those of his students he sent on to his alma mater, that "we really got Harvard in homeopathic doses." There was also the tall, striking West Indian, J. Arthur Harley, who expressed his ra-cial pride in ways that drew Locke's attention and constant respect. Harley's presence would extend beyond Locke's graduation. Some friendships had a directly esthetic foundation, such as the brief union Locke formed with John Hall Wheelock, whose precocity extended to the publication of a small book of his poems while still an undergraduate. Eventually there developed a sense of rivalry with other students—chief among these was Van Wyck Brooks—and other cliques. For many years after the class of 1907 left Harvard, Locke and his close friends would measure their own careers by comparison with the publication record and reputations of Brooks and his cohorts, some of whom, such as Maxwell Perkins and Edward (Ned) Sheldon, had distin-guished careers in editing and theater respectively. In fact, Sheldon had his first play produced on Broadway the year after Locke graduated.[3]

Technically speaking Locke was not a member of the class of 1907. Since he entered as a freshman in 1904, he belonged on the official roster of the class of 1908, but almost all his best friends were members of the preceding class. Receiving advanced credit for his previous courses, he was able to graduate in 1907, after only three years of attendance. From the start Dr. Brandt had told him he could receive advanced standing based on the coursework he had completed at the School of Pedagogy in the two years prior to his enrollment at Harvard. Locke went to work on this right away, though it took consider-able bureaucratic savvy to accomplish it. (In fact, the then recently reformed curriculum, with its emphasis on "free" electives, made graduation in three years generally easier.) In the meantime his entrance exams showed him de-ficient in three areas: Elementary History, Algebra, and Physics. He needed to do what amounted to remedial work in these subjects, so during the aca-demic year 1904–1905 Locke worked extremely hard. He was able to keep his grades up by relying on the study habits and frequent writing he had prac-ticed at Pedagogy. At the same time he developed a sophisticated social life.

The course of undergraduate study at Harvard at the turn of the century was extremely rigorous compared to previous and later periods. This was combined, however, with a recent reform of the curriculum, initiated by

President Charles Eliot, that did away with required courses and substituted a system of electives. Allowing undergraduates to pick courses that were especially important for their career plans served as the main justification for the changes. A sizable portion of the faculty objected to this, fearing such an orientation would only develop commercial and business mentalities. Some suggested this added to the split between those undergraduates who cultivated their esthetic sensibilities and those who strove to prepare themselves for leadership roles in business and public life. This split was, of course, becoming evident in the general culture of an increasingly prosperous mercantile society and had already been, and was to be, one of the dominant themes in American literature for decades. Locke, by virtue of his race and his individual talents, would see this split from a special angle of vision.

The philosophy department drew Locke's attention from the start, and since his literary interests led him to focus as well on the esthetic side of things, he did very good work as a student of the humanities. At the time he entered Harvard, the philosophy department was enjoying what has been referred to as its Golden Age: Hugo Münsterberg, George Herbert Palmer, Josiah Royce, George Santayana, and William James were all lending their talents and reputations to the luster. On the literary side, the English department also included a number of influential teachers and critics. There was Irving Babbitt, from whom Locke took a course his senior year, who later went on to be the center of the conservative movement known as the New Humanism. There was also Charles T. Copeland, the much admired writing teacher fondly known as "Copey," who set a very high standard in his English composition course. Barrett Wendell, a high-minded esthete who had earlier taught Wallace Stevens, was another teacher of writing, and his advanced class was much sought after. Locke was influenced by all these men, though he resisted the plain direct style favored by Copeland, and he never actually studied with William James. Perhaps the single most important teacher for Locke in terms of intellectual interests was Münsterberg, whose work would lead Locke not only to his Oxford thesis but also to the year at the University of Berlin in 1910–11 and a lifelong interest in the philosophy of value. He also absorbed from Josiah Royce an intensified interest in value theory. But at one point he told his mother that Palmer, with whom he took courses all three years, was "one of our teachers—he is peculiarly mine."[4]

The intellectual atmosphere at Harvard in 1904 was formed by an unstable mix of Protestant moral perfectionism and late Romantic estheticism, held together by a genteel Anglophilia. The Protestantism was reflected in the concern with value theory, where it was understood that one was to hold central values very firmly, and—if possible—with some rational justification. The estheticism was reflected in the pursuit of an idealism that went beyond (often without really challenging) the materialist bounty of America's propertied class. As for the Anglophilia, as far as Locke was concerned, it would reach its peak with the Rhodes Scholarship, but it was also there in his Bowdoin Prize essay on Tennyson and in his reading, which at one point was concentrated on Kipling and Keats. All these intellectual and cultural ingredients had in common a tremendous stress on individualism, of the sort for which William James was the leading spokesman. Locke's elitism and self-confidence were nurtured by this individualism, and it was not until after he left Harvard that he began to see that it was not the only framework for his intellectual vocation.

———•———

Locke arrived in Cambridge on September 16, 1904, and at first stayed at Palmer House. He intended to put an advertisement in the local paper for some furnished lodging, evidently feeling the dormitories were déclassé. For the first term he secured a rented room and lived there in fairly high style, but then he was forced by economic stringency to become a participant in dormitory life, moving into Grays Hall in the spring of 1905 and into Holyoke Hall his second year. His first impressions of his fellow freshmen were hardly positive, and he wrote home describing them as "a funny looking lot, dudes about 20–22 years of age, some eccentric with heels 2 ins. or more high skin tight jackets and colored hander chiefs [*sic*] tied around their rough rider hats." By the end of September Locke was able to wire his mother "Passed and Admitted," and to further report that "Blue Monday," when freshmen were mercilessly hazed, had been suppressed. But there were some more serious concerns as well.[5]

One of them was what attitude Locke would adopt toward the other students of his race. Locke's years at Central High in Philadelphia had conditioned him to being one of the very few members of his race in an elite environment dominated by whites, and he had absorbed the attitudes of that city's favored African American community, which did not look with special indulgence on lower class people from any race. At first he reported back to his mother that he attended a party where there "were 5 niggers all Harvard men. . . . I staid the visit out for fun but I might as well have that one experience. It's my last." Locke felt it was fine for such individuals to get an education, but they were not gentlemen. He complained that he could not understand how Negroes could "come up here in a broad-minded place like this and stick together like they were in the heart of Africa." Later he attended a "cake walk" at the black students' house and he found it "so funny that I would willingly have watched them longer if it had not been that I was on my dignity." He resolved not to be bothered by the group and eventually decided not to acknowledge them when he was in the presence of a white person. Of course, he also felt most Harvard students, even the graduate students, were "coarse." He described himself to his mother as quite "fashionable," even though he could not afford personalized stationery and needed to seek a tutoring job in order to make ends meet.[6]

Locke at first felt that Harvard should not be a place where separatism prevailed. In his second year he told his mother that "by common consent, [the black students have] unanimously chosen to occupy a separate table together. Now what do you think of that? It's the same old lifelong criticism I shall be making against our people." But issues of race and group identity were a fairly constant source of consternation and even anger, and they were not restricted to African Americans. For example, several Jewish students were sent away from a dining table, and two of Locke's friends with Jewish names went with them in sympathy. Locke resisted the idea that this was straightforward anti-Semitism, telling his mother that it was "the same old mistake our colored brothers make, for the objection was not to them as Jews but as disagreeable, ungentlemanly fellows."[7] And later when some black students complained of being "jim-crowed" in the dining hall, Locke told one of them that he was not on the lookout for discrimination. Locke never joined the social clubs at Harvard, preferring his associations to be built on academic interests, such as he found in the Philosophical Club and the Ethical Culture Club. Perhaps he never pursued such membership in the "exclusive" social clubs because he did not want to face or force the issue. But clearly such incidents in the dining halls kept the question of race in focus, however it might have been complicated by questions of class and sensibility.

Group identity and the individual's role in it drew Locke's attention and analysis all his life. Whatever paradoxes he might observe in the tensions between these two poles, he felt that he must make the widest possible network of friends and contacts at Harvard, and he set about doing so with purpose. In the fall of his second year he wrote home to say:

I am ever pursuing my policy of making good friends gradually and cautiously and by the time I leave here expect to have a goodly collection of what a book collector would call first editions. (ALPHU 164-50/17)

With a letter of introduction from Brandt, where the mentor described his student as "apt in philosophical subjects as in languages," Locke met Josiah Royce in his first semester, having read one of his recent books while at Central High. He was told that the philosopher had earned the nickname of the "modern Socrates" because of his ugly appearance. Locke not only admired Royce's library, he made a point of reading another one of his books before the meeting and told the professor how much it had done for him. In the first term, he also connected with Dickerman, a fellow Central High School graduate, and Dickerman successfully nominated him for membership in the Ethical Culture Club. He also introduced Locke to a man named Blumfield, who was a powerful politician of the time and the head of the Civil Service House. Dickerman did volunteer work there, teaching a group of young Jewish boys, and Locke also considered joining in the effort. His impulse to follow his parents into a vocation as a teacher was obviously not based merely on economic need, but on this occasion he decided to husband his time.

Another way the race issue was focused for Locke arose with the ongoing interest he shared with many in the fortunes of Booker T. Washington. Before coming to Harvard he had met the most famous leader of the race in 1903, at an annual meeting of the Unitarian Book Room Association in Philadelphia, and it was clear that Locke and his mother looked up to him. While at Harvard, Locke routinely visited a black barber in Cambridge, and this man talked all the time about Washington's fortunes as the leading spokesman for African Americans. Locke regularly read the African American press, and he remarked to his mother about the virulent attacks on Washington launched by the Boston *Guardian*. Founded by the African Americans William Monroe Trotter and George Forbes in 1901, the *Guardian* promoted a spirit of radical activism and resistance to racial oppression. The newspaper's office was in the building that had previously housed the abolitionist William Lloyd Garrison's *Liberator*. Locke told his mother how the editor, Monroe Trotter, had caused an uproar in 1903 when he disrupted a meeting of the National Negro Business League in Boston. Trotter ended up serving a thirty day sentence for disturbing the peace. This incident brought to a head the rivalry between Du Bois and Washington, as Du Bois was now forced to side with Trotter and his allies. Sentiment in Boston was largely anti-Washington, since the liberal blacks of New England saw his Tuskegee idea of practical education as far too accommodationist. The struggle between Du Bois and Washington would one day play an important part in Locke's own understanding of the question of black leadership.

Locke managed to keep up his interest in music while at college. He told his mother that he was interested in taking piano lessons at the Conservatory in Cambridge, but it appears that he was unable to afford them. He went with a fellow student two or three times a week to play on the Aeolian organ at the Holden Chapel on campus. He also attended concerts given by the Boston Symphony and would often mention details to his mother, praising and dispraising with firm conviction. His taste in music supported one of the more elitist strains in Locke's temperament and would often be cited against him in later years. A lifelong inveterate concertgoer, his knowledgeable love of music was one of the pillars of his esthetic enjoyment. He made a point to hear the famous Jubilee Singers, who had won renown for their versions of the sorrow songs and whose national tour raised funds for Fisk University. At first things went well, and he felt the two or three plantation melodies were beautifully sung. But then the singers went into the sort of "ragtime one hears at a cheap Bowery theater." Locke told his mother that "your touchy offspring could not resist the temptation to get up immediately and leave." Questions of esthetic purity came up often in Locke's mind, and he always seemed to have very clear responses to them.[8]

In November 1904 he attended a party at Phelps Brooks House, where he met President Eliot, whose radical curricular reforms were still the subject of much talk and some resistance, and Mrs. Eliot as well. The president mentioned Brandt, and it was clear to Locke that he had recalled the strong recommendation Brandt had written for his star pupil. At term's end Locke was able to tell his mother that the valedictorian of Central High's class of 1903 had gotten three A's his first term and Locke had garnered four. Meanwhile he was socializing with Dickerman and the circle around Blumfield. Blumfield invited Locke in February 1905 to a party honoring the novelist Israel Zangwill—who coined the term "melting pot"—and, though Zangwill was prevented from coming, Locke enjoyed the ethnic dancing and costumes.

Dickerman, an excellent student and aspiring poet, became a fairly constant companion, and in fact he and Locke sustained a correspondence for almost four decades after graduation. Dickerman was homosexual, and he and Locke may partly have based their friendship on this shared orientation. After college Dickerman was to be involved in a number of promiscuous affairs—about which he wrote Locke in some detail—but he also desired a stable relationship. Prone to unsuccessful affairs of the heart, Dickerman was constantly being thwarted in his search for a soul mate. In college he exhibited certain charismatic qualities, for his other friends, such as Dap and Downes (whose father was the arts editor of the *Boston Evening Transcript*) remained concerned about him for many years after their college days were over. It was Dickerman who sent Locke a letter of congratulations "from table 28" in the dining hall when the Rhodes Scholarship winners were announced. It was probably also he who gave Locke the nickname "Lockus," while reserving for himself the similar "Dickus" in their correspondence. The chances are they collaborated on the two-act mock play Locke and his friends wrote, called *Volpone's Apotheosis, or the Foxe's Death*. This sophomoric effort included a good deal of doggerel, and parodies of several genres, especially the Aesopian tale. Though largely obscure in plot and detail, its moral is announced very clearly at the end: "Never pretend to be what you're not." It is hard to know if this satire had as its target the social pretensions of all undergraduates, or was a covert protest against the need of Locke, Dickerman, and others to conceal their sexuality. Though Dickerman's aspirations as a writer seem to have come to naught, Locke sent him his stories and essays for comments throughout the first several years of his academic and literary career. The familiarity with which Dickerman discussed his own homosexual experiences and desires would lead one to assume that Locke reciprocated the level of intimate trust, though no letters from Locke to Dickerman survive.[9]

After Dickerman nominated Locke for membership in the Ethical Culture Club, they were to hear a number of notable lecturers in the next three years, and it may have been through this club that Locke met Harley, who became one of the officers of the club in 1906. There was also Henry James's appearance on his brother's campus in the spring of 1905, when he made the visit to his native soil that produced *The American Scene*. But on this occasion the novelist lectured to a large audience on Balzac; Locke told his mother he understood only about three-fourths of it, and that much only because he sat close to the podium and was used to English inflection. (In an unpublished review of a book by H. G. Wells that Locke wrote while still at Harvard, he described *The American Scene* as written like a diary, for the author's eyes only.) Locke also joined the Philosophical Club, and though he applied to work on the *Crimson* he evidently was not accepted. He heard a talk by Kelly Miller from Howard University, an expert on the subject of race relations; Miller would later become Locke's colleague and good friend in Washington, D.C. There was a lecture by Henry George, the social reformer best known for advancing the famous single-tax theory, about his visit with Tolstoy. In Locke's senior year he heard a series of lectures on early Greek poetry by Gilbert Murray, this after having become tolerably fluent in the ancient language. Frequent lectures by such established figures ensured that self-culture and service were constantly discussed and debated in public and private arenas.

Locke's academic work was rigorous and may appear daunting compared to today's undergraduate standards. In his final philosophy exam in 1907, for example, he was faced with the question, "In what sense are you yourself, personally considered, a fact? In what sense have you value?" Of course, the split between facts and values was one of the great themes of modern philosophy, and Locke's struggle with this split centers much of his early concern with value theory and persists into the 1930s.. The exam question also strongly implies that it is the philosophy of individualism that will give the issues their purchase. In Philosophy 4, which he took with George Herbert Palmer in the spring of 1906, he studied moral perfectionism and the question of ends and means in ethics, writing a paper called "A Critique of Utilitarianism" and another called "Free Will as the Primary Sanctum of Life." In one of his final exams, he writes out an argument that seeks to overcome the fact/value split by positing a "higher" unity that is a version of an ideal form. Eventually Locke would become dissatisfied with this approach, preferring instead the pluralism of James and yet later that of Dewey to the idealism of Santayana and Royce. But strains of idealism are never completely absent from Locke's writing, especially on esthetic issues.[10]

Some of the seeds of Jamesian pragmatism can be detected in an answer Locke wrote for his mid-year exam in Royce's Philosophy 9, just about one year later than the Philosophy 4 exam:

Experience . . . is not coterminous with perception [or] with consciousness, but is especially reserved for that realm of the external meaning, that field of the verification of mental facts, which by reason of its apparent externality and objectivity seems to be a realm of independent validity that confirms or refutes our mental purposes, as they are expressed or attempted to be expressed in actions. (ALPHU 164-154/13)

This harkens to the beginning of a philosophy of experience, as pragmatism is sometimes known, where mental "truth" is subject to confirmation or refutation on grounds other than its mere coherence or formal aspects. But Locke was still some distance away from holding to the tenets of pragmatism. In an undated letter he describes how he "hurried over to hear Prof. Dewey a famous philosopher—Like all of his kind he was tedious, read from his manuscript a while a lot of drool about Utilitarianism, pragmatism and lord knows what." Later he would change his mind considerably, and Dewey's writings would become central to the courses Locke taught in philosophy at Howard.[11]

There was also a class, misleadingly called Economics 3, where Locke's answers to a mid-year exam in January 1906 showed that he was studying what today we would call political theory. In replying to the question "What are the chief factors tending to promote the improvement of the race and what are the chief factors tending to deteriorate it?," Locke ignores the ethnocentricity of the formulation and weaves together a set of explanations based on theorists as disparate as Spencer and Walter Bagehot. From the latter he borrows the observation that progress is never verifiable because there is no test or criterion of ultimate value. This would later enter Locke's thought as part of his rejection of all forms of absolutism. He also quotes Carlyle to the effect that the supreme gift of man is that he can "will to do as a thing most to be desired what he has to do." This would constitute something like moral perfectionism, for in Carlylean self-discipline and the love of duty he seems to find and approve an intensity of commitment that serves as its own measure.

Very high-minded approaches to literature and the arts vied with philosophic ideas for Locke's attention. In Irving Babbitt's English 46, during the winter of 1906, the class built upon the Renaissance as the source of modernity, since it was then that the characteristic fact of a world tradition was reinterpreted and transformed by the modern idea of nationality. This idea could have been drawn from any of several critics, but perhaps it is most clearly traceable to Sainte-Beuve, whose analysis of literature into the triad of race, milieu, and moment served as the historicist backbone of many literary surveys of the time. Locke himself would adapt and employ some of these ideas when he came to write his essay on "The New Negro," but because that essay was in the optative mode it relied less on historicizing accounts of the "background" of literature and more on its potential for expressing and guiding cultural change. For English 46 he also wrote a paper called "Impressions of Dante," where he argued that "fact becoming tradition, and tradition fact" was especially important, and added that sociologists have been studying this scientifically as "the power of idealization." This idea influenced his essay on Paul Laurence Dunbar, which played an important role in his literary development, as it set out his concern with the use of a literary tradition, a notion analogous to his idea of ancestry. Throughout his career Locke was to negotiate the differences—and the charged relationship—between the recovery of a neglected tradition in need of a more faithful audience and the assertion of a tradition not yet fully formed.

Locke wrote home often, describing his experiences and surroundings with animation and directness, saying that "I don't put on literary flourishes for my home letters"; his mother was always able to play the role of confidant and friend. She was clearly delighted with her son's successes, often telling him about the neighbors and relatives who inquired as to his progress and asked to be remembered. At one point, with a bit of waggish humor, she proposed calling the organization she had formed for her seventh and eighth graders the Alain Locke Literary Club. But she made a point of adding more seriously that he taught her a great deal and she was passing it on to her students. A strong-willed woman, despite her widowhood and near penury she never stopped conveying the correct social attitudes to her son. Once she told him about her attendance at a musical concert at William Penn High School, where she was the only black in the audience. Even though her knees were sore (probably from arthritis) and the pain caused her to feel mildly nauseated, she stayed through to the end of the concert. It was typical of her to notice that she was the only black there, yet she refused to use that as an excuse for not enjoying the entire concert. Awareness of prejudice without retreating into false piety, destructive anger, or restrictive self-denial: this was to be the complex and balanced reaction that Locke, too, often adopted in the face of the effrontery of racism.[12]

Locke often showed genuine solicitude for his mother, urging her to slow down, work less, and enjoy herself with cultural pursuits and simple leisure. His letters are also filled with advice about which bills to pay first and which books she should be reading. As to the advice about evading debtors, he told her that "I think I was made for diplomacy or something equally deceitful and oily." The debts were constant, an elaborate set of interlocking cycles of payments to cover previous loans and repayment in a Byzantine sequence of priorities. Mary Locke would often borrow money from her neighbors and fellow teachers, striving to make the most out of her modest teacher's salary. Locke remarked how funny it was that he became fatherly when financial matters were broached. Clearly she needed some support, if nothing other than a friendly ear to whom she could recount the myriad small amounts due or paid. A letter to Cambridge would sometimes include a dollar or two that she had managed to shelter from other pressing needs. And often the end of the month budget letter Locke sent home would include a column of figures, carefully totaled.[13]

As to books, Locke's recommendations to his mother included Ibsen's plays and Hawthorne's *Marble Faun;* he also dipped into the French symbolists but was unable to recommend them. She, however, was able to brag that she had read Du Bois's *Souls of Black Folk* even before he had. But when he did read it, in the fall of 1905, he did so twice and pronounced it "perfectly wonderful, truthful, though pessimistic." He also reminded her that Brandt had suggested that he should one day write like Du Bois. Earlier on his mother had expressed a preference for a law career for her son, but he had responded by mentioning his attraction to journalism. His own ambition was taking on a decidedly literary cast. Almost all of his close friendships formed around literary or philosophical interests, and his reading inside and outside of class always aimed at self-improvement or esthetic cultivation. He told his mother that Dickerman was moody but quite a good poet and "wouldn't it be funny if he really turned out to be a great poet—If so this letter may live in his biography as evidence of his early genius—Therefore don't burn this letter."[14]

His skill as a literary critic became evident quite early; his class papers were written with a facility that earned him not only good grades but the respect of his fellow students. This became most obvious in the background of an incident that Locke described in detail to his mother. One of his classmates, John Hall Wheelock, was a precocious poet who had built up a reputation as one of the special young men at Harvard. Eventually he would go on to a career as an editor with Scribner's, and his *Collected Poems* (1936) won the Golden Rose Award of the New England Poetry Society. Solidifying his college reputation was Wheelock's decision to bring his poems out in pamphlet form while still an undergraduate. He and fellow student Van Wyck Brooks issued *Verses by Two Undergraduates* (1905), and it was for a time quite a sensation. Locke wrote home to say that Bliss Perry, the editor of the *Atlantic Monthly*—then perhaps the most prestigious cultural magazine in America—was interested in Wheelock's poems. More important from Locke's point of view was the fact that he himself "played the part of the critic and watched their little pamphlet grow." One night at the dining hall Wheelock had brought the proofs with him and asked Locke to read through them, all the while keeping them under the table so as to maintain the element of surprise. It was the first time—but not the last—that Locke was to play the midwife to someone's artistic achievement. (Interestingly, Locke tells the story as centered on Wheelock without mentioning Brooks by name; Wheelock, in apparent recompense, tried unsuccessfully to get Locke on the staff of the *Harvard Monthly*.)[15]

Locke's own possible artistic fame was on his mind. Moving from Philadelphia to Cambridge meant changing his name as well as his prospects; from now on he would be known as Alain, instead of the more familiar Roy, which is what his mother always called him. Remarking that his friend David Pfromm had told him that Pfromm meant pious in German, he told his mother that this was "one more example of the powerful might of a name; why Alain may make me famous some day, who knows? I hardly think Le Roy will." The French form of Alain had appealed to him for its esthetic overtones, though he may have pronounced it in an Anglicized way. Earlier he had said that he had "taken liberties with my name. I have stumbled into quite artistic company—Alain Rene Lesage and Alain Chartier are among the most celebrated of French literary geniuses." The right artistic-sounding name was important, but he kept enough of a sense of wry humor about himself to remark that "God might not recognize me if I made any more changes."[16]

Part of his literary ambition was clearly fueled by the responses he got from his teachers about work he did for class. Copeland and Wendell, very literary in their tastes, based their approach to writing on imitation of the classics and the belletristic tradition. Locke, with his Philadelphia background and high verbal manner, fit in quite well, and his teachers seemed truly to take an interest in him, especially in his final year—Copeland, for example, made a point of asking Locke to correspond with him after graduation. In the spring of 1906 he was able to report home that "in spite of the grudge Professor Palmer must have had for my audacity in introducing literature into philosophy he gave me a good mark."[17] Freely mixing his interest in philosophy and literature would be a hallmark of Locke's identity as a writer. Not every one of his teachers fully appreciated Locke's somewhat florid prose, however. An instructor named Fuller gave Locke a B in his spring 1905 class. From his home in Camden Locke wrote to him in July to argue for a higher mark. Fuller seemed to reconsider Locke's case but eventually decided to leave the mark unchanged. "Your style was often too involved, too wordy to warrant this higher mark," he told the petitioner, who apparently accepted the verdict.

Locke did better, however, with the teachers who most intrigued him. Barrett Wendell was a source of some fascination for Locke and his classmates. The esthete had recently returned from a year abroad lecturing at the Sorbonne, polishing the otherworldly airs for which he was well known. When Locke went to his office to discuss his work, the goateed Wendell would twirl his cane, and Locke noted that he wore garters. A few years earlier Wendell's book, *A Literary History of America,* had appeared, and in its Anglophilia had presented American literature as culturally impoverished and hardly worthy of serious study or praise. He was one of the voices at Harvard often raised in argument against the sterility of American commercial culture, using this as an explanation for the country's failure to produce a great artist. To go with these judgments, there was also a considerable dash of snobbery or even worse, as his letters mention his aversion to immigrants and the lower orders. The year after Locke graduated, Wendell published a book called *The Privileged Classes,* which made his snobbery all too apparent. He was probably one of the people Locke had in mind when he described the New Englanders who constantly looked back to better days.

Whatever Locke felt about Wendell's social views, he may have approved of the professor's fin-de-siècle temperament and attitude, considering them as at least more genuine than those adopted by undergraduates. In any case, Locke had reason to be pleased with Wendell's judgment in at least one instance: in class Wendell caught Locke quite off guard when he praised his Tennyson essay, the same one that was eventually awarded the Bowdoin Prize in his senior year. Addressing the class with an air of mystery and drama, the professor averred that at least one student's thesis made an original contribution to its subject, and that was Locke's. He was prepared to award it an A, the only one earned by the group of forty-eight students. To the copy of the paper, Wendell added the written comment, "A remarkable piece of work." This approval may have convinced Locke to submit the essay for the Bowdoin Prize, given for the best undergraduate essay each year. Locke also decided to submit his paper on Dunbar to Wendell's appraisal, the essay having recently come back from the *Atlantic Monthly,* where Locke had "audaciously" sent it. Locke seems not to have maintained close ties with Wendell and seldom if ever mentioned him in later years. It is, however, possible that some of the spirit behind Locke's initial trust in the possibilities of an esthetic Renaissance in 1925 may have been a rebuke to Wendell's etiolated sensibility.[18]

Copeland, popular with many students, was also a model of literary sensibility, but one that was more committed to journalism than to the rarefied models offered by Wendell. Copey did well under President Eliot's reforms, for he felt that educated men should engage in the business of life, if not make their sole purpose in life the pursuit of wealth. Locke was introduced to him by Dickerman and was thereafter included in some of Copey's "soirees," usually attended by fifteen to twenty-five students who would sit around the professor's living room for an hour and a half while "literary chat ensue[d]." Copeland, a chain smoker, would consume ten to fifteen cigarettes an hour, according to Locke's count. Locke thought of these gatherings as a "shrine of eminently respectable New England culture," pointing out, with a certain sangfroid, however, that this sort of behavior was "not the base simple kind of the days when there was real culture—the Emerson and Lowell days— but the later modern up to date culture that lives on memories of the past." This expression of a distinction by Locke between a usable past and a merely revered one is loaded but also considerably ambivalent. Locke went to visit Concord his first term at Harvard and saw there the graves of Hawthorne, Emerson, and Thoreau, among others. The sight impressed him, but he had enough distance to observe "that New England was God's country but that unfortunately the New Englanders knew it." This was in a letter to Albert Rowland, a Central High graduate with whom Locke had a brief correspondence. Rowland responded to Locke by observing that "Harvard is just like the old maid you might expect an unmarried blue stocking to be, she gets on your nerves, and worries all of us more than she harms." Locke and his friends seemed to possess in full supply the sort of ironic distance from their own experience that budding writers are frequently encouraged to cultivate.

One meeting at Copeland's in particular was memorable, for it featured the oracular appearance of none other than Horace Traubel, Whitman's famous companion and biographer.[19] Copeland made preparations by taking a moment to dust off Traubel's book and cut open its pages before the man himself arrived. Traubel, for his part, did not fail to entertain the group with an anecdote about Whitman. A minister came to preach to the good gray poet, and, finally exasperated, Whitman rose up and exclaimed, "Oh Hell." "Is that all you have to say, Mr. Whitman?" the minister asked. To which the poet replied: "What more would you have me say? I can do it if you want to listen." At that the minister left, and Whitman turned to Traubel and said, "Wouldn't you say "Oh Hell" covered the case pretty thoroughly?" Locke would later invoke Whitman in an essay he wrote about American culture, and he was one of the few non-black writers in the American tradition that Locke commented on in print during the early years of his writing career.[20]

Locke became close friends with Harley, who was president of the Ethics Club, and in many ways he measured himself against him, since he was apparently the only person of color with whom Locke was close during his Harvard years. When Locke won the Rhodes, Harley told him: "Go and prosper Locke. You have acted the part of a man always. Your reward has come and with sincerity I congratulate you." Harley had intentions to go into the ministry, but Locke saw this as something he himself could not contemplate. Locke knew all too well that "by selecting the ministry he [Harley] will have to depend on the colored people for his living—I, thank goodness, don't have that obstacle among the many before me, if I had I should give it up as a hopeless task." Harley also brought considerable attention to himself when he dated white female students from Wellesley; indeed, it had become known that he had a young woman in his room without a chaperone. Harley also told Locke that someone had written to the dean of the seminary where he studied after Harvard to say that Harley should not have been admitted as he believed in "the fundamental antagonism of the races." Locke described Harley to his mother as someone who "doesn't hesitate to sling mud and sarcasm when he gets good and ready." The two young men discussed racial issues, and Locke often expressed various opinions to his mother as well. In the fall of 1906 he wrote that Du Bois's famous "Litany"—composed after the Atlanta race riots and widely circulated in the black press—was "weak and namby-pamby and as literature is unmentionably sentimental and slushy." The first part of this opinion may have come from Harley; the second is clearly Locke's own. He also went on to say that this proved that Du Bois was ill equipped to work in the South as Booker T. Washington could, adding for good measure that he himself would never cross the Mason-Dixon Line. Some years later he would break this vow, drawn to the South by Washington's authority.[21]

Harley also told Locke about an incident that was all too typical for people of color when they left the relatively broad-minded precincts of the Harvard campus. In August 1907, Harley was traveling on one of Boston's trolleys when he noticed that "an aged, shriveled, repulsive looking negress" wanted to get off at her stop. However, the conductor chose to ignore her for at least three stops. Harley spoke up sarcastically and asked if this wasn't a fine thing to do and then to laugh about it. The conductor immediately took up the challenge and told Harley that if he cared to, he could report the incident. At this further provocation, Harley decided to do just that, getting off at the last stop and going straight to the supervisor's office. Though he "urged age as the point" in lodging his complaint, Harley clearly knew the rudeness was racist and told Locke so. Locke was impressed with this story and retold it to his mother in detail.[22]

The essay Locke wrote on Paul Laurence Dunbar especially reveals his race consciousness at Harvard, and even addresses some of the tangled issues of race and esthetics that Locke contemplated throughout his life. Conscious as he was of the New England tradition of letters so resplendently on display at Harvard, Locke wanted to stake out some tradition of his own. He began the essay upon reading Dunbar's obituary (the poet died in 1906), and he planned immediately to send it out for publication. Locke showed the essay to Wendell and sent it to the *Atlantic Monthly,* clearly proud of what he had produced. He also delivered the essay as a lecture at a black church in Cambridge, probably invited to do so as a result of the notice the Rhodes Scholarship brought his way. After speaking to an audience of eighty-five people at the church, Locke joked wryly to his mother about his first such effort, saying that he "just uncorked the champagne of oratory and I was soaked with all sorts of mixed metaphors." He also said more seriously that "I think I can handle the masses quite as effectively as Father." (He may have remembered here his father's oration on the centennial of the Emancipation Proclamation.) Leadership for the African American tradition is often tied up with the homiletic style, and taking on the voice of the father at this point was something that resonated for Locke even as it caused anxiety and satisfaction. The essay began by claiming that no one had yet taken Dunbar's place as the representative Negro poet. Most important to Locke was that Dunbar respected his birthright of a race tradition and never sold that birthright.[23]

The essay confronted several literary subjects: the question of group representation, the need for high moral standards, and the right use of a cultural tradition. Calling Dunbar "a minor poet of very great significance," Locke argued that "in all that has been written about the Negro since *Uncle Tom's Cabin,* and even in that to a certain extent, the true Negro has been conspicuous by his absence." He boldly and directly admonished his audience, clearly one of African Americans, that when they read Dunbar's poetry, "you should recognize your race traditions in it, and first be humbled, and then thoughtful, and then be proud." After this rather complex admonition, Locke raised one of the central themes of his career when he insisted that "you can't pay for civilization except by becoming civilized, you can't pay for the English language and its benefits except by contributing to it in a permanent endowment of literature." In conclusion, and while saying that he did not wish to moralize, Locke insisted: "If we are a race we must have a race tradition, and if we are to have a race tradition we must keep and cherish it as priceless—yes as a holy thing and above all not be ashamed to wear the badge of our tribe." Being a part of a race meant recognizing and revering its traditions. A tradition became a fact by how those who had access to it treated it and used it in their own group definition. The same arguments he had used in his English 46 paper, "Impressions of Dante," were here being put to more local use, though Locke was still committed to seeing them as having universal application.

The theme of not forgetting his birthright weighed heavily with Locke, starting from his early memories of the ancestral fathers looking down on him as he did his genealogical research in the Philadelphia Merchants' Library. The note of race pride in the Dunbar speech might, however, seem at odds with Locke's disdain, even condescension, toward the other African

Americans at Harvard. Locke might have argued that the group of students he found offensive were so because they did not have enough self-regard, and they seemed unwilling to "pay" for the opportunities of their civilization by educating and refining their sensibility—especially in regards to language and literature—as called for by the theory of culture Locke embraced at that time. Locke himself, it must be said repeatedly, was never ashamed to be a member of his race, and he turned that belonging into an active commitment to what he called a "race tradition." He seldom separated this commitment from the other concern that motivated much of his thought and effort, namely the German sense of education and self-discipline—conveyed by the word *Bildung*—which he absorbed at Harvard and then even more so at Oxford and Berlin. But it would be mistaken to think of this "other" concern as something added to Locke's character in his twenties and thirties, for it was with him as soon as he could comprehend his parents' language.

This concern for self-discipline, both at odds with and fulfilled by an obligation to provide leadership for others when necessary, was something Locke articulated in many ways. One striking example of this is his work on an essay about the classical figure of Prometheus, an effort he referred to as his "literary high-water mark." In this myth about the defiant hero who brings great advantage to his people while incurring the wrath of the gods and unending punishment, Locke was clearly mediating some of the tensions he felt between his own elitist self-regard and his commitment to wear his group's race identity as a badge of honor. Locke had written on the subject as one of the many essays he wrote during his time at the School of Pedagogy. He had also been fascinated with it as a young child, and reminded his mother in a letter from Harvard how he had pasted an account of it to a door jam in the Camden house. Working on it during 1906, he brought it to completion in the following year. Perhaps most importantly he submitted it for consideration for the Bowdoin Prize. In fact, in a note he wrote to the Bowdoin judges he said that he preferred the Prometheus essay to the other he had submitted, and if the rules of the contest allowed only one submission per student, he would withdraw the Tennyson in favor of the Prometheus. The judges chose the Tennyson, perhaps because it fit in better with the Anglophilic literary sensibility then dominant. In many ways, however, the Prometheus essay is more intellectually challenging, and it says more about Locke's attitude toward some of the tensions that were driving him even as his Harvard career was drawing to a close.[24]

The essay is entitled "The Prometheus Myth: A Study in Literary Tradition," and the last word of the title is clearly one of the keys to its import for Locke. Casting a fairly broad theoretical framework, Locke discusses the relation between myth and narrative and argues that mythic narratives are always symbolic. Using Plato's writing on myth, Locke is able to argue that allegory and symbol are forms that result from the "various methods of combining interpretive narrative and universal truth that are at the disposal of literary art." He then gathers the various famous versions of the Prometheus legend, from Hesiod to Aeschylus and on to Goethe and Shelley, paying special attention to Browning's "few score lines" in his "Parley with Bernard Mandeville." What all this shows is that literature self-reflexively creates its tradition by constantly reinterpreting its own truths. This anticipates by more than a decade T. S. Eliot's famous 1919 essay on "Tradition and the Individual Talent,"[25] even as it expresses a special literary sensibility:

> If the study of literary tradition can show that the succession of interpretation and reinterpretation in literature is the perpetuation of truth, if it can demonstrate that the forms of literary symbolism are means to this end, it has answered its own question and has proved the evolution of literature.

At heart this formulation resembles Northrop Frye's theory of literature as an integrated self-enclosing system of symbolic meanings. It also draws on Locke's budding formalism, his sense that any undertaking gains value through being unified on its own autonomous basis. Locke arrived at these reflections in part because of his concern with the "race traditions" that he had explored in the Dunbar essay, and he would later refer to some of these same things by the phrase "ancestral legacy," which for him meant the sort of active historical and group memory that is important to the African American cultural and social experience.

Comparable to the Prometheus essay, in terms of scale and the amount of apparent labor he put into them, are two other essays Locke thought good enough to submit to the Bowdoin Prize competition. One was "Tennyson and His Literary Heritage," which won the prize Locke's senior year, and the other was "The Romantic Movement as Expressed by John Keats." The Tennyson essay tends to overpraise the part that convention plays in art, though this may have convinced the judges of its author's maturity and good taste. Locke argued: "Art, in its generic sense, is simply a conventional form of expression, a heritage of craftsmanship. The genius may be an iconoclast and may ignore the conventions of art-tradition, but the artist, never." This was a view of Tennyson that prevailed at the time (and often made him the foil of modernist innovators) and that dominated a canonical anthology like Palgrave's *Golden Treasury*. Locke never completely abandoned the formalist notion behind Tennyson's high standing, namely that a lyric poem justified its truth or value by the very skill with which it was composed; the "extra-poetic" truth it urged on its readers, or used to structure its claims, was of decidedly secondary importance. On many occasions, however, Locke concentrated on what the literary work offered as a claim about the world.[26]

For the Romanticism essay Locke used some of the work he had done at the School of Pedagogy on an essay about John Keats. Keats at this time was often considered the predecessor of Tennyson, essentially a lyricizing poet whose transcendent longings produced a melodic beauty allegorized as a form of spiritual freedom and striving. Locke created a context in which Keats became the epitome of Romanticism, stressing the way the movement took over much of the ethical framework of Christianity by placing it in a secular version of art as a redemptive, transcendent force in civilization. By so doing, Locke chose to stress the "spiritual" aspirations of the movement rather than its political iconoclasm:

> . . . that yearning for the Ideal, that desire for personal and direct vision which tolerates no intermediary of past insight, no restriction of past tradition, in short, that religion of personal art and philosophy which is its own High Priest, and constructs its own Holy of Holies, runs throughout all Romantic poetry. . . . Romanticism is above and beyond all else a spiritual Renaissance in literature.

Here Locke does not concern himself with an attempt to harmonize this view with his sense that tradition is of the essence in literature. Among other things, this shows that the contradictions between Protestant moral perfectionism, drawn perhaps from Emerson, and estheticizing self-cultivation, a result of his study with Wendell, could be experienced by Locke as non-canceling alternatives, even perhaps as versions of the same aspiration. But harder, more insistent choices lay ahead.

Locke's literary education at Harvard was a highly advanced one, as was his philosophic study, and they provided him with considerable advantages as a critic in later life. When he came to argue about the uses of folk art and ancestral traditions, or when he came to see many literary critical issues as needing a broader horizon in order to be properly appreciated, or when he struggled with the tensions between personal expression and group representation as the key elements in literary value, he would draw on his Harvard essays. And when he quipped about Palmer's "grudge" against bringing literature into a discussion of philosophy, he evinced his sense of the close relations that exist between various branches of the humanities. Even as early as 1906, when he wrote an answer on his midterm exam in his ethics course (Philosophy 4), he was able to combine an argument about ethical value with an esthetic sense that was also informed by the terms of evolution:

> The conception of goodness in general as that perfection of internal organization which makes possible the active perfection of something outside itself, in short, the philosophic conception of the organism as applied to goodness I consider above criticism. . . . This conception of goodness in general is merely a deduction from the universally accepted conditions of an organism and evolution which are, to my thinking, unimpeachable.

The thinking here is clearly indebted not only to evolution but to organic formalism, the notion borrowed from Romantic esthetics and German idealism that unity is the highest state of being and therefore possesses the highest value. Notions of "internal organization" and individual autonomy, borrowed from the natural sciences, served in part as a model for metaphysical formulations. As for the idea of evolution, it was rampant at Harvard in the early years of the twentieth century, and Locke absorbed it eagerly. However, he was to use it in special ways, turning it into one of his more important notions, namely the belief that all ideas are historically derived, as are the social and political forms to which they give rise. Such change and derivation in ideas—as well as in ethical values and imperatives—would also provide Locke with more than a few ideas of use to help critique those social forms that had led to false notions of supremacy, absolutism, and fixity.

The year 1907, his final one as an undergraduate at Harvard, started well for Locke, as he was elected to Phi Beta Kappa in January, pointing out to his mother that Brandt himself had not won this high honor. This was to be only the first of many accolades Locke won in his senior year. But his mind was also on his growing sense of authorship. Using a copy of his essay on Dunbar as a calling card, Locke sought and obtained Copeland's permission to join his English 12, an advanced class in writing. He was especially keen about this, as Copeland exercised considerable influence with editors. In the spring Locke told his mother of reading to Copeland two short stories he had written for the class. The development of his literary sensibility was beginning to equal, and perhaps for a while to outstrip, his interest in philosophy. These two stories are probably those that are included among his papers from Harvard. One of them, undated, is called "The Rain" and is more like a belletristic essay than a short story. The other is called "The Ebb Tide" and is about a Norwegian fishing village and bears the date of January 4, 1907. At least one of them is quite revealing about Locke's inner state, his ambitions during his final year at Harvard, and his already striking ability to delve into questions of sensibility as well as social tension.[27]

"The Rain" begins with an epigraph from Verlaine's well-known poem: "Il pleut dans mon cœur / Comme il pleut sur la ville." The first sentence sets the decidedly damp mood: "There can be nothing more depressing than a ride in an express train through a rainstorm. . . . " The atmosphere stays gloomy as the narrator encounters the man sitting opposite him on the train. Unable to decipher anything about him from his clothing, the narrator studies his face and deduces from his "repulsive lips" that he is "an ascetic and a sensualist." This paradoxical character does not approve of umbrellas and makes a habit of studying the rain. Soon the gloomy specter tells the narrator the story of his life. It turns out that one day in a fit of childish pique he spilt some ink on a book and was sent upstairs to his room. There in anger he spit out the window. Just then his mother entered the room to announce that his younger brother has just died and adds "God will punish you now." On the way to the brother's funeral the grandmother observed that the older boy has never cried. The narrator all the while thinks the man's story is trivial but still realizes the man is deep in thought. At the funeral the boy was finally able to cry while standing in the rain, and now the man says reflectively "I hate the rain and I love the rain too." The narrator refuses to be indulgent toward the man and says of him only that he "could not formulate a philosophy of the rain." The train goes through a tunnel and by the time it passes out on the other side the two men again feel like strangers. As they leave the train and part, the narrator can only admit that "everything that came into my head to say was either trite or unspeakable."

Though in the margins of the story Copeland wrote, rather ungenerously, that it was "on the whole painful and not too profitable," the story belongs to an important tradition of modernist narratives that explore the disjunction between interior states and social experience. It recalls the alienation and anomie of the sort that is explored in Rilke's *Notebooks of Malte Laurids*

Brigge, for example. The details of the train ride are skillfully handled, especially for an undergraduate who had not yet published his first story, and the
story-within-the story, though melodramatic, manages to express a certain
lurid period psychology that rings true. The narrative offers clues to Locke's
imagination and self-image, either in the role of the narrator or the man who
recounts his trauma. As the narrator, Locke explores his sense of how social
standing—all the external details of our communal existence, which might
include such things as skin color—only serve to frustrate our desire to know
one another. (This also signals the dissatisfaction Locke felt with realism
and naturalism.) Only if we tell our most guilty inner secrets can we come
to share in another's subjectivity; yet that, too, is condemned to frustration,
since many of our most painful experiences will seem trivial to others. As
the man who relates his trauma, on the other hand, Locke may be exploring
his own standing as an only child, one who has cultivated an aloof reserve
to protect himself from his envy and guilt. The paradox at the center of the
story—"I hate the rain and I love the rain too"—affirms the possibility of the
external world expressing, or symbolizing, our inner states, even as it shows
us the inescapably mundane quality of that interiority.

The other story, "The Ebb Tide," is not as successful as "The Rain."
Some reader—judging by the handwriting it is probably not Copeland—has
written on the title page the observation: "Both Maeterlinck and Yeats succeed from time to time in a sort of imaginative triumph of the vague." At least
this response recognizes the tradition that the story operates in, and its suggestion that excess vagueness often defeats short stories is near the mark. The
story concerns Hilda and her husband, Oscar, who are living in an unnamed
country when they are visited by a male American friend and his child. The
husband and the friend leave the next morning in a boat; after the men eventually go their separate ways, the friend sails for America and later returns to
the village. Oscar, on the other hand, attempts to return by sea in a dangerous tide. After he is found dead in his boat, the villagers remark: "Yes he
came in with the flood, but was going out with the ebb when we found him."
Since most of the motivation and the natural occurrences are not clearly represented, it's hard to make out what Locke was after. The story's atmosphere
is morbid and its sense of fate stifling.

Even more obscure than this morbid story is a poem Locke wrote, called
"The House of Death." It offers a possible clue to his psychology if read
loosely and symbolically. Consisting of two stanzas of uneven length (the
second may be incomplete), with variant lines for the close of each stanza, it

employs the stilted diction and funereal tone of much verse of the period. But its odd ending may suggest something:

> When I shall come before the House of Death
> Confronting there my journey's instant end
> Let me salute the sun as one salutes the friend
> Who toward some further hostel hurrieth
> Before the night fall; or else like one
> Who gladly would companionably abide
> But that some ancient feud unsatisfied
> Proscribes the inn, {though there were only one
> {Death may not house the sun[?]
> II
> And entering there, let me resign myself
> To all the customed usage of the place
> Condoning the rude manners of the inn
> Put off the body {idly as a cloak (though the sun shine)
> {gaily

The argument appears to concern a traveler who wants to shed his outer being as a way of transcending the roughness of the world and its injustices (the "ancient feud unsatisfied"), which could be read as a covert allusion to racial prejudice. The "rude manners" could very well suggest the "coarse" fellow students Locke objected to at Harvard, and the insouciant salute to the sun could reflect Locke's sense of disdain and self-reserve. In any case, the feelings are obscure even without being read biographically or symbolically, for the traditional Christian sense of death does not seem to be what the poem wants to convey—it more closely resembles Bryant's "Thanatopsis" than it does an orthodox religious poem. The speaker seems at once almost grandiose ("Let me salute the sun") and self-pitying ("let me resign myself") in his gestures, which are in any case clearer than his thoughts.[28]

Locke was, however, very clear-minded in his pursuit of the Rhodes Scholarship. As early as the spring of 1906 he had to secure the applications for it, and early in the academic year of 1906–1907 he set about arranging for references from his teachers, especially Royce and Copeland. He took the written exams for the Rhodes Scholarship at the new Harvard Medical School in Brookline in the second week of February. In between the Latin and arithmetic sections he took a break and surveyed the anatomical museum in the building, telling his mother that he saw "the most horrible and gruesome specimens." It was an odd way to relax, but presumably it worked. He passed the written exams for the Rhodes Scholarship and then faced the decision of whether to apply as a candidate from Massachusetts or Pennsylvania. He thought that the competition, which grew very keen at the next stage when a personal interview was required, would be less if he applied from Pennsylvania, his home state. He in fact did apply from there, though his current residence in Camden, New Jersey might have created a problem. The post-exam interview was scheduled for March 9. By the first week of April he was notified that he had won. He was the first of his race to be awarded the benefits of the enormous wealth of a man associated with imperialism, and no other African American was to win one while Locke was alive. The award was mentioned constantly throughout Locke's life. It immediately established him as a member of the "talented tenth," and he soon received attention from several Negro colleges and educators. He had joined a group singled out in the "contributionist" history of African Americans, one of those "firsts" that lent great credit to the race.[29]

He quickly prepared his applications for what Oxford referred to as "Senior Foreign Student Standing." He also had to apply to various Oxford colleges, admission to which was normally assured by winning the Rhodes. Writing to a Mr. Wylie, who served as the secretary for the Rhodes Foundation in charge of the scholarship winners and their arrangements, Locke applied to several colleges at once. He told his mother he preferred Magdalen, saying confidently that "I shall meet some of the best blood in England—a rather literary set and my introductions will take me farthest there." In the meantime he continued to serve as coxswain for a rowing team, since athletic achievement was a necessary part of a Rhodes Scholar's profile. The fact that Locke's rheumatically weakened heart kept him from more arduous forms of competition would make some of his British hosts skeptical about his complete satisfaction of this particular term of Rhodes's legacy. It was not the only issue on which he and his hosts would not see eye to eye.

The race issue was still there, coming up as it did in connection with his pursuit of the Rhodes and also between him and people he wished to cultivate. A measure of how racism operated among the genteel in America (and similarly among the British) can be gathered from the way President Eliot of Harvard explained his views of the situation, which included being sympathetic to Southern leaders:

> Perhaps if there were as many Negroes here as there, we might think it better for them to be in separate schools. At present Harvard has

about five thousand white students and about thirty of the colored race. The latter are hidden in the great mass and are not noticeable. If they were equal in numbers or in a majority, we might deem a separation necessary.[30]

The question of numbers, and of the role of a majority in a democratic society, would stay a part of the race issue for the next hundred years and beyond. Locke's sense of his own individuality at this point—despite how forcefully the Rhodes Scholarship would make him "noticeable"—kept him from dealing explicitly with the issue in these terms. But before long he would begin to formulate a way to be more explicitly antiracist in terms of a social collective.

An especially complicated sense of racism was that reflected in a book by Professor Royce, which would appear just after Locke left Harvard. Drawing in some ways on the approach of the pragmatists, Royce saw that the category of race was itself of limited accuracy:

[M]y present skepticism concerns the present state of science, and the result of such study as we have yet made of racial psychology of man is distinctly disappointing to those who want to make their task easy by insisting that the physical varieties of mankind are in our present state of knowledge sufficient guides to an interpretation of the whole inner contrast of the characters and of the mental processes of men.[31]

This passage obliquely expressed the then minority view that race was not a rigorously scientific concept, a view that Franz Boas would later develop in anthropology and a view that Locke also considered valuable. Other passages in the book were less circumspect. Royce felt that the Southern problem was a result not of racist theories but of a failure in what he called "administration," and it might well be cured if only Southerners would let blacks police their own communities. He justified this suggestion by referring to what he had seen of the problem in Jamaica and praised it as "the English way." In fact, Royce faced up to some of the aspects of racism, but his genteel Anglophilia kept him from exploring the issue with the sort of rigor that Locke would use in another eight years or so. When the student turned to his teachers for instruction in the issue of race, he was not likely to find any aggressive antiracist sentiment or reasoning. But Royce was a special case.

Royce was antiracist but also a paternalist, and Locke also saw him as "a crank on the Negro problem [who] goes on a regular tirade at the slightest provocation." For his own part Locke insisted that he did not "care for this muddling of a purely personal issue of my life with the race problem"—and then, perhaps recalling one of the famous passages from *Souls of Black Folk,* argued against it by insisting that "I am not a race problem."[32] Winning the Rhodes Scholarship did more, nevertheless, than anything else to place Locke in a position of representing the race. Mention was made in many newspapers throughout the country, black and white, such as the *Tuskegee Student* and the Wilberforce college newspaper, as well as the Springfield *Republican,* two Rochester papers, the *Catholic American,* and many more. The *Philadelphia Bulletin* ran a picture of Locke pointing out that he had won out over fifty competitors. The *Press,* another Philadelphia newspaper, expressed considerable local and national pride and editorialized that

> the solitary success speaks for little, but Mr. Locke belongs to a class growing rapidly of colored men whose families have had the advantage of education for three generations. Mr. Locke's success is a record of steady creation among 9,000,000 of our colored fellow-citizens, of men and women not only with personal training and education, but with the indefinable but none the less real advantages of a family tradition of liberal learning. (*Press,* April 21, 1907)

There were also negative reactions, such as a letter to the editor of one paper that said Locke's being awarded a Rhodes would tend to put the famous scholarship under a cloud in the South. So when Paul Elmer More, the famous editor and critic known for his role in the conservative New Humanism, served as a judge for the Bowdoin Prize that Locke won, he took pleasure in telling his mother that it was "an ironic slap at the Southerns." But the majority of journalistic notices were favorable, and the intensity of interest, though it greatly pleased Mary Locke, seemed to catch her son up short. He even received a request from a man who wanted to know if he could distribute pictures of Locke in a fundraising scheme to help build a new church building. The *Independent,* a left-wing African American newspaper, approached him to write a journalistic account of his impressions of the English university, a request to which he eagerly consented.

Though he eventually came to accept this distinction as related to the destiny of a larger group, at the time it was awarded Locke felt that his personal accomplishment was being distorted or even co-opted. In one particularly long letter home, he detailed the congratulations from relatives, neighbors, and hangers-on, often questioning the sincerity of the well-wishers. Not only was the event widely covered in the press, people dunned Mary Locke for information. Locke told her to resist: "I wouldn't give people clippings—just tell them where to get them—it's more dignified—If I ever really do become a public man you don't want to deal in newspapers, do you?" At one point upon his return to Cambridge from Camden, an especially intrusive reporter from the *Boston American* accosted him, insisting that Locke say something about Booker T. Washington or he would make up a quotation; "I have some privacy and I mean to keep it," Locke complained to his mother, and said that in angrily telling the reporter he had had enough, "I made the air blue."[33]

Pressure of publicity also sparked a series of complaints from Locke that were charged by some of the feeling that must have developed throughout his years at Harvard. At one point he said: "It is a typical Harvard attitude to make you prove what you can do—I hardly see how they can ask much more of a Negro." He protested that "whatever credit I take to myself I take because after a certain fashion I have always believed in myself." The adolescent arrogance and self-assurance he carried with him from Philadelphia, and that his mother had warned against, remained steadfast. But he also complained that he was not "a dime museum freak," and he refused "to be put on exhibition," meant to serve as an illustration of what the race could accomplish. In a final fit of rebellion against his group identity (the "them" are clearly Negroes, especially those whose congratulations he felt were not totally sincere), he concluded by saying:

> [W]hen I sail I'll leave them and they won't figure in my life again unless I have the objectionable bothersome task of leading them some day— and really I'd rather not—if I ever do it will be forced upon me.[34]

Though the level of his frustration was high at this moment, Locke was clarifying for himself the balance between what he called self-culture and service that he had spoken of a few years previously. The shadow of race leadership was felt as burdensome. Locke's insistence on the personal dimension of his accomplishment was strong enough to be reiterated. He wrote home in another letter with considerable determination that he meant to accept the experience only on his own terms. Yet even here he could not completely escape the question of group consciousness, or at least one of its most bedeviling aspects, the question of leadership, which continued to come up again and again:

I'm not going to England as a Negro—I will leave the color question in New York. . . . [T]he only condition on which I will take up the Negro question again is the race leadership in America—Otherwise none of it for me.

Also at this time Locke met a millionaire named Shipman, who was going to China but who was also considering philanthropic support of Negro education when he returned. He wanted to hear Locke's views, and they discussed the issues for five hours. Locke told his mother that "I discovered for the first time that I had a definite system of the race problem"—adding, in response to Shipman's question about the desirability of separate churches, that "I answered the same way I would answer the question of separate schools." Locke was not specific about his views at this time, though it is fairly clear that he felt people of all races should attend the same schools; only later did he express a separate sense of Negro culture, in part by maintaining educational and ecclesiastical traditions that are properly derived from Negro experience. He was also able to meet William Lloyd Garrison in the summer before he sailed to England and to discuss the race question with him; Garrison's cousin was working as editor of the *New York Evening Post,* and was curious to know if Locke was interested in working as a journalist. William Lloyd Garrison's grandson was Oswald Garrison Villard, who would soon play a role as editor of the *Nation* and a board member of the NAACP.[35]

The award of the Bowdoin Prize, announced in June, was not as significant as the Rhodes, but Locke took special satisfaction in it, for it conveyed a highly developed sense of literary talent and achievement. The prize carried a cash award of $250.00, a bronze medal, and the chance for a public reading— and what he called "more popularity[,] or notoriety as it seems in my case." It also meant that when Mary Locke made the trip up for the Commencement Exercises, she would be able to see her son's name set apart from his classmates in the official program. The Rhodes Scholarship, the Bowdoin Prize, Phi Beta Kappa, magna cum laude, Honors in Philosophy—it was indeed a most impressive array of prizes. Mary Locke must have been near to bursting with justifiable pride, and one can only wonder how much it was tempered by the awareness that the Rhodes victory meant a voyage filled with anxiety for her and many months of separation for both of them.[36]

The summer was filled with preparations for the first transatlantic voyage Locke was to make; by the end of his life he would be a seasoned visitor to European ports of call. Unlike Greener, his fellow Harvard graduate, Locke would find his talents and his education fully exercised on both the personal and social levels. Meanwhile some of his classmates were moving into places in the literary establishment. Van Wyck Brooks, for example, had already sailed in steerage to Europe and would within a year or so write the book, *The Wine of the Puritans,* that would launch his career as a major American critic. Locke was set on a different path, however, shaped by circumstances at once predetermined and self-willed. Having absorbed a great deal of philosophy and esthetic education, he had also managed to reflect critically on the intersections of race and culture. His own private Harvard legacy would sustain him for many years, and a decade later he would return to Cambridge for yet more education. Because of the Rhodes prize, however, he was in the midst of a congratulatory atmosphere that was perhaps as intense as any other he would experience. Whatever misgivings he may have had about his ability to meet the next round of study and self-cultivation, publicly he expressed no hesitation. He left Harvard Yard with as little obvious anxiety as he had first entered it. For now he was leaving with a sense of genuine adventure. It was on September 24 that he wrote his first letter from the ship, just beyond America's edge: "Am on board all right sailing out into the ocean now—just out of sight of Liberty statue. . . . I feel very hopeful just as if one had a new world to conquer."[37]

CHAPTER THREE

Oxford and Berlin

Though Locke left a thickly structured social life in Harvard, he arrived at an even thicker one in Oxford. While looking for housing, he wrote his mother that at Oxford "good locations have a lot to do with an entree into social life." As was the case in Harvard, Locke recognized quickly how to read the social codes and practiced them with seeming ease. The next three years would be a social whirl, spinning with introductions, calling cards, riding lessons, and visits to the tailor and specialty shops along the High Street. There would be essays published, a long thesis written, and a new set of stimulating and cosmopolitan friends that he entertained and traveled with to the continent. At times it might have seemed to Locke that it was Harvard replayed with a finer tone; at other times Locke felt weariness and disappointment when a certain intellectual sterility showed through the pleasant surfaces. Like many other travelers, Locke felt the experience threw national differences into high profile. Moreover, the issue of race would play out in various ways, and the issue of homosexuality as well, as Locke was struck by the fate of Oscar Wilde at the hands of his compatriots.[1]

On the first day of October 1907 Locke wrote his mother from Ward's Private Hotel on Upper Bedford Street near Russell Square. He was in the company of Downes, a Harvard friend, who was to study for a year at Oxford before going back to take a Ph.D. at Harvard. Locke described himself as having arrived in England "penniless as Columbus," continuing the explorer metaphor that he used when he sailed off to cross the Atlantic for the first time. Shortly after arriving in Oxford he secured rooms for himself at

20 Banbury Road. The autumn and winter seasons saw him using his connections adroitly. He was able to meet Thackeray's niece and was even promised an introduction to George Bernard Shaw. More importantly, he continued his friendship with Horace Kallen, who had been an instructor at Harvard and had come to Oxford with introductions from James and Royce. He was, according to Locke, "a brilliant Boston Ghetto Jew" who was already "hobnobbing with the chief intellectual lights of Oxford." It was Kallen who had promised the introduction to Shaw, and Locke saw his new friend as "working himself up and I am holding on to his coattails so to speak." Kallen would later become an important friend for Locke in terms of his connections with American pragmatism, but not before Kallen would play a role in some of Locke's unpleasant experiences of racism while at Oxford.[2]

By December Locke's social life was so active that he was changing his clothes four or five times a day. He told Mary Locke that "I have almost forgotten I was colored."[3] This was in a context of reporting that in seven weeks he had entertained at twenty-five lunches, and had been a guest at twelve others; at five of these he was the sole guest. There were also trips to London, which allowed him to describe many sights to his mother, chief among them the opera and the National Gallery. Two clubs, the Union Liberal and the United Arts, were soon to have him as a member. He took advantage of the shared services of a man servant, who was also employed by five or six other students. Some sense of his lifestyle can be garnered from his bills. One arrived from Frank Cooper, a warehouseman and wine merchant at 83 High Street, where Locke ordered camembert, claret, Green Chartreuse, Mysore and Mocha coffee, figs, a Genoa cake, and three bottles of Moselle. His tailor was hard at work as well, for Stamden & Co., also on the High Street, sent him a bill for his single-breasted Chesterfield, lined in black satin, and other items, for just over twelve pounds sterling; the special velvet collar was seven shillings, six pence extra. For three pounds thirteen more, he was the indubitably proud owner of a black dress Shetland dinner jacket. His riding fees at the Clarendon Hotel Stables for two months came to over four pounds.

Friendships from Harvard served to bridge the cultural distance between America and England. In addition to Kallen, there was the exuberant presence of Harley, whom he described as being swell-headed as usual. Harley was still pursuing his divinity studies, and Locke went to hear him preach in Gloucester and Banbury. Locke told his mother that he and Downes "have grown to like each other immensely and the friendship is . . . intimate and companionable"; Downes was characterized by Locke as being "at times . . . very taciturn." But then again he could be "most communicable—a great deal

FIG. 3.1. This was apparently taken while Locke was at Oxford, 1907–10, when his riding lessons added to his expenses. Moorland-Spingarn Research Center.

more so than any deceitful person like myself can ever hope to be." Locke may have felt that the pressures of a new social order called on him to exercise that "diplomatic" aspect of his character he had polished at Harvard. Seeing to it that he was made coxswain of a rowing crew, he suggested he was improving enough that he might even row for the university team, and so give a "black eye to those people who said I did not qualify athletically for the Rhodes Scholarship."[4]

By the middle of the winter he was thinking about the piece he had been commissioned to write for the *Independent* about his Oxford experience. Thinking in terms of his possible career in journalism, he told his mother he hoped it would secure him an entree to the *Nation*. Through Kallen he had become involved with what he referred to as the WaWa people, "the society of young American composers who are trying to found an American school of music on Indian and Negro melodies." At the same time he was busying himself at the piano, playing the music of Edward A. MacDowell; all of this showed that his sense of his own American identity was still firm. He also met Tennyson's niece, a Miss Weld, and was given a letter of introduction from one of his Harvard teachers to Professor Baird, the successor to Benjamin Jowett, the late master of Balliol College. But Baird was in his dotage and asked Locke absent-minded questions and spilt his food. Locke did not seem particularly interested in finding an Oxford professor or don who would serve as a role model or mentor, as did Palmer or Münsterberg at Harvard. Other observations about local customs led Locke to complain to his mother about "Oxford superficiality and insincerity."[5]

Locke continued to express such a negative reaction off and on all the while he was at Oxford. It came to a head in a letter he wrote in the spring of 1909, at the end of his second full year there. In it he talks about the case of Oscar Wilde and the way the disclosure of his homosexuality ruined his reputation. But for Locke the real issue is less Wilde than it is the mindset of the people at Oxford:

> [T]hey [Oxfordians] are particularly stupid priggish people[,] witness the disowning of Oscar Wilde. They don't seem to mind as long as a man keeps his private life away from public knowledge and censure— for instance Oscar Wilde's defects were well known and the subject of risqué gossip while he was yet at Oxford—Swineburne [*sic*] they disowned because he was a confirmed erotic and drunkard. (ALPHU 164-57/26)

Locke at one point complained about his roommate, whose "apologetics" regarding some unspecified incident he called "unmanly and a break of friendship etiquette," adding somewhat bitterly that "at Oxford everything Oxfordian is right." This side of Locke—his insistence on straight talking between friends and coworkers—was clearly at odds with his own self-described ability, and in some cases his willingness, to be "diplomatic" to the point of deceitfulness. The conflict here can be explained in part by the cultural gap between Americans and Oxfordians, and Englishmen generally. Locke began gravitating toward people of color in some of his friendships at this time, especially students from the British colonies. Unlike his aversion to the lower-class blacks at Harvard, Locke's attitude toward people seemed to change in the direction of more tolerance for, and interest in, individuals, especially those who were themselves somewhat eccentric in their attitude toward establishment values.

Many of his new friends found Locke impressive, and he was soon to be sought after for both social and intellectual companionship. At Harvard he had held back at some of the social functions, being careful not to drink to excess as many of his classmates were inclined to do. At Oxford the taking of tea in one's room, and the more formal atmosphere which encouraged using the dinner hour more socially, appealed to him, and he collected calling cards from several people in and outside his closest circle. Remarking to his mother at one point that he had met the Rhodes Scholars from Maine and South Dakota, he added that he was quite content to let them come to him, perhaps indicating that some of his new English friends were more interesting than American ones. Clearly, and paradoxically considering his estimation of what was revealed by the Wilde affair, a certain amount of Anglophilia was entering into the picture. He started out reading Classics, a traditional English approach, buoyed by his good grades in Greek at Harvard. Eventually, however, he found the pronunciation of the ancient languages difficult to master, and he shifted to philosophy. By October 17 of his first term he had matriculated at Hertford College, and according to his letters home, he was quite well and happily settled.[6]

How quickly Locke adapted himself to the Oxford scene can be gauged by the article he was asked to write for the *Independent*. This was a liberal newspaper that ran news items, cultivated a world perspective in its reporting, and also included a literary section. In the July 15, 1909 issue Locke's essay, entitled "Oxford Contrasts," appeared; it was reprinted unchanged three months later in the *Colored American Magazine*. Quite perceptive and elegant in style, the essay is obviously balanced in its views. The word "contrasts" is one that took on special meaning for Locke, suggesting the important knowledge that derives from contact between cultural or racial groups, and its use here shows that he approached this article seriously, not just as some undergraduate travel piece. For Locke, Oxford is "a society of scholars, a scholar-craft for the perpetuation rather than for the extension of learning." This means, among other things, that the "typical Oxonian's philosophy is a philosophy of manners," and that cultivation, especially by the dons, or tutors, is "very like a prudent gardener who relies a prayerful lot on the sun, and the wind, and the rain—on his system and the natural laws of growth."[7]

Reliance on such a system means that innovation and personal incentive are not particularly valued, in contrast, say, to the individualism fostered by James at Harvard. People who leave Oxford to teach do not intend to set up "little Oxfords all over England" but rather want to have people consider Oxford itself a "great Mecca." This "medieval" attitude has virtues and drawbacks, especially considering that it survives into the modern age:

> Oxford [has] a sort of religious dominance over the province of knowledge that certainly makes the right to teach, and too often the right to be taught a matter of apostolic succession, and excommunicates all education that does not subordinate itself as directly preparatory to that system.

Clearly Locke includes himself among those who were educated in a way that was not "directly preparatory" for Oxford, and so he speaks as a subordinate, an outsider. But by using the vocabulary of Catholic theology he is twitting his hosts, who were notoriously anti-Catholic. The word "medieval" also conjures up, at least for American readers, a world of religious superstition and repression, so that the action of excommunication is likely to be seen as an act of tyranny. The word "Mecca" further suggests the persistence of a zealous fidelity.

Locke grants certain points in the university's favor, for example its development of an extension program and its new schools of sociology and engineering. He insists, nevertheless, on the medieval nature of the place. When, however, he says Oxford is consistent, "and one must either take issue with the system or with nothing at all," it is clear he prefers the former alternative. He approves of the fact that "every university function, every university custom is both the occasion and the cause of some little bit of wholesome social life." Appreciating Oxford as a place of "select retirement," he suggests that the urban location of most American universities may keep them from being "the home of scholarship, of beauty and repose." However, he is most impressed with what he calls "the beauty of impersonal service," which allows Oxford to "consecrate . . . even the most aristocratic of all aims, self-culture, and makes one wish democracy did not need to be so blatant, so self-assertive—but it does need to be." The tension between self-culture and service appears in nearly perfect balance, though the American approach, with its individualism and energy, persists as the ultimate, even the inevitable, standard.

Before concluding, Locke opines on two more issues: the purpose of the Rhodes Scholarship and the English attitude toward race. On the first point, he defines the Rhodes man in terms that were dear to his own heart and sets out what could be seen as a plan for his own development over the next few years: "If he has served his time and purpose well, he will be . . . a man whose sympathies are wider than his prejudices, whose knowledge is larger than his beliefs, his work and his hopes greater than he himself. He will be an ideal type—a rare type, indeed—a patriotic cosmopolitan." The last word resonates throughout all of Locke's Oxford experience and is plainly his ego-ideal, but the contrastive adjective that defines it is also important. The essay itself is an example of how one can be paradoxically both patriotic and cosmopolitan.[8]

The final reflections in the essay have to do with race, and Locke injects a personal note when he speaks as "one who has lived upon the cleavage-plane of so great a class distinction at that of races in America." Locke wryly points out that such distinctions are "marvelously subtle things," which are "sometimes . . . ridiculously unreal, self-contradictory," and yet they "manage to evade the keen edge of logic which splits a hair instead." England has class distinctions but no race distinctions that Locke can see, at least not any which "have taxed [his] blunt democratic vision." What he has seen is indifference, recognizing that peculiar form of Anglo-Saxon ethnocentrism which often proceeds simply by assuming that ethnicity does not matter. He says:

> But racially, I prefer disfavor and that most proverbial and effective of disciplines, persecution even, to indifference. One cannot be neutral towards a class or social body without the gravest danger of losing one's own humanity in denying to some one else the most human of all rights, the rights to be considered either a friend or an enemy, either as helpful or harmful.

The argument here contains several complexities. Locke says he "prefers race prejudice to race indifference," while alluding to the notion of hardship as educative, seeing in persecution the chance to develop discipline that is not only useful but a source of wisdom. The matter will be aggravated, moreover, when Locke sees that what he here calls indifference may be more purposive and directed than that word suggests.

Locke's experience of Oxford and its styles and mores led him in several directions. These new developments were in large measure shaped by two experiences: the question of racial discrimination, especially in regard to the question of which of the colleges would admit him, and his membership in the Cosmopolitan Club.

The first issue took shape even before Locke reached England, and it influenced his assessment of indifference on the part of the British, or the habit of hiding their prejudices with sangfroid. Shortly after being informed about the Rhodes Scholarship, Locke applied to various colleges at Oxford. Admission to any college was not guaranteed by the award of the Rhodes. Instead applications were handled and sent on to the individual colleges by the secretary for the Rhodes Fund at Oxford; when Locke applied, this office was held by Francis J. Wylie. Locke wrote to Wylie in May 1907 to say that five colleges had refused his application: Madgalen, Balliol, Merton, Brasenose, and Christ Church. At first Locke seemed unperturbed and said that he would reapply, and if still rejected he would accept provisional status "to any one of the smaller colleges." In August Wylie, writing from St. Petersburg where he was apparently vacationing, responded that Locke should not come over too early. He added some statistics about the colleges, pointing out that though Balliol had rejected only one of the twenty-four foreign students who had applied, three of the other colleges had rejected more than they had taken. Obviously the question of race hovered in the background. Wylie was apparently trying to defuse the situation, mentioning that New College and University College had recently adopted a policy of accepting no more Rhodes Scholars whatsoever; he then suggested Hertford, which was the college Locke eventually enrolled in and remained a member of throughout his time at Oxford.

Unknown to Locke, Wylie had worked diligently to rescind his Rhodes' award. He had researched Locke's birth certificate, used the fact that his name on the certificate was "Arthur" and that it falsely read "white" as the race to defame Locke to the Rhodes Trust, organized a meeting to reevaluate Locke's January 1907 exam, and supported the white students at Oxford who refused to reside at their college if Locke were admitted.[9] Wylie's deceptive behavior could be seen as foretelling behavior Locke would too often encounter at Oxford. Wylie even wrote Locke, supplying advice on how to manage the personal and racial slights Locke was receiving. He told Locke "that you have in this question an interest which is racial and not merely personal. That interest will no doubt give to your work here a special zest. It may also sometimes bring its own difficulties." By turning an insult into an occasion to demonstrate one's superiority, this might have mollified Locke, though its condescension may also have rankled. In any case, Locke accepted Wylie's advice and even managed to form a friendship with him, as attested by their correspondence which continued for several years after Locke left Oxford. Wylie evidently never revealed to Locke his leadership role in trying to rescind Locke's award.

The question of English attitudes toward racial matters was something that was never again to leave Locke's awareness. He remarked to his mother shortly after his arrival that all the people in Oxford seemed eager to discuss the issue. There were other black men at Oxford at this time; in fact, one of them, a Jamaican author named Dr. Theophilus Scholes, was introduced to Locke early on.[10] Scholes had been a medical missionary in Africa and had written a book on the British politician Joseph Chamberlain (1863–1914) as well as a survey of race relations. The student who provided the introduction was another black man, Pixley Seme, from Natal, South Africa, who was to become a very close friend. Seme was sophisticated and cultured, a student at Jesus College, and he also had lodgings in London at the Middle Temple, where members of the legal profession resided. He had graduated from Columbia University in 1906 and would return to South Africa to help found and eventually become the second president of the African National Congress. Locke enjoyed trips to London and the continent with him. He recorded on a calling card the fact that he and Seme had breakfast together on March 3, 1908, and talked of Tuskegee; this apparently was an occasion where Locke could explain his views on the merits of the industrial and practical education stressed by Booker T. Washington. One of the several people of color that he met at Oxford, Seme helped turn Locke's attention to racial matters as a subject of intellectual analysis as well as personal commitment.

In fact, when it came to speaking of Tuskegee and Washington's approach to the problems of race relations, Seme could speak with more authority than Locke. Seme was born in 1881 at a mission outside Durban, South Africa. Following the lead of a friend who had come to America and studied at Oberlin College, Seme arrived in 1897 and began studying at the Mount Hermon School in Northfield, Massachusetts. Raised as a Christian in South Africa by a Congregationalist minister, from whom he took his surname, Seme was to go on to study at Columbia while living in Harlem. At Columbia he delivered a speech entitled "Regeneration of Africa" that announced the theme of Pan-Africanism. Africans, he claimed, "although not a strictly homogeneous race, possess a common fundamental sentiment," and more importantly, perhaps, a "common destiny." After Columbia, he traveled south and heard Washington speak at a conference of the Negro Business League of America. Later, after founding the African National Congress, he would invoke this moment, describing "the great vision of national power I saw at Atlanta." He studied for the bar in London before going up to Oxford where he met Locke. Hounded by debtors, as was Locke, in part because of their commitment to

FIG. 3.2. Pixley Seme. Graduation photo from Columbia University, 1904. Pixley Ka Isaka Seme, one of three founders of the African National Congress, South Africa; member of the Cosmopolitan Club. University Archives, Columbia University.

sartorial excellence and high culture, Seme never lost sight of his goals to return home and forge a political movement with his fellow Africans based on a heightened consciousness of race and its role in world affairs.[11]

Seme and Locke shared many things beyond their refined tastes. The question of leadership and the way one prepared for it by an advanced education, not to mention the threat of resulting alienation, gave the two plenty of material for conversation. Continental travel and further education acted as forces of deferral for both men, keeping them for a while from their vocations as leaders in racial matters. In 1910, for example, after a time in Holland practicing his Dutch so that he could address the Boers in his native land, Seme wrote to Locke from Johannesburg that he "could not stick the continent any longer, so I resolved to come home and earn an honest living as I could not play the Duke with only an income of two guineas a week." Locke would take up many of Seme's ideas about Africa in the next several years, and he would also find himself making hard choices about his place in the world that resembled those of his elegant and jovial friend. Unlike his experience at Harvard, where his fellow blacks were not sufficiently of a social class to suit Locke, at Oxford the friendship of Seme and others put the question of racial identity into a different context.

But the issue of race was never far from the surface. Horace Kallen, the German-born Jew from Boston, who had served as the section instructor in the course that Locke took with Santayana at Harvard, privately shed light on just how thickly complex the question would be, not only at Harvard but also at Oxford. Kallen was with Locke at Oxford, as a Sheldon scholar, in 1907 and 1908, and he later credited Locke with helping to germinate the idea for which Kallen is best known: cultural pluralism, or multiculturalism. In a series of letters to Barrett Wendell, Kallen discussed Locke in revealing and disturbing ways. As Kallen described the origins of his relationship with Locke, he told of the germination of an important idea:

It was in 1905 that I began to formulate the notion of cultural plural-ism. . . . I had a Negro student named Alain Locke, a very remarkable young man—very sensitive, very easily hurt—who insisted that he was a human being and that his color ought not to make any difference. . . .

Two years later when I went to Oxford on a fellowship he was there as a Rhodes scholar, and we had a race problem because the Rhodes scholars from the South were bastards. So they had a Thanksgiving dinner which I refused to attend because they refused to have Locke.

And he said, "I am a human being," just as I had said it earlier. What difference does the difference make? We are all alike Americans. And we had to argue out the question of how the differences made differ-ences, and in arguing out those questions the formulae, then phrases, developed—"cultural pluralism," "the right to be different."

Wendell responded to this concern for Locke by adding to gentility his out-right racist sentiment. He advised Kallen to treat Locke with respect, but at the same time he, Wendell, could not manage to expunge his own feelings.

Keeping up appearances, a bourgeois sentiment dear to Wendell, set a standard of conduct toward all members of the black race: "It would be disastrous to them, if they are gentlemen at heart, to expose them in private life to such sentiments of repugnance as mine. . . ." Kallen responded by agreeing, "you have phrased my own feeling toward the race," but he told Wendell that he had managed to invite Locke to tea and introduced him to various of his friends. Perhaps Kallen did not feel the same repugnance that was animating Wendell.[12]

Kallen maintained a courteous friendship with Locke for many years, and later they contributed essays to periodicals together. The summer after the incident of the southern students' rejection of Locke, Kallen sent him a postcard from Cambridge. Locke presumably had told Kallen about his desire to study value theory, and Kallen was encouraging: "Subject is excellent—a practically virgin field," he wrote. Since presumably there had been a subsequent dinner for the Rhodes Scholars, apparently to mark the end of the first academic year, Kallen added another bit of encouragement: "Glad you went to the banquet & photo. You'll never need to go again, but this first time was very important. Damn the cotton-belters." Both men seemed willing to share the credit for the formulation of the important antiracist idea that came to be known as multiculturalism. Kallen would go on to write a number of important essays about ethnicity and immigration in the 1920s, which were collected into a volume called *Culture and Democracy in the United States* (1924), though they almost completely ignored the issue of race. If Locke ever knew of the explicit accounts and feelings that Kallen and Wendell shared about his race, he apparently never recorded the fact.

The racial issue entered again into Locke's experience with his application for a degree, which involved the submission of his thesis on value theory for approval. Even though he was able to resist the conclusion that the rejection was based on racial discrimination, when he made notes on the incident many years later, he connected the experience with two others:

> I should have had to complain of discrimination which so far as it related to the degree examination itself was in my best judgment personal rather than racial but which would immediately have been construed as racial by public opinion, especially in view of the frequent recurrence in my Oxford career of instances from other sources of racial discrimination, two instances of which had already appeared in the public press. I thus deliberately resorted to a strategic coverup at the great risk of personal honor and peace of mind.

One of these "instances" referred to was perhaps the outcry of the American press in the South to his selection for the Rhodes, while he was still at Harvard. However, there were two other separate incidents of a similar nature, which occurred at Oxford, and they might have been what Locke was referring to.[13]

The first of these—alluded to in the quotation above from Kallen—took place shortly after Locke arrived. There were altogether almost eighty Americans studying at Oxford at this time, and they formed a club which each year held a Thanksgiving dinner. But in 1907, apparently spurred on by Americans from the South, they refused to invite Locke. One of his teachers, Professor Dyer, invited him to his house instead, causing dismay among the white students. The second incident made matters worse. In 1909, when the American Ambassador, Whitelaw Reid, had invited all the American Rhodes Scholars to lunch at a London hotel, Locke was invited. The southerners, however, asked him not to accept. He told his mother that he attended the lunch, but "premeditatedly" decided to be the first to leave. He meant this as a way of taunting his prejudiced countrymen: "they were sore I came but sorer still that I should be the first to leave." These two instances, plainly caused by Americans and their racial prejudice, were connected by Locke with the English rejection of his degree. Although he felt the English attitude in his examination may have been personal rather than racial, and thus may have been one of "indifference," he saw that underneath there was still the "frequent recurrence" of benighted illusions about racial superiority. The reference in the *Independent* article to English attitudes toward race certainly was in his mind as well. His "strategic coverup" was not something that he was prepared to repeat indefinitely.[14]

Locke's relation to the Cosmopolitan Club served as a powerful influence on his views, strengthening his commitment to a broader sense of racial themes even as it formed the center of a network of friendships and intellectual investigations. Locke helped found the club, along with Seme and his friends the Scotsman Percy J. Philip, the Ceylonese Lionel de Fonseka, and others. The club's charter said that its purpose was "to promote mutual knowledge and sympathy between members of different nationalities residing in Oxford." It met every second Tuesday during each term of the year, and the "debate" speeches were of fifteen minutes' duration. *The Oxford Cosmopolitan*, the first issue of which appeared in June 1908, was the club's journal, and it was dedicated to "removing many a narrow national or racial prejudice by coming into contact with new ideas and ways of thought." The first year featured lectures mainly on literary subjects, but with a decidedly

FIG. 3.3. Locke with members of the Cosmopolitan Club. Locke was a member of this Oxford Club that engaged in anti-imperialist cultural criticism. Locke is fifth from the right. Moorland-Spingarn Research Center.

national focus; there was a lecture on Norwegian literature and another on Whitman; there was a talk by Philip on Thoreau and one by Murkerjea on the Bengali novelist Bunkim.

The formation of the club clearly grew out of the experience of several of its members as colonial subjects of the British Empire, men who impressed Locke with their commitment to return to their various countries and serve the interests of their people. In the spring of 1909 Locke wrote home to say that he was planning on sitting for the BCL—the Bachelor of Civil Law—degree at Oxford in a few years. This was a direct response to Seme and others who were "formulating plans for the admission of Asiatic and African peoples into the jurisdiction of international law." In the same letter, he observed that "Chesterton was right about Oxford—it is a training school for the governing classes—and has taught your son its lesson—Many thanks." Such a career plan was the result of the contact and friendship Locke had established with the members of the Cosmopolitan Club, and the club helped determine Locke's sense of himself for the next several years.[15]

If the formation of the Cosmopolitan Club produced nothing else in Locke's life and thought than his own unpublished essay on "Cosmopolitanism and Culture," it would have played a major role in his development. Like a number of other important efforts in his life that remained unpublished, Locke's work on this topic represented an advance in his intellectual range and an ample demonstration of his self-confidence and aptitude as a thinker. This essay, which exists in several partial versions, shows that Locke was formulating a sweeping cultural criticism that combined historical schematizing, philosophical reflection, and social analysis in a style that is a forerunner of that of intellectuals throughout the period of high modernism, that is, roughly from 1910 to 1950. Some of the piece's passages anticipate the style or content of such broad-ranging modernist attempts to offer a critique of twentieth century culture as T. S. Eliot's *Notes towards the Definition of Culture*, the essays of Ezra Pound and T. E. Hulme, and the criticism of Edmund Wilson. Locke's viewpoint was, to be sure, deeply rooted in tolerance and racial justice in a way that separated him from such figures as Eliot and Pound. As was the case with many of these figures, however, Locke's argument both diagnosed what was wrong with modern culture and attempted to identify within it the liberating potential of its cultural and social energy. It would not be amiss to read cosmopolitanism as Locke's word for modernism.

"Cosmopolitanism and Culture" should not be viewed only in the context of Anglo-American modernism, however, since it is the essay in which Locke first exhibits his interest in a worldwide view of culture and modernity. Markedly influenced by his friendships with men from nonwestern countries, he was beginning to separate himself from a view of racial difference that was restricted to the American experience. Though for the time being Locke did not focus on race as the central problem of the twentieth century, nevertheless he was thinking through the problems of what sociologists call a "restricted group," one that has developed its own ethos and particular point of view. This particularized viewpoint meant that the question of integration into the larger dominant culture, and the less explicit question of leadership in the small group, would always be in the background, proximately or remotely affecting the shape of the argument. Add to this the sense of strangeness that Oxford induced in Locke, despite his earnest efforts to fit in with the British as well as to downplay his American experience with its always present racial theme, and a struggle results between a disinterested, elite point of view and a critical, barely concealed autobiographical allegory about his own powers as an analyst of social values and arrangements.[16]

The essay on "Cosmopolitanism and Culture" had two brief essays as part of its immediate context. Locke gave a speech entitled "Cosmopolitanism" to the Cosmopolitan Club on June 9, 1908, at the end of his first academic year at Oxford. The talk was given in the rooms of Hamed El Alaily, who would four months later give a talk in Locke's rooms on Egypt. Locke then published what is presumably a small fraction of the talk in the first issue of the club's journal, the *Oxford Cosmopolitan,* which appeared shortly afterward; this was titled, enigmatically, "Epilogue," and could perhaps be read as the summary statement of principles that animated the club's formation. Just three paragraphs long, the piece defines cosmopolitanism in a somewhat nervous and elliptical way, indicating how Locke had mixed feelings about the attitude—one might say the ideology—that was to dominate his thought for the next several years. In it, he sets out something like a personal code, reminiscent in part of the ideal gentleman of Victorian England and the Anglo-American esthete of Harvard Yard. Looked at somewhat differently, Locke was justifying his protracted education and the personality he had developed while engaging in it.

The "Epilogue" begins on a defensive note, complete with images of games and children. Only because of its place at the end of the journal, after a number of serious essays, and because of what we know of Locke's commitment to education and high culture, do we know there are serious issues at stake. But Locke presents them playfully:

> If ideas are worth anything, said a cynic, Cosmopolitanism would have put the world into intellectual bankruptcy long ago. But it is an innocent and enlightened gaming, this pastime of eclectic societies: where in the name of cosmopolitan culture they play their sweepstakes of the imagination, lending each other their mental vices and borrowing each others ideas; but what serious man will chide them! 'Tis innocent as child's play and no economic waste at that.

The cosmopolitan thinker uses up ideas in a spendthrift fashion, circulating them one after another with little sense of retention, and cultivated people are indifferent to whether it is ideas or vices that are being exchanged. Locke announces that cosmopolitanism is an exercise "of more or less pure disciplinary value" and suggests that, if it's a game, it is one played with strict or rarefied rules. As a game it produces diversion but also an altered awareness; this is perhaps the core of this brief presentation:

> It [cosmopolitanism] is all a shifting of the attention and the interest, a juggling with the centre of a predetermined but movable circle, and most of us are convinced and some of us are perplexed on finding that

we carry our horizons with us and are unable to see through other eyes than our own.

The paradox that obtains between all that "shifting" and all that fixity ("unable to see through any other eyes") will not be easily resolved. Locke had apparently absorbed some of Wilde's esthetic irony as well.

Some resolution is just what Locke has in mind, however, as the essay's last paragraph begins: "Cosmopolitan culture, then, if it is to be truly cultivating, is a sense of value contrasts and a heightened and rationalized self-centralization." This resolution, as much hoped-for as provable, is clear enough in its first part, for seeing the contrasting values of other peoples would come rather readily to anyone with the leisure or wealth to travel or study abroad. The second part still shows the signs of Locke's straining under the weight of his own individualism. Actions of heightening and rationalizing one's self can be read as an ongoing process ("cultivating") that is opposed to the tendency to centralize all experience, indeed all horizons, in one's ego. Concluding with a strict formulation, the argument claims: "The only solution is an enforced respect and interest for one's own tradition, and a more or less accurate appreciation of its contrast values with other traditions."

Using the cramped terms of the "Epilogue" provides some guidance to the larger and more inchoate views partially worked out in "Cosmopolitanism and Culture." (This may distort as much as it clarifies, however, since the longer work does not offer an explicit statement of its thesis.) Locke chooses to start "Cosmopolitanism and Culture," his first major work of cultural criticism, with late eighteenth-century literary culture, and especially with the notions that sympathy and a catholic appreciation are crucial to culture and that all learning is each person's province. These notions are supported by the belief that "knowledge and sympathy are if not the same thing, conditional on each other." This joins a key belief about cosmopolitanism as a set of ideas, but also more than that: "It started with the French Encyclopedist reaction with the discovery that ideas were social forces." Here the ideas behind his Harvard essay on Keats and Romanticism are broadened and deepened to provide the framework of a world culture. But a world culture involves not only extending the power of domination but the power of understanding, and the ability to see other peoples' values sympathetically.

Locke leavens his claims about the dynamics of cosmopolitanism with an array of citations from various cultural authorities. First, he cites Goethe's claim that he saw nothing contradictory in being a patriotic German and a citizen of the world. Then he buttresses this with a quotation from Santayana:

"There is a certain plane on which all nations must live in common, that of morals and science." Using the Enlightenment's tendency to universalize its claims, Locke goes on to agree that for the imperial idea, civilization "is an extended thing," and, for the national idea, "civilization is the corporate possession of the utilities of civilized life." Cosmopolitanism must draw from the strengths of both these outlooks, the universal and the local. He quotes Sainte-Beuve, who said: "The only unity I am ambitious of is that of comprehending everything." From this network of ideas Locke builds up a picture of a world civilization that is based on harmony and tolerance, saying as a working definition that "cosmopolitanism will be the intellectual courtesy by which [other people's] contrasted ideas will pass as of equal worth with our own." This is the core of Locke's idea of the need for "cultural reciprocity" and his special sense of multiculturalism, which he would spend the next several decades developing and promulgating. Madame de Staël is another of his authorities, and he uses her to argue that the sympathetic power that culture induces is "the most masculine production of the faculties of woman." The blending of gender qualities here also says something about Locke's growing exploration of his own sexuality, as well as his hope that tolerance would become a central value in cultural transactions.

All is not that simple, however. Culture, it must be admitted, could easily have negative manifestations. In one passage which he crossed out Locke said that "this ambassadorial function of the romantic mind is the spiritual counterpart of the colonizing army." From his Oxford companions he must have come to realize that the universalizing or imperial sway of cosmopolitanism might be too idealistic a formulation. Nevertheless, he firmly denies that cosmopolitanism is merely internationalism based on the commerce of the industrial order, which would be one of the serious charges brought against it. There is also another danger: "By some strange fatality modern culture . . . seems committed to imperialist illusion, and with an empire in its grasp and reach, forgetful that real empire is not extent but authority, not in subjects but in citizenship." The vexed relation between the Enlightenment's universalizing in the realm of ideas and imperial domination in the arena of physical force bedevils the structure of the essay and may even be one reason why it was never completely finished. (Locke would, however, turn in the 1940s toward a firmly anti-imperialist view.)

Locke adds to the essay some formulations of the role of art and the critic's responsibility in interpreting it for a modern audience, and these contribute to its complexity. Such reflections were part of what Locke was beginning to evolve at this time, namely a modern form of cultural criticism. This involves a mixture of historical schematizing, philosophical reflection, and social analysis, but often it uses as its evidence the practice of art and instances of criticism as cultural activities that provide the best occasion for such wide-ranging formulations. Though he quotes Emerson as having said that "culture is the measure of things taken for granted," Locke also saw modern art as a challenge to our ideas and our actions, an Arnoldian criticism of life. Indeed, cosmopolitanism originated as a view of art and culture, as Locke made clear in his historical framework. By calling for a culture that went beyond what he identified as "interpretive criticism," in which the critic apparently played a subordinate role to that of the artist, he posited the possibility of a critical awareness and sophistication in the field of esthetics that would become a substitute for metaphysics, producing a "system that expands and incorporates as its content grows."

Such a new criticism would work alongside art as a form of cultural truth-seeking; Locke invokes the figure of Oscar Wilde, who combines the roles of artist and critic, as a model for the new culture that is fully engaged with modern life. Following such a model would not be easy: the movements of the Symbolists and Parnassian poets show that art is not at home in the world. The critic too often must act as surveyor or guide to a realm that is remote and obscure. Art, Locke claims, used to be narrow in its claims and influences because of external conditions, but now it chooses to be so. Locke suggests that many modern artists are willfully obscurantist or only mystically universal. Ibsen and Tolstoy, however, demonstrate that nationalism and cosmopolitanism can be in harmony. They serve as positive examples of how the larger social use of art must somehow remain consonant with the individual's experience of it. This is true because "what culture and reflection are to the individual, history and art are to the race."

At one point Locke invokes the experience of his own race and alludes to the sort of thinking that lay behind his essay on Dunbar when he asserts that civilization is more than material advantage. He speaks directly about African Americans:

[T]he ideal heritage of that transplanted race will reassert itself . . . not as political ambition or economic greediness, but as a distinctive and vital national idea embodied in a race literature, a race art—a race religion and a sense of corporate history and destiny. There will be a divided nationalism within one political nation, an ideal difference within a geographical unity, and you will be surprised to hear me say a cosmopolitanism within a nation.

Here Locke posits a political dream, one that he prefers to a mere eclectic mingling of different cultures. What he envisions is what he will later describe in detail in "The New Negro," namely, a scheme where suspect difference becomes instructive contrast and antagonism is transformed into a healthy respect for other people. He was developing a concept of cosmopolitanism as confraternity that would seem to lend itself to a romantic vision of society.

However, Locke does not indulge solely in visions of utopian harmony. He realizes, as he says, that civilization "has destroyed so many nations and disintegrated so many bodies of tradition." He even says at one point that modern culture is "atomic," invoking the sense of urban alienation and social anomie that he would soon study in detail with Georg Simmel, one of his teachers at the University of Berlin. While some of the "border contacts of our civilization" have been harmonized, "further separations and new units have been springing up in the very heart" of the modern world. What can be felt as danger points are transformed in Locke's view into two distinct but positive phenomena: "one is the contact with any very divergent and assertive non-European race or nation, and the other, the persistent and insoluble tradition of several bodies of assimilative peoples resident in the heart of our home civilization." Here the experience of Locke as an African American and his newly heightened awareness of the experience of colonial peoples are brought together. The conversion of these danger points into possibilities is the sort of political theorizing that is characteristic of Locke, who always clung to a trust in the progressive myth of civilization advanced by the Encylcopedists. At the very end of the essay Locke admits that the development of true cosmopolitanism is still in process, though the ultimate goal is clear; he both warns us and comforts us when he says that we "must work out our own cosmopolitanism, but we can hardly hope to produce anything better or different." The end of the essay thus raises the issue of self-culture, one of the most abiding of Locke's concerns, even as he sets this process of criticism and improvement against a noble ideal.

———•———

It is fairly clear that Locke meant the unfinished "Cosmopolitanism and Culture" to be the major summing up of his views on a number of subjects:

modernity, criticism, cultural differences, race relations, even, in a way, self-culture. The fact that he wrote several pages of it on the back of pages of his rejected Oxford thesis, "The Concept of Value," also suggests that he may have connected it with the notion of value theory—at the very least, all of his work at Oxford revolved around this essay and the thesis. His inability to finish the work should be understood in the context of its impressive scope. Just as he would work over the Oxford thesis in 1917 as part of his Harvard Ph.D., he used parts of "Cosmopolitanism and Culture" in a number of essays he published in the late 'teens and early 'twenties. But it would not be until "The New Negro" that Locke would once again allow himself the scope and depth that he has essayed so energetically in the "select retirement" of his Oxford residence. The essay shows how much Locke absorbed from his Oxford friends, and, fueled by his increasing interest in national identities and cultural power, how many ideas he was willing to articulate and pursue.

Locke's life as a club member was not restricted to the Cosmopolitan Club. In October, when he first arrived, he became a member of the Oxford University Musical Union and the Oxford Union Society. At one point he was invited by Farid Nameh to discuss the formation of an Oriental Club at Oxford, but nothing seems to have come of this. There was also the African Union Society. This was a group that Locke also helped bring into existence, as he had done with the Cosmopolitan Club. Taken all together this roster of clubs shows that Locke spent a great deal of time with people who were thinking through the problems of the imperial world-system and that he had become increasingly serious about political and cultural issues, especially as they involved questions of racial identity and leadership. He was reflecting on his own identity more and more.

There is a partial copy of a speech Locke gave to the African Union Society in 1909 that reveals a great deal about how he was thinking about racial identity. In it he complains of "too much dramatization both of the tragedy and the comedy of color . . . and too little problem work, too little action, too little race service—far—far too little." Trying to approach the problem rationally and constructively, however, has its limits, for the problem remains that it is individuals who live racism, and, at this time for Locke, individual responsibility has to be at the center of the problem: "The man who doesn't know why he is a Negro will never be one—at least one of the right sort." This does not mean, however, that one can by a simple act of will or self-discipline remove oneself from the racial situation or control its irrational aspects. The possession of a culture does not automatically follow from having paid for it in time and labor: "Good manners cannot remove the sense of being in somebody else's drawing room." Locke alludes to a passage in Du Bois's *Souls of Black Folk* when he says that it is a vain boast to join Shakespeare and Plato above the color line.[17]

Locke's speech shows he was continuing to think about the problems of race in the context of a worldwide system. Leadership remained one of the key issues in his thought on this subject; equally important was the way he connected this issue not only to an African but also an African American context:

> . . . the admitted fault of our race leadership both in Africa and among the Afro-Americans has been not so much deficiencies in the qualities of leadership as in their own unthinking enlightenment[;] they have not known where they were going. . . .

Here the phrase "the admitted fault" may conceal a certain amount of presumption on Locke's part; his sense of mission may be leading him to describe things as generally agreed upon when in fact it is only his circle of friends who have decided on the nature of the situation. In any case, the African Union Society took the trouble to print up its constitution in 1908, and it was signed by Locke, who was listed as the "Hon. Secretary" of the organization. Its stated purpose was "to meet for the general discussion and interchange of special and personal knowledge concerning the unhappy Fatherland," and for the "cultivation of thought and social intercourse between its members as prospective leaders of the African Race." Locke's activities with the African Union Society appear less extensive than those with the Cosmopolitan Club, but in future years the proportion of his interests in these two areas would be reversed.

Not all of Locke's friends at Oxford were people of color. He formed a close and lively friendship with Percy J. Philip, whose family home was the Manse of Kells, New Galloway, Scotland. Philip was serious but also a bon vivant who could write to Locke about his lunching on partridge and sparkling burgundy. He had worked for a while with Sir James Murray on editing the *Oxford English Dictionary*. Locke admired Philip's love of nature, reflected in his Cosmopolitan Club talk on Thoreau. Locke proclaimed that "I should not be afraid of wild nature in his company." When Philip returned home from Oxford for the holidays, he often wrote Locke while engaged in the leisure activities of the upper classes; once he spent his vacation on a yacht sailing to Guernsey in the Channel. In September 1910, he reported with his bantering tone a conversation he had recently heard (though this may be a teasing fiction):

> What is your opinion of Locke nowadays? He seems to us to be going rapidly to Romanticism and seed. He talks of memories like a French decadent. He reminds one terrifyingly of Rousseau. Will he ever get back into the world again?

Philip supported Locke for the presidency of the Cosmopolitan Club in 1908 and was instrumental a year later in helping defeat a radical group of students who tried to take over the leadership of the club. In February 1909, Locke told his mother how the "crowd of extremists [who] had gone in for intellectual radicalism of the most virulent sort" had suffered a vote of no confidence. Eventually Philip would become the Paris correspondent for a New York paper, and Locke saw him several times in later years.[18]

Locke also maintained in Oxford his continuing interest in a career as a writer. This was manifest in various ways. In the spring of 1908 he testified to his mother that "you cannot write without experience and cynicism— self-esteem and even a self-centered interest in life are a cheap price for experience—many others pay more and get less." This concern with experience and self-centeredness—really a part of his interest in individualism, which he first developed at Harvard—did not always sit easily or translate readily into finished writing. Locke even selected a title for the novel he was planning to write, saying slyly to his mother that the title is the most important part of the writing of a modern novel. He seems never to have completed this project, though he also lists at one point the titles for several stories; again, it is hard to know what state of completion he achieved for these. He was able to finish one story at Oxford, which he called "The Miraculous Draught." In early February 1909 he sent the manuscripts of more than one story to Mary Locke so that she might mail them out to various magazines. At the same time he was planning to enter a poem in the contest for the Newdigate Prize, the subject for which was Michelangelo; this, too, seems not to have materialized. Tracking the progress of some of his classmates at Harvard, he observed that "the other set [Van Wyck] Brooks [and Ned] Sheldon etc." had accomplished a lot their first year out, but consoled his mother and himself by reminding her of the "proverb of the rocket—to change the figure bet on the dark horse."[19]

Writing for Locke did not always take place within a competitive framework. Locke apparently combined for a while his creative impulses and his interest in race and the question of Africa. Among his Oxford papers is a sheet that again lists titles, this time of poems, some with dates, but no finished texts to go with them. However, the titles alone are revealing:

"Race Poems"
I.   To Ethiopia 1910 Oxford
II. Sonnet "I felt an ancient quarrel in my veins" 1907[?]
III. "O mother race, despised of Men"
IV. The Poet to his People
V.   The Pageant 1915
VI. Rhodes 1911 {The Colossus}
                 {The Burden}

> No other burden but thyself
> I bring thee, soul-fettered as thou art
> A song weight on thy heart
>   (ALPHU 164-60/5)

Included in this set of papers is a partial version of "To Ethiopia," whose last stanza reads:

> Now is the time when our winged destiny
> [?] and sings and shapes [?] its wings
> Tomorrow the [brooding?] of [preening?] care
> Today the song of the untried [sovereign?] air
>   (ALPHU 164-60/5)

In October 1908 he had told his mother, in connection with meeting Seme, who was "blossoming out in African exuberance into everything," that "[t]he African mind and temperament is not self-divided nor self-despising[.] Thank God for it." [20] There is also another fragment, which echoes some of the same sentiment and probably belongs to the third poem listed above, "O Mother race, despised of men." In part it reads:

> Too long have I lisped in civilization[']s ways
> Mocking my perverse thought with empty phrases
> Teach me o mother race to sing thy praise
> . . . .

To sing the song that hums low in my veins
To distill the lyric that dwells on my tongue
To throw off the weight that oppresses my chest
(ALPHU 164-60/5)

Some of this sentiment can be identified with primitivism, the modernist notion which argued that the primitive spirit was less spoiled by civilization than was that of refined or urbanized people, a sentiment that concealed its own racist component and an idea that would play a large part in Locke's life after he met Charlotte Mason nearly two decades later.

Locke combined with his continuing interest in the writer's vocation an increasingly keen delight in travel. Again as part of his friendship with Seme, he told his mother: "I'll visit every part of Africa the climate will allow me." It was not only Africa where he wished to go; by the end of his first term he had made plans to visit several places in Europe. By January 1908 he was in the French resort of St. Malo, overeating, painting, and sketching. His first visit to Paris took place sometime in February. These vacation trips were usually taken with one or more of his friends and frequently involved meeting others at predetermined places en route. Occasionally plans would change, and sometimes they would be cut short by an absence of funds. Later, in the winter of 1908, he planned to travel to Paris again with Seme, meet Percy Philip there, and then stay for a while by himself to try and get some writing done. But bad weather in the Channel seems to have changed these plans altogether. This was the beginning of Locke's engagement with travel, a honed skill that he would raise to a high level in subsequent decades.

During a spring vacation in 1909 he crossed the Alps and arrived in Venice, which he found too "touristy," thinking that Turner's paintings had made it too familiar. He passed through Paris, where he saw the new musical setting of Maeterlinck's *Monna Vanna*. Going on to Florence, he spent Easter week in Rome with Lionel De Fonseka, where he spotted Rudyard Kipling at a nearby table.[21] One of the classmates he rendezvoused with, named Arthur Lee, was able to introduce the table of students to Richard Strauss. "I shall know how to live," he boasted to his mother, "and if you saw the people who have the means and don't know how—you would understand how joyfully subordinate the where-withall really is." These early trips were thoroughly enjoyable, judging from his letters home, and they helped Locke treat his lifelong love of travel, especially to European capitals, as a form of enrichment removed from the growing habits and values of tourism. While he admired scenery, and took delight in modest hikes in the countryside, he usually spent his time taking deep draughts of a city's cultural life, visiting the theater, the opera, and the museums.[22]

From the start of his Oxford stay Locke planned to have his mother come and visit him. This, too, became a regular event, and for many summers after her first transatlantic trip in 1908, Mary Locke would join or accompany her son and travel with him throughout Europe. She first set sail across the ocean on July 4, 1908, with a berth on the *Ertruria,* embarking from New York City, since there were no steamship companies in Philadelphia that both had empty places and would sell a ticket to a Negro. While with her son, she was able to meet some of his friends, especially Seme and Philip. Because they were together, of course, there is no correspondence to tell how the trip went, though after returning to America in mid-September Mary Locke is able to report that the sail went smoothly. The next year she sailed on June 30 aboard the *Lusitania,* and she returned on July 29 on a Holland American vessel that was not as smooth sailing as the others. She was not home for long before she could report seeing the publication of his essay, "Oxford Contrasts," in the *Independent,* which she referred to as his first published article.

While back home in Camden, Mary Locke continued to send her son information about her daily rounds and also about the constant piling up of small debts. These debts grew into a major problem in subsequent years. She also dutifully relayed to him a steady stream of reports about Booker T. Washington and other black leaders. These formed the backdrop to the transoceanic conversation they were having about Locke's understanding of black leadership and what he came more and more to think of as his vocation in this regard. As early as the spring of 1909, Locke remarked of Washington: "They will play dice for his toga when he dies and then find that no one of them can wear it. He is really a big man." A few months later Mary Locke mentioned Du Bois's biography of the insurrectionary abolitionist, John Brown. Then in February 1910, she was able to say that she has heard Washington lecture, sponsored by the Armstrong Association of Philadelphia, and that he "speaks now with the confidence of victory." At about this time Locke told his mother of a plan that she reacted to with amazement. She replied that "I admit I was fairly staggered at first by the 'colossal' scheme—it made my poor head swim." The plan involved Locke meeting Washington, "to make your initial bow to him," and thereby gain his approval and financial support for a trip to Africa and India. Locke's interest in Africa, and the general conditions of colored peoples throughout the colonial world, had begun to take form as a desire to study these conditions and then examine the "contrasts" that obtained between them and the plight of American blacks. The theoretical musings of "Cosmopolitanism and Culture" were to be tested in the field.[23]

It is clear, at least in outline, that Locke presented his scheme to Washington; what is not clear is how. He sailed to America in March 1910 aboard the *Mauritania,* and he probably sent Washington a letter while at home in Camden, without arranging a personal meeting. Mary Locke wrote on June 28 to Locke, in Oxford, to say how she regretted that Washington had declined to support Locke's proposal. Mary also wrote letters in August to say that a failure to meet Washington would be a setback in Locke's career and that expressed the hope that he could sound Washington out about the possibilities of a job at Howard University. Mary Locke wrote to Locke in the early fall, while he was in Heidelberg, to express the opinion: "There seems to be great rivalry between them"—obviously referring to Washington and Du Bois— "but no comparison, for Washington is way on top." Around the same time, she sent details of the founding of the *Crisis,* the magazine of the National Association for the Advancement of Colored People, which was to receive financial backing from Oswald Garrison Villard and be edited by Du Bois. By March 1911, her sentiments seem to have shifted, for she expressed a concern that Washington may put obstacles in the way of Locke's career; she no longer trusted him. This mistrust may have been occasioned by the famous incident that same month in New York City when Washington was set upon while wandering through a district frequented by prostitutes. Details of the incident were widely disputed, but Mary Locke probably came to a firm conclusion about the meaning of them. It would be one more reason for her to worry about the possible negative consequences of her son's exposure to the public eye.[24]

Even as events arose that complicated Mary Locke's views of her son's prospects, he was busy talking to her, and to himself, about a decision that felt at times as if it had been waiting for him all along. Personal destiny was not a concept Locke shied away from, nor was it something that he took lightly. Perhaps his fullest commentary on it, one that seems marked by a reading of Nietzsche or Max Stirner, with its emphasis on self-shaping will, came in a letter of May 5, 1909:

I really long to get back to America and into my position—it will be a stormier and shorter reign than Booker's, but so much the better—I want a long arm and the will to use it—Heredity has given me both[.] I only need the favorable environment—I have realized definitely and finally at Oxford that I am cast for a practical career, and my scholastic pretensions have dwindled to mere ideals of personal culture. . . . (ALPHU 164-57/28)

Locke remarked on the "dwindling" in other letters, as he mentioned how he was "tiring of Oxford—it is too relaxing mentally and physically"—this in January 1909. Locke went on in the letter of May 5:

[S]trength will and autocracy are tragically useless and at the same time grotesquely comic when exercised in the cramped environment. . . . [I]n the meantime I shall have as much as I can do ruling myself—a turbulent battlefield of contrasted heredities. . . . [E]very blasted one of the young race-leaders here at Oxford would like to see me secured for his work, his field.

Locke's pride plainly combines, with his typical sense of paradox, a sense that he will need all his strength and a great deal of support if he is to stand any chance of succeeding. Adult plans still combine with a student's self-image: "I have made up my mind to serve a great apprenticeship." This does not, however, prevent him from delivering a strong judgment on his superiors. "My greatest immediate concern is to me[et] Washington on neutral ground . . . he has practically crowned himself now—and it is the beginning of his end—you see if he does not get too aristocratic shortly." Locke's vaunted pride in his ability to judge people took on a justified glow in this instance.

Locke had come back to America for his brief stay in the spring of 1910 because Mary Locke had not been well enough to travel abroad. In May 1909 she had been struck in the face by a student. This incident caused her great distress; the boy at first claimed he was sixteen years old, but later it was discovered that he was eighteen. She had him arrested in any case, and with the backing of her principal, Mr. Cornish, she went to court to testify against the student.[25] As early as the spring of 1908 she had suffered what her doctor called a "complete breakdown of the nervous system" and had also been diagnosed as having a heart murmur. Locke was extremely concerned, as Mary Locke was nearly sixty years old, and though she did make the trip to Oxford that year and again in the summer of 1909, it was for a rather short stay. Throughout this period she had recurring dreams about finding money. Locke, for his part, seemed intent on ignoring his mounting debts and was happily benefiting from his riding sessions. His weight was up to one hundred and twelve pounds; he was about to turn twenty-five as his days at Oxford drew to a close.

It was during the spring of 1910 that Locke probably was working on his short story, "The Miraculous Draught." This was one of the rare instances in which Locke felt it was worth trying hard to get his creative writing published. Late in 1909 his old Harvard friend David Pfromm wrote to him at Oxford and mentioned that Dickerman had told him one of Locke's stories would soon appear in *Scribner's Magazine*. This was premature, but it indicates the anticipation his friends had for him and perhaps also Locke's own confidence in—and certainly his commitment to—this particular narrative. Written in a very dated period style, the story's sensibility is largely fin de siècle, rooted as it is in assumptions about the spiritual purity of an idealizing main character and his relationship with a "primitive" society. The allegory centers on a young man, profoundly troubled by his vocation, who must rely on his faith in himself and the "higher" meaning of his destiny to work out his problems. The story reads well and contains signs of polished writing that could easily have portended publication. It exists in two versions, one titled "The Miraculous Draught" and the other "The Pardon of the Sea." The former is nearly complete, containing fourteen typed pages, while the latter appears to be an earlier draft of only three pages.[26]

As with his Harvard story, "The Rain," Locke creates a narrator and a central figure, both of whom could stand in for the author. The narrator of "The Miraculous Draught" is trying to understand the "primitive" faith of the fishermen in Plomodiem, a Breton village, especially as such faith is set against the highly self-conscious main character, a seminarian named Etienne studying in Rome. The story opens with the narrator observing the villagers attending a religious service, an "indulgent concession to the pagan childishness of the Breton fisher folk." Meanwhile Etienne is being carefully watched by a cardinal, who knows of his ambition and senses that he may even one day be pope. The cardinal, referring to a religious folktale, muses "on the possibility that the ancient mullet with Peter's signet still in its cold entrails might flounder one day into the nets of Plomodiem."

The cardinal, effetely ironic, sends Etienne to Plomodiem to help and perhaps replace the dying abbé, who sagely cautions the young man against self-pity. Once there, Etienne discovers that the fish have not appeared, threatening the village with catastrophe. The volatile leader of the fishing fleet, Le Bourrouec, "stormed as long as others were meek and quiet, but sneered and shrugged his shoulders as soon as they in turn were aroused." Etienne becomes his antagonist, especially when Bourrouec wants to rush out with the fleet when he hears about his father's vision that the fish are returning. He wants Etienne to bless the fishermen with holy water, but when the young man is slow to appear, Bourrouec does it himself. The seminarian accosts him: "Bourrouec! You heathen! You dare?" Bourrouec, who "stood by like a detained schoolboy, shifting and twirling his cap," calmly but sacrilegiously replies that he would pray to the devil himself if it would help catch the fish.

The fleet takes off after the fish, and Etienne impulsively joins them. At first he "watch[es] . . . intently in order to excuse his own uselessness." Surprisingly, the catch turns out to be hugely successful, and, as the dawn breaks, the men impulsively credit Etienne with a miracle: "a mad chorus of response filled his ears with the blasphemy." Etienne struggles to explain that this is not the case, but words fail him. His last steps are ambiguous, either "heroic strides or a frightened scurry," as he steps out of the boat and drowns himself, his small biretta "bobbing like a small black cork on the sun-lit waters." It is left to Bourrouec to turn Etienne's last act into the stuff of legend. It is in fact Etienne's biretta that the narrator had earlier seen hanging in the villagers' chapel as a votive item.

The story's themes reflect many of Locke's concerns: the role of leadership, especially when two authority figures clash; the nature of one's vocation, especially in relation to the older generation that one is destined to challenge and replace; and the possibility that one's actions will always be misunderstood by those who are too simple to understand the way the world works. Richly ambiguous, each of these thematic issues presents the line between right and wrong, effective and misguided, as wavering. One can see the dying abbé as a representation of Booker T. Washington, for example, weakened but wise, just as the fishermen are the unlettered blacks that Locke is called upon to serve, strong but easily misled. The struggle between Bourrouec and Etienne might reflect Locke's own inner struggle, or, to stretch the point perhaps, can suggest the possible difficulty Locke foresaw if he challenged the impulsive Du Bois for a leadership role after Washington's demise. As for the notion that this sort of reading also implies that Locke had enough ambition to imagine himself an exalted leader, there is the letter where he tells his mother that he would one day consider being the leader of the university where his father studied law:

I should ultimately like and accept the presidency of Howard. . . . [I]t may be the first great cosmopolitan university—but this is crude—I do not do my day dreams justice. . . . (ALPHU 164-56/6)

Of course the work of fiction is only a virtual mirror of the author's state of mind, a trying out of forms of action, belief, and emotion. Here the story's ending seems to say that Locke could not reconcile his ambition with his trust in himself. Certainly the Oxford years tested Locke's self-image. Locke was dividing his allegiance between the dedication he was lending to the cause of racial justice (in which friends and fellow students saw him as a desirable colleague if not yet a leader), and the recurring temptation to tend his own garden, as the metaphors of cultivation in "Oxford Contrasts" would have it.

Locke's confidence, meanwhile, received a shock when he found out in 1910 that his thesis would not be accepted and that he was thus denied an Oxford degree. He had told his mother about the subject for the thesis sometime late in his first year. By October 1908 his plan was accepted by Dr. Ferdinand C. S. Schiller, though his tutor at Hertford objected to it because it left him off the committee that would judge the finished work. Schiller's *Studies in Humanism* (1907) had established him as a follower of William James's approach to knowledge. He was one of the few tutors at Oxford with an appreciation of value theory and sympathy toward its methods of making broad claims about psychological traits. The subject, "The Concept of Value," was something Locke had contemplated when he studied with Perry, Royce, and Münsterberg at Harvard, and he would pursue it further at the University of Berlin, before transforming it into his doctoral thesis in 1917. Locke often recycled his work for convenience's sake, even from his days at the School of Pedagogy and at Harvard, but this subject was one he meant to sound fully. He started work on it in earnest by the spring of 1909; in the fall he hired a German tutor to help him read some of the untranslated source material from the Austrian school of value theory. He was able by the end of the year to tell his mother he was enjoying the work on it.

The opportunity to work on his thesis was the result of a long and often trying sojourn. Kallen contacted Schiller on Locke's behalf and initiated a meeting between the two.[27] Locke met with Schiller, and in a note to himself, Locke wrote: "Went Monday the 18—found Dr. Schiller alone—very [ ] etc—selected subject The Concept of Value in philosophy—Stewart Williams + Schiller—Thanked him most heartily and walked over with S to James lectures. This is a great day—when I met Schiller—the whole prospect of my work and life seem different."[28] Locke thus attended at least the first of the eight Hibbert Lectures by William James, titled "On the Present Situation in Philosophy," on May 18, 1908. The lectures would be the basis of James's 1909 *Pluralistic Universe: Hibbert Lectures at Manchester College on the Present Situation in Philosophy.*

Locke also attended the ceremony at which James received an honorary D.Sc. from Oxford. Kallen, the consummate friend and promoter of pragmatism, sent a note to Locke: "As D[ownes] + I are going away, it remains to you to collect all the Harvard men –etc. about, and to bring them to the degree giving on Tuesday—and many other Americans as possible — + to give James a proper Rah! Rah! When he gets his degree. . . . "[29] For Locke, James's lecture and his meeting Schiller were welcome relief from his usual interactions with philosophers at Oxford.

Locke originally elected to pursue a B.A. *Literae Humaniores* degree, popularly known as "Greats." This degree required that Locke attend weekly meetings with his tutors, study assigned works in Latin and Greek, and take an Honours exam. The Rev. H. H. Williams of Hertford College was his advisor and tutor, and the Rev. E. M. Walker of Queens College was also his tutor.

Locke said of at least one, if not meaning both, of his Oxford tutors, the Rev. Williams and the Rev. Walker, that he was a "closed-nosed clergyman with a wig."[30] Locke requested a change to the B.Sc. degree from Williams after meeting with and gaining the support of Schiller for his thesis project. This degree option required a thesis, without weekly tutorials or an exam. Williams rejected the request on grounds that his thesis topic was "frightfully unorthodox," even though Schiller supported it. Locke persisted. The change was approved in October 1908, but Williams assigned J. Cook Wilson of New College, the Wykeham Professor of Logic, as his thesis supervisor and advisor. Wilson was a noted philosophical realist. As a realist, Wilson believed that reality is ontologically independent of human conceptual schemes. This was probably Williams's expression of disdain toward Locke and his project, since Wilson shared the same attitude as Williams toward value theory—that it was an unorthodox subject not worthy of serious attention. Learning German, gaining access to the current work in value theory in Austria, developing an interpretation and creative arguments were all assiduously, if inconsistently, pursued by Locke without the aid of his advisor. Wilson's comments on work Locke submitted to him on Christian von Ehrenfels reveal that he provided no substantive comments on Locke's interpretation of von Ehrenfels or his arguments about the elasticity of value categories. Rather, Wilson wanted greater technical presentation of quotation marks and footnotes so that he could understand Locke's understanding of von Ehrenfels.

Shortly after returning from his visit home and failed effort to secure support from Booker T. Washington for research in Egypt and India, Locke received a blow to his status at Oxford. His finances had been stretched for some time; Pixley Seme had written to Locke the previous November: "I pray that you may be saved from proctors who lay about for you in the night and from tradesman who trouble you by day."[31] Now, in the months following his March 1910 sailing to America, they had been stretched beyond his capacity. In a letter dated May 31, 1910, Locke was given four days to leave Hertford by the Vice-Chancellor's Court, having failed to satisfy debts to local vendors.[32] In the same letter Locke was also informed that to obtain his B.Sc. degree he would have to submit his thesis by October 10, 1910.

Although only recently settled in Berlin, in September Locke mailed his thesis to Oxford and in November 1910 was informed by his supervisor, Wilson, that it "was not regarded as adequate by the examiners."[33] The rejection occasioned the sentence "I should have had to complain . . . " to Mary Locke in 1910. Locke needed "peace of mind" and did not file a complaint against his advisors. He was also aware that protesting the racial exclusion and lack of deference he received might jeopardize the chance of a Negro receiving a Rhodes Scholarship in the future. He did not want to bear the "blame of being largely responsible for the non-election of Negro candidates for these scholarships."[34]

In April 1911 Mary Locke wrote to say how sorry she was the thesis had been rejected, but added that "if one dances, one must pay the fiddler."[35] This suggests that Locke's periods of lassitude and self-indulgence may have contributed to his failure to win acceptance. The philosophic orientation and prejudices of his tutors were certainly an obstacle that he may not have been able to overcome so as to secure their acceptance as a person let alone a philosopher. By the fall of 1910, however, he was already settled in Berlin, taking more courses and continuing his work on the subject of value theory, but also expanding his knowledge of modern life.

THE BERLIN INTERLUDE

When in September 1910 Dickerman called Mary Locke to get her son's address, she told him that Locke had decided to study for his doctorate at the University of Berlin. Though his three years of study at Oxford were over, Locke was addicted to the student's life. But back in May 1909 he had also told his mother: "I am cast for a practical career, and my scholastic pretensions have dwindled to mere ideals of personal culture." The conflict that occupied him between the fall of 1910 and the spring of 1911—a conflict between esthetic indulgence and academic discipline—was at once part of an interlude during which he tied together some loose strings in his sense of a practical vocation as a race leader and a period when he appears to have indulged his taste for esthetic experiences and even dissipation. Locke's daily life during this period is somewhat hard to trace, as he uncharacteristically went for long periods without answering his mother's letters, which on occasion grew quite fretful. Disappointed not to have taken his degree at Oxford, he nevertheless took courses at the University of Berlin (then known officially as Friedrich-Wilhelms-Universität and later to be renamed Humboldt University) that fed his imagination as it grappled with artistic questions and the rigors of modernist culture.

Drawn to Berlin because of his interest in philosophy and his "ideals of personal culture," and perhaps because one of his Harvard professors, Hugo Münsterberg, encouraged him to go there, he enjoyed the very liberal atmosphere of the city. For him, European culture generally meant Paris and other places, but it eventually came to mean chiefly Germany, and he would return to Berlin virtually every summer from 1911 to 1914, and then again from 1919 to 1935. Because he was fluent in German he could take full advantage of all the city's pleasures, and he probably developed his lifelong appreciation for German culture starting in 1910 at the latest. Whether or not he indulged in frequent homosexual liaisons when he attended the university there is unknown, but Berlin would have made it easy to do so, especially considering its greater tolerance for homosexuals when compared to Oxford. It is clear that Locke was quite impecunious at this time, and it was all his mother could do to send him the small amount of money she could spare from her teacher's salary.

His reasons for choosing Berlin were various. There was already a tradition of advanced study at German universities, most notably in the case of Du Bois, who had spent two years in Berlin but left without a degree. Indeed, this was the period when American institutions of higher leaning, chief among them the John Hopkins University, redesigned themselves to imitate the German research model. Locke may also have been drawn to Berlin because of its student life, as many young scholars went there on relatively little funds to be supported by a generous state system. In the academic year 1910–11, when Locke was resident there, Berlin had at least one hundred and sixty American students, about half of them women, registered at the university. As for the overall enrollment, the German universities went from 21,000 students in 1880 to 61,000 in 1914. Moreover, universities in Germany were involved in the policies of the state in complex ways, and professors enjoyed a social status that was enviable, and all this enabled Locke to form a view of academic life which, combined with his years at Harvard, probably presented a life of study and teaching as a desirable vocation.

Berlin was at the time still an imperial city, the capital of a state ruled by an emperor, Wilhelm II, who claimed certain aspects of his legitimacy from divine right. But class divisions were sharp and getting more so, in part due to the massive growth of industry, some of it planted squarely inside the city boundaries. Many students were enrolled in youth organizations that were often based on a desire to do away with the stiffness of Wilhemine society and to reaffirm a nationalistic ethic based on volkish sentiments, in reaction to what seemed an inevitable intensification of industrial and commercial society. Students who formed youth clubs spent vacation periods on long romantic hikes in the countryside, and Locke apparently joined them on occasion. In contrast to the colonial subjects who had come to Oxford to become part of the managerial class in the British Empire, the students whom Locke was likely to meet were involved in explorations of the Romantic sensibility, Idealist philosophy, and the emphasis on *Innerlichkeit*, or inwardness. All of this, combined with the decidedly modern urban nature of Berlin, made the change from the relative pastoralism of Oxford a striking experience.[36]

Also acting as a draw on Locke's educational desires was the presence of famous scholars. Locke enrolled for two courses—one each semester—with Georg Simmel, who was then in the process of redefining modern sociology. Some important aspects of Simmel's thought are reflected in Locke's later works. Perhaps chief among these is Simmel's claim that social formations had abstract structures that could be separated from the content of social interaction and independently studied. In fact, this is what led some to think of him (as well as his colleague and teacher, Ferdinand Tönnies), as one of the founders of modern sociology. This notion can be compared to Locke's later sense that in cultural contact a reciprocity can take place, largely because people can critically investigate the role that certain cultural values and activities play in the overall cultural framework. If such a role in one culture has some analogue in another, then a greater—and mutual—cultural "translation" can occur, even if there is a significant difference between values in the two societies. Such cultural reciprocity increases understanding between peoples and aids in the elimination of oppressive stereotypes and destructive feelings of group or racial supremacy. Simmel also stressed that such formal analogues were not, however, to be taken as unchanging universals, and this too would have appealed to Locke.

Simmel published a series of articles with the word "culture" in the titles, and most of them relied on a distinction between subjective and objective culture. *Geist,* a trans-subjective entity, is in opposition to, but a source of, subjective creativity and the objective world of cultural things. Modernity is often described as the mediation between the objective world of things and subjective development. The subjective sense of culture was based on the individual cultivation of one's mind and emotions, aimed at producing "the purely personal harmony of knowledge, feeling, and aspiration in the fully developed individual." Carrying such a notion at least since his Harvard days when he wrote on ideals of service and self-development, many years later Locke would speak often on this subject to his students at Howard. This notion of culture was pervasive throughout higher education in Germany, of course, and was often identified as the main goal of the mandarin intellectuals who taught in the universities there. *Geist* might also be analyzed as a group phenomenon, and Locke could have adapted Simmel's treatment of it as a way of adapting Du Bois's idea of the "talented tenth" with its implicit sense of the group advancing through the agency of its most expressively developed members. Simmel also postulated a sharp tension between objective and subjective forms of *Geist,* since the subjective form could never be fully realized in the objective expression. This could have helped Locke explain to himself the sense of paradox he felt when he later came to wrestle with the conflicts between the autonomy of the individual artist and the demands of the group, and the group's experience, of which the artist was the expressive force.

Simmel wrote seventy essays as well as six books, as well as a great many articles for newspapers, and he ranged widely among various sociological subjects. This caused him to be disregarded by those who prized above all the specializing expectations of academic disciplines, and so greatly delayed his advancement in the faculty hierarchy. Locke would eventually face opposition at Howard from a professor in the art history department, for example, who felt that Locke's interest in African art was infringing on the boundaries of the academic disciplines as they served to structure university governance. By taking the large idea of culture as his subject, Simmel was a polymath who was led into a wide variety of problems and intuitions, approaching them with a skepticism about empirical studies; such studies struck him as weakened by their propensity to ignore the element of "subjective" *Geist.* One can even read Simmel as a cultural critic and as someone who took as his overarching subject the nature of modernist culture. Locke's career as a writer and teacher was preoccupied with questions of culture in similar ways.

Another draw for Locke was Hugo Münsterberg, whom he looked upon him as one of his favorite professors. Münsterberg had returned to Germany, to teach in Berlin for a year or two, just as Locke was arriving in the city. He was known by all as a generous teacher, tolerant, and with a lively sense of humor; he also inherited a strong esthetic sense from his artistic mother. His research was largely devoted to what would eventually become the field of industrial psychology, but in addition he wrote an early study of film and its psychological effects on the audience. He shared with the Austrian value theorists, whom Locke had begun to study at Oxford, an interest in the typical post-Kantian problems of how the mind interacts with the physical stimuli of the external world to form comprehensive cognitive structures. In terms of how the mind functioned on the physiological plane, he was an empiricist, but from a value standpoint he saw the mental realm as one marked chiefly by a sense of freedom. This enabled him to be more or less at home in the German Idealist tradition, even as he equipped his own home laboratory with scientific apparatus to pursue his work in experimental psychology. His exchange professorship between Harvard and Berlin was undertaken with an eye toward fostering harmony between the two nations. When the war broke out just a few years later, Münsterberg was torn in his loyalties, and he was ostracized in America for his German sympathies. He would die in 1916, while beginning a lecture in Cambridge.[37]

In the fall Locke enrolled in Simmel's course, on the philosophy of the preceding century, from Fichte to Nietzsche and Bergson. He also studied in two courses with Münsterberg, on "Idealistic Theories" and "Problems of Will." He took advantage of the spring offering by Simmel, "The Problem of Modern Culture." This course was briefly described in the catalogue as dealing with "the controversies of principles of art, the religious problem, [and] objective and subjective value." There were also two courses on Kant by Professor Riehl. Kant, of course, was the philosopher who, more than any other, shaped the way philosophy was taught in Germany. Kantian idealism, with its questioning of sensory experience and its emphasis on the structure of logical forms and subjective experience, was not something that Locke pursued in later years. He may, however, have been impressed with Kant's three critiques, with their respective focus on epistemology, ethics, and esthetic experience, at least in the sense that they offered a way of articulating several different bodies of knowledge into a comprehensive structure.[38]

Near the end of his second semester in Berlin, by matriculating at the University of Berlin on May 6, 1911—an action recorded in his official grade book, part of the German university's sense of bureaucracy—Locke showed he was still hoping to take a doctorate there. He had earlier informed his mother that he planned to get the higher degree at Oxford or Berlin or even in America, and thus secure his academic credentials. But one year of study at the German university was all he would complete in terms of structured courses. The year at Berlin, which began in the fall of 1910, saw Mary Locke increasingly apprehensive about her son's vocation. Knowing the schedules of the steamers that went to Europe from Philadelphia, she timed her letters, which meant she wrote twice a week, on Tuesdays and Saturdays. Locke replied from his address on Grossbeerenstrasse, only to tell her that he had missed seeing Washington on his trip to Berlin. Mary Locke continued being nervous; she asked her son to be careful what he wrote to Helen Irvin, a close family friend, as gossip might spread, and Locke had said something indiscreet about Jessie Fauset. Fauset, who eventually became an editor and novelist of note, was a friend of the Lockes for many years, and she and Locke grew up together; their families apparently knew each other well. (Their relation would sour many years later when she played an important role in the Harlem Renaissance.) His mother also kept him informed about events in the world of black leadership, for example the founding of the *Crisis* in November and its editorship under Du Bois.

Locke often failed to respond to every one of Mary's letters, and this increased the sense of gloom in her correspondence, filled as it was with concerns about Locke's debts from Oxford as well as ever mounting financial pressures. "Sometimes I almost wish you have never gone to Oxford—only sometimes when I feel how they are harassing you with the debts," she complained. Mary relayed an offer to be the principal of a school, perhaps hoping to focus his attention on the completion of his studies and eventual employment. Sometime before the spring Locke moved his quarters to Kantstrasse, though whether this was because of money troubles it is hard to say. In any case, in January she insisted he stay in Berlin and get his degree; in May she repeated this suggestion, linking it to a plan to avoid paying his Oxford debts. Meanwhile, he told her that Münsterberg had suggested he return to Harvard and work for an advanced degree there, an idea that would come to fruition several years later. She responded pessimistically, saying "I think your plans may all miscarry for a while[;] it is the penalty of having had so good a time." But in the same letter she reminded him of his obligations: "you cannot afford to fail as the first and only one of your race," apparently referring to the Rhodes.[39]

However studious Locke set himself to be in Berlin, there were also signs that he was preoccupied with esthetic issues. Some of these had persisted from his interests in literature at Harvard and Oxford, and he had begun, however tentatively, to start his career as a writer. He mentioned to his mother that in late summer of 1911 he was quite startled when he unexpectedly saw his recently published essay on "The American Temperament" in a magazine in a library. But the liberal atmosphere in Berlin would have its effect, too. The course on modernist culture with Simmel, the long conversations with De Fonseka on the difference in esthetics between East and West, his own lingering desire to write stories and poems, all came together in Berlin to distract and tempt him, on the one hand, but also to develop his sensibility. Later in life Locke would author a style of criticism that included a certain prescriptive streak, animated in part by his acute sense of what would be best for the cultural expressions of Negro experience. But his prescriptiveness may also have had some of its origins in his sense of himself as someone who had, for a time at least, been a creative writer as well as a critic.

Locke saved a number of writings from his days in Berlin, most of them very fragmentary, but they indicate that his ambitions were headed in certain directions. On a small scrap of paper he had written: "Decoration not expression is the end of art. . . . Convention occupied the place in eastern art which personal emotion does in Western art." This is the main thesis of De Fonseka's book, *On the Truth of Decorative Art*, published in London in 1913. Taking the form of a "dialogue between an Oriental and an Occidental," the book is rife with paradox and provocation. The Eastern speaker continuously attacks what he sees as the emotional indulgence of Western art, especially of a Romantic sort, and praises Eastern art in all of its aspects. As his Western interlocutor objects, the Easterner turns the argument in elaborate ways, continuously formulating paradoxes ("Hieratic art is the only democratic art," for example) in order to answer and further confound the Western man's rather too-logical objections.

Throughout the book a tone of reflectiveness dominates, and though the two viewpoints are diametrically opposed, there is no sign of rancor or satire on either side. The book may well have been composed with Locke's help, or at least with his participation in some of the discussions that are clearly reflected in its structure. Locke would have reveled in the book's disposition toward framing all argument through paradox. He had also pondered in recent months, years even, questions of national identity and how it is reflected in cultural suppositions and expression. Another of the book's main themes—that all art is made for practical purposes and is best dedicated to the art of life rather than the need for self-expression—could easily blend with Locke's formality. Later in life he would say that, though he was himself an esthete, he did not like highly estheticized art, and he always disparaged both sentimental and overly conventionalized work. On another scrap Locke wrote, "Fonseka's subject The Obsession of Personality," which may have been a working title for the book; in any case it would strongly emphasize the need for the artist to balance individual expression with a sense of responsibility to group ethos. De Fonseka's surety in esthetic matters, which comes through despite the dialogical structure of his book, was impressive, and it may well have had its contribution to make in terms of Locke's critical standards.[40]

Unlike the papers and exams he kept from his Harvard days, Locke's writings while in Berlin seem to indicate experimentation as a part of his esthetic. One fragment claims: "This victorious assimilation of the new is in fact the type of all intellectual pleasures." At another point he writes, apparently quoting William James: "Genius in truth means little more than the faculty of perceiving in an unusual way." He also copied out a passage from Santayana's *Three Poets,* which began: "Here we have a program of a new philosophy. . . . " Emphasis on innovation constantly came to Locke's attention in Berlin, in marked contrast to what he had seen in Oxford, and his attraction to modernism led him to that movement's stress on a new approach to sensory experience, in which the poetic image would be one of the main instruments of representation. One fragment reads: "gas jets enclosed in wire cages—always the smell of escaping gas in cheap lodging house—as if the feeblest light had to have a fender to keep these tattered burnt moths out of the struggling [?] flame." On a separate sheet he wrote out what appears to be a table of contents for a projected book of short stories. The influences of Oscar Wilde's estheticism and, say, the orientalism of Flaubert, are evident:

> London Stories   London Nocturnes
> I   The Lace Hankerchief
> II   John the Baptist
>   (Embankment
>   (A Jordan of Deliverance)
>   to Lionel De Fonseka
> III The Coffins
>   (to P. J. Phillip)
>
> IV   Cleopatra's Needle
>   Poem Preface or Story
>   (Nile Dreams)

On yet another page, which also resembles a tentative table of contents, Locke wrote "The City," and under it two categories: "Essays London Paris" and "Stories London." This scrap is dated June 20, 1912, or a year after Locke left Berlin. This may indicate that his plans to publish stories and poems survived his return to America, but otherwise nothing described in these scraps was ever published under his name.

———•———

In several of the publications that the Rhodes people published to record the scholars' careers after Oxford, Locke lists his activities in the period right after Berlin variously, but in one entry he describes the time as spent on "travel and research." Whatever he meant to cover by this phrase, it is certain that his finances suffered considerably. The period from the fall of 1910 through the summer of 1912 was unsettled for Locke's advanced education, and apparently he was learning as much about himself as he was about scholarly subjects. He returned from Europe by the early fall of 1911, rather seriously in debt and, though still driven by his "colossal" scheme, uncertain as to his future prospects.

Locke's decision to return to America was shaped by several factors. Fatigue after nine uninterrupted years of higher education probably had its effect, especially as the last year was conducted in a language which he had only recently mastered. Certainly his mother's health weighed in the balance. She reported her "startling and terrifying dreams" in the summer of 1911, and she had declined to cross the ocean, hoping to save money and allow Locke to finish his degree in Berlin. In fact, the financial worries that had made Mary Locke dream often about finding money were getting to the point that something had to be done. In early 1911 she warned Locke about the bill collectors, saying they will "pounce" on him when he returns to America. The financial support he had tried to solicit from Washington was becoming a more remote option. To complicate matters further, there was the debt he had compiled with Mrs. Addis, his landlady at Oxford. This was to be a source of constant irritation, indeed panic, for Mrs. Addis took some unsettling means to recover it. First of all, she still had some of Locke's possessions, which he had left behind when he went to Berlin. Chief among her devices, however, was the enlisting of aid from a Mr. A. Parker Fitch, who threatened to write to people in America and discredit Locke. Mary Locke felt this would ruin her son's chances at the start of his career.[41]

The clash that resulted from Mr. Fitch's letter-writing reveals something about Locke's character and frame of mind at this time. On May 11, 1911 Fitch wrote to Mary Locke on behalf of Mrs. Addis and said that unless the debt was settled, he would inform Locke's "employers." Of course at this juncture Locke had no employer, but the threat seemed to involve Harvard being notified. Fitch wrote on stationery from the Andover Theological Seminary in Massachusetts, so his status would add gravity to the charge. Locke was informed of the situation by his mother and drafted a reply. It is not clear whether the letter was sent, or perhaps sent with the rather furious and cutting tone softened. But Locke was in no mood to be polite: "I don't acknowledge the authority or jurisdiction of your court, which I take it, is the bar of Public Opinion," he said. He did, however, add that he thought Mrs. Addis could recover some of the debt by selling the personal effects he had left behind, but he also complained that she had already resorted to "several of these extra-judicial and indirect appeals." His own patience was clearly at an end, and he knew his mother was unable to bear the psychological pressure of the situation, which had been considerable at least since the scramble for scholarships back at Harvard.[42]

To these negative reasons for returning, however, should be added the positive pull of what was becoming his vocational call. All through the last seven years, since he began at Harvard, Locke was engaged in a conversation with himself and others about racial problems and the part leadership might play in alleviating them. His education was always considered, at least in part, a possible preparation for such leadership. Locke sought but missed an opportunity to meet Washington during the leader's tour of Europe in 1910. In the summer of 1911 Mary Locke hoped that he would be able to attend the "Race Congress," as she called it. This obviously refers to the First Universal Races Congress held in London during the last days of July that year. De Fonseka had invited Locke to attend as his guest, and the two men stayed part of the summer at De Fonseka's residence in Cheyne Walk, in London. This meeting, modeled in part of the first Pan-African Congress of 1910, featured many papers that discussed all aspects of racial thought, from scientific and sociological points of view. Locke drew on it a few years later when he gave his series of lectures on interracial relations at Howard University.[43]

The opposing call of self-culture, however, would sound very loudly at times. The year or so in Berlin, though not detailed in many letters to Mary Locke, was apparently for Locke a time of self-indulgence; her reference to "paying the fiddler" may speak to more than an inability to attend to his studies. Hints from his correspondence with Dickerman, who was having a hard time shaping his vocation, suggest Locke enjoyed the open atmosphere of Berlin. Dickerman had come to visit Locke, and they had spent time in London together. There Dickerman met De Fonseka and also went to dinner at the Liberal Club with his old friends Downes and Dap. He wrote Locke an undated letter in which he glosses some homosexual argot, explaining how the word "so" meant homosexual, as in "I didn't know he was so." Dickerman added some details about a liaison he had with a Cockney sailor on the boat back to America. Locke had obviously written to Dickerman, though the letters are lost, and spoken of his relation with a young man named Phillip. Dickerman said in reply: "I'm awfully glad about Phillip. . . . Also that's why you're not coming over, nicht Wahr? Why not bring him?" Dickerman was usually discreet in his letters as far as mentioning Locke's sexual experiences, but there are more than enough references to establish that when together the two men discussed their various relations openly. Locke, however, was aware that openly homosexual relations were not something he was temperamentally prepared for in America. Bringing a friend back home was not an option.[44]

Before he returned to America Locke was able to publish one of his important statements about the country and its culture. "The American Temperament," which ran in the *North American Review* in 1911, is perhaps Locke's most impressive published essay before the appearance of "The New Negro" almost fifteen years later. He sets out to define the national character by using the form of the belletristic essay; there are no statistics, no demographics to guide the argument, only reflection and cultural analysis. This is especially apt because one of the essay's chief claims points to the irony that the American temperament "should of all temperaments [be] the least reflective, and for all its self-consciousness, should know itself so ill." Locke even tweaks his fellow Americans by a certain coy use of the passive, impersonal voice, set against their assertiveness, and suggests that "one may point to the need for self-analysis and expression." When, in November 1909, Locke gave a talk to the Rationalist Society at Oxford entitled "The American Temperament," he was probably reading from an earlier version of the essay. At that occasion he said, in a passage removed from the printed version, that he was faced with "the alternative of either making a composite portrait or drawing an ideal sketch—if forced to choose I should prefer the latter. . . . [I] would rather present you unashamed the bare outlines of pure thought." This choice, of course, left Locke considerable freedom in his approach.[45]

A hint of the reformer appears in his approach, for he dares to suggest what is most crucially missing in the national psychology during times of crisis: "Historical-mindedness and patience while the natural equilibrium is reestablishing itself are two traits, most lacking and most needed, in the American temperament." He harbors no illusion about his own ability to influence these and other traits with any real lasting impact: "Public opinion in America asserts itself violently, impulsively, and more often than in any other country perhaps, accomplishes its immediate aims . . . , owing to the plastic and tentative nature of our institutions and our ideas." The readerly delight of this essay comes from Locke's way of characterizing his subject as difficult to define ("plastic") and his still proceeding, through recursive loops and rhetorical swerves, to say something illuminating about it. The essay can be read as Locke's way of reentering America, studying paradoxically as a stranger and a native son the internal contrasts of the country he had been away from for three years.

Much of what the essay proposes as a delineation of the national temperament was available to Locke from a myriad of sources, ranging from Emerson to Tocqueville. But the essay impresses with its own maturity and insight. It appeared four years before Van Wyck Brooks's *America's Coming of Age*, fourteen years before William Carlos Williams's *In the American Grain*, and a number of years before the essays and books of Randolph Bourne and Lewis Mumford on the subject. Speculation about the national character, a literary activity since the republic's earliest days, was rampant in the early years of the twentieth century and into the 1920s; Marianne Moore wrote a poem about it (called, ironically, "England"), and D. H. Lawrence's *Studies in Classic American Literature* (1923) is obsessed with it. While at college Locke had reviewed H. G. Wells's book on the subject, *The Future in America*. The atmosphere at Harvard must have been at times marked by discussions of the issue as well, as Brooks's and Locke's efforts appearing so soon after graduation would suggest. Santayana stands as an imposing figure in this context, as his *Character and Opinion in the United States* (1920) makes clear. Many of these efforts centered on the question of American art, and while Locke takes up this aspect briefly, he is more concerned to represent American habits and values.

If there is a controlling trope in Locke's essay, it is the notion that the American temperament is something that is staged, and staged in part because of the evasiveness that is at its center. Locke introduces this figure of speech in the essay's second paragraph, showing that his recent experience as a foreign traveler has highlighted his own Americanness, as well as his perplexity in trying to represent just what this is:

> The histrionic demeanor of Americans abroad, at times so very like the behavior of actors off the stage, exacting calcium-light duty of the sun, is a real clue to the national temperament. If only by the reactions of others do we achieve any definite notion of what we ourselves are, it is small wonder that we have cultivated the actor's manner and practice his arts, only it is a strange art for an otherwise inartistic nation, a curious dependence for a free people.

Locke's Philadelphian sense of propriety shows through here, as surely does a dose of Harvard's strict social expectations. But to these elements in his background has been added the Oxford experience of the clash of national differences and the English reserve and studied indifference that he felt keenly.

The question of art is broached more than once in the essay, though without sustained esthetic theorizing, except for one paragraph where Locke seems to be rejecting the genteel tradition that had reigned at Harvard. However, he is unprepared to explain exactly what will take its place. Though wary of the esthete as a type, he is not reluctant to speak about some sharp alternatives:

> America is wise, after all, in preferring to remain artless and unenlightened rather than accept contemporary art as a serious expression of itself. . . . To force an art first to digest its civilization in all its crude lumpiness is, after all, a good and sound procedure, and it is safe to prophesy that in America either the result will be representative and unique or that there will emerge no national art at all.

The "lumpiness" figured in many of the discussions about art that followed in the next several decades, as Locke and others wrestled with the widespread dominance of realism and naturalism, with their "low" subject matter and deterministic ideas. Locke at this point had no way of knowing how the "almost expatriated" artists would become physically absent from America in large numbers in the next two decades. A key point here, still implicit and undeveloped, is that a purely formalist approach to esthetic matters would not satisfy Locke. The "reflective and representative arts" will eventually always "make for that sense of institutions, which, beginning in jingo patriotism, ends in sound traditions."

So far the American arts cannot tell us what we need to know about our national character. It is best understood as "something more than . . . commercial-mindedness and personal self-assertiveness." Pushing beyond this often cited charge, Locke turns to a description of it as "a mental atmosphere . . . something spiritual . . . free, accessible, contagious." The temperament takes on a political cast on "festival days" and is often thought of as "corporate prosperity." Locke alludes to the ethos of the robber baron here, but he would not settle for that as the highest expression of the nation's striving. At its core the American temperament, based on individualism, "is really a very limited and simple system of conventional ideas." This system is, frankly, "shallow and contentless . . . as an idea," but "the pragmatic verdict will prevail," for it works as a cohesive social force. The American's idea of himself is "Protean and even puerile," and his naive individuality is unquestionable, "because it is so plastic it knows no self-contradiction." Its evasiveness is its greatest anomaly, and this quality results from the rush of "self-willed energy" and the "modern demand for material progress." Locke even suggests, with some of the wry detachment of a Henry Adams, that the ultimate goal of this energy is the "securing [of] a final and restful mastery over the means of life."

Power and prosperity lie at the root of American patriotism for Locke. At one point he indulges in a comparison that would later serve as a common theme for Robert Lowell and Gore Vidal, when he compares America to ancient Rome: "A country that worships power, respects the autocrat, and may even come to tolerate the tyrant. Indeed, the analogies between the republican temper of Rome and that of America may well worry those who believe that history repeats itself." But he also sees that the reductive charge of crude materialism misses the point. The temperament, though made up of "superb eclecticism, . . . voraciousness . . . [and a] collector's instinct for facts and details," somehow generates a "public spiritedness [that] prevails to a marked and unusual degree." In describing "that phenomenon of our civilization, the millionaire philanthropist," he is able to show that "if Americans worship money, they worship it as power, as cornered energy and not in an intrinsic and miserly way."

Locke does not mean this as an apologetics for accumulated wealth, and the satiric bite comes in just in time to suggest that Locke had seen enough of accumulated wealth at Harvard and Oxford to recognize how insensitive it often makes people:

The process of accumulation, becoming automatic, discharges him; he takes to his new vocation of giving, but as far as the muscular reactions are concerned there is very little difference between shoveling in and shoveling out.

This passage captures some of the resentment of the scholarship student who realizes that the largess of wealthy benefactors does not always guarantee their commitment to the highest ideals of those they support.

Locke ends the essay by saying that "as long as the American temperament remains its own excuse for being, one cannot expect it to be humble and unassertive." Having worked around and around his subject, balancing each formulation with a qualification or a paradox, Locke's sense of the temperament as "its own excuse for being" suggests something like a final value. This value draws heavily on esthetics, a tactic that Locke will repeat many times in the future. Here he analogizes the national temperament with the acme of formalist esthetics, invoking the notion of art for art's sake. The essay rather cannily combines elements of political analysis, social psychology, a historicizing sensibility, and an esthetic imagination to try and represent something "so wholly vital and unique and interesting as the national character." Provoked in part by his reflections on the English character in his essay about Oxford, Locke tries to balance praise and censure when describing his own national identity. Some of the complexity of the writing, and the associative nature of the argument at various points, can be put down to the author's paradoxical need to embrace his country and hold it at arm's length. In any case, the essay is Locke's first step in recognizing that America's problems, though certainly unique, could not be immune to probing analysis and frank criticism. Both these features would be present in nearly everything he wrote after "The American Temperament."

———•———

Mary Locke and her son were constantly discussing his prospects when he would return to America. In the spring of 1911, she wrote to express her anxiety about his choosing an academic appointment. "I do not want you at Howard les[t] they dismiss you in disgrace, as they have done Montgomery Gregory of Harvard." Gregory, a young drama professor at Howard, had been seen exiting a saloon during the middle of the day by what she cryptically called the "Official of the lust." She added that the president of the university had given him fifteen minutes to write his letter of resignation. Fortunately,

Gregory was rehired a year later, in part through the intercession of Booker T. Washington. He and Locke were later to become close friends, working together to develop interest in Negro drama at Howard and throughout the country. When, in August 1911, Mary Locke saw the copy of the *North American Review* that contained "The American Temperament," Locke was still in Germany. She wrote to say that he should "Keep Alain[,] drop that silly old LeRoy—as I see you have." She added, referring to his "colossal" plan to travel extensively in Africa and the Middle East: "Now if you can make Egypt go." Locke's authorial identity had been definitely christened by the "Alain" and his appearance in a major intellectual journal, as well as by the bold and broad formulations in "Cosmopolitanism and Culture." His vocation was still fixed on the idea of seeing the world in order to understand its complexity of racial and cultural identities. The chances of seeing the world had so far hinged on the beneficence of various well-endowed educational enterprises. Now, however, it was beginning to be an unignorable fact that, despite an African American leadership that was often divided, limited, and overly cautious, he would have to make a living for himself in the service of his race. For that, America seemed the right place.[46]

CHAPTER FOUR

Howard: The Early Years

Locke's entry into the academy as a professor initiated what would be a forty year experience, rich with many rewards and scarred with more than a few frustrations and defeats. He never let the difficulties—the low pay, the academic disputes, the unappreciative administrators, the longing to travel and spend more time in purely cultural pursuits—erode his genuine delight in instructing young minds. Howard University, however, seemed to him almost like a consummation devoutly to be avoided. On the one hand it offered the possibility of a position of race leadership, but on the other it tied him by demanding a great deal of his time and energy. Almost from the start he ran afoul of a conservative college president, and yet in his first few years he managed to increase his credentials with an earned doctorate in philosophy and to put to excellent use his polymathic interests in many academic fields as well as a broad range of esthetic activities. The two public roles he had been preparing himself for, cultural critic and race leader, were soon to be in his reach. Another role, which he would characterize ironically as "midwife to the arts," would also present itself with greater and greater clarity. He approached all these roles with his usual self-awareness and the felt need to use those diplomatic skills that his long and learned maturation had provided.

In the Secretary's Second Report of the Harvard Class of 1908, published in 1914 on the eve of the First World War, Locke begins describing himself by reminding his fellow alumni that he had graduated in three years, thereby "losing the compound interest of the Senior year." The resort to financial metaphor was only partly tongue in cheek. He goes on to say his three years

at Oxford and one and a half years in Berlin would have been a waste of time
but for three reasons:

> first, one had a chance to balance one's education in the scales of two
> standard systems,—instead of transferring my allegiance from schol-
> arships to scholarship itself, as would have been best, I temporarily
> abandoned formal education for the pursuit of culture—yet fortunately,
> without money enough to collect blue china. . . .

After he waggishly overlays the concern with money with a reference to one
of Oscar Wilde's esthetic preoccupations, Locke continues:

> second, in the midst of a type of life that is a world-type simply be-
> cause it is so consistently itself, one had every facility for becoming
> really cosmopolitan—it was a rare experience in the company of many
> foreign students to pay Englishmen the very high tribute of not even
> attempting to be like them, but to be more one's self, because of their
> example. . . .

Here he paints the moral—which is as much an esthetic as an ethic—derived
from his contributions to the Cosmopolitan Club and the emphasis on self-
culture, while very discreetly distancing himself from his English hosts. He
goes on to the final reason:

> third, [there] is a brief corollary, for me the same fact was the very rare
> opportunity to choose deliberately to be what I was born, but what the
> tyranny of circumstances prevents many of my folk from ever viewing
> as the privilege and opportunity of being an Afro-American.

Locke's emphasis on a personal choice is foregrounded, but still he must bear
up against the tyrannical circumstances, even though they seem to affect his
folk more than himself. His racial identity has become a corollary of other
choices, but it, too, has been deliberately made. As if writing a capsule Bil-
dungsroman, Locke tells the familiar story of how the main protagonist has
become that most startling character: himself. Heredity and environment
have become virtually inseparable.[1]

Answering the class secretary's request for information in the third report,
in 1920, and the fourth, in 1923, Locke supplied many more factual details of
his activities, choosing not to reflect on his attitudes and values but instead

emphasizing his work, largely by listing his Howard University position and publications. The years between his return to America in late 1911 until the appearance of *The New Negro* in 1925 can be seen as a sobering period for Locke, forced in part by circumstances to abandon one lifestyle for another, not altogether of his liking. The relations Locke was to experience with Howard University often left him frazzled and frustrated. Most surprising, perhaps, was not the pressure of teaching and committee assignments and academic politics of a particularly unpromising sort, but rather the fact that he produced a good deal of writing and managed to expand and refine his interests in a number of areas. Neither cosmopolitanism nor culture would be neglected. His health was, relatively speaking, strong for a good number of years, and he used the summer vacations not only for travel but also research. Friendships were formed, especially with some of his Howard colleagues, and his social life branched out considerably. Almost from the first, he set up the lifelong pattern of visiting New York City often, usually leaving Washington by train on Thursday evenings and not returning until Sunday night or Monday morning. Often he was tired, but even more often he was busy.

Before Locke began his long career at Howard, however, he tried again to put into place a scheme that would allow him to increase the scope and depth of his knowledge and experience on the issues of race and race education. Here is how he recounted it in the second report to the class of 1908:

> . . . on my return [from Berlin], 1911, I spent six months visiting institutions for the special training of Negro youth in the South and West, a trip requiring all my philosophy and experience, but rich in return. My present job, teaching at Howard University . . . is a matter of deliberate choice and satisfaction. Teaching, with the race question as in some part a necessary, and in some part a gratuitous avocation seems very much like life-work to me at present.

The race question and education were to mingle in Locke's life as vocation and avocation. On the trip referred to Locke met Booker T. Washington and traveled with him throughout the deep South. At the turn of the century 90 percent of all African Americans lived in the South. For many black intellectuals and writers, such as Locke, Jean Toomer, and Du Bois, a trip down south meant something like a pilgrimage to the nation of black folk. Such a trip was often transformative, as the cultured urban dweller of the northeast was confronted with the poverty and the harsher discrimination of those states where clearly the failures of post-Reconstruction politics were most evident. But one could also see large numbers of black people in one place, and realize that, in terms of their culture, they had not only survived but in some ways prevailed.

What stands out from the reports he sent to his former classmates is that his sense of himself as a race-conscious intellectual was already formed and taking on an aspect of genuine dedication. By invoking "the privilege and opportunity of being an Afro-American," he was also introducing what he would later refer to as one of his "imperatives"—that is, a sense of value that shapes the course of one's activities and the meaning of one's experience. In the immediate foreground of his awareness, however, was a sense of himself as an educator. This would lead him to pursue two large projects in the next decade: a thorough study of the concept of race and the return to scholarship in the form of a Ph.D. at Harvard on the subject of value.

But before his sojourn in the South, an important event for Locke occurred in between his studies in Berlin and his return to America; he attended the First Universal Races Congress in London in 1911. While at Oxford, he and his friend Seme had formed the African Union Society, which was dedicated to "All men of Africa or Negro extraction who are interested in the general welfare of the Race both in Africa and in the other parts of the world," as the society's constitution expressed it. The society was a vivid expression of Locke's interest in Africa, which stretched from his high school essay on the Alhambra to his presence at the opening of the tomb in Luxor in 1924 and beyond. Locke wrote to his mother that De Fonseka had invited him to attend the congress, which took place at the University of London from July 26th to the 29th. His mother encouraged him to go, and she perhaps knew that the idea for the congress had originated with Felix Adler, the founder of the Society for Ethical Culture and a strong influence on Mary Locke's approach to teaching. (Adler was also a visiting professor for two years at the University of Berlin, shortly before Locke arrived there.) Among the papers presented at the congress in London was "The Instability of Human Types" by Franz Boas, which featured an argument that would influence Locke throughout his life and that was reinforced by his readings in pragmatism. Boas used his field experience to undercut the then dominant scientific claims for the perdurable categories of racial types. The anthropologist had earlier formed a professional friendship with Du Bois and had lectured in Atlanta at Du Bois's invitation. Further, his skeptical work on the vexed question of race classification in his own scientific field led Boas to become a source of intellectual support for a number of leading black intellectuals. In revolutionizing the field of anthropology and training a whole new generation of followers, such as Zora N. Hurston and Melville Herskovits, Boas helped form the phalanx of opposition to the biologically based racist theories of the nineteenth century.

A high level of intellectual discussion was also generated at the congress by the contributions of Adler, Du Bois (who served as the American secretary for the congress), Ferdinand Tönnies, and Felix Luschan, among many others. But the idealistic promise of the congress unfortunately was never realized as the next gathering, planned for 1914, came to nothing as a result of the commencement of the Great War. Fifty years later, however, Du Bois was to characterize the congress in his autobiography as "a great and inspiring occasion bringing together representatives of numerous ethnic and cultural groups and bringing new and frank conceptions of scientific bases of racial and social relations of people." For Locke the occasion was one that served to confirm the relations between imperialism and racism and that set him on a course where he could begin to delve deeply into the subject of race that would preoccupy him for decades.[2]

In early 1912, recently arrived back in America, Locke began a six-month-long project to learn about Negro schooling in the South by setting out to join Booker T. Washington. Locke had first encountered Washington in 1903, when he came to Philadelphia to speak at the Unitarian Book Room Association. Through the courtesy of a Professor Poser, perhaps a teacher at Central High School, Locke, then only seventeen years old, was able to hear Washington's speech and to talk with him briefly afterwards. Clearly the event impressed Locke, and a few years later the impression was still shaping his thoughts about race leadership. When, in 1909 and 1910, Locke had shared with his mother his scheme to meet Washington, he desired not only to work toward a "practical career" but to measure himself against the leaders of his race. Mary Locke had responded, in 1910, when Locke further detailed his career plans, that his "colossal" scheme had made her head swim. Locke planned then not only to meet Booker T. Washington but to travel extensively to Egypt and India. Now that he had arrived back in America after his years abroad, it was time to present his travel plans again, this time in person, and ask for the support of the Wizard, as Booker T. Washington was commonly known. Washington, of course, was the most famous race leader in the country at this time, and though his accommodationist approach had many detractors, his approval would be most valuable for the aspiring Locke. This "colossal" project would allow him to see black peoples in many different countries and to write about their cultures. But he had other motives in mind as well; he went to the South with an eye toward acquiring some position at Tuskegee, and simply to learn about the social conditions of his "folk" in an area of the country where he had never previously ventured. He traveled with Washington for several weeks in early 1912, as the older man went about displaying his oratory in a number of southern states, and though the details are obscure, he was clearly impressed with the heat, the poverty, and the cultural textures that he was seeing for the first time.

Some of what he faced in the South deeply discomfited him, but he felt the trip was important and instructive. He wrote his mother a letter in February 1912, from Jacksonville, Florida, in which he said he "made a bullseye with Washington." Later that same month he traveled to Montgomery, Alabama, to rejoin Washington after a short, unexplained separation. Even the train travel proved revealing. "As I write this an old confederate opposite sits and glares—I guess it makes him angry that I can write," he quipped to his mother. Locke wrote to his mother in early March when he was still in Jacksonville, and a week later he had returned to Tuskegee. From there he went to Atlanta, all the while saying he had been serenaded and showered with affection. He meanwhile completed his application for a Kahn Fellowship from Columbia University, designed to support his travel and research plans. For the time being it looked as if his scheme could be fully implemented.

In March he testified that he had been on his best social behavior, but he did so with the usual self-critical tone, mixed perhaps with a large dose of irony. He told his mother:

> I have seen a lot and been seen by a great many more—and as to using my eyes and ears—they are both sore—my tongue never tires as you know—indeed it is oiled to an appalling slickness—you will think me an arch hypocrite when you see me—I don't know that I can even be sincere with you though I shall try.

The irony directed at his self-presentation—calling himself "an arch hypocrite"—reverberates through many of his letters to his mother, and his commitment to what at a minimum can be called social unction earned him considerable enmity throughout his life. However teasing he may have been about it to his mother, part of his self-justification lay in his requiring it for leadership. But a working union with Washington never occurred, and so Locke turned his efforts to a different sort of teaching. As the late spring and summer of 1912 arrived, Locke was back in Philadelphia, increasingly focused on an academic position. "Colossal" as they might have seemed, Locke's plans were to be put into motion, albeit in a different form, as he slowly decided to begin his career as an academic. Traveling around the world to know more and more about questions of race and cultural contact would, however, always form part of his avocation. In some ways, the trip to the South bore little fruit, yet it provided Locke with firsthand knowledge of a region where black culture flourished, and it introduced him to a famous race leader. It may also have helped him see that an academic position would be the best solution, for the time being, to the question of his vocation.[3]

Locke's article on "The American Temperament" had appeared some months earlier, in 1911, and he was told by Alexander Crummel, the founder of the Negro Academy in Washington, D.C., that he would be nominated for election to that relatively new but prestigious body.[4] During the early months of 1912, the time Locke traveled in the South, he mulled over an invitation to speak at the International Congress on the Negro, to be held at Tuskegee in April, but he eventually declined. He also visited New York City, where he had lunch with Du Bois in March. It may have been at this time that he began to shift his interest from the compliant Washington to the more activist Du Bois, recalling how his mother had notified him of the latter's founding of the *Crisis* in 1910. Near the end of 1911, even before he had started his travels in the South, he had told his mother that if Lewis Moore, the dean of the Teachers' College at Howard University, would support his appointment there, so, too, would Kelly Miller, and he would be able to teach both literature and philosophy courses. This represented a change in Locke's attitude from his noncommittal response to a letter he had received in Berlin, in which Professor Cook, a friend of Pliny Locke, had mentioned the possibility of employment at Howard. Mary Locke had meanwhile secured a teaching job at the Whittier School, at the corner of Eighth Street and Chestnut in Philadelphia, where she was to teach until her retirement in 1915. At this time Locke remained uncertainly suspended between assimilating the lessons of the travel with Washington and his more and more likely decision to accept an academic appointment.

Now that the trip to the South to visit and travel with Washington was over, Locke's search for a place to teach took on new urgency and focus. He faced considerable pressure to settle down, as he and his mother were burdened with many of the debts accumulated during his study and travel abroad. There was, too, the real question during the late spring of 1912 as to which black university might he chose to offer his services. For a while

Wilberforce seemed a possibility. Mary Locke meanwhile felt that one day Booker T. Washington might "put obstacles" in her son's way; apparently she had heard from Locke what had gone awry in the plans on that front. Of course, Howard University seemed a logical choice, as it was where his father had studied law, and he had already interviewed with Kelly Miller and Dean Moore. With her usual maternal protectiveness, however, Mary Locke, writing to Locke in Berlin, had alerted her son to the problem that Montgomery Gregory had had with the morally censorious administration at Howard. Nevertheless, Howard remained the leading choice. And so in the fall of 1912, Locke's teaching career at Howard, which was to stretch for four decades, began among a number of uncertainties. Starting at an annual salary of one thousand dollars (which would slowly rise to just over four thousand by 1946), he began as an assistant professor in the Teachers' College. There were fewer than two hundred and fifty undergraduates at Howard at this time, and only thirty in the graduating class. But he had a position, and he meant to do well at it, even slowly redefining it to suit his talents.

From the start of Locke's appointment, Kelly Miller, though twenty-five years his senior, would become one of his close friends and a soldier-in-arms, so to speak, in the many battles that would ensue at Howard. Miller was an activist and spokesman for racial causes, a man of considerable energy. Born in South Carolina of a father who was a freed slave, as a child he exhibited considerable intelligence and won a scholarship to Howard. A decade before Locke joined him as a colleague, he had proposed that Howard support the publication program of the Negro Academy, only to be rebuffed by the trustees. But Miller was nothing if not persistent. Of his own student days, he later said it was "difficult to overestimate the advantage of such cultural contact to a country boy of the crude surroundings and contacts such as I sustained prior to my entrance to Howard University." Though primarily trained as a mathematician, Miller had studied graduate-level physics and astronomy at Johns Hopkins, where he was the first black to be admitted, but he left without taking a degree. He taught at Howard and served in the administration there, chiefly as a dean, from 1890 to 1934.[5]

Adding sociology to his wide learning, he became an outspoken theorist about the race question. He tended to steer a middle course between the accommodationism of Booker T. Washington and the agitation of the Niagara movement that led to the founding of the National Association for the Advancement of Colored People, and he argued that industrial and technical education was not antipathetic to the higher educational ideals of the arts and humanities, but that the two approaches had to be blended into some balance in an overall scheme. He matched this view with a partly journalistic approach to writing that was aimed at mass audiences. Like many other black sociologists trained by an earlier generation of teachers who were often clerics, Miller used the frame of Christian ethics in his work. As late as 1936 he could argue: "The Negro embodies the assemblage of Christian virtues and graces to a degree unequaled by any other member of the human family. Meekness, humility and forgiveness of spirit are undetachable coefficients of his blood." Locke never completely shared this set of values, and, being of a later generation than Miller, he was educated in a more secular tradition. But he did share Miller's concern with that perennial topic, "the advancement of the race."

It was in large part through Miller's influence that Jesse E. Moorland, an alumnus of Howard and a notable leader in the NAACP, was convinced to donate his important collection of books to form the nucleus of an important research library at Howard. Able to work well with Howard's presidents such as Wilbur Thirkield (1906–12) and Stephen M. Newman (1912–18), Miller eventually clashed with J. Stanley Durkee (1918–26), after which his influence in the administration was curtailed. With less sway on the campus, he was eventually to enjoy considerable success with his syndicated newspaper column, which earned him an estimated quarter of a million black readers. But he clearly recognized early on the merits of Locke's academic training and saw in him a future scholar of distinction. Locke graciously accepted Miller's friendship and support, but he well knew that he was qualified to teach at Howard, though he may have viewed such a position as merely a way station along his path to a fuller role as a race leader.

In the fall of 1912 Locke arranged to live within walking distance of the Howard campus, at 1309 R Street N.W. in Washington, D.C. Later he moved a few doors down to a modest apartment at 1326 R Street, where he resided for the rest of his life in the capital. As a resident of Washington, D.C., Locke was restless; as he snobbishly put it, "Washington externally is like a real capital—it only lacks the proper people—." But he took part fully in the society that had been created by the most extensive population of middle-class blacks in the country. Many of his neighbors were Howard faculty, and some were leading intellectual and cultural figures who made the neighborhood near Howard, often referred to as Shaw West, the center of black culture in the nation's capital. The relatively prosperous area was nicknamed after a local high school which commemorated the heroism of Robert Gould Shaw, a white New Englander who led a black regiment in the Civil War. It was a vibrant neighborhood with a strong sense of history. The industrious and enterprising historian, Carter Woodson, lived only a few blocks away from Locke, and in 1912 he founded the Association for the Study of Negro Life and History. A year later he began the important *Journal of Negro History* and also started Associated Publishers, devoted to bringing out the work of black authors. Tireless in his efforts to recover the lost history of black people, his agitation led in 1926 to the forming of Black History Week, which was later expanded into Black History Month. Woodson was born in West Virginia, the son of former slaves, and he went on to be the second black to attain a Ph.D. from Harvard, after W. E. B. Du Bois. Along with Kelly Miller, he lent considerable luster to Howard's faculty, though such merit often failed to strike the college's administration in the proper light.[6]

Locke's house on R Street placed him not only close to the Howard campus but in the middle of a neighborhood with many bourgeois features. Among these was a literary salon, run by the genteel Georgia Douglas Johnson, where Locke often attended evening gatherings devoted to high literary discussion and readings of poetry. Across the street from Locke's house, at 1327 R Street, was the MuSoLit Club, where musical, social, and literary activities had been featured since 1905. This society was the focus of a satirical attack written by W. Calvin Chase, the editor of a local newspaper called the *Washington Bee*. Chase excoriated the elite's "colorphobia," suggesting that there was "more intelligence excluded than included." Every February the club hosted a Lincoln-Douglass birthday celebration, considered by many the highlight of the year's social calendar. This was also the society and neighborhood that had provided the background for Duke Ellington and others who cultivated a sense of refinement and style, perhaps not at the level of the London and Paris Locke had come to know in his travels a few years earlier, but sufficient unto the day. The "talented tenth" was busy recognizing itself through a host of cultural activities.

Shaw West was only part of the story, however. A more raucous area, called Shaw East, stretched along Seventh Street, with its many theaters and pool halls, and the Howard Theater, the most prestigious of black playhouses in America. It was this area, populated with many working-class people, that so attracted Langston Hughes, who spent time in Washington on several occasions, even being employed for a while as a clerk in Carter Woodson's office. On Seventh Street, Hughes applauded the impoverished blacks who "looked at the dome of the Capitol and laughed out loud." Jean Toomer also depicted the area in a section of *Cane,* his lyrical novel that appeared in 1923, referring to its "crude-boned, soft-skinned wedge of nigger life." Though later Locke would identify Harlem as the race capital for blacks in America, he clearly could see a modern urban black society around him every day when he walked to his classes on the Howard campus.[7]

In the summer of 1913 Locke made a return visit to Harvard with his old friend Dickerman to attend a Phi Beta Kappa ceremony, and they both went around to look at the rooms where they had lodged. Neither graduate was experiencing any financial security. Locke's financial woes persisted, and his mother told him of one of her dreams in which she saw "large silver dollars— but too large to be natural I fear—they looked more like turnips." Locke frequently rendezvoused with Mary in Philadelphia, where they often attended concerts together. She made a point of telling him that when she went by herself she always sat in the middle of the audience when seeing motion pictures, for she refused to be "Jim Crowed." Even as the possibility of his promotion to associate professor was progressing, Locke told her that he meant to raise the question of his salary with the university's president, anticipating an explosive issue that would cause considerable difficulties a few years later. But he was also elected as secretary to the Teachers' College faculty, and given a place on the council that lobbied Congress for the annual budget appropriation for Howard. At the end of 1913, Mary Locke wrote to compliment her son: "It is a great satisfaction that you are becoming a public speaker. It was always the height of my ambition for your father so the son is making up for many disappointments along that particular line." Locke answered with a confession to his mother that "I am not the sybarite I used to be." He busied himself, however, staying informed about all the ferment in contemporary efforts to mount a political forum for black people.[8]

He constantly increased his knowledge about all the affairs of the rising black middle classes. Referring to the many flourishing black newspapers as his "classics," he protested that "I almost bankrupt myself buying them."[9] He told Mary in January 1914, probably referring to a recent shift in the politics of the National Association for the Advancement of Colored People (NAACP): "It is disgusting to see the way these Negroes down here . . . flop over at the slightest change of fortune—they are all Villardists now," referring to Oswald Garrison Villard, one of the founders of the organization.[10] On more than one occasion Locke described a group of Negroes as either untrustworthy or self-encumbering; his elitism tended to be unforgiving, and it was hard for him to separate his idealism from his impatience. One of the struggles that most engaged Locke in this period was his desire to come to some personal understanding with the mass of under- or uneducated blacks. But he also realized it was a larger social issue. In 1911 he had drafted an article for the *North American Review* on the issue of racial progress, perhaps hoping that his success with "The American Temperament" provided him an opening. Announcing the notion that "one of the highest desiderata is to find an adequate simple test of Negro progress," he said that this should be more than "a program of justification for the Negro." But the question remained: how do you judge a race? Rejecting the Anglo-Saxon standard of "assimilative imitation," Locke insisted on the need for "a new standard of judgment—to do justice to the Negro and decrease white hysteria." He openly advocated a rational approach and the need to agree on shared and empirical standards. The article never appeared, but its ideas were suffused throughout much of his work in the following decades.

Even as he was preparing to begin his academic life, Locke formed a professional relationship with John E. Bruce, an activist and journalist who wrote to introduce himself to Locke in November 1911. Bruce, the son of slaves, was born in Maryland in 1856, and though he attended Howard University for a short period, was largely self-taught. His militant writings and speeches earned him recognition by audiences throughout the country. In the 1880s he became well known through his syndicated column in Cleveland and New York papers; the column bore the title "Bruce Grit." Along with Arthur Schomburg and others, he founded the Negro Society for Historical Research in 1911. Wanting to enlist Locke in his political activism, he invited him to visit at his farm in Yonkers, New York. Bruce early on spoke very openly of his opinions and shared with Locke his strongly held views about various black leaders. In a letter from 1912, he bolstered Locke's ego by saying: "You will soon get your stride now that you have gotten the edge of the wedge under you. And you will have little difficulty in pressing forward to the mark of higher calling." Then he went on to comment on Booker T. Washington: "The Wizard is a long headed diplomat and he plays the game to win. When he wins so does the other fellow." Six months later, it was Du Bois's turn to be described: "The Crisis space is too limited and its editor does not appear to be as broad gauged as some of us could wish. The Doctor is not a good mixer, his pride of learning is his greatest handicap so he will never be a popular Negro idol, because he is too stiff in manner and lives too much in the upper ether." Bruce could be forgiven for not realizing the irony of his remarks, for these were the charges that would eventually attach themselves to Locke. Meanwhile Locke listened and absorbed information from the autodidact.[11]

Bruce went nearly blind in old age, but he continued to correspond with Locke until his death in 1924. He shared unstintingly with Locke his disillusionment with civil rights progress after the war and described how he joined Marcus Garvey's Universal Negro Improvement Association (UNIA). He grew increasingly cranky, and even opined that Du Bois had framed Garvey, presumably on the charges of fraud that led to his deportation. He joined with Schomburg and others to support Locke generously in many ways, especially in the academic projects that he felt would strengthen American blacks' awareness of Africa as well as civil rights. When he died, the Garvey organization staged three different memorial services for him, and Garvey himself delivered one of the eulogies. Bruce's life as a race leader, and a man of admirable energy, probably could not have served as a direct model for Locke, perhaps, but at the very least his efforts paralleled Locke's work in giving black people a sense of pride through a greater knowledge of their own past. Locke also became more immediately aware, in yet another way, of how large and approachable the black audience was and of the many voices that were trying to sway it.

———————

Though little of substance seemed to have come from Locke's meeting with Washington, in March 1912 Washington had nevertheless written a strong recommendation to Nicholas Murray Butler at Columbia University, supporting Locke's application for the Kahn Traveling Fellowship and speaking of how the project to explore race relations would address "these questions as a world problem." This plan was a modified version of the colossal scheme that had earlier made Mary Locke's head spin. Locke's application was rejected, however, because the fellowship was designed for someone who had already established a reputation as a teacher. Locke, meanwhile, resolved not to be disappointed and settled into his academic routine, eventually teaching philosophy as well as literature classes. Not long after his initial appointment Locke met the disfavor of his university's administration on a crucial issue. It was in 1913 that Locke first mentioned to his mother that he had proposed to teach a class on the question of race. But by late 1914 he planned to turn his research into a series of public lectures, although, at the time, with uncertain sponsorship. He hoped finally to be able to bring together all his learning and reflection on the race issue and so use his academic position to further his role as a race leader. It was a bold plan, equal in some ways to what he had proposed for the Kahn Fellowship, though without the travel and yet retaining the broadest of contexts.

Locke first proposed presenting the lecture series in 1914, and the Board of Trustees approved the request. However, the board stipulated that they be given only on one day, hardly enough time to present the lectures Locke intended to give. In the summer of 1915 Locke proposed to offer a course on the topic of race that would incorporate his lectures, but his request was rejected presumably because the administration wanted to avoid incorporating courses on controversial political topics into the curriculum. Locke nonetheless secured the board's permission for his lecture series. First presented in the fall of 1915, the series was poorly advertised, and Locke was disappointed that hardly anyone attended. He worked to make sure that did not happen again. He delivered the lectures a second time, beginning at approximately 4 p.m. on Monday, March 27, 1916, and continuing for the next four Mondays, in Carnegie Library's large lecture hall at Howard with such notables in attendance as Kelly Miller, Dean of the College of Arts and Sciences, and Lewis Moore, Dean of Teacher's College.

The Howard administration's reluctant approval of the lecture series, and its unwillingness to sanction a course on race, are representative of the widespread self-censorship and conservative anxiety that afflicted the Howard community. The administration, especially in the person of the university's white president, the Rev. Stephen M. Newman, staunchly opposed ideas that would attract the attention of the Congressional committee that oversaw the government's allocation of funds. (It would be 1928 before Congress passed the legislation that allowed Howard to receive a secure annual appropriation.) Not only Howard but all the other black institutions of higher learning at this time were forced to look over their shoulders at their white benefactors, and their curricula were often severely limited as a result. Since the administrations of the black universities, and a good percentage of their faculties as well, were white, such self-censorship was standard. Further, as late as the second half of the 1920s, only four of the Negro colleges in the country, out of more than sixty, were nonsectarian. This meant their attitude toward the question of race was often tempered with a call for Christian humility. It would also be decades before several colleges at Howard would receive full academic accreditation. Locke's persistence in presenting his thorough research into the questions of what he called "race contacts and interracial relations" was a tribute to the seriousness of his earlier career plans.

For the next few years, from 1913 until 1915, Locke worked on his lectures, which were published posthumously with the title *Race Contacts and Interracial Relations.*[12] During his Oxford and Berlin years Locke absorbed a great deal of philosophical and sociological reading, and this led to focusing his main interests on the issues of value and race. Among the main influences were Georg Simmel, Franz Boas, and W. E. B. Du Bois, and the work of these important thinkers cross-fertilized in Locke's thought and experience. Simmel was something of a renegade in German academic life, being essayistic in his approach and favoring a style of investigation that owed as much to social psychology as to the accumulation of observed data. His work on questions of alienation and the effects of mass urbanized society became better known later, when his contributions were often read as part of a compendious theory of modernization. In addition, in the spirit of Simmel, Locke favored a sociology that was interpretive rather than merely empirical. The more he studied the issue of race the less he trusted merely empirical data, and he was often to speak against the elevation of scientistic values above all others. He shared with Simmel a suspicion about any academic discipline that offered itself as a cure-all for solving problems and settling disputes. By nature and training a multidisciplinarian, Locke knew that any approach to learning involved the activation of values, just as he was willing to subject values themselves to analytic scrutiny.

Boas, whose work Locke came to know as a result of his attendance at the First Universal Races Congress in 1911, helped him formulate his idea of "cultural reciprocity." In his battle against the pseudoscientific discourse on race, Boas argued for an approach that would grant value to all forms of culture, and he proposed a research program to consider each group's cultural expression as part of a specific approach to life and therefore worth consideration in its own terms. Thus Boas further helped Locke reject—or at least refine—the paradigm of scientific positivism as the dominant model of all rigorous knowledge. The two issues of race and value became linked in Locke's mind, and he would also continue to develop them throughout his life. His Ph.D. was to be the culmination of his concern with the philosophical analysis of value. For the issue of race, it was his lecture series, a virtual compendium of many of the ideas he had heard at the International Races Congress, that served as the occasion to display much of his evolved thinking.

When Locke delivered the lectures in March 1916, the series had three sponsors. First was the Howard chapter of the National Association for the Advancement of Colored People, which had been formed in large part as a result of the Niagara Movement. The adult education section at Howard, called the Teachers and the Commercial College, joined in, along with the Social Science Club. The rationales of the three sponsors reflected Locke's approach, which was meant to instruct people as to the mechanism and ideology of racism, so as to facilitate its eradication. Locke amassed a very impressive amount of reading and reflection in the lectures, and it remains a puzzle as to why he did not seek to have them published as a book during his lifetime. The brief summary of the lectures, including a short bibliography for each lecture, which he arranged to have privately published as a modest pamphlet, hardly did justice to the nuances of his presentation. In any case, he took pains to have the lectures recorded by a stenographer, whom he paid with his own funds. It is safe to assume that the young professor, then just thirty years old, was able to show his colleagues that his academic training and public speaking were of the highest order.

The five lectures are filled with important and subtle claims and perceptions, but three of their main points can be easily summarized. First, Locke maintained that there was no scientific basis for race or racism. Its persistence as an idea had to be accounted for, however, and for this Locke argued that it was a cultural construct and so had become "second nature" to many. Second, the cultures of people were complex and hybrid historical phenomena, and they were formed by contact between groups. These groups derived and contributed cultural meanings to other groups in a reciprocal way that often defied precise analysis, but the reciprocity was always pervasive. Such cultural borrowing between peoples allowed each distinct social group to appreciate, as Boas had suggested, the values of other groups.

Locke significantly differed from Boas in two major respects, however. Boas maintained that races could not be scientifically proven and that they were unstable; nonetheless, he consistently maintained that a race, and particularly the Negro race, was likely to remain a permanent category. Locke did not accept the idea that races were permanent. Races would be understood by Locke, in many respects, as cultural groupings. In addition, Boas promoted minority group assimilation or miscegenation as a solution to racial problems; Locke argued for the continuation of cultures and cultural exchange in an equitable and reciprocal fashion.

The third main point argued that the group and its values were best understood as represented by a "civilization type." This resembled Max Weber's ideal type, was compatible with Simmel's notion of an abstract sociological form, and was commonly used by Alexander Crummell. "Civilization type" means the dominant cultural representative in any given society, one who epitomizes its values; consequently, the first time Locke uses the term he then queries: "In what kind of society do you wish to live?" This civilization type would persist as both an expression of, and a stabilizing force in, group identity, but could in the future—so Locke would argue—be freed of any strictly racial basis. This line of argument allowed Locke to conceive of social structures that were at once stable and yet, because they were embodied through lived experience, amenable to change. These three main points anchored the manifold reflections in the lectures.

Locke was especially impressive in assimilating his influences. Simmel was involved in the development of modern sociology even when Locke studied with him, and the German philosopher felt an urgent need to define the "true" subject matter of sociology, which he saw as abstract forms of group relations and individual types. Locke may well have responded positively to Simmel's method mainly because it went beyond empirical data to formulate more lasting, and potentially universal, social patterns. Locke's approach to "civilization type" distances him from the then dominant American schools of sociology, represented by such authors as Franklin Giddings, Charles Cooley, Edward Ross, and William I. Thomas. These authors considered civilization a 'white' creation and racial antipathy natural. Civilizations were, at best, composed of unequal racial kinds, with whites at the top. Obviously Locke rejected this school of thought and turned in part to a theory of race that borrowed from Du Bois, who, at this point in his career, occasionally treated race as a transhistorical phenomenon. Races frequently changed their social status and changed how they were defined, yet there was an unbroken sense of black African civilization. Whether drawn from Alexander Crummell, John Bruce, or Du Bois, this sense of race was quite popular among authors, showing as it did a link between Africans, African Americans, and the Afro-Caribbean.

The arguments in Locke's lectures invoke a range of methodologies and disciplines, as he draws from sociology, history, psychology, and philosophy. But the way his mind works is plainly on view throughout. One of his telling habits of mind is his penchant for finding the way between two extreme positions, the mediation of a pragmatist turn of thought. Here is one example, from the third lecture:

> I fancy we shall have to mediate between two rather natural and yet very dangerous positions, the one regarding race contacts as wholly automatic, and the other regarding them as wholly deliberate. They span both the voluntary and the involuntary actions of peoples in groups. We somehow or other regard race feeling . . . as different in kind from the same kind of group feeling which prevails in social classes. I fancy that is a fundamental mistake. . . . (RCIR, 44)

When Locke points out "rather natural but dangerous positions," he is arguing like a pragmatist, since only with a reconstruction of philosophical ideas would we be able to separate the "rather" natural position from the dangerous one. Locke's habits of refusal are visible here: a refusal to see any social phenomenon as unique and therefore inexplicably cut off from other similar phenomena, and a refusal to allow any problem to be exclusively defined either by an extreme statement of the situation or its possible solution.

Locke remained far from believing that racism could be easily eliminated, but—relying on an Enlightenment trust that clear thought was ultimately corrective—he suggested that a full explanation was also a full condemnation of such a destructive social attitude. The lectures present a compendium of early twentieth-century racial theorizing and contain observations and arguments which were to become commonplace in the decades that followed. Locke's skill at extended argument was best demonstrated in his fourth lecture. Here he broke racist thought into five fallacies, invoking the "idols of the tribe" of Francis Bacon, who sought to separate superstition and delusion from critical and supportable thinking. The first fallacy was the biological justification of racial superiority. Here Locke was brief and blunt: "race purity as such (purity of ethnic strain or blood) is impossible under [the] conditions of life." The second fallacy he called "the fallacy of the masses," which led to a common contradiction: when people thought of themselves as superior they measured people as individuals, whereas when someone judged a group to be inferior, the basis of judgment was the aggregate. The third fallacy was borrowed directly from Boas, and Locke called it "the fallacy of the permanency of race types." Even dominant groups are subject to change: "in fact, the more representative they are, the less permanent they are apt to be," and the changes brought about by "environmental adaptation and under what we term modern social growth and development" make it impossible to "fasten any set of judgments upon any group of people."

The fourth fallacy was one that Locke wished he had had time to discuss more fully: he called it the "fallacy of race ascendancy." Essentially this was an argument for the separation of the races, with the proviso that the smaller or less powerful group in society should "duplicate the larger social organization within itself and keep to itself, maintaining its solidarity with the rest of society only through the merest sort of economic cooperation." Locke goes on explicitly to identify this fallacy with Booker T. Washington and credits the separatist argument as having been derived from the practice of the Austro-Hungarian empire. While signaling his distance from the sage of Tuskegee, Locke casts the references to him in very balanced and polite terms. He admits that such a fallacy can produce, under certain historical conditions, an acceptable social structure, but he very clearly states that it is finally a self destructive arrangement. Further, in such a system of apartheid what invariably happens is that the dominant group uses, as it sees fit, economic or social stringency to support its privileged position. The discussion of this fallacy concludes by Locke observing: "You will find that all the handicaps placed on colored peoples come under either one of these two areas." As far back as his Harvard days Locke had vehemently argued against separate educational systems for black people, and his mistrust of separatist "solutions" would only grow more thorough.

The fifth fallacy is labeled the fallacy of "automatic adjustment." This would argue that society is automatic in its forms and forces and so is not subject to remedial measures. Locke counters this by suggesting that activism is necessary in order to change "false habits of judgment as well as false social standards." Because he had earlier argued that the biological and scientific bases of racism were demonstrably false, he now argued that the standards of judgment must be challenged and changed. "Now it is toward false social standards that our activity must be directed if we wish to controvert false race creed," he insisted (RCIR, 78). By forcing society to "controvert the standard," the "whole life of society" would be upset. This catches the spirit of Locke's attitude nicely, since it shows that, because of the virulence and persistence of theories of racial supremacy, one should proceed rationally where possible, gradually where necessary, but always unceasingly until society itself is founded upon a surer and more democratic sense of values. By using a phrase like "controvert[ing] the standard," Locke was referring to the realm of values where his own contributions were most likely to have the greatest effect.

In his final lecture, Locke made a number of arguments and claims, so many in fact that the structure seems rushed and overly full of references to experts. He speaks of a reactionary form of nationalism, which supports racist feelings, and he mentions his earlier interest in eugenics, while he also reaffirms his trust in rational thought: "The history of progress has been the history of the redemption of ideas." One of his most important ideas—the "civilization-type"—is not as fully developed as one might wish, especially given how Locke uses it to formulate his views on the possible future of a world without rabid and persistent racism. Locke believed that group identity was inevitable, and the only way to manage it was to make it possible to have groups offer reciprocal tolerance to each other and for each to encapsulate its values into a representative type. The broader and more cosmopolitan such a type was, the higher and more fulfilled the civilization. Borrowing from Du Bois's idea of the "talented tenth," Locke projects a future where the representative of what he calls the "secondary race consciousness" (by which he means that of the group that is a numerical minority) not only adapts to the larger, dominant group but—and this is crucial—prevents the secondary group from losing its identity. He makes this point:

> Now this is not a doctrine of race isolation. It is not even a doctrine of race integrity. It is really a theory of social conservation which in practice conserves the best in each group, and promotes the development of social solidarity out of heterogeneous elements. (RCIR, 98)

The use of the word "conservation" echoes the famous essay of Du Bois, "The Conservation of the Races," but Locke shifts the category to one of "social" rather than "racial" conservation and invokes his own emergent ideas of multiculturalism to complete his thought. Locke from the beginning avoided any suggestion of chauvinism or separatism.

Stretching as far back as the abolitionists Richard Allen, William Lloyd Garrison, and Frederick Douglass, the justification for the use of racial solidarity by churches and political unions for purposes of organization has been debated. Many of the early abolitionists believed that churches and political organizations using race as a criteria of membership, even for the purpose of organizing networks of support to help defend the enslaved, were perpetuating the evil of racial division. Du Bois, and with him Locke, entered the continuing debates and supported the idea of racial solidarity for defense. Crummell had prepared the basis for this approach in his "The Relations and Duties of Free Colored Men in America to Africa" (1861) and "Civilization: The Primal Need of the Race" (1898), even before Du Bois lectured to Crummell's American Negro Academy on "The Conservation of the Races." Negro institutions, lead by the "talented tenth," were necessary. "Conservation," in Locke's nuanced treatment, is instrumental.

Ending the concluding lecture by seeing in the idea of race classification a social good, Locke says that "the race issue has performed a social function in society because it has blended two heterogeneous elements [that is, two different racial groups] into a homogeneity of which either one in itself would have been incapable without the collaboration and help of the other." Then, he concludes: "Whatever theory or practice moves toward it [the blending of heterogeneous elements] is sound; whatever opposes and retards it is false."

Whatever optimism or meliorist thought animated Locke's lectures, one of the chief ironies is that he delivered them as some of the highly civilized nations of the world were about to try to destroy one another. In September 1914, six months before he delivered his lectures on race contacts, he delivered a talk to a group in Yonkers, New York, and made this bracing claim: "[L]et us realize and confess that the civilization which is at war with itself is not ours in the intimate sense that we owe it a blood debt or even an irrevocable allegiance." Such a confession would seem inevitably to lead to outright opposition to the war. Finally, though, he was no pacifist and no separatist. By the end of the war he had shifted his thinking considerably. At the start of the war, in letters exchanged with his mother and between him and Dickerman, Locke expressed his support for Germany. Obviously, his intellectual debt to his year in Berlin and his cultural preference for German music were influences here. For a brief period he was to argue strongly against the war altogether, seeing it as the blind struggle of a civilization against itself. But as the war progressed, his own patriotic feelings surfaced, as, of course, they did throughout the country. To adapt the comment of one historian, all racial difference melted like butter in the frying pan of nationalism. By 1917 he was instrumental in helping to prepare students at Howard for service in the armed forces of America.[13]

Locke gave these lectures a number of times at Howard, and he was concerned to print the syllabus as a booklet and offer it for sale, for $1.00. Despite having trouble with the printer, he saw to it that the booklet appeared, since, as he told Mary, he did not want others to steal all his work. But various other projects also occupied Locke during his first years at Howard. In March 1915 he was in conversation with the NAACP and wrote to tell his mother that "I had an interview with Miss Lerney of the NAACP and it promises developments. You know I'd never kow-tow to Du Bois for a chance there— she had heard of my series of lectures—which begin Tuesday by the way— and thought they would be fine as part of their extension work—at other colleges—so next year there is a chance of getting a really good hearing through them." Presumably the project involved traveling throughout the country lecturing on race and race theory. The reference to Du Bois hints at what would later be a considerable rivalry. Earlier in 1915 he had proposed to the Board of Trustees at Howard a project for an encyclopedia, to be called "Negro-Americana," drawing on the gift of Jesse Moorland's library, with himself as editor, but this seems never to have developed. In November of the preceding year he complained that "teaching is really dragging work—I am surely going to try something else someday." Later he would complain to Mary Locke that "I don't go in for 'pleasing' people as much perhaps as I ought to—but its [*sic*] such a concession and such a drain on one's private time."[14]

Private time offered some certain pleasures. His travels through Europe having whetted his appetite for museums and concert halls, Locke adapted himself to Washington by spending time at the Corcoran Gallery, looking at pictures and further developing his interest in the visual arts. He was especially struck by one picture: "Young William James, Professor James' son—the small boy whom I used to know when I lived across from them on Irving St. has an interesting portrait study of a girl's hand." Equally notable was Thomas Eakins's portrait of Henry Ossawa Tanner, the important Negro painter. His colleague Kelly Miller was having his portrait painted by May Howard Johnson, who invited Locke to her studio. His reaction to her was decidedly mixed: "She is really talented—but so erratic—and so unconventional—I can't stand for [*sic*] unconventional women." Contradictions between personal distaste and esthetic approval, or the reverse, would be a constant worry in the ensuing decades, as it exemplified the split he felt between public probity and personal expressiveness.[15]

Keeping up appearances and maintaining social contacts were unending concerns, especially as Locke (with his mother's concurrence) saw himself as destined for a life of public notice. Mary Locke notified her son of the death of Booker T. Washington in November 1915, and he responded by saying: "Wasn't it sad—and dramatic too. Mr. Washington's death—all the little [?] are on the move. You might have thought they really had known him—George Cook and the President have gone to represent Howard—I telegraphed Mrs. Washington." A week later Mary sent a stern warning: "You must be wary with these Negroes—can't trust one of them—Washington was grand master of tact—wasn't he—one just begins to see how well he managed 'the herd.'" Washington's death left the field of leadership more open than it had been, though it also had the effect of magnifying the standing of Du Bois. Washington had been a race leader in ways that were seldom equaled by others, and his use of underhanded means to insure his power did not always endear him to many black people. What Mary Locke saw as tact others viewed as duplicity. Perhaps Locke realized that power on that scale always involved some manipulation. The prospect of leadership brought with it frustrating questions. After completing his lectures in 1916, Locke was told by some people at Howard that surely he would one day be the president of the university.[16]

In the wake of Washington's death, Locke received a telegram from William Stanley Braithwaite, editor of the *Citizen,* asking him to write a memorial of the famous black leader, emphasizing his literary side. Locke complied, but the essay seems not to have been published, and Mary Locke even asked her son if he were able to place it some where else. Locke kept his draft of the essay, and it shows that he was able to approach Washington in unsentimental terms. Beginning by describing the leader as someone who "never could have become sophisticated enough to have been a man of letters," Locke characterized him as being "great as a writer because he was great as an orator." Locke saw Washington as someone whose vision grew during his life, but one who could not speak with one tongue to his divided audiences. In a short typescript essay, apparently from a later date, entitled "Strategies of Southern Reconstruction," the evaluation was more negative. Here he chastises Washington for allowing his policy to become unprofessional and even reactionary, and refers to the famous separatist sentence from the Atlanta Exposition speech of 1895, about the "fingers of one hand," as being "false." Locke's estimation of Washington would always be divided, since he found much to admire in the style and the scope of the public figure, and much to lament in the thinker and strategist.[17]

———•———

The first few years at Howard exhausted Locke in many ways, but he never let his academic and scholarly ambitions flag. When he decided to complete his doctorate at Harvard it was a considerable commitment, one that would strap him financially and yet boost his academic standing. The 1915 lecture series on race had placed Locke in a public position unlike any other he had faced, as it was attended by faculty and members of the community. However, Locke was teaching and hoping for promotions and increased salary without the accreditation of the terminal degree. He needed to see to it that the resources normally granted to whites as a matter of course were made available to an eager and very highly qualified African American. Many of the young white men who were normally enrolling or applying for graduate work were instead enlisting in the military services. From his studies at Harvard, through Oxford and the University of Berlin, and the lecture series on race, Locke had the basis—in terms of philosophical sophistication and scholarly training—for a full development of his value theory. Locke went to Cambridge and spent the academic year 1916–17 there. Because he had done so much thinking and writing about questions of value and value theory, he was able to submit his doctoral dissertation, "The Problem of Classification in the Theory of Value," to Ralph Barton Perry, the chair of his committee, on September 17, 1917. In effect, Locke's doctoral dissertation was written between 1907 and 1917, and his stay in Harvard proceeded rather smoothly in academic terms.

Locke requested a leave of absence from Howard, not something routinely granted, but Bishop Walters, a strong supporter of his and a recently elected member of the Board of Trustees, promised to push Locke's application. Locke, still concerned about his debts and expenses, went to Cambridge in February of 1916 to "lobby" for a fellowship, and in April he was notified of his being given the Austin Teaching Fellowship in Philosophy, which carried a stipend of $350.00. This was eventually supplemented in June by a grant from Howard that covered part of his salary, eliciting the rare observation that "Howard isn't so bad after all." The summer of 1916 found him searching for housing in Boston and facing prejudice doing so. His mother, who was to spend the year with him, counseled him not to try and find room in a white apartment house and face "the risk and trouble of being put out." She reminded him he would need his "quiet mind and peace" if he were to finish all his work inside one academic year, which was his ambitious plan.

After arriving at Harvard and taking courses in the fall term, Locke completed his registration for the Ph.D. program on January 7, 1917. He listed his special field of interest as the "Theory of Value." He also mentioned that he was planning to publish his lectures on race as a book and that he was working on a bibliography of Afro-Americana, presumably the project he had mentioned earlier as having been submitted to the Howard trustees. He described his planned thesis for the doctorate: out of "the solution of methodological problems of the theory of value" he would derive "a new and fresh adjustment of the philosophical discipline" and so generate "a reinforcement of the human value sciences, social and cultural." This would result in a "classification of value," and he mentioned that he "deplored the increasing intrusion of metaphysical bias into the subject of values." In writing out his plans, he specifically thanked Hugo Münsterberg, with whom he had studied at Harvard, for help in developing this thesis. But there were strong debts as well to Royce, whose earlier work on loyalty was important to Locke, and also to Perry's 1914 essay on "The Definition of Value." Because Royce had recently died, Locke decided to work with Perry. Clearly Locke had done a great deal of reading while at Howard, and the experience of his work in philosophy at Berlin and the lectures on race had led him to analyze prejudice and racism as key problems of human valuation. He saw social phenomena in a broad philosophical context, and he now wanted to contribute something of importance to the field of academic philosophy.[18]

There is no mention of race in his dissertation, yet Locke had spent nearly two years working out the details of what "race" was as a socially constructed category and why categories, even when well defined and objectively verifiable, can also be understood as instruments of understanding. The problem he considers in his dissertation is a classical one in the philosophy of the natural and social sciences: Do classifications actually picture objective reality or do classifications arbitrarily shape our picture of reality? Theories of classification differ over whether classifying can be best explained by logical structures, rather than, say, psychological dispositions. However, what was once called a "unified theory of science" would provide a way of appreciating psychological as well as natural categories, thus ending the dispute. For example, the International Congress of Arts and Sciences, held in St. Louis in 1904, attended by Münsterberg, its vice president, and an international gathering of scholars, including Felix Adler, Jane Addams, and John Dewey, was intended to advance the search for, and present the details of, a unified science.

Locke meanwhile questions the claim that esthetic psychological values were the basis of most value systems: "As a result aesthetic values have become the classical example of a group of values where the ground . . . has always been a psychological rather than a logical one—and this psychological basis of differentiation has rarely been questioned. . . . " This suggests that Locke will attack the standard views. He rejects the alleged incompatibility between judgments as logical or scientific, on the one hand, and judgments as psychological or emotional on the other. This frees the way for esthetic judgments to have more cognitive force. "Art could never successfully carry the amount of representative and symbolic content that it does if there was an ineradicable incompatibility between [logic-based] judgments and esthetic states of consciousness." Both logical and psychological judgments convey knowledge; both are important. This reaches all the way back to his undergraduate essays and his exam answers about the relations between philosophy and the arts.[19]

Alexius Meinong, and Christian von Ehrenfels, the chief representatives of the Austrian School of value theory, and Wilbur Urban, the highly noted American value theorist from Dartmouth College, whose work Locke had studied in Oxford and Berlin, considered beauty and ugliness to inhere in us, not in the nature of esthetic objects. It is dependent on humanity to make beauty and goodness cohere. There simply is no guarantee that moral goodness would be supported by artistic or literary products. Instead, as Urban wrote, "it is the development or realization of selves that constitutes the 'good' . . . and the theory of ethics which makes this the locus of value is called the ethics of self-realization. By this is meant that the locus of the good is not found in pleasure, nor in organic survival or welfare, but in the complete energizing of our capacities as selves or persons. . . . " Urban locates the "good" in self-development the way Locke locates the good, in a sense drawing on the German tradition of *Bildung* or self-refinement, an argument that often led to Locke being criticized as elitist. It is, nonetheless, the expression of a hope in the midst of a world that offers no guarantee that beauty and goodness will occur together. The ethics of realization and a relativism toward beauty and goodness finds a compatible role in Locke's philosophy.[20]

Locke offers in his dissertation a new theory of value: a "Dynamic and Genetic Theory of Value." Locke's theory differs from purely logical theories of value because they consider human values well formed and fixed structures which can be captured by a unified science. The "Dynamic and Genetic Theory of Value" considers that categories, as such, are always subject to change. Here is the second section of his dissertation "Outline," where he sets out the various types of value classifications:

II. Types of Classification in Theory of Value
  1. Criticism of Theory of Value Groups as Ultimate Undefinables (Moore. Sedgewick. Lipps. Simmel.)
  2. Criticism of the Biological Classifications (Eisler. Avenarius School, & Behaviourist Theories.)
  3. Criticism of the Analytical Psychological Classifications (Allgemeiner Wert-theoretische School: Meinong)
  4. Restatement of the Dynamic or Functional Psychological Classification (Schwartz-Ehrenfels-Urban.)
  5. Correlation of the Dynamic and Genetic Interpretations as the basis proposed for Value Classification.

The first four of these types—the logical, the biological, the analytical psychological, and the structural or functional psychological—Locke rejects. In doing so, he implicitly rejects the search for a unified science of values, even though such approaches had been developed by his dissertation chair, Perry, and were representative of the dominant pragmatist orientation, including Dewey's logic of values. He also rejects the reigning approaches of Georg Simmel and Alexius Meinong. However, Simmel and Meinong remain important to Locke, along with Christian von Ehrenfels and Wilbur M. Urban. The best way, finally, to describe Locke's view is "Lockean." Working by means of synergy and synthesis, avoiding extremes while understanding their roles in shaping views, Locke was always a navigator among many landmarks.

One way to see Locke's unique approach is to consider his communications with Perry prior to his return to Harvard, a series of exchanges meant to prepare the groundwork for his return. Locke wrote an extensive review, "A Note on Bosanquet's Doctrine of Judgment as a Basis for the Logic of Values." It was handwritten and signed December 4, 1916. The "Note" concerned a book by Bosanquet, *Logic, or the Morphology of Knowledge* (1885), in which he offered a coherence theory of truth which was quite appealing to pragmatists. Bosanquet's esthetic theory makes use of a number of principles he developed in his coherence theory of truth. For example, in art as in logic, no element is "isolated"; starting from any particular, we are led to the "system," which he calls, in metaphysics, the "Absolute." Art allows access to the Absolute through "feeling" or esthetic consciousness. Other topics discussed by Bosanquet are the forms of esthetic satisfaction and different "kinds" of beauty. He suggests that nothing is genuinely ugly in art, and instead speaks of "difficult" beauty, cases where, because of some feature in the object or some failure in the individual observer (e.g., of education, imagination, or effort), there is a failure to appreciate the beauty of the object.

Locke was, as he said in his review essay, "interested really in only one phase of this possible logic of values, and that [is], the value-norms can be regarded as stereotyped qualitative kinds, which are the actual psychological bases as feeling references or what Meinong calls 'presuppositions' of certain types and classes of judgment." This meant that all value judgments had a typical basis in feeling and yet had substantial structures that prevented them from being purely subjective. No one, Locke argued, is satisfied with the "rigidly objective or the rigidly subjective interpretation of values." This was typical of his seeking the resolution between opposites. However, according to Locke, Bosanquet has a weakness when it comes to accounting for the possibility of change in values. For Locke, "qualities must be shown to develop genetically into kinds through quantitative variations introducing new constituent qualities." One kind of value judgment could change into another. Consequently, he goes on, "I can see scarcely any point in calling the analysis 'logical' or 'psychological' in contradistinction." That is, treating thinking as compartmentalized into logical, psychological, or emotional spheres of judgment is not helpful, nor are the distinctions reducible to one another. Values can and will commingle, even as they form and support coherent standards.[21]

Locke wrote another review, "A Criticism of the Bosanquetian Doctrine of Judgment and Forms," more telling and twice as long as the first, in which he puzzled over the difficulty of explaining how values change. This was also handwritten and submitted to Perry, who wrote on the paper, "An exceedingly interesting piece of work, which I have read with pleasure & profit." Locke conceived of valuation as a process that creates new objects (e.g., ideas, thoughts, preferences, judgments) that differ from the initial moments of valuation. (Account for value change would also often occupy Perry's work especially after his role as Locke's dissertation advisor, although to what extent is a matter of speculation.) Locke classified Dewey in his dissertation as a member of the "Logical" system of value approach, along with H. W. Stuart, J. S. Moore, and Hugo Münsterberg. According to Locke, they were looking for a system of valuation that would depict the character of value change. However, valuation itself creates new objects of thought and thus a system accounting for change will fail. The Austrian School of value theory, broadly including Ehrenfels, Meinong, and Urban, whose work Locke had studied in Oxford and Berlin, featured in his dissertation as well. Locke consistently rejected, at least from his days at Oxford, systems of logic that depict value change in a formulistic fashion, and he rejected metaphysical systems that depicted values as traits reducible to or deducible from stable categories of thought. Locke contended in his critique of Bosanquet that movement from "the indeterminate concrete to an abstract type of universal, and then back again to a main concrete type which is nevertheless universal" is a method that fails. Such a method describes value changes by seeing them as shifting from one single concrete act of valuation to a different universal and fixed value judgment.

Although such an approach begins with accepting value change, it is inadequate because it treats such change simply as a variant of 'universal types' or absolutes. In short, value absolutes remain, and they determine all value judgments. "The scheme reunites on the very principle on which it divided,"

FIG. 4.1. Locke at the time of his Harvard Ph.D., 1917–18. Locke spent the academic year in Cambridge with his mother. Moorland-Spingarn Research Center.

as Locke concisely put it. Accepting the idea that categories, kinds, or 'indeterminate concrete' acts of valuation are the source of universal values (rather than the other way around), as Locke did, also means accepting the idea that the exchange between categories, kinds, and concretes are always in flux. Their affiliations, contrary to Bosanquet, cannot be mapped by a rigid logical system. The absolute stability of value categories is rejected by Locke, all the way down.

Perry's "Dewey and Urban on Value Judgments" (1917) focused on a central issue addressed by Locke, namely the difficulty of a theory to account for value creations when valuation is defined as a process which itself creates new objects of value.[22] Perry's article addressed works by Schiller, Dewey, and Urban on the difficulty in accounting for value change. Schiller had played an important role in Locke's life at Oxford, supporting his "Concept of Value" thesis project; Urban and Dewey figured in Locke's dissertation. All three at different times in their lives wrote articles critically assessing the concept of value in each other's works. Locke's view of valuation is thus "Lockean," indicated by his approach to Bosanquet, Dewey, and others in the pragmatist community.

When Locke argued that racial categories are social constructions, or created by us, he relied not just on contemporary sociology and anthropology but also on his views about the social and psychological basis of all categories. And when Locke argues that literature is a source of universal esthetic values expressed by a particular cultural voice, Locke is not only trying to show that there can be representations involving new values but also that racial and ethnic literature can convey universal themes. Locke's approach is not intended to serve as a closed and comprehensive system, since that would limit the possibility of novelty, creativity, and unsettling insights that change the boundaries of accepted categories.

———— ◆ ————

Meanwhile Locke continued to develop a number of important friendships and to expand his contacts in the literary and cultural worlds. His February trip to Harvard to seek scholarship support was in the company of Montgomery Gregory, who would ally with Locke to advance the level of the dramatic arts at Howard. They stayed in Boston with William Stanley Braithwaite, the anthologist and poet who would correspond with Locke for the next several decades. Braithwaite, best known as a reviewer for the *Boston Evening Transcript,* edited a yearly collection of poems that was a virtual institution on the literary landscape. He was, like Locke, elitist in his tastes, and for many years his role in the New England and national literary scene was so traditional that some of his readers assumed he was white. In later years Braithwaite's conservative tastes in literature would make him one of the leading opponents of some of the Harlem Renaissance writers. Locke also kept up with other, earlier friendships in one way or another. In January 1916 he was busy reading Horace Kallen's book on James and Bergson. There were also Harvard friends whose correspondence with him would give Locke a way of measuring his own progress.

Two classmates from Harvard, C. Henry Dickerman ("Dik") and David A. Pfromm ("Dap"), were especially reliable correspondents. They shared with Locke an interest in the classics, and thus their nickname for him was "Lockus." Pfromm, who first knew Locke during their high school days at Central High, was the secretary of the Philosophy Club at Harvard, and he went on to study law, telling Locke that "New England intellectualism bores me now." After completing law school, he joined a Philadelphia firm and eventually transferred to Boston, where he was admitted to the bar at the end of 1913. He mentioned a short story that Locke sent him in manuscript (probably "The Miraculous Draught") and also thanked Locke for giving him a copy of De Fonseka's *The Truth of Decorative Art,* which Dickerman and Locke were trying to place with an American publisher. The correspondence indicates that Locke's estheticism was something he shared freely, even joyfully, with his classmates, but he was also interested in their political and social attitudes. Dap eventually turned socially conservative, commenting on the Boston police strike of 1919 as proof that unionism must be "curtailed." And later when he read Locke's *The New Negro,* he confessed that he had "lost too much in the modern symbolism. When you come you must take time to explain." Serving in part as a conduit of news about their other classmates and friends, Dap kept Locke well informed about all sorts of developments. The friendship, or at least their correspondence, persisted for several decades beyond Harvard, for Dap acknowledged receiving Locke's Christmas card in 1952.[23]

With Dickerman, the friendship was more complex. He was homosexual, witty and playful, and the bond he had formed with Locke at Harvard helped to maintain a long, frank, and intimate correspondence. He often used his correspondence with Locke to describe his troubled inner life, which involved esthetic aspirations and romanticized attachments. Friendly with Locke for many years—he too had gone to Central High—Dickerman was unable to settle on a vocation, switching from teaching to journalism and back again, and he moved often in the twenty years after his graduation. Teaching appointments included the Wilson School in Fishkill, New York, a high school in Boston, where he hoped to get a permanent job at Boston Latin, Mt. Holyoke College, and Denison University, where he underwent psychoanalysis in 1926. Journalistic positions included being on the rewrite desk at the *Boston Herald* and the *Philadelphia Press.* He visited Locke in 1908 while Locke was in Oxford, and then he went alone on to Paris. A poem of his was accepted in a journal called *Transatlantic Tales,* and he published some literary and musical criticism in the *Nation.* He also stayed with Locke at Howard and went to supper with him and Montgomery Gregory. Rather decadent in his literary tastes, he teased Locke at one point by saying, "I must say your prose style is becoming a most violent combination of Wilde, Wine, and Wanderlust; a purple tailed dolphin cavorting through exotic meres and leaving in its wake a fugitive path of beer foam." Willing to suffer Locke's high standards, he sent along one of his poems in manuscript, a quatrain that is apparently heavily coded:

> Hold up thy mouth magnificently high
> Like a saint's aureole where I may aspire;
> Cast down upon the ground thy cloak of Tyre;
> Clasp me like brimming Baal, and let me die. [24]

During a trip to London, Dickerman visited De Fonseka, whom he had apparently been introduced to by Locke; the two dined at the Liberal Club with Pfromm. The network of friends thus included Harvard and Oxford, and extended to two continents.

In 1914 Dickerman disagreed with Locke's pacifist views, and he insisted to Locke that "you must admit to yourself if you reflect frankly, to too strong feeling for the Germans." He told Locke about a homosexual experience he had in Worcester, Massachusetts, and how he was almost blackmailed by someone who evidently saw him cruising. Various places where Locke might also indulge were suggested: "The Park is a sort of Gomorrah these days. . . . Don't neglect City Point, about midnight, these days. I suppose you have discovered the desirability of the bathhouses at Revere. . . . " Presumably Locke was frank about his own homosexual experiences when writing to Dickerman, but Locke's side of the correspondence does not appear to have survived. Dickerman also knew Braithwaite and sent him an article for possible publication, and the two spent time together, sharing literary gossip, while Dickerman was training at the Naval Reserve Camp in Hingham, Massachusetts in 1918. While an assistant professor at Denison University, in Granville, Ohio, Dickerman lamented about his teaching and his apparently decreased sexual activity: "the urge is far less insistent these days: it has degenerated into a sort of gentle lyricism in the blood, between the tissues. . . . " He adds that he is including the work of John Addington Symons to his course, and then comments: "What an idea—to start such propaganda, such a cenacle, in this biblebacked place! It fascinates me at moments until I am afraid of doing something uncanny."[25]

One can assume from Dickerman's tone throughout the correspondence that Locke remained interested and sympathetic toward his friend, whose tensions between his private and public identities were unrelenting. Locke would later be quite adept at counseling friends with similar conflicts, in part because he was able to live with his own in a way that was at once self-accepting, frank, and controlled. Dickerman resigned his post at Denison in 1927, and there is a long hiatus in his correspondence with Locke. Then, in the last letter that survives, Locke writes to Dickerman in London in 1943: "Here's the best of good luck and friendly remembrances." That Locke would preserve the friendships for such a long period of time showed not only that he was comfortable with well-educated whites but that he maintained and enjoyed various forms of group identity.[26]

It was not only the faculty who had to contend with the repressive atmosphere created by Howard's administration. In April 1916 Locke told his mother of how the discipline felt by the students was becoming unbearable. The protest strike they mounted at that time foreshadows some of the conflict that Locke himself would face in a few years time. He told Mary how Montgomery Gregory was openly partisan on the side of the students. Locke, too, was very sympathetic: "The students have been very manly and have stuck together bravely—and the deans have been like a tottering dynasty in the upper palace chamber." Later that spring Locke would escort some of his students from the Stylus Club, the organization for hopeful writers which he had helped found with Gregory, to see the nearby Fredrick Douglass homestead in Anacostia, Maryland. He was constantly challenging his students to expand their cultural horizons and discover their own history.[27]

Besides being a considerable figure in more than one field, Montgomery Gregory was an important and valued friend for Locke. Along with Kelly Miller, the activist sociologist, Gregory was probably closer than any of the other Howard colleagues to Locke in terms of interest and temperament. Roots at Howard ran deep for Gregory, for not only was he a native of Washington, his father was in the first graduating class, and his mother, an impressive woman of Madagascan descent, was well known for counseling the female students there. Handsome in a dashing way, with a striking goatee, Gregory was a Harvard graduate in the class of 1910, which included T. S. Eliot and Walter Lippmann. He served as the president of the Harvard debating club and would later form Howard's division of Dramatic Art and

Public Speaking. Outspoken on racial issues, he believed that cultural and artistic expression formed a crucial element in race pride. He published an essay arguing this point in the *Citizen,* the Boston magazine edited by Braithwaite. "If art is self-expression, it is necessarily race expression," was how he put it, in a way that echoed Locke's position. Since they were often together at Howard, there is no correspondence between them, but the mutual efforts of Locke and Gregory to address the arts at Howard demonstrate their affinity. The two men co-founded the creative writing journal at Howard, the *Stylus,* and the literary club that published it, and Locke helped Gregory with the organizing of the Howard Players, a theater troupe that achieved national recognition. In 1927 they joined in co-editing *Plays of Negro Life,* which included works by Jean Toomer, Richard Bruce (Nugent), Georgia Douglas Johnson, and Eugene O'Neill, among others. That same year Gregory contributed the article on "The Negro in Drama" to the fourteenth edition of *Encyclopedia Britannica.* He had scored a notable success with his production of O'Neill's *The Hairy Ape* in 1921, starring the famous black actor, Charles Gilpin. Like Locke, Gregory nursed large ambitions for his cultural commitments, and he wanted to use Howard as a base to build a national black theater. His strong views on the esthetics of theater were shared with Locke, and their belief in the power of cultural expression to improve racial consciousness led both men to resign from the Drama Committee of the NAACP; they were objecting to the tendentious "race problem" plays that the organization favored, which they considered esthetically weak. In 1924 Gregory left Howard and accepted a position as Supervisor of Negro Schools in Atlantic City, New Jersey. He told Locke his main reason for doing so was to have a better salary.[28]

No sooner had Locke returned to Washington from his Ph.D. work at Harvard in the late spring of 1917 than he became involved in the war effort. His involvement focused on racial issues, and he argued strongly that black soldiers should be officered by black men. This argument was made at Howard with special urgency, for it was there that the lobbying effort to convince the War Department to accept the idea took place most visibly. An account of the entire episode was co-authored by Locke with two of his Howard colleagues and published in the *Howard University Record.* Though this account does not specify which faculty members took which part in the episode—serving, for example on a committee to lobby congressmen—by being a named co-author of the article, Locke made his views on the matter quite clear. Joel Spingarn, of the NAACP, had begun the public discussion of the issue when he visited Howard and encouraged faculty and students to set up an Officers' Training Camp in New York state. Along with a committee of many people from the Washington area, Spingarn approached the War Department with this plan but was rebuffed. Soon Spingarn was called into active service, but the Howard community, in the form of a Central Committee of Negro College Men, took up the agitation for themselves. After petitioning Congress by letters and personal visits, they were told eventually that if they could summon one thousand men for the effort, the War Department might favorably consider the plan. Howard students and faculty then appealed to the several black universities throughout the country. Soon the recruitment proved impressively successful, and in June 1917 a camp was started in Des Moines, Iowa, for the training of black officers. The camp saw the commissioning of six hundred and fifty-nine officers, of whom ninety-five were Howard students and faculty. As the article put it, "one is at the outset well nigh overwhelmed by the extraordinary enthusiasm, resourcefulness, confidence, race loyalty and patriotism exhibited by the students of Howard University." The phrase "race loyalty" bears the stamp of Locke's position. However, the United States Army remained thoroughly segregated.[29]

Shortly after the conclusion of the war, Washington, D.C., was ravaged by a vicious race riot, sparked in some measure by sensationalistic newspaper headlines about a crime thought to have been committed by a black. Both blacks and whites were killed in the violence, though Locke makes no mention of the events in any of his letters. Indeed, his life during the immediate postwar period seems to have been comparatively settled. As for his personal standing, he was made private in the army in November 1919 as part of the Students' Army Training Corps. This may have had some honorific or merely symbolic status, though he was granted a pass that read: "Private Locke can enter or leave day or night." He had earlier taken the medical test after having been declared 1A in October 1918, and the records show that he weighed but ninety-four pounds and stood five feet, two and a quarter inches. His nationality was listed as "AA." His papers show that he had had cardiac trouble for a number of years, and to the question, "Do you consider that you are now sound and well?," he answered, "No."[30]

CHAPTER FIVE

Howard and Beyond

With the significant accomplishments of his Ph.D. dissertation and the lectures on race behind him, Locke's horizon widened considerably at the start of the decade to include many new friends, interests, and activities. Though he sometimes felt university teaching to be constraining, he used his writings and public lectures to establish a growing national reputation. He met several important writers who would influence—and be influenced by—his ideas on esthetic issues. Political questions joined social ones with a sharpened sense of the problems of group identity and the snares of jealousy and intrigue that often complicated the development of race leadership. He also began to define more carefully his conception of culture. At the same time, personal growth would vex and enrich him, as the long maturation preceding his Howard appointment continued, though deepened in tone and substance. The Twenties were to be one of the most storied of American decades, and for Locke they were to unveil some of his most resounding triumphs. More than a small measure of leadership was to come his way, and it came in more than one field. His ability to conceive of "colossal" projects persisted, driving him energetically to increase his learning, use his skills, and shape his sense of worth and purpose.

As the decade of the 1920s began, however, Locke faced the prospect of his mother's weakening health. She was in her late sixties and had retired, finally, from her teaching duties in 1915. Her letters to Locke reveal her to have been a quiet person in her manner, and her training in the Ethical Culture of Felix Adler contributed to her firm sense of right; she was often able privately to express strong opinions to her son. He clearly inherited from her a deep self-regard and an unwillingness to tolerate condescension or prejudice. Seen from one angle, she embodied that sense of remote Philadelphia gentility about which Locke was frequently self-conscious and self-ironizing. From another angle, they shared a sense of propriety that was occasionally more fierce than reserved. It was in 1917 that she eventually planned to move from Philadelphia into Locke's residence at 1326 R Street in Washington, D.C. This arrangement followed the academic year spent together in Boston as Locke pursued his Ph.D. It was from Boston that she decided to make the move and live with Locke for the remainder of her life. She sold all the furniture in the rooming house she ran in Philadelphia, telling a friend that "Roy is determined, he wanted to increase his salary or get a better position at Howard by continuing his studies here [at Harvard]." Two years later she sent a note to Locke, who was lecturing at a college in North Carolina, and she assured him: "I miss you so much—but have not had the blues—I have followed strictly the rules laid down—even to the 'Soda'—[and] feel first rate." Apparently he had prescribed the soda to alleviate a digestive problem; the domestic burdens had shifted, as he was now taking care of her.[1]

She traveled overseas with her son several times. Sometimes she took the steamship to join him, and after he finished his years in Oxford and Berlin they would sail to Europe together. Ranging throughout Europe, they greatly enjoyed the cultural monuments. Their tours were focused by Locke's interests, and they seem to have covered a great many sites, proceeding much in the manner of nineteenth-century ritualized tourism. As far back as 1908 she had visited Paris with him while he was summering there during his Rhodes Scholarship. She also had the pleasure of the company of Pixley Seme at dinner during that trip. Another summer she kept a notebook which recorded the dates but not the year (it may have been while Locke was still studying abroad), and she listed there how the two of them visited many museums, traveling to Amsterdam, Antwerp, the Hague, and Brussels. The gardens in Dordrecht were declared the "finest scenery so far." In Brussels atop a hill the Palace of Justice, a neoclassical behemoth with an excess of grey stone columns, was declared the largest and best building in the world; she was also impressed by the sight of French speaking barristers wearing their wigs. She took special note of the Rembrandts in Amsterdam, but took time to visit the docks there as well, and she was pleased to see some "Negro Slave Bronzes" by a van Hove, in Rotterdam. She also made a special note on August 26: "Glorious day—walk with R[oy]."[2]

Familiar with all of her son's friends, she received letters from Dickerman and Gregory, among others. These friends addressed her informally and always reported positive things about his accomplishments. Of course she doted on her "Roy," but as he grew they also became intellectual companions. Their letters to each other are marked by what seems total agreement on most questions of taste and manners, sharing his devotion to German culture, for instance. Their trip to Germany in the summer of 1914 proved fateful, and dramatic, as mother and son shared the historical experience of being in the city when martial law was declared while the country mobilized for war. She witnessed the riot-like conditions, and saw a number of Russian men shot and arrested in the street; one Russian had been dragged from the house where she was lodging. The English ambassador's car was stoned as he tried to leave the city, and the police even came into Locke's room looking for other Russians, but they left after they "saw his black face." It is a measure of her vitality at that time that she described all this as "thrilling sights."[3]

On April 23, 1922, Mary Locke died at the age of seventy. Her obituary notice in the *Crisis* said "the deceased was a member of an old Philadelphia family, educated at the Institute for Colored Youth, and was for a period of thirty-six years a school teacher in Camden and Camden County." Locke had a death notice printed on small cards, bordered in black, that said "Internment private" and added the note that one should "Kindly omit flowers." However, he decided to hold a wake to commemorate his mother. He had her dressed in a pretty grey dress and laid out on a couch, with a minimum of flowers set about the room. A number of his students and friends were invited, because, as Locke said, he wanted them to have this last scene remain with them all their lives, to help them see life whole, with death as a beautiful part of it. Some people in the community were put off by the wake, and it became the subject of anecdotes and gossip for years after. Often the stories suggested that Locke was deranged or perverse in this situation, as if he thought his mother were still alive or he might be able to speak to her. Nonetheless, the ceremony borrowed from the form of traditional Irish American wakes and plainly expressed Locke's wishes.[4]

It was in the emotional aftermath of his mother's death that Locke prepared his first will, which is dated June 30, 1922. Never physically robust, he may have acted out of both grief and premonition. In any case, he named Helen Irvin Grossley as his executrix; she had been a supervisor in the Camden schools where she and Mary Locke formed a fast friendship. Locke knew her as Helen Irvin; she had married her second husband, Richard Grossley, and moved to Jackson, Mississippi, before Mary's death. When she went with Mary to Oxford to visit Locke in 1909, she wrote to thank him for the best summer of her life. Always very fond of Locke, she encouraged him to apply for the position of president of Lincoln University in Missouri in February 1922, as a friend of hers was a member of the board there. In other parts of his will Locke specified a gift of $200.00 to a Reverend Mitchell as a memorial in the name of his mother. He also set aside a small amount for student prizes, "or some worthy object." Finally, he asked that a small foundation be set up to bear the names of his parents, "in honour of their great sacrifices for me." The lifelong commitment of both his parents to the ideals of education and ethical training reverberated throughout Locke's life. His mother had lived to see him achieve many of her fondest dreams for him, and he also knew how thoroughly he had made her dreams his own.[5]

Despite the passing of his mother, Locke was able to continue very productively as a writer and scholar in the postwar years. If anything, he seems to have redoubled his energy and commitment to race leadership. During these years he published different kinds of essays for a widening audience and further enhanced the polymath nature of his intelligence. His interest in questions of race and race leadership led him to pursue several different academic disciplines, generally displaying little hesitation in speaking to what he saw as the central problems, no matter the field of study. One of the more striking examples is the journalistic piece he wrote on "Impressions of Luxor." This essay recounted his experience at the opening of the tomb of Tut-ankh-amen, in February 1923. Locke participated in this historic undertaking while on leave from Howard in 1923, during which he traveled for several months, accompanied by his friend Seme, in the Near East, visiting Egypt and Sudan. His interest in the African basis of African American culture originated as early as his Oxford days and his participation in the African Union Club. This interest continued and broadened throughout the 1920s as he increasingly devoted time and personal expenses to the collection of African artifacts. The essay itself, a rather masterly piece of cultural journalism, combines philosophical reflection, travel descriptions, observations on people and academic disciplines, and esthetic formulations. Like a compendium of his interests at the time, the "Impressions" addresses one of his main ideas. As he puts it, the discovery of the tomb serves as "a confirmation of the broadest and most natural of all hypotheses—namely, that great cultures are the result invariably of the fusion of several cultures, the impetus given to the one culture by contact with others,—the fermenting of one civilization by another." Locke formulates this claim in part by pointing out that Egypt's culture was polyglot and contained not only African elements but "possibly even Negro components."[6]

The essay buttressed Locke's preoccupation with culture and the contacts between peoples, though clearly that notion was one of the main reasons he undertook his travels in the first place. But he was also able to turn his attention to the state of Egyptology itself, where he felt that the archaeologist would soon be joined by the philosopher, as the material evidence would eventually yield to cultural and spiritual insights. Meanwhile, the discipline of archeology had to increase its sensitivity. The English team of archeologists operated under the leadership of Howard Carter, an amateur who had considerable early experience and was the discoverer of Tut-ankh-amen's tomb; the team was financed by George Herbert, the fifth Earl of Carnarvon. Locke contrasted the English unfavorably with the French team, headed by Pierre Lacau and Georges Foucart, the latter of whom had helped sponsor Locke's attendance at the opening of the tomb. Foucart, as Locke acknowledged in the essay, was the director of the French Institute of Oriental Archeology, and he had visited Howard to supervise a program for the comparative study of African archeology. Locke wryly noted of Carter that "even his best friends cannot claim diplomacy, tact, sympathy or even courtesy as among his outstanding qualities." Locke pointed this out because of "the question of Egyptian national pride, newly asserting itself after the victory of the nationalist party, galled by the preferential treatment of the English press and of foreign visitors, and chronically piqued by the assertion of authority which until recently had had to be tolerated."

What Locke saw in the tomb, and what he made of it, was evidence for a period of cultural efflorescence, what he went on to call "this first great cultural renaissance." Locke, of course, was not able to examine the contents of the tomb at length or in detail. This makes his formulation of their significance more revealing about Locke than about the immense subject of Egyptology. But confident as always about his own taste and judgment, Locke did not hesitate to bring the phenomena under the aegis of his own concerns. "Even from cursory inspection this art would seem to be highly composite, both culturally and artistically; it may be a turning point in art theory as well as the unexpected filling-in of another great art period in the chronicle of human culture," he wrote. Locke signs off in the article by again referring to a situation that can be read as an allegory of his concerns and that comments on the discipline itself:

Native archeologists of training are scarce. . . . There is in process of training a fair number of junior men, but the field is much larger than the prospective supply. It is going to be interesting to watch these developments. Our own racial cultural problems and points of view have too many analogies, not to say points of contact, and possible connection for us not to be additionally concerned and interested in this aspect of the matter.

Much of the essay reads like an anticipation of the concerns and viewpoint that Locke would bring to the Harlem Renaissance. It also serves as a demonstration of how Locke's concern with African culture and the creation of a usable past, to use the phrase from his Harvard classmate, Van Wyck Brooks, was a part of his unceasing commitment to defining the way forward for the culture of his community.

Unlike some major race leaders of the early 1920s, such as Du Bois, Garvey, and Washington, as well other important cultural leaders such as Jesse Fauset, Charles Johnson, or Walter White, Locke had visited Africa. He commented on various African questions, having first published a short news article on nationalist movements in Egypt and Turkey in 1907. Locke's Pan-Africanism would gain momentum with a fortuitous meeting when he enjoyed a chance to meet the Abyssinian leader, Ras Tafari. This possibility originated in November 1923 when Locke was in Cairo, as part of his visit to the tomb of Tut-ankh-amen. There he met the Egyptian Belata Heroui, who had been helpful in gaining Abyssinia's entry into the League of Nations. Heroui was in Paris in September 1924, and there he introduced Locke to Ras Tafari at the Hotel des Deux Mondes. At the time, Ras Tafari was acting as regent—a position to which he was appointed in 1917—and was effectively in control of the government, as the empress had turned her attention to religion and other matters. A few years later, in 1928, after the death of the empress, Ras Tafari would be crowned king; in 1930, he was designated Emperor Haile Selassie I, Conquering Lion of Judah, Elect of God, King of Kings. He set about modernizing Abyssinia—now called Ethiopia—by eliminating slavery, improving education, and producing a written constitution. He reigned for over forty-five years and was generally much beloved, although he was both vilified as a tyrant by those who deposed him in 1974 and also venerated by Rastafarians, who consider him to be God incarnate.

Locke wrote up notes on his meeting with Ras Tafari, but a later chance to publish an article on the event, by invitation from Du Bois for the *Crisis*, apparently came to nothing. His friend Heroui left the two men alone at the hotel, and Locke asked Ras Tafari if he thought Abyssinians were Negroes. "We are all Africans—that is enough," was the reply. Locke enquired if it were a good idea to have American Negroes come and work in Africa. "I think a man can always come home," Ras Tafari answered. Locke's notes include a brief reference to the possibility that he might act as the tutor and guardian for Ras Tafari's children. Years later, in the 1930s, Locke would meet a nephew of Ras Tafari—Malaku Bayen—at Howard and helped raise money for him. A plan to have Howard students set up an exchange with Ethiopia, however, never materialized. Locke kept the question of Negro identity in the forefront of his mind and thought of it in the context of African descendancy. In the early 1920s, moreover, Locke's interest began to be focused on African art, spurred by his travels in Egypt, and he was to develop an esthetic that would, at least in part, incorporate a Pan-African consciousness.[7]

Publications of his academic efforts occupied Locke's time and brought him notice in various fields. He sometimes made use of local publications, such as the *Howard University Record*, to see his academic work into print. "The Ethics of Culture," published there in 1923, began as a lecture he gave to Howard freshmen in 1922; it is the purest expression of Locke's elitism and his ethics of self-realization. As with most of his ideas and attitudes, one can appreciate the nuances and even the paradoxes of his formulation. He begins by circling his subject, as if knowing that the difficulty in defining the concept of culture was tied up with its ethical necessity and complexity. While arguing that culture has an intimate relation with personality, he admits it operates in and through the group, though it exists more purely in the individual. Trying to convey how evanescent it can appear, his characterization of culture culminates when he says that "it is that which cannot be taught, but can only be learned." He then turns to how the senses and the mind must reciprocate their powers, and so culture is "warrantably judge[d]" by "manners, tastes, and the fineness of discrimination of a person's interests." Locke attempts to move beyond Victorian ideals, and even beyond the Wildean irony that appealed to him in his Oxford days, to a more rigorous philosophical sense of culture, especially when he argues that if one's taste "should be merely a veneer, then it is indeed both culturally false and artistically deceptive."

Turning to a more discursive argument, Locke lists the five charges most often brought against culture—that it is artificial, superficial, useless, selfish, and over-refined—and addresses each in turn. The worst thing to do in the face of such charges is to "shirk the blow and attack of such criticism [from] behind the bastion of dilettantism." Each of the five answers is detailed and reverts to Locke's concern with culture as the work of personality, and this in turn leads him to a strong defense of individuality. His claims reach all the way back to his Harvard essay on the tensions between self-expression and service, and he ultimately cuts the Gordian knot by proclaiming that "the highest intellectual duty is to be cultured." Then he addresses the group's responsibility by adapting a witticism of Wilde's:

> A brilliant Englishman once characterized America as a place where everything had a price, but nothing a value, referring to the typical preference for practical and utilitarian points of view. There is a special need for a correction of this on your part. As a race group we are at the critical stage where we are releasing creative artistic talent in excess of our group ability to understand and support it. . . . [A] group which expects to be judged by its best must live up to its best so that that may be truly representative. (PAL, 182)

Locke would soon make similar arguments in the context of the Renaissance, where they will be intertwined with the question of the representativeness of group identity.

Locke takes pains in the essay to distinguish what he considers true culture from the many false versions of it as well as from the vulgar understanding of it as mere pretension. When he warns against what he calls the "'pull' of the crowd," he goes on to insist that "there is no individuality in being ordinary: it is the boast of sub-mediocrity." Yet it is the social collectivity that serves as one of the truest measures of culture successfully attained:

> [P]ersonal representativeness and group achievement are . . . identical. Ultimately a people is judged by its capacity to contribute to culture. It is to be hoped that as we progressively acquire in this energetic democracy the common means of modern civilization, we shall justify ourselves more and more, individually, and collectively, by the use of them to produce culture-goods and representative types of culture. (PAL, 184-85)

Sounding a very American note, by balancing the claims of the group and the individual, this passage picks up two of the key political terms of the time, "progressive" and "energetic," while also arguing for the need to display, even to dramatize, value by creating representations of it that can be read and imitated by all. There is also a strong echo of his idea of the "civilization type" from his lectures on race. In its defense of an elite sense of culture, the essay is unrelenting but not monolithic. The right version of elitism opposes the flawed; as he puts it: "Exclusive, culture may and must be, but seclusive culture is obsolete." This is not only a way of saying that culture is as culture does, but that culture must constantly renew itself, for "it has to be earned and re-earned, though it returns with greater increment each time." Read autobiographically, the essay might be seen as Locke's self-admonition against his excessively sybaritic days in Berlin. Read as a moral lesson, it is a recommendation for self-realization through the aegis of culture. Culture became one of Locke's key concerns, and he defined it in nuanced ways, though always aware of its renewal as its greatest necessity.

Drawing again on the work he had done for his lecture series, Locke crafted an essay called "The Concept of Race as Applied to Social Culture," which he published in the *Howard Review* in 1924. It did not add substantially to the arguments he had made in his lectures on race contacts, but it does show how completely he mastered the academic discourse of sociology and anthropology. There should be three methodological principles when discussing race: the "principle of organic interpretation" (that all presumably race-derived behavior be seen as part of the entire society where it occurred); the "principle of cultural relativity" (which saw each culture in its own terms and yet comparable to others; this was to form the core of his notion of "cultural reciprocity"); and "the dynamic and social interpretation of race" (which involved seeing race and culture as historically changing social forces and traditions) (PAL, 187–200).

Locke kept remarkably busy throughout his early years at Howard, fostering his status and sense of himself as a race leader by giving lectures outside of the academy. In the early 1920s his speaking engagements grew in frequency as his reputation took on a national scope. In 1921 he spoke on "The Problem of Race and Culture" in front of the Negro Academy in Washington, which had been founded by Alexander Crummel and now had Arthur Schomburg as president; Locke himself was on the Executive Committee. His relationship with Schomburg, both personal and professional, would continue for many years. Locke returned to the Negro Academy in 1922 to speak on "The American Literary Tradition and the Negro," and in the following year on "Notes Made at Luxor, Egypt." In early 1924 the Society for Ethical Culture sponsored a three-day public conference on "Interracial Harmony and Peace." Locke chaired a session there, and Boas spoke, as did James Weldon

Johnson and Jane Addams. Later that year Locke spoke at the Fifteenth Annual Conference of the NAACP in Philadelphia, addressing the question of educational theory as applied to the race problem. In October 1924, he addressed a "Convention for Amity" under the auspices of the Bahá'í movement, in Philadelphia, on the subject of "Negro Art and Culture."[8]

Perhaps the most impressive of Locke's public appearances was one at a conference that paradoxically amounted to very little in the long run. This was a gathering of many black notables in Chicago during the second week of February 1924; it was called the Sanhedrin, named after the ancient Jewish group of judges. Locke served as the secretary of the conference, which had been largely organized by Kelly Miller, who wanted to create a coordinating movement that would bring together various black organizations for the purpose of increasing their political effectiveness. Sixty or so organizations were present at the conference, and they agreed on a list of topics and goals that included education, religion, fraternal organizations, the women's movement, labor, culture, and so forth. There were three main points of consensus: (1) the conference should be made permanent, (2) a Commission of Public Information would be set up in Washington, D.C., and (3) the conference would only act to coordinate and it would not infringe on any organization's right to define its own purpose. Kelly Miller was charged with editing the proceedings, but it appears that no such publication ever appeared. At a session where Jessie Fauset spoke on "The Importance of Race Literature," Locke's presentation was on "The Afro-American Relation to World Wide Race Movements." Only a portion of his speech survives in typescript. It says in part: "The problem that confronts us then is that of the utilization and development of our spiritual assets in this enterprise of group success and group salvation. Our chief wealth and resources, our primary natural endowment is after all spiritual . . . we compete at great odds in the most materialistic civilization of all time."[9]

That this impressive gathering did not produce anything more permanent is regrettable, though its mere occurrence is evidence that the political and social consciousness of black people was definitely mobilized during this period. Remarkably, the NAACP and the Urban League organized themselves and started their journals, the *Crisis* and *Opportunity* respectively. Within the past fifteen years or so, there was strong anti-lynching agitation in different arenas, and the Great Migration after the recent war had markedly altered the demographics of black life in America. The growing black press and the discussions of many spokespeople for greater freedom and rights for blacks were all forums for the growing political consciousness that was more and more set against the era of Jim Crow and legally sanctioned segregation. Locke was aware of all of this, to be sure, and he was involved in several different forms of expression and development as he attempted to exert his sense of leadership. In some sense, his personal evolution epitomized the larger social and political growth of African American society.

Locke was to become active on the issue of Pan-Africanism, as his travels in the Near East showed, but he was also building friendships in various other locales as well. In 1924 he exchanged observations with René Maran, a Martinique-born writer whose novel, *Batouala,* won the Prix Goncourt in 1921. The novel was a poetically evocative portrait of an African tribe that depicted the colonial settlers as marginal though oppressive, while at the same time conveying a rich sense of the tribal culture in its relation to natural forces. Locke felt, in reviewing the work in *Opportunity* in November 1923, that the novel was an important contribution, as it showed that black folk material could serve as the basis of a serious literary work. He recommended it to many of his friends with great enthusiasm.

Not only did Maran host many African American visitors at his Paris apartment on the rue Bonaparte, he also edited a journal called *Les Continents,* which published many African American writers and kept its readers informed about the American struggles over racial equality. He and Locke exchanged observations when Locke wrote an article, "Black Watch Along the Rhine," for the January 1924 *Opportunity,* where he argued that the French army has managed to integrate its fighting forces without any sense of racial division. He recounted what he saw in Germany, where French troops, made up of men from various racial and national backgrounds, were the occupying force:

> I have heard it repeatedly said—often as if it implied something desirable, that the colored Frenchman was merely a Frenchman who happens to be colored. One may well get the impression from a small class of the Parisian-trained gentry. But here, among the average and ordinary, there was observable something quite different and, in my judgment, something finer and more desirable. . . . Indeed, freed from the pressure of prejudice and the repressions of social stigma, the sense of race among these men was very marked.

Locke was idealizing somewhat, for what he describes is a multicultural blending of the sort he had implicitly argued for in various ways. Maran took exception, nevertheless, and in the September 1924 *Opportunity* suggested Locke had been deceived, as the French were still using "pretense" in their "benevolence . . . toward subject races." Locke defended himself in a rejoinder by pointing out that he was commenting on French soldiers in Europe and not in Africa, and in any case he was not endorsing French colonial power. He also pointed out that "some things are possible for the black man in France which are not yet possible for him in America," a sentiment shared by a number of expatriated African Americans. Locke's contemporaries weighed in on both sides of this issue: was French society truly more accepting of black people, or was such acceptance an illusion caused mainly by the favorable contrast with the Jim Crow era in America? In any case, Locke and Maran remained good friends, and Locke would go on to foster the ideas and ideals of a transnational sense of racial solidarity that extended not only to Europe and Africa but the Caribbean as well, indeed throughout the African diaspora.[10]

Locke formed another friendship around this time that was to have long-term consequences. Charles S. Johnson, one of the leading figures of the Harlem Renaissance, had become the editor of *Opportunity* in 1923, and shortly thereafter Locke began to publish often in the magazine. Though it was the official organ of the Urban League, as the *Crisis* was for the NAACP, Johnson had a somewhat more committed interest in esthetic and cultural expression and the role that it might play in black affairs than did Du Bois. Like Du Bois, Johnson was a sociologist, but he trained at the University of Chicago under the tutelage of Robert E. Park. Park shifted the focus of black sociology away from its basis in nineteenth-century racialist thought and concentrated instead on questions of social disorganization and what he called "marginal man," a social type caught between two cultures. (This concept resonates with Locke's notion, adopted from Simmel, of the "civilization type.") In Johnson's mind such marginality existed in the black experience of the time as exemplified in the southern blacks' migration north and in the corresponding change from a rural to an urban society. He himself had been a part of the migration when he moved to Chicago in 1917.

Johnson, seven years younger than Locke, was born in Virginia as the son of a Baptist preacher who introduced him to higher learning. After receiving his Ph.D. from the University of Chicago in 1918, he served in the 803rd Pioneer Infantry Expeditionary Forces in France and returned to the States in 1919. As a result of his schooling, Johnson was appointed to study the 1919 race riot in Chicago, which he had experienced firsthand. Serving as associate executive secretary of the Commission on Race Relations, he concluded the riot had been caused by inadequate housing as well as racist employment practices. Johnson then went on to take the important post of Director of Research and Investigation for the Urban League in 1921. When he took over the editorship of *Opportunity*, he dedicated much of the magazine to cultural and literary issues, making sure, for example, that all books by black authors were reviewed.[11]

Throughout the 1920s *Opportunity* and the *Crisis* were crucial information sources, exemplars of black literature and journalism. They became important beacons for black readers. Locke published more frequently in the former, and, even after the Renaissance was considered over, Locke published year-end surveys of black literature in *Opportunity* throughout the 1930s. Though Locke and Du Bois co-authored an essay on young black writers, it was with Johnson that Locke had a fuller relationship, and it was Johnson's journal that more actively promoted the esthetic and even experimental side of the Renaissance. It was also Johnson who organized the Civic Club dinner on March 21, 1924 that was to stand for many as the originating event of the Harlem Renaissance. Johnson went on to an illustrious academic career and eventually became the first black president of Fisk University. For several years he and Locke, among others, would share the work of sponsoring an important movement with progressive social and esthetic aspects that would seek to examine and improve African American life. Their correspondence reflects feelings of true friendship and mutual intellectual respect.

Through the first part of the 1920s, as Locke expanded his contacts with publishers and editors and continued to develop his ideas on value and culture, he also involved himself in esthetic issues that had personal dimensions. Some of these arose out of friendships that Locke formed at this time. Especially important were the relationships he enjoyed with three talented writers who would go on to literary fame: Countee Cullen, Langston Hughes, and Jean Toomer. Locke saw these three, and others, as members of a younger generation, and there was at this time much talk about the role and nature of generational change in American society. By concentrating on the cultural force of generational change, Locke was for a short time allied with Du Bois. Their single collaboration on a published article was devoted to what they termed "The Younger Literary Movement." When the article appeared in the *Crisis* in 1924 it was an exaggeration to speak of a movement, since the figures discussed did not all know one another, nor did they share any specific esthetic principles. What most united the writers was that Locke and

Du Bois—who began the article calling themselves "we writers of the older set"—took an interest in them. But significant changes were in the offing.

The article generated interest on several grounds. First, most readers, upon hearing that Toomer and Jessie Fauset were the main subjects of the article, would probably have guessed that Locke discussed Toomer and Du Bois wrote about Fauset. But the opposite was the case. The piece begins by telling the audience of the *Crisis* that the two books under consideration "will mark an epoch." After the general introduction, which uses the plural "we" to cast its opinions, Du Bois shifts to the singular and speaks about Toomer's *Cane,* then just published. He praises Toomer's daring in that he was able to "emancipate the colored world from the conventions of sex." "It is almost impossible for most Americans to realize how straight-laced and conventional thought is within the Negro world," the often proper Du Bois claimed, and this made it all the more important that Toomer was "the first to hurl his pen across the very face of our sex conventionality." Though he complained about what he felt were the obscure passages in the book, Du Bois ended by saying, somewhat paternalistically, that "Toomer strikes me as a man who has written a powerful book but who is still watching for the fullness of his strength and for that calm certainty of his art which will undoubtedly come with years."

Du Bois had intended to write about Fauset's first novel, *There is Confusion,* but when he received a review of it from Locke, he "gladly yield[ed] to him." Locke is fairly unstinting in his praise, and since he knew Fauset well, and knew that she was currently Du Bois's editorial assistant at the *Crisis,* he begins by saying this is the novel that "the Negro intelligentzia [*sic*] have been clamoring for." The novel is not "merely a race story told from the inside, but a cross section of the race life higher up the social pyramid and further from the base-line of the peasant and the soil than is usually taken." Locke goes on to argue that by treating of four generations in one family, Fauset avoids the error, common to the bulk of Negro fiction, of "growing rootless flowers or exploring detached levels" of society. The story is essentially one of "blood and ancestry such as might be expected to come from the Philadelphia tradition which the author shares." This anticipated the reception of Fauset's work, which was sometimes dismissed as too bourgeois for black readers and insufficiently sensationalized for whites. Locke read all social novels as being in a genre of high seriousness; this novel had what he "maintain[ed] is the prime essential for novels with subject matter—social perspective, social sanity." Otherwise, he argued, one ends with a "raw and brutal cross-sectioning or . . . unpalatable propaganda." Some of the same demanding esthetic principles would appear in all Locke's criticism. One can only regret that he and Du Bois did not collaborate again, and indeed their esthetic common ground would become rather more limited in the coming years. The same is true for Fauset and Locke, whose relationship, despite the balanced graciousness of this review, would eventually end in estrangement.

Locke came to know Countee Cullen when the younger poet—he was born in 1903, eighteen years after Locke—approached him in the fall of 1922, seeking a reference for his application for a Rhodes Scholarship. Cullen would soon introduce Locke to Langston Hughes as a correspondent. At first, in the spring of 1923, Locke and Hughes knew each other only through their letters, and it was not until the summer of 1924 that they met in Paris. Their relationship actually began as a nuanced and flirtatious triangle among Cullen, Locke, and Hughes, with the men sharing poems, artistic advice, and gossip. Cullen and Hughes had met at the Harlem Branch Library in 1923, when Cullen was a student at New York University and Hughes had been attending Columbia. The two poets were beginning to be published in magazines but had not yet brought out their first books. Cullen, for reasons that are not clear, broke off his friendship with Hughes a little while later, but not before sharing his poems and his affection with the shy and self-deprecating Hughes and introducing him to many luminaries in Harlem. Both poets were younger than Locke, and both admired the older man's learning and willingness to support struggling writers. It is possible that none of the three ever enjoyed sexual intimacy with the others, but it was not through lack of trying, as their three-way correspondence served as a form of flirtation. Their esthetic values were distinguishable enough to provide a fruitful dialogue and express temperamental differences at the same time. Their friendships formed prior to the Renaissance, and though they had somewhat drifted apart before 1925, their roles in the artistic and cultural events of the movement remained complexly intertwined.[12]

Cullen's first letter to Locke, the one requesting a recommendation for a Rhodes Scholarship, set the respectable tone one would expect: "you are our race's sole representative as a Rhodes scholar." Trained in the lyric tradition of Keats and Edna St. Vincent Millay, on both of whom he wrote essays while at NYU, Cullen was ambitious not only for his poetry but also for his place in the literary world at large. He was the adopted son of a fundamentalist preacher, Frederick A. Cullen, the eleventh child of a couple who had been slaves in Somerset County, Maryland. His adoptive father instilled in Cullen not only a love of higher learning but a strong sense of Christian rectitude, yet the poet would struggle throughout his life against what he felt was the failure of Christianity to deal forthrightly with racism. The Reverend Cullen founded what had become a large church in Harlem, was a social activist, and had helped James Weldon Johnson and Du Bois organize the 1917 march down Fifth Avenue protesting the East St. Louis riot in which many blacks had been killed. Cullen's devotion to his poetry led him to a sense of political commitment rather less active than his father's.

The poet was not wholly without social concerns, however. Speaking at Town Hall in New York in 1923, he set out the terms of the youth movement which he saw as a worldwide "spiritual and intellectual awakening." Using the term "New Negro," Cullen implied he himself represented this movement, marked as it was by a commitment to higher education and a sense of self-shaping. Cullen's preoccupation with questions of identity, as well as his strong sense of scholarly duty and a devout sense of obligation to his adoptive parents, and perhaps most of all a love of high esthetic ideals, all provided points of friendship with Locke. Both men constantly dealt with racial issues, refusing to back away from the demands and promises of race pride, while at the same time seeking and believing in a realm of universal esthetic values. By the winter of 1922–23 the two had met in person, and Cullen visited Locke in Washington on occasion, even as Locke continued to come quite often to New York, where he rendezvoused with Cullen. In a letter apparently written in 1923, Locke offers Cullen a full measure of advice and reveals something about himself as well:

> I do not want to claim any special breadth of view—but I must say a propos of your remark that one's intimate confidences often seem foolish even to the best intentioned confidants. I think I may assure you of but one standard of judgment,—and that is the law of a man's own temperament and personality. But one cannot often discover this, especially if there are convention-complexes[,] except through confessional self-analysis. I have always thought that the wisest institution of the Catholic church was the confessional. Its only drawback is its moralistic background and condescension. If I were inventing a religion I would try to work out some beautifully ritualistic mode of reciprocal confession and make all conception of punishment and reward psychological and self-inflicted.

Locke rather gloomily opined that "a few of us surely may outrun the slowly inevitable," adding that his "listening ear is as kindly as it is acutely receptive." Locke's personal ethic always displayed this liberal attitude, and his need for a ritual that would insure "reciprocal confession" apparently entails doing away with any "third person" sense of punishment and reward. There is in this letter a feeling that draws on his Philadelphia boyhood, and the strong divide between the public and the personal.

The correspondence between the two men remained warm and even intimate, as they shared their fears, hopes, and experiences. In January 1923 Cullen had already given Locke Langston Hughes's address, saying that "his is such a charming childishness that I feel years older in his presence," though Hughes was actually born the year before Cullen. He also asked Locke to keep faith with the younger writers, sensing that Locke's literary standards were sometimes so high as to be punishing. Later the same month, having shown one of Locke's letters to Hughes, Cullen writes that he and Hughes will gladly join a "group" such as Locke was suggesting, probably a reference to the circle of Locke's gay friends in Washington and New York. Cullen added that Locke should not encourage Hughes to continue his studies, as if he preferred the childishness that many people remarked about in Hughes's character. But he wanted Locke to send his, Cullen's, poems to Braithwaite but not to J. Weldon Johnson, since he "did not want to curry favor." Thus began a series of mild intrigues and projects and competitions involving literary reputation and emotional intimacy that would last for several years.

As winter turned to spring in 1923, Cullen wrote often to his new mentor. He referred to a poem of Locke's which Locke had failed to include in his letter. Locke had earlier told him that he wanted a "most professional reaction" to one of his poems as "an exchange courtesy which I have been following with friends now for a number of years." Locke added: "I write verse for private circulation and consumption only." Cullen hoped that his book of poems would appear before his interview with the Rhodes committee. On Locke's recommendation, Cullen read Edward Carpenter's *Iolaus,* the anthology of gay writing that discreetly presented itself as a book about male camaraderie through a wide range of literature, from the Bible and the classics to modern times. He found it most revealing; "I loved myself in it," he said. Frankly full of desire, he told Locke, "I suppose some of us erotic lads, vide myself, were placed here just to eat our hearts out with longing for unattainable things." The two discussed other books by Carpenter in their correspondence, using the material to refer to their discussions of homosexual issues with an idealizing vocabulary of "perfect friendship," in part adapted from Greek classicism. In March Cullen wrote that his father had given him permission to spend the Easter holidays with Locke and that he was looking forward to meeting Georgia Douglas Johnson. In New York, he and Hughes had gone to see the Moscow Players' production of Gorky's *The Lower Depths,* and Hughes had promised to write Locke and send along some of his poems. In April, a letter from Cullen included two poems of Hughes's, with a note asking Locke not to send them out for publication. Later that month Cullen refers to some rupture in a friendship that Locke had enjoyed with someone, and Cullen offers the consolation that Locke still has "recourse" to Rudolf Dressler, a lover of Locke's in Germany. Meanwhile, Locke had given one of his former students, C. Glenn Carrington, Cullen's address and urged him to correspond with the poet. Carrington, Cullen's contemporary, was a graduate of Howard and greatly interested in the performing arts; he had been socially initiated into Locke's circle of gay friends, and Locke and he would be correspondents for the next three decades or so and would often rendezvous when Locke came to New York City.

Advice flowed in both directions between Locke and Cullen. The two men avidly shared their idealization of Hughes, but they also opened their private lives to one another in ways they did not usually employ with many other people. Cullen referred to Locke's "spiritual and mental anguish" and went on to say: "By all means keep a racial heart if you can do so without injury to yourself. But this cannot always be done." This came in a letter that expressed Cullen's happiness that Locke and Hughes had begun to correspond. Locke was planning his trip to Egypt, and Cullen suggested Hughes might accompany him. "Oh it would be wonderful if he could go with you this summer . . . each of you will be such inspiration to the other." In a letter of May 31 he offered to step aside where Hughes was concerned and let Locke take over in Hughes's affections. "I would be willing to make the sacrifice could it ensure your happiness, " he said. But in July, Cullen and Hughes were to spend four days together, and Cullen reported to Locke that some misunderstanding had occurred which caused some alienation: "He [Hughes] is probably unaware of what he has done, and, doubtless, blames you."

Meanwhile Cullen celebrated his twentieth birthday in Washington with Georgia Douglas Johnson, and the two talked for three hours; "she really has the soul of a poet," he testified to Locke. Though Scribner's had rejected his book of poems, he had a promising offer from Boni and Liveright. Cullen wrote to say that he was less committed to pursuing the Rhodes and would concentrate on his poetry. In the summer he responded to a letter Locke apparently wrote from Berlin while in the company of his friend Rudolf Dressler and told him that he was glad to hear that he was "reveling in the ecstasies of a perfect friendship which is enough to inebriate your senses." Locke had met Dressler in Dresden, and the two men carried on a correspondence in German and apparently joined each other during Locke's subsequent summer visit to Europe. Cullen continued with more advice. "Act prudently," he tells Locke, because "There are some people in Washington who would give their hope of heaven for a chance to hurt you." Still, Cullen was able to offer a positive suggestion: "surfeit yourself this summer." In the same letter he told Locke: "Recently I met Yolande Du Bois," the daughter of W. E. B. Du Bois, "and I am near the solution of my problem. But I shall proceed warily." It would be almost five years until Cullen married Yolande in an ill-fated union that did not successfully obviate the difficulties Cullen faced about his own sexual orientation.[13]

By the fall of 1923 Cullen had met Jessie Fauset, who relayed news from Locke, and he praised parts of Toomer's *Cane,* which he liked "immensely," and asked Locke, "were you like this—hot and cold by turn—when you were young?" He was also studying German so that he might write to Rudolf. Taking note of Hughes's return from his African trip, he observed that he is "looking like a virile brown god" and added that Hughes was considering going to Howard. It was also around this time that Cullen met Harold Jackman, who was to become his lifelong friend. Jackman, like Locke and Cullen, spent much of his life as a teacher and a patron of the arts and was especially active in the drama field. Many people took it as a given that Cullen and Jackman were lovers, and when Jackman later went on a transatlantic cruise with Cullen shortly after Cullen married Yolande, it was the subject of many jokes in Harlem.

By the spring of 1924, Cullen had arranged for the Imagist poet Witter Bynner to write the introduction to his first book of poems. He wrote to Locke that he "would much prefer to have you do the introduction, unless you think there would be more point to one outside the race." Locke may well have felt slighted by Cullen's choice of Bynner to help launch his poetry. But Locke offered advice in a professional tone and let Cullen know that an article he was preparing on his work would have to be adjusted accordingly:

> As to the matter of the preface, I appreciate your attitude, but I have no suggestion to offer as long as Bynner has a mind to keep the agreement. I only thought he had defaulted and wanted to know whether to hold back some things from the article on "The Younger Generation." As this will not be finally edited until early November, you can keep me posted as to developments: as it is, I will write out the paragraphs and include or cut as the occasion requires. You should by all means see his

preface before deciding. A preface beyond one's first volume is I think undignified and not exactly "comme il faut."

In fact, Bynner felt several of the poems Cullen wished to include in the volume were not of sufficient quality, and Cullen suggested to Locke that he might use this as a way of removing himself from the agreement to have Bynner write the introduction. Another misunderstanding occurred between Cullen and Locke at the turn of the year, when Cullen spoke directly to the editor of *Survey Graphic* to ask for a higher fee for his poem, "Heritage." In January 1925 Locke wrote to terminate their friendship, presumably feeling Cullen's ambition for his own work was leading him to act improperly. Cullen, however, rejected the termination and insisted that their friendship continue. As it turned out the book of poems, *Color,* would appear in 1925 with no introduction at all.

A few months later Locke returned one of Cullen's poems to him, "corrected" in a way that Cullen felt was too severe. He said to Locke: "Very few people can reach you. Do bend down a little." Locke firmly believed that black writers should use their racial identity in their art, drawing on a tradition rooted in folk culture and yet still strive to attain a universal meaning. For Cullen, the burden of being a lyric poet was enough; adding to it a responsibility for group expression struck him as excessive. He also complained to Locke that things were not going well with Yolande and that Hughes had fallen for a young English girl in Paris. This news was accompanied by Cullen's heartfelt declaration: "I have come quite definitely to the conclusion that I shall never again love any one with all my heart and soul. If I must be a libertine in order to preserve my health, my sanity, and my peace of mind, I shall do so; I shall make no further sacrifices." Despite what seems a vow to indulge his sensuality, Cullen continued to remain very discreet about his private life, and in this he and Locke were also sharing an important common experience.

In the fall of 1924 Locke took advantage of an invitation from Cullen to come and speak at his father's church, which had grown to be one of the largest in Harlem. At the same time, Cullen was anxiously awaiting news from the Rhodes committee, which eventually rejected his application in December. Cullen's reputation as a poet had grown considerably by now, and a student of Locke's from Howard, Llewellyn Ransom, began a serious study of Cullen's work, though the poet was a bit apprehensive about this and asked Locke if Ransom were sincere. Several letters from Cullen to Locke contain cryptic references to a "L.R.," apparently Llewellyn Ransom. It is possible that Ransom and Cullen were sexually intimate at this time. In any case, Locke and Cullen had shared friends in the past, and Cullen's view of his mentor was deeply appreciative on both esthetic and personal grounds. Months earlier he had said, in regards Locke and Hughes, that "I am deeply happy at your friendship for one another and proud to be its instrument." As for Cullen and Locke, they would work together as poet and critic, though perhaps less closely as friends, throughout the Renaissance years.

With Hughes Locke experienced some of the same sort of intimacy he shared with Cullen, but Hughes was much more reserved with the older man, as he was with almost everyone who knew him. Though Hughes had read widely when at Columbia before meeting Locke, he recounts in his autobiography, *The Big Sea,* that he threw all his books overboard when he sailed on a merchant ship to Africa; "it was like throwing a million bricks out of my heart," he wrote. Drawing upon the culture of working-class blacks and the proletariat, Hughes wrote a poetry strikingly different from Cullen's, and most readers took note. If Cullen were to be hailed as the poet laureate of the Renaissance, Hughes wanted to be the "poet lowrate," as a Chicago newspaper quipped. As such, Locke tried to convert Hughes to his sense of European culture and high estheticism, but by and large the poet balked.

As for Locke's part in the friendship with Hughes, it reflects a willingness to be revealing about his inner life more than in any of his other relationships and correspondences. The first letter in their correspondence, dated January 17, 1922 but clearly written in 1923, begins: "Everybody it seems who is a particular friend of yours insists on my knowing you." The "particular" here may refer covertly to the homosexual, or at least homosocial, world that Locke and Hughes shared, the main figure of which was Cullen. "You must write to me in more detail, " Locke insisted, "or you will have to remain a rather intriguing phantom. . . . If you do write, and I hope you will, let it be in some considerable degree of definiteness and detail." Locke mentions their friend in common, Jessie Fauset, who had recently praised Hughes, but Locke withheld the remarks she made, quipping that "I don't usually repeat compliments to young poets in their twenties." But in the next letter, dated February 10, 1922 (again, clearly written in 1923), Locke is a little more direct, and proposes meeting Hughes where his ship is docked, at Jones Point in New York. The nuanced language continued, however, as Locke began to suggest on what basis they might form a relationship:[14]

> . . . what you are enjoying at Jones' point on the level of naïve and un-
> sophisticated expression, one can find and enjoy best in Germany on
> the level of sophistication and the exchange of ideas as well as of senti-

ment. Indeed within their own boundaries, the Germans have a perfect genius for friendship, which cult I confess is my only religion, and
has been ever since my early infatuation with Greek ideals of life. You
see I was caught up early in the coils of classicism.

The reference to Greek ideals is a coded way of establishing a homosexual
framework, while at the same time carrying on a literate dialogue in which
references to Laocoön would be understood. Responding to a remark in one
of Hughes's letters to him, Locke praised the world of sailors: "I agree with
you that sailors are of all men most human, and that for a writer the sea, and
the broad perspective it gives, is the best and most developing discipline to
which he can submit. . . . [A] poet needs primarily spiritual deepening, and
not always the intellectual kind of development." Here Locke presents himself in worldly terms, offering the kind of advice that Hughes would appreciate, since it would confirm many of his attitudes. Nevertheless, Locke tried to
be honest about his own character: "Poor me,—I am all leaden intellectuality
and have to content myself with being a friend of poets," Locke lamented.
But by "being in at the feast and watching the succession of the spirit," he
could offer Hughes some genuine gifts.

Obviously stirred by the reports he had from Cullen, and in part from a
photograph Hughes sent him early on, Locke opened his heart to Hughes.
In what appears to be one of two early handwritten letters, both undated but
clearly written in early 1923, Locke would tell Hughes how he was "too battered and disappointed in human relationships at present (perhaps he [Cul-
len] has told you how) to be anything but quiescently fatalistic even about
you." Locke offers no name, so it is difficult to know to whom he is referring.
But the mood of confession permeates the letter. In an earlier passage, he tells
Hughes: "[M]y tragedy is I cannot follow my instincts—too sophisticated to
obey them, not too sophisticated not to have them—even though you mayn't
have a book-knowledge of psychology—you can, I am sure, appreciate the
tragedy." Locke, ever a lover of paradox in thought, was equally divided in
his emotions, telling Hughes plaintively: "Sooner or later, I must meet you—
and it would have been better sooner—especially with Countee as a sort of
shock-absorber—in case of—well in case of disillusionment on your part or
fatal loss of poise on mine." Thanking Hughes for the photograph of himself
he had sent, Locke somewhat teasingly responded: "I would send you one
in return—but I must give my spirit a chance to interpret and break through
its ugly mask—otherwise it couldn't possibly hope to mean anything worth
while to you."

In what is probably the second of the handwritten letters he sent Hughes, Locke focused on the artistic plans and hopes that supported the two men's relationship for the next several years. Locke wrote: "Countee is a wonderful lad. I only wish I could be located somewhere nearer you and be the mentor of a literary and art coterie—we have enough talent now to begin to have a movement—and to express a school of thought." This same letter said that he "had quite gotten over the pique I felt at your not permitting me to come to Jones Point to see you." Perhaps appealing to what he knew was Hughes's wanderlust, Locke mentions his own plans "for another summer abroad" and the possibility that he would take a leave to visit Egypt: "I just must shake off the academic bookshelf dust with the dust of the road—but I don't take to American roads or the American scenery." Hoping to lure Hughes to Washington, he also offered his apartment on R Street for use as "headquarters, if you are so disposed."

From the start Locke wanted to be an artistic guide for Hughes as well as a deep friend and lover. Describing his temperament and esthetics, Locke said that "I am pagan to the core—and how I love the Hellenic view." Then he went on to say that he taught philosophy and psychology and, explaining his recent experiences abroad, referred in part to the ethos of the Weimar Republic:

[T]hat is how I come to know so much of Germany, but the new Germany is more Hellenic and pagan than most people suspect—especially the new Youth movement which intrigues me terribly. My dearest friend is a member of it—this summer, he may even succeed in getting me in knickers, sandals and blouse—at any rate we are going to 'wandervogel' together for some happy weeks.

The "dearest friend" is probably Rudolf Dressler, the writer of a series of three letters that Locke preserved. Written in German from Dresden, the letters are signed "Rudolf," and clearly date from the early 1920s (a partial date of 192- is visible on one of them). This would be the same Rudolf mentioned by Cullen as being an intimate of Locke's. The letters tell of a chance meeting and intense relationship that Rudolf and Locke shared starting in the summer of 1922 and continuing for many years after. Rudolf speaks expectantly of Locke's return to Germany and clearly has made plans to extend their relationship. He says specifically at one point: "Wie schon wird es werden, wenn wir beide ganz allein durch die schone Natur wandern werden Arm im

FIG. 5.1. Langston Hughes, signed "to my friend." Hughes included this photograph with some of his poems which he sent to Locke before the men first met, in 1924 in Paris. Moorland-Spingarn Research Center.

FIG. 5.2. René Maran. This French intellectual was a good friend of Locke and introduced him to various figures in Paris. Moorland-Spingarn Research Center.

Arm?" (How nice it will be when the two of us will hike through beautiful Nature, arm in arm?)

The relation with Rudolf forms part of the background against which Locke met Hughes and can serve as a gloss on it. "Soon it will be June and you will be here," Rudolf writes, adding, "Oh I am feeling happy like a little kid, you too?" He offers to pick up Locke at the harbor, if Locke will send him the name of the steamer and the port of entry. He includes some of his poems in one of the letters, expressing in rather stilted literary diction his hopes for their reunion:

> Es kommt der Tag, in Juni bald.
> Wo wir uns sehen werden wieder,
> wir werden dann uns Aug' in Aug'
> Ins tiefe Antlitz schauen.
> Vorbei ist dann der Sehnsucht Traum
> Und alles—alles, wird wahr?

> The day will come, [so] soon in June
> When we will see ourselves again,
> We'll then see one another eye to eye
> Peering deep into the visage
> Gone then will be yearning's dream
> And all—all will come true?

The other two letters from Rudolf suggest that he was an unemployed worker, affected by the uncertain politics of Weimar, and that Locke had met his family and they were grateful for Locke's "benevolence." He also expressed the hope that he and Locke could live together, and he was saving the money Locke had sent him so that he might buy a suit to wear for Locke's arrival. Unfortunately Locke's letters to Rudolf do not survive, and the story is thus incomplete. However, Locke did save Rudolf's letters and the poems that came with them. He clearly felt strongly about Rudolf and saw the possibility of their time together as a way of extending his love of German culture and the longed-for pleasure of his summers in Europe.[15]

Not merely escapist, however, the feelings Locke developed for Hughes were entwined with a desire to share a deep and serious appreciation of poetry. Locke, in his second letter to Hughes, comments on Hughes's poems—which Hughes had apparently sent him in one of the first of the letters that passed between them: "Your estimate of your poetry is about correct—the newer technique is too strained—the other is not quite mellow enough. By the way—hasn't Cullen mellowness to a fine degree?" Locke's taste, trained in more classical standards, would have been drawn to Cullen's technical skill, yet Locke eventually appreciated both poets equally, though years later he would also lament what he saw as a falling off in their inspiration. Locke offered to send some of the poems to magazines. But there were strictures as well: "I don't think you are very successful in getting the exact touch which sometimes transmutes the colloquial into the poetic. Toomer has that gift," he told the poet, and then added, "each his own gift—my boy—each his own gift."

Hughes tried to make his esthetic stand very clear early on, as he wrote to Locke in a letter of May 1923. He remarks on having heard Cullen's speech to the League of Youth and goes on to display some of the paradoxical attitudes toward art that likely frustrated and entranced Locke:

> You are right that we have enough talent now to begin a movement. I wish we had some gathering place of our artists—some little Greenwich Village of our own. But would our artists have the pose of so many of the Villagers? I hate pose or pretension of any sort. And especially sham intellectuality. I prefer simple, stupid people to half-wise pretenders. (But perhaps it's because I'm stupid myself and half-ashamed of my stupidity. I don't know. I never studied psychology. . . . I wish that I had.

Locke would go on for some time trying to seduce Hughes, in both the sexual and literary senses, and Hughes would sometimes respond quite positively. But the roles that had been assigned to them—poet and critic, young man and older confidant, wanderer and academic—made their friendship one of shifting attitudes and defenses.

Shortly after Cullen arranged for the two men to correspond, Locke apparently asked Hughes to join him in Europe in the summer of 1923, though Hughes said he was unable to do so. At the time he was waiting on a ship docked in New York harbor, prepared to go to sea. Hughes was to use *The Big Sea* to recount the early epistolary contact, and the coy tone reveals and conceals at the same time:

> Meanwhile, there came to me at the fleet, a letter from a gentleman in Washington named Alain Locke. Written in a very small hand, it commented upon what he felt to be the merits of my poems he had seen in

the *Crisis,* and he asked if he might come to Jones Point to see me—
evidently thinking I lived in the village. I couldn't picture a distinguished professor from Howard, a Ph.D. at that, clambering over the
hundred-odd freight boats that made up our fleet, slipping on the wet
docks and balancing himself over precarious runways between rock-
ing old vessels. So I wrote back, "No." I didn't want to see him anyway,
being afraid of learned people in those days. (92-93)

Hughes has some sport at Locke's expense here, waggishly rewriting the moment to create an image of Locke as hopelessly otherworldly and at the same
time concealing his own real, though furtive, interest in his literary ambitions
and developing taste in great books. He also neglects to mention that in one
of his return letters to Locke he wrote that he was thinking about going to
Howard to complete his studies when he returned from his travels. Hughes
could be as reserved and sly as Locke, though in a different way.

Within two months of the beginning of their correspondence, Hughes
sent Locke a packet of his poems with the coy remark that Locke "must be a
charming friend for poets." He spun a fantasy that he must have known Locke
would appreciate: "how wonderful it would be to come surprisingly upon
one another in some Old World street! Delightful and too romantic!" Then,
mentioning he was going to send Locke an autographed picture of himself,
he ended with a gesture: "there are other rivers in the world to see besides the
Hudson. And Oh! so many dreams to chase." This only added to the mixed
signals he sent Locke, contrasting with his stance of anti-intellectualism.
A few months later, in the summer of 1923, Locke would write to him from
Egypt, and Hughes replied by asking Locke if he might join him. But their
meeting would be often delayed. This prompted a complaint from Locke: "I
cannot describe what I have been going through, it has felt like death—but
out of this death and burial of pride and self there has suddenly come a resur-
rection of hope and love. Langston!" He asked Hughes on three occasions
to join him, but Hughes continued to be evasive. "What whoredom is this!"
Locke protested. This was probably the "misunderstanding" that Cullen
had referred to. In any case, Locke was to persist and Hughes was to relent.

In April 1924, Hughes wrote from his Paris address in the fifteenth ar-
rondissement, where he was working in a cabaret. He was seeing "the other
side of the smile," as he put it, probably referring to the French habit of being
less charmed by American blacks once the enchantment wore thin. Locke
wrote a letter to Cullen while on board the ship headed to Europe, setting out
some of his thoughts about approaching Hughes. "I am going to land at Cher-

bourg and go to Paris—I shall look up Langston right away before the mood of 'incog' comes over me—but I give due notice that I have abandoned my code—altruism on my slender resources was threatening to land me in either the mad or the poor-house—it was just a question which." Despite the quandary he felt, and obviously overcoming his reluctance, in July Locke went to Hughes's apartment at 15 rue Nollet. Finally they were together, and both men seemed to enjoy one another. They spent time together in Paris, seeing various museums, and then traveled to Italy. Before they left Paris they each wrote a postcard to Cullen. Hughes said: "I'm enjoying my last two weeks in Paris more than any others because Mr. Locke is here. I only wish you were with us, too. Today we are going to see the fountains at Versailles. Sincerely, Langston." Locke was considerably more wry about the situation. He told Cullen: "'See Paris and die'—Meet Langston and be damned'—Sorry I can't carry out instructions to the last syllable. I have seen Paris and met L.—but it looks as if I might live and be blessed. Certainly I am grateful for the friendship of both of you. Thanks. As ever, Alain Locke." A month later, a card from Verona was briefer. "Dear Countee: Salute e baci, as the Italians say. Sincerely, Langston." Locke added, "We are together here again—wishing we were three instead of two. As ever, Alain Locke."

After their meeting in Paris in the summer of 1924, Hughes wrote a postcard to Locke to tell him: "Your company in Paris has spoiled me for being alone." As for Locke's reaction, he wrote Hughes a very romantic letter:

Today, the atmosphere is like atomized gold—and last night you know how it was—two days the equal of which atmospherically I have never seen in a great city—days where every breath has the soothe of a kiss and every step the thrill of an embrace. . . . I needed one such day and one such night to tell you how much I love you in which to see soul-deep and be satisfied—for after all with all my sensuality and sentimentality, I love sublimated things and today nature, the only great cleanser of life, would have distilled anything. God grant us one such day and night before America with her inhibitions closes down on us.

Locke apparently proposed that they travel together through Europe, but before the summer was over they had gone separate ways. Later in August other postcards arrived from Hughes. The poet had visited Romeo and Juliet's tomb and had recently finished reading *Madame Bovary;* he enjoyed a fiesta on the shores of Lago di Garda and asked Locke to "Write me soon, dear friend." Yet another card said: "I like you immensely and certainly we are

good 'pals,' aren't we? And we shall work together well and produce beautiful things." Locke arranged for Hughes to meet Albert Barnes, the art collector from Pennsylvania, and Paul Guillaume, whose collection of African
art in Paris Hughes went to see later that year. Hughes was grateful to Locke,
who seemed to him "a gentleman of culture, happy to help others enjoy the
things he had learned to enjoy."

Hughes returned to America in 1924, but too late to attend the awards
dinner sponsored by *Opportunity* magazine in May that some saw as the beginning of the Renaissance. His own return, however, was marked by his
luckily attending a benefit cabaret party thrown by the NAACP, at which
many notables, including Du Bois and James Weldon Johnson, greeted him,
and there met for the first time Carl Van Vechten, the white dandy who did
much to advance Hughes's career and to whom the poet would dedicate his
first book of poems. His friendship with Cullen dissolved later in the year,
for unexplained reasons, and he then went on to Washington, D.C., where,
among other things, he worked for Carter Woodson's Negro Life and History
research project. While there he saw little of Locke. But he did record in his
autobiography his attempt to enroll at Howard:

> I spoke with Dean Kelly Miller at Howard University about the pos-
> sibility of trying for a scholarship at the college. . . . But it seems that
> there were no scholarships forthcoming. I spoke with Dr. Alain Locke,
> who said my poems were about to appear in *Survey Graphic,* and who
> declared that I was the most racial of the New Negro poets. But he
> didn't have any scholarships up his sleeve, either. (*The Big Sea,* 204)

Eventually Hughes decided not to attend Howard, and his correspondence
with Locke would be sporadic until later in the 1920s. Locke remained a
strong supporter of Hughes's poetry, however, and would in a matter of a few
years serve as one of his sponsors to Charlotte Osgood Mason, one of the Renaissance's leading patrons. Hughes, for his part, was always more than a bit
uncomfortable with the idea of joining a group, and he resisted being closely
or exclusively identified with the Renaissance. But for the time being Hughes
would pursue an esthetic, and a lifestyle, that would keep him at least one
remove from Locke.

Jean Toomer's relation with Locke showed a somewhat different pattern
from those Locke formed with Cullen and Hughes, in part because Locke
and Toomer shared time together among the black bourgeoisie of Washington. Toomer was a native of the capital, but his childhood was spent in sev-

eral places. Though his father had been a slave, his mother was the daughter of a black man who had been governor of Louisiana during Reconstruction. Both parents were light skinned and hence could easily pass as white, which they did. This interracial experience affected Toomer deeply and provided the basis on which he eventually thought of himself as beyond racial categories. After the death of his mother in 1909 he lived off and on with his maternal grandparents and his uncle, who was later to be the manager of the Howard Theater; his father had earlier left the family, in 1895. After attending a number of colleges during the war, Toomer moved often among the cities of the north. Desperately in search of a vaguely defined "unity" that was at once psychological and esthetic, Toomer tried his hand at several different activities through the late 1910s, including the study of agronomy and sociology. Later, when his literary career began to open out, he befriended a number of authors and artists in New York City, a group that included Waldo Frank, Lola Ridge, Hart Crane, Alfred Stieglitz, and Georgia O'Keefe, all of whom were intent on developing an American esthetic that would be at once indigenous and transcendent. In 1919, he was forced to return to Washington to attend his dying grandfather. Then, in 1921 he taught for a short period in an agricultural and mechanical school in Sparta, Georgia. This experience, which at least glancingly recalled Locke's travels with Booker T. Washington in the winter of 1911–12, affected Toomer greatly, and he incorporated it into his novel, *Cane,* which was to be published in 1923.[16]

Toomer and Locke had come to know each other as early as 1919 and became close in the next few years, in part through their participation in the literary salon of Georgia Douglas Johnson, called the Saturday Nighters. Over the years visitors to the salon included Zora Neale Hurston, Bruce Nugent, and Jesse Fauset; Toomer also met Countee Cullen around this time, perhaps at one of Douglas's Saturday evenings. Hughes was to refer to such intellectual gatherings as "arid as the sides of the Washington monument." But Toomer needed a sense of artistic community, and Locke helped him to some extent in this regard. Like Toomer, Locke could well be described by James Weldon Johnson's phrase as a "marginal man." Both men found Washington more than a bit suffocating. But the literary group also devoted time to reading books, some of which Toomer used to deepen his sense of Negro history. Toomer wrote to Locke on January 26, 1921, to call on his erudition:

> I have managed to hold two meetings of a group . . . whose central purpose is an historical study of slavery and the Negro. . . . The aim is twofold, first, to arrive at a sound and just criticism of the actual place

and condition of the mixed-blood group in this country, and, second, to formulate an ideal that will be both workable and inclusive.

We need something to cement us. And that something can only spring out of a knowledge, out of certain fundamental facts which we have in common. It is to a lack of such a basis that I largely attribute our failure to get together in the past. The meetings should at least provide material for conversation other than the commonplace and trivial.

The first group came together a week ago Wednesday. I outlined the purpose of the meetings, and tried my best to throw a little fire in their hearts. . . . The subjects may be a trifle elementary for you, but now that we seem to be underway, I certainly would like to have you join us—whenever the time will permit. And if she would enjoy it, bring Mrs. L. by all means.

That Toomer would think to invite Locke's mother as well is an indication of the closeness of their friendship. Though the manners of the group may have been staid, the subjects discussed were serious and of great interest to Locke. Moreover, since activists such as Angelina Grimke were among the attendees, the discussion could not have always been completely placid. Grimke, coincidentally, had taught English at Paul Dunbar High School when Toomer was a student there, but apparently he was not in her class.

The correspondence between the two men suggests they often discussed the intersection between the issues of race and esthetics. Toomer's views on racial identity were already in a state of flux, if not confusion, and he might not have been able to adopt Locke's more philosophical approach. Locke arranged for Toomer to send his work to Dickerman and also introduced him to Montgomery Gregory. It is not clear how much Locke helped Toomer work out the material for his novel; obviously it was the close relationship Toomer had with Waldo Frank that was most deeply formative as an influence. But Locke did aid in arranging for the first of Toomer's publications in a major journal; the *Crisis* took a poem called "Song of the Son" for its April 1922 issue, and a few months later ran "Banking Coal," another poem. Late in 1922 Toomer attempted to find a patron who might support him while he continued to write, and he enlisted Locke's help in this regard. Locke warily approached a Mrs. Elbert on Toomer's behalf. Toomer mentioned it in a postscript to a letter he wrote to Waldo Frank:

Curious—just as I was about to mail this, a letter came from Locke. The tone is all right. Sincere. Delay unavoidable. Doesn't think so well of Mrs Elbert (glad I got the letter off to her!) but wants to see me as soon as possible. "It [raising the money] should be done through some channel in justice to your talent. For Washington is stagnation." I'll drop around to see him this evening.

Later Locke would be deeply involved in securing patronage for the writers and artists he knew; New York turned out to be a more favorable place for such activity than Washington, D.C.

An outsider's view of the capital's social set was preserved when Waldo Frank visited Toomer in Washington and wrote down his impressions of Toomer's then current set of literary associates:

I got the feel of what was then . . . the most conscious community of American Negroes: the poets, the intellectuals, the scholars of such institutions as Howard University, the bureaucrats with government jobs. They were aware of their ghetto and their awareness corroded their instinctual relation with the Negro peasant and with the earth of the South. They were intelligent, sensitive, neurotic. Toomer's trauma was deeper than the others'.

Calling the Washington milieu a "ghetto" is a harsh formulation of the separation of the Negro middle class from both white society and the "Negro peasant." Although Locke expressed his disdain for the city more than once, he would likely have been divided about Frank's emphasis on the "Negro peasant" as the cure for any modern lack of instinct. Toomer's "trauma," on the other hand, even if it were not cured, was to be fully registered in his novel.

Cane was a way for the deracinated Toomer to find a stabilizing sense of place and identity. As he put it, referring to his months in Sparta: "My seed was planted in myself down there. Roots have grown and strengthened." The novel meant a great deal to Locke. Its experimental form—the use of highly lyrical prose and a fragmentation that recalled several works of high modernist style, such as James Joyce's *Ulysses* and T. S. Eliot's "The Waste Land"— made it one of the most remarkable novels written by a black author at that time. Toomer also included sections—"Box Seat" and "Theater," both based on his working in the Howard Theater—that treated of Seventh Street in Washington; other sections are set in different urban centers as well as in the agricultural society of the Deep South. Though integrated in its form by its musical sweep more than its overall plot structure, the book combined many of the textures of a folk society with a very modernist sense of alienation and anomie. Toomer, whose unease over his own racial identity extended to his sense of class as well, shared Hughes's disdain for aspects of the social style of the black bourgeoisie. As Hughes was later to describe them, "They were on the whole as unbearable and snobbish a group of people as I have ever come in contact with anywhere"; in fact, to him they "seemed to [be] lacking in real culture, kindness, or good common sense." But Toomer also poeticized aspects of life in the capital. He wrote a letter to Waldo Frank in 1923 that included a description of the Seventh Street neighborhood:

> Washington is budding to Spring. From open windows come the sound of victrolas, jazzing the latest music, laughter, and soft women's voices. Mating birds chirp shrilly as they dart among tree limbs, heavy with buds. Chicken cackles, auto-claxons, news boys calling the scandals of the yellow papers, hammers driving nails, their thuds on boards of pine and oak. . . . And at evening, when the theatre signs are lighted, Washington opens to a dusk-bloom. Negroes leave their houses for the streets. They sway along on rubber-heels. Their rhythm approaches the soft slow music of the black-belt South. Budding above the stems of streets and pavements, their faces are deep clusters of macadam-flowers.

Toomer's poetic was one that relied on transformation, as here the urban textures slowly yield something like a folkish flavor. It was what charmed all his critics, and for Locke it demonstrated a unique talent.

Montgomery Gregory reviewed *Cane* favorably in *Opportunity*, and the essay in the *Crisis*, "The Younger Literary Movement," co-authored by Du Bois and Locke, presented the novel in very favorable terms. Locke later reprinted two of its sections in *The New Negro*, despite Toomer's reluctance by 1925 to be identified as a Negro artist. A few years later Locke would praise "Kabnis," a portion of *Cane* that Toomer converted into a staged monologue, as "cryptic but powerful." And he would include Toomer in his anthology, *Four Negro Poets* (1927), describing his work as a "probing into the sub-soil of Southern life [that] is only a significant bit of the same plowing under of Reconstruction sentimentalism that has yielded us a new realistic poetry of the South." Toomer later felt the novel was unsuccessfully received, and his conflict about his sense that he did not want to be identified as a Negro author extended to his unhappiness with Waldo Frank's introduction to the novel and his publisher's advertising for it as well. He wrote to his editor, who had asked for an author's statement to go with the press material: "For myself, I have sufficiently featured Negro in Cane. Whatever statement I give will inevitably come from a sympathetic human and art point of view; not from a racial one." Locke, mindful of the universalist claims of high art, might well have sympathized with Toomer's feeling in this instance, though he would have also appreciated the paradox of this feeling originating from the author of a novel so deeply expressive of racial consciousness.

Toomer was almost certainly the only writer in America who visited literary groups as diverse as Johnson's Saturday Nighters and the *Seven Arts* circle around Lewis Mumford, Sherwood Anderson, and Waldo Frank. But rather than form a bridge between such artistic groups, an almost impossible prospect considering the racism of the society, Toomer, questing for spiritual fulfillment, joined Gurdjieff's mystical cult in the later 1920s, spent a short period in France with the guru, and brought his teachings back to America. In a sense his esthetic combined, in part, those of Cullen and Hughes, using as it did a strain of high lyricism and a feeling for the marginal members of society. Such a paradox produced and reflected tensions that would eventually lead him away from any sort of membership in the Renaissance. His friendship with Locke, however, had left its mark, and Locke would refer to *Cane* for years afterward as a book that pointed the way.

The three writers that Locke met in the early 1920s—Hughes, Cullen, and Toomer—earned his highest esthetic judgment and his deep friendship. Generous to each, he also derived from them a strong sense of what the African American artist was capable of doing in poetry and prose. Though he knew creative artists in all fields throughout his life, the few years in the 1920s when Locke met the "young generation" at first hand left him feeling especially close to the esthetic values he embraced.

———

Meanwhile, things at Howard were increasingly unsettled. Budget crises were common, and Locke's continual decade-long tensions with the college's administration—over salary and curriculum and commitments to a plan to make Africana studies a field for high scholarship—showed no signs of abatement. His sense of the necessity of constantly setting challenging goals for everyone in the community earned him the reputation of being impossibly high-minded. And he had little more than contempt for President J. Stanley Durkee himself. Despite Locke's impressive productivity during his first decade or so at Howard, and disregarding his increasingly national reputation as a black intellectual, the president of Howard decided to fire him. It was in the spring of 1925 that Durkee made his decision to dismiss Locke along with three other professors. Rumors of the impending dismissals were circulating a few days before the decision was announced, though Durkee was busy denying them. Evidently the various department chairs would not acquiesce in the wholesale dismissal, so Durkee himself drew up the charges of "unsatisfactory work." Earlier, he had forced the resignation of Carter Woodson, the admired editor of the *Journal of Negro History*. So Durkee, bluff and autocratic, was far from shy in such matters. But the ensuing outcry may have alarmed as well as surprised him. The atmosphere became even more charged when the students went on strike in the spring. The reasons behind the strike were confused in several accounts, but they included a rule that made attendance at chapel compulsory and a plan that would result in failure or dismissal if a student missed a certain number of R.O.T.C. or physical education classes.[17]

Durkee pleaded that the dismissals were the result of economic pressure, even invoking President Coolidge's call for national belt-tightening, but Locke saw them as the result of the faculty members' absence of "personal loyalty and political service to the administration machine." Strikingly, the lie was given to Durkee's rationale that the firings were due to financial stringency, since all four men were in fact offered raises in their salary during their last year of service. Durkee, meanwhile, was under attack by the faculty and the alumni on several scores. Chief among them was the issue of faculty salaries. In fact, Locke himself had served as the secretary on a faculty committee that stressed the need for higher salaries; this may very well have brought him to Durkee's special attention. There was also the question of Durkee simultaneously holding the presidencies of Howard and the Curry School of Expression—though this dual position had been approved by Howard's Trustees—and when this became widely known, along with the fact that the Curry School did not admit Negroes, Durkee had to backpedal. He resigned the Curry position, but much damage had been done. There were also charges that he had mismanaged increased funds from Congress, doling out salary increases and rollbacks on the basis of personal favoritism.

Locke took immediate and strong action when his dismissal was made official. He contacted a lawyer in Washington, but he was told that Durkee was within his rights. In June, Locke wrote to the Board of Trustees, who responded by referring the matter back to Durkee, who happened to be out of town at the time. By December Locke had a meeting with the trustees, but they could do no more than offer him a year's pay. It was left to the alumni to create pressure and bring public light to the situation. Mr. T. B. D. Dyett was the secretary of the Special Alumni Committee, and he went to work on Locke's behalf. There was an editorial in the *Messenger* and a trustee, J. L. Parker, wrote to the dean of the Divinity School at Yale to protest what he called the board's neglectful actions. Other black writers sent their support. Countee Cullen wrote in June to say: "This world is more of a hell than my worst moments have conceived it if there are not open arms for you the country through." Du Bois used the *Crisis* to editorialize, and he received a three-page letter from Locke detailing the insulting behavior and racist remarks of Durkee. Rumors proliferated, and the one Locke repeated to Du Bois said that Durkee at one point referred to Kelly Miller as a "contemptible cur." In defending himself Durkee claimed that Miller threatened him and he responded by calling the dean a "pup." In any case, it was established before a faculty meeting investigating a number of charges against Durkee that the two men had decided to "let it be." Not stopping with the pages of his own journal, Du Bois meanwhile went further and wrote a strong piece for the *Nation* exposing in some detail just how poorly run the nation's black colleges were in the hands of white administrators. For example, he described the administration of Wilberforce College, where he began his teaching, as "vindictive, and without discipline or ideal."[18]

Locke wrote to Franz Boas at Columbia on December 3, 1925 to thank him for his help and to keep him informed of the developments. A special meeting of the trustees was planned, and Locke felt there was little chance they would do anything but approve of Durkee's handling of the matter, but there was some hope for a deferred decision. This meant at least that the pressure from the Alumni Committee might be brought into play. The Board of Trustees met on December 10 and made the dismissals look like part of a retrenchment and reorganization, trying thereby to diminish the personal aspect that had been generated by Durkee's approach. Emmett J. Scott, the secretary-treasurer, recorded in the minutes that the board passed two motions: "1. . . . the action of the Executive Committee and the Budget Committee . . . is ratified as carrying out . . . the reorganization plan of the University as adopted in June, 1925," and "2. . . . the Trustees hereby grant leave of absence to . . . four persons, beginning July 1, 1925, for one year,—full salaries to be paid. . . . At the end of the year, June 30, 1926, all connections of these persons with the University shall cease." Locke wrote to Franz Boas to tell him of the developments. "Our special trustee meeting turned out to be a complete endorsement of the Durkee administration," he said, despite the Alumni's Committee's eight-hour presentation opposing it. He closed by telling Boaz:

"There is some reason to think the Board may have given Dr. Durkee its vote in order to facilitate his going—but I dare not credit this, as really they are collectively as stupid and arbitrary as he is individually." Eventually the pressure would be too much even for Durkee, and he resigned in 1926. He left to become the pastor at the Plymouth Congregational Church in Brooklyn.

Locke was able to take the academic year 1925–26 off from teaching, and he then spent a year as a visiting professor at Fisk University, in part through the intercession of Du Bois. Meanwhile, Howard hired its first black president, Mordecai Johnson, whose father was a former slave. Johnson was a highly educated divinity student, with degrees from the University of Chicago and Harvard Divinity School. In April 1926, Emmett J. Scott approached Johnson after hearing him deliver a series of lectures on religion and offered him the candidacy for president. At first he declined the offer. Shortly thereafter, the trustees drafted him, and so he became the university's eleventh president. He was successful in securing more reliable funding from Congress to support Howard, and in increasing the quality of the faculty and the size of the student body. Many people, both those who liked and detested him, agreed that Johnson had a "Messianic complex." He once remarked of himself that "God tells me when to speak, but He doesn't tell me when to stop." It was unclear, according to some witnesses, whether this was said in jest or seriously. His tenure as president would last from 1926 until 1960, far longer than that of any other person.[19]

In September 1926, Locke wrote Johnson, asking for his job back. The Alumni Association was also at work trying to get the new president to reverse the actions of his predecessor. Locke reported to his friend Paul Kellogg that a discussion with Johnson had revealed that the delay in Locke's reappointment was due to Johnson's feelings that the others who were looking to be reappointed as well were not "up to scratch." But whether or not this was Johnson being self-servingly protective, he eventually realized Locke's value, and by June of the following year Locke sent Johnson a letter accepting a position at Howard. In the fall of 1927 Locke was to begin his second stint at Howard, this one to last for twenty-five years, almost twice the length of the first one. But first he had to deal with the New Negro and the Harlem Renaissance.

CHAPTER SIX

The Renaissance and the New Negro

The preferred name for it, as far as Locke was concerned, was the New Negro Movement. Many others often called it the Harlem Renaissance, though some felt this neglected Chicago, Detroit, and other cities that saw cultural ferment in the 1920s. But even Locke himself referred to it as the Renaissance on occasion. The terminological debate reflected some of the mixed opinions and conflicting commentaries that the movement elicited. Such a broad spectrum of opinion cast doubt on whether it even constituted a movement. Locke treated it as such, however, and saw himself as one of its chief movers. Using his wry sense of self-presentation, he later called himself the "midwife" of the new attitudes and expressions that hearkened not only to the "new" culture but to a wider, more engaged sense of group identity. Locke's philosophical bent and temperament led him, early and late, to ponder the issues of group identity and cultural legitimation in polemical and analytic terms. Some of the events and interpretations of the issues fostered by the Renaissance turned out to be virtually imponderable. Later generations would argue about its success or failure, its ultimate purposes, its origins. Twenty years after his involvement in the movement Locke offered one of its most soberingly negative assessments. But in 1925 the surge of new feelings took many directions, and Locke's sense of value moved with it.

As for Harlem itself, the Renaissance drew a great deal of its vitality from the historical circumstances of a neighborhood that was becoming fabled even as Locke saw it as the capital of a new Negro nation. The sociological and demographic facts, much commented on by later writers, were part of

Locke's lived experience. He traveled to Harlem frequently in the 1920s and thereafter; he came to know all its political and artistic leaders, and its social life as well. Washington, D.C., was in many ways the center of the black bourgeoisie in America, but Harlem was something new. It offered a diversity of people with a considerable array of personal origins—from throughout the African diaspora, and especially the Caribbean islands—and this led to a variety of classes and sensibilities. As with any national entity and its capital, Harlem served to confer on the New Negro a putative unity, as much an idea as an actuality. Locke reflected this important aspect in the articles he selected for the anthology that placed him in the center of the new movement.

Locke brought back with him from Oxford and Berlin a current of modernism, that innovative awareness of personal autonomy and the secular sense of historical consciousness. Locke knew, as did many others, that to be modern was to be urbanized, and to be so in the context of a mass society. Many visitors to Harlem remarked on the way it offered the black population a startling sense of self-awareness and self-identification, and with it the promise of self-shaping. "Hundreds of colored people! I wanted to shake hands with them, speak to them," is how Langston Hughes registered the sentiment when he first walked out of the subway stop at 135th Street. "Done died an' woke up in Heaven," says one of the characters in a story by Rudolph Fisher, a naive bumpkin of a character, amazed to see how Harlem works, and who will shortly be gulled by its inhabitants. And Aaron Douglas, an artist who would eventually be influenced by Locke, retrospectively described his first sense of arrival: " . . . an enormous outdoor stage swarming with humanity and spreading roughly from 116th Street on the South to about 143rd Street on the North, and from 5th Avenue on the East to St. Nicholas Avenue on the West. . . . Here one found a kaleidoscope of rapidly changing colors, sounds, movements. . . . And yet, beneath the surface of this chaotic incoherent activity one sensed an inner harmony. . . . " Reactions like this from many observers contributed to the impression of Harlem as a city within a city, an impression intensified by the issue of racial identity.[1]

Modernism for Harlem and for Locke also meant a break with the past, another way of implementing—at least at the level of attitudes—that sense of secular historical consciousness that is close to the heart of the modern. "Liberal minds today cannot be asked to peer with sympathetic curiosity into the darkened Ghetto of a segregated race life. That was yesterday." This was Locke in his "Foreword" to the anthology of 1925, with his voice poised between the polemic and the analysis of a manifesto. Speaking of and for Harlem, the philosopher is speaking to it, rousing it to agreement, moving it beyond the imposed category of a ghetto into the status of a capital. The cultural effect of the anthology called *The New Negro* ramified in the wake of the consciousness and idiom that had been fostered by modernist culture. As Locke put it, again in the "Foreword," "we have . . . concentrated on self-expression and the forces and motives of self-determination."[2] Openness, autonomy, newness, experimentation, the ability to think and experience across and beyond boundaries of genres and disciplines: all these aspects were already part of Locke's writings and thought in the ten or more years since he began at Howard. Harlem was at once the metaphor and the evidence for Locke's modernist declaration.

The social energies of the new race capital were vibrant and complex. Migration to northern urban centers by southern blacks on a large scale in the first two decades of the new century was fueled by poor conditions in the South and a severe labor shortage up North. A week's wages for female domestics in the Deep South, for example, could be earned in a day in Manhattan. Between 1910 and 1930, the black population in New York City increased two and a half times, from ninety thousand to over three hundred and twenty-five thousand. A building bust in Harlem, first developed for prosperous whites, made vacant housing there suddenly available and affordable in the early 1910s, and blacks poured out of the Manhattan slums known as Tenderloin and San Juan Hill to occupy newly built and spacious apartments and houses above 125th Street. Harlem itself had over 100,000 citizens in the signal year of 1925, and the population was over 95 percent black. Much of the rental property was still owned by white developers, and the community was less than successful in creating a sustaining entrepreneurial class. These facts, combined with rising rents and the need to overcrowd the living space in order to shoulder those rents, would in the 1930s develop into social problems of worrisome force. But for the time being, blacks had a race capital and at least the beginnings of an audience for cultural expression unlike any they had previously experienced in America.[3]

For Locke in particular Harlem was a place that he came to know well. He had first traveled to New York City as early as 1912, when he was plotting his first career moves while developing his vocation as a race leader, and he had traveled there frequently for a number of years. In 1925 he shifted his base of operations from Washington, D.C., to Harlem on an almost permanent basis, taking up residence in a rented room. His situation was described by Arthur P. Davis, a young man, later a student at Howard, who knew him at the time he was editing the *Survey Graphic* issue and *The New Negro,* the publications that would be the basis of his claim that he served as a "midwife" for the younger generation of artists who made up the core of the Renaissance:

> During the time that he was producing these works, Locke lived in a top floor room of a brownstone house in (I believe) 139th Street. It was a typical Harlem room-to-let, bare, ugly, and often quite cold (as I remember it, Locke occasionally worked with a blanket around his feet to keep off drafts). Young writers and artists and college boys were constantly dropping in on Locke to seek his advice on writing, to submit material for The New Negro, or just to talk. To those of us who were preparing for an academic career, Locke with his Harvard-Oxford background and his interest not only in literature but in music, drama, and art as well—Locke was a revelation. He represented a kind of continental sophistication and learning that we had never seen before—at least that I had found in my teachers. Moreover, he was easy to talk to; as his interests were broad and decidedly unconventional, he could and did talk brilliantly on many things our teachers had not discussed with us—folk songs, blues, African art, and modern painting. Incidentally, Locke was the first person I heard who discussed seriously the blues and other folk material.[4]

This picture of Locke offers a rare account of his actual working conditions, and it nicely captures the breadth of his interests and the pedagogic role that he enacted throughout his career.

Locke had been preparing for the Renaissance for almost two decades. From his essay on Paul Dunbar, written while at Harvard, up to his grappling with the possible uses of African art in the early 1920s, Locke wanted to fashion a usable past for black people. This past, in the simplest sense, became a source of esthetic material and, more complexly, a way to measure racial identity through historical gravity and social development. Perhaps most important, a shared past enabled black people to take hold of a rapidly changing present and so enjoy greater autonomy in the future. The metaphor, or conceit, of Harlem as the capital of the race facilitated this elaborate set of historical and social possibilities, and Locke was determined to make things happen. Dreams of race leadership seldom appeared more likely to come true. All of Locke's reading and research and study could be brought to bear as sources of intellectual and critical power, and the tensions between individual expression and group service, reaching back to his college days, might be fruitfully resolved. More than once his personal balance between explainer and shaper would falter and need to be righted, but what he showed least often were any signs of hesitation.

If the locale of the Renaissance served as a subject of discussion and dispute, so, too, did the time frame of the movement and the origin of the term "New Negro." The term had appeared in the black press just before the turn of the twentieth century, and disputes proliferated regarding its intellectual origin and correct definition, as well as about the traits a person needed to be a New Negro and about the historic mission of such persons.

There were several popular but competing definitions. Booker T. Washington, in his *The New Negro for a New Century* (1900), defined the "New Negro" as patriotic, committed to local community development, and firm but not belligerent in expecting recognition of personal dignity. The historic mission of the first "New Negro" was thus economic development and social accommodation. Marcus Garvey offered a radically different definition. Garvey's organization, the Universal Negro Improvement Association (UNIA) published the *Negro World*, which had the largest circulation of any black-owned or controlled publication throughout the 1920s, with impressive circulation in the Caribbean, Africa, and Europe. Garvey's "New Negro" was defined as an African population promoting race loyalty, unity, and separately controlled institutions. Claude McKay, Zora Neale Hurston, Eric D. Walrond, J. A. Rogers, Arthur Schomburg, and W. A. Domingo (a *Negro World* editor in 1919) published in the *Negro World* prior to their works appearing in Locke's *The New Negro*. In 1921, "The New Negro, A Genuine Negro Melodrama" by A. Lincoln Harris was staged in Philadelphia. "The old Uncle Tom" type is shown as a servant of the Hon. Marcus Garvey, while the New Negro stands up in the person of the son of Marcus Garvey and demands equality with other races. Weana, an Indian girl, and Garvey's son want to marry; however, the senior Garvey stops the marriage because she is not black, and the father wants his son to continue his work. Near the end of the play it turns out that Weana really is black, and all live happily. The "New Negro" pursued dignity through race loyalty and independent institutions.

Others used the medium of stage presentations to explore the themes of racial equality and simultaneously to present their own definitions of the "New Negro." Du Bois emphasized the importance of the "New Negro" as an active civil rights campaigner. This was the animating theme of his great pageant, *Star of Ethiopia*, first performed in 1913 in Washington, D.C., and later in Philadelphia in 1916 and Los Angeles in 1925. A bust of Abraham Lincoln was carried across the stage in the parade of black figures representing accomplishments from Egyptians, abolitionists, and physicians. The first performance used approximately three hundred fifty actors. Du Bois's *Star of Ethiopia* was in many ways his theatrical version of his *Souls of Black Folk* (1903).

Different publications used different tactics and stressed a variety of issues. The *Call* defined the "New Negro" as a socialist, engaged in a struggle, including violent action, against capitalism: "The New Negro is here; and there will be more of them to enrich the Socialist movement in the United States." The *Messenger* published pictures condemning the lynching of blacks, especially during the numerous riots in 1919. The *Messenger*'s pictures had captions beneath cartoons. One caption in June 1919 read: "Following the Advice of the 'Old Crow' Negro," lampooning Du Bois, Robert R. Moton, and Kelly Miller, and another in July 1919, "The 'New Crowd' Negro Making America Safe for Himself," pictured a black man shooting whites, with a flag with the names of cities with recent white mob violence against blacks, including Longview, Texas, Washington, D.C., and Chicago.

African Americans confronted vicious forms of social oppression in often desperate ways, and cultural expression was therefore quite various. Langston Hughes published his "Johannesburg Mines" poem, a fact-based attack against the owning class, in the *Messenger* in 1924. Locke, alert to the possibilities of Negro poetry, emphasized the values that cultural products demonstrate when they employ such traits as rhythm, balance, and style, all of which aid in creating the universally appreciated achievements of Negro culture. This was the way James W. Johnson understood a newly emergent group in his *Book of American Negro Poetry* (1922): "[T]here is only one measure by which [a people's] greatness is recognized and acknowledged—[the] amount and standard of literature and art they have produced."

Some, even as they acknowledged the importance of cultural struggles, would date the intellectual origin of the "New Negro" as early as the publication of Du Bois's *Souls of Black Folk* in 1903. Others, with a sense of public occasion, invoked the return of the demobilized black regiment that paraded down the streets of Harlem in 1919. There was also a sociological marker in the arrival of Marcus Garvey in Harlem in 1917, and his UNIA marshaled the largest mass movement of the decade. On a more literary note, the publication of Jean Toomer's *Cane* in 1923, and Claude McKay's first book of poems, *Harlem Shadows,* in 1922, were omens of an important stirring. Likewise the end of the movement was to be questioned: certainly the stock market crash of 1929 offered itself as a definite watershed, but so too did the Harlem race riot of 1935. Locke was involved in all these events, often as commentator or critic, remotely or closely connected.[5]

Several contemporary forces and abiding concerns converged to lead Locke into the position where he could edit the anthology that was to be the chief group presentation of the values and interests of the Harlem Renaissance. His interest in race was foremost, but more specifically he faced the questions of the relation between racial identity and artistic expression. Locke, however, for all of the perennial discussion of this issue, felt that its clarification could only take place in a pluralistic context of varied voices and different forms of knowledge. He used his national standing and his wide network of friends and colleagues to put forth a polyvocal collection of Negro expression, experience, and examination. The issue of the *Survey Graphic* would include articles on art, music, sociology, anthropology, and history, as well as original drawings, poetry, and fiction. Personal differences would be elided, and some of the larger, intractable questions could be put aside or at least reframed for the moment. Pluralism was part of what Locke had taught himself for the previous two decades and what he had been applying in several different fields.

There was also the question of how political and social advances might occur for blacks. Often supposedly progressive figures turned out to be less so in practice. Woodrow Wilson, for example, saw fit to segregate the public buildings in the nation's capital, thus extending the reign of Jim Crow. The aftermath of the Great War caused many to seek in nationalist sentiment a security that was otherwise threatened by an unstable international order, and this sentiment rigidified the status quo. The years following the armistice of 1918 were a time of progressive politics in some areas, but there were retrograde forces at work as well. The issue of immigration, and the restriction of it by Congressional action in 1924, caused the subject of racial purity to arise as an instrument of reactionary politics. The so-called nativist movement, which spread specious theories about "mongrelization" and fueled the vicious lynching campaigns of the time, stood in direct opposition to Locke's sense of the great social values of pluralism and tolerance. Locke's sense that cultural expression would serve the ends of social progress was developed in this context.[6]

The resurgence of nationalist sentiment after the Great War had swept Locke along in his activities at Howard. Other black leaders felt the same reaction. Du Bois affirmed, in a May 1919 *Crisis* editorial, that he would fight the Great War again, even as he insisted: "The faults of our country are our faults" and that America's blacks should fight to eliminate "the forces of hell in our own land"; despite the tension in his feelings, the editorial earned him a certain amount of scorn. But Locke wanted to add to his own nationalist sentiment an ongoing concern with internationalism. This concern would have a part in the Renaissance, which Locke considered, in part, a transnational movement. Charles S. Johnson had devoted an issue of *Opportunity* in May 1924 to African art, which included a poem by Countee Cullen on Rene Maran's novel, *Batoula*. The imprint of Locke's taste and concerns was clearly present in this. Locke also contributed a brief essay, in French, to the journal, *Les Continents* later in the same year. In it he introduced "La jeune poesie afro-americaine," as the title put it, which included a brief discussion of McKay, Hughes, and Cullen. (The essay was an early version of his "Introduction" to *Four Negro Poets*, which would appear in 1927.) There was also the article from a 1925 issue of the *World Tomorrow*, called "Internationalism: Friend or Foe of Art?" Locke's emphasis on culture was not something that was used merely to help set up bright lines around national groups; it was a part of his view of cultural reciprocity that all national sentiment must eventually lead to a more universal understanding. The theory of race that he had set out in his lectures on race contacts he now applied to cultural expression as a force in group identity.[7]

Others formed part of the dialogue about the complex intertwining of race, politics, and cultural expression. W. E. B. Du Bois, for example, could argue in an editorial in the *Crisis* in November 1922: "We Negroes have gone fast forward in economic development, in political and social agitation; and we are likely to forget that the great mission of the Negro to America and the modern world is the development of Art and the appreciation of the Beautiful." A little more than a year later, he and Locke co-authored the piece in the *Crisis* on the youth movement in the arts. The two men implicitly accepted the notion that even a generation could serve as a political entity. Politics in the modern metropolis took on different aspects at different times. The fight against racism, and the struggle for social justice, was many-sided; no one had a monopoly on tactics or strategy. Locke's role as an educator at Howard for the preceding ten years had led him to believe that it was best to work incrementally but also in many different arenas at once. Though Locke was trained to question received truth, and to go about enunciating first principles with a healthy and affirmative skepticism, he nevertheless could see no reason why a developed and nuanced cultural expression could not bear social and political fruit.

———•——

Charles S. Johnson had the idea to stage a celebratory dinner as a way to honor Jessie Fauset's new novel, *There is Confusion,* and announce the prizes that *Opportunity* would bestow on promising black writers. Such dinners and awards, self-conscious acts of community spirit, became popular and even commonplace in Harlem in the 1920s. On March 21, 1924, the dinner was held at the Civic Club, and the crowd of one hundred or so attendees, comprised of black and white cultural leaders, was illustrious. Johnson used the occasion to arrange for Locke to meet with Paul Kellogg, knowing that the latter had plans to make Locke a special offer. A special number of the magazine Kellogg edited, *Survey Graphic,* would be devoted to the idea of Harlem as the Mecca of the race, "The Greatest Negro Community in the World" as the opening section of the issue would label it, with perhaps forgivable chauvinism. Kellogg needed a guest editor and offered Locke the task. Locke accepted, though there was an imposingly short deadline, as the issue was due in twelve months' time. Locke worked hard and swiftly, and the issue appeared on time in March 1925, with two dozen contributors offering essays, fiction, and poems organized into three sections. Besides the opening section on the "greatest" community, there were groupings called "The Negro Expresses Himself" and "Black and White—Studies in Race Contacts," the latter obviously echoing the title of Locke's lecture series. The first and third were heavily sociological in their emphases, covering such topics as black urban workers, by Charles S. Johnson, and the role of women in black society, by Elise Johnson McDougald. The middle section included the poems, Winold Reiss's graphics, Locke's essay on the "ancestral legacy," and Albert Barnes and Arthur Schomburg, respectively, on Negro art in general and Negro history. The issue was a great success. Two printings quickly followed, and some white benefactors bought large numbers of copies for free distribution.[8]

The special number of the *Survey Graphic* resulted from the forward-looking attitudes of Paul Kellogg. Kellogg was born in Kalamazoo, Michigan, in 1879, and he had come to New York to study at Columbia in the early years of the century. Unstintingly progressive in his views, he had assumed the editorship of a journal called *Charities and the Commons* in 1907. After using the journal to sponsor a thorough sociological study of Pittsburgh, he decided in 1912 to change the name to the *Survey*, in an attempt to stress its sociological methodologies. Kellogg believed in an activist sociology and group action, and he joined with other progressives of his era to enlighten the public on many issues. In 1920 he was one of the founders of the American Civil Liberties Union, and seven years later actively campaigned to stop the execution of Sacco and Vanzetti. In 1921 he again changed the name of his journal; this time it was called the *Survey Graphic*. Actually this was a separate journal, a new incarnation of Kellogg's commitment to using print and graphic art to convey the important values of progressive politics to a wider audience, and it ran alongside the more sober and sociologically focused *Survey*, which continued to address an audience of specialists and academics. Before and after the Harlem issue appeared, other issues of the journal treated a wide range of social concerns, such as feminism, family life, the need for government control in the power industry, and the threat of fascism.[9]

In many ways the *Survey Graphic* was a perfect instrument for Locke's ideas. Kellogg associated with intellectuals who owed a debt to the kind of social thought known as "efficiency progressivism," which stressed the use of social science and pragmatism to solve the persistent problems of modern society. Dewey later contributed to the journal, and his arguments about the need for balance between public awareness and the use of scientific authority would find an analogue in Locke's editorial policy. The "talented tenth" would be praised in Locke's editorial control and content of the Harlem issue, but there would also be an emphasis on the role of the larger audiences, not least the constituency made up of the younger generation. The contents page of the issue offered an overview of the journal's contents, introduced with a paragraph called "The Gist of It," which was probably written by Kellogg himself:

> The *Survey* is seeking month by month and year by year, to follow the subtle traces of race growth and interaction through the shifting outline of social organization and the flickering light of individual achievement. There are times when these forces that work so slowly and so delicately seem suddenly to flower—and we become aware that the curtain has lifted on a new set in the drama of part or all of us.

The sense here of progressivist amelioration and an interplay between large forces and individual talent, all cast in the esthetic vocabulary of the dramatic art, animated Kellogg and Locke equally. The paragraph mentions similar cases of nationalistic "awakenings" in Mexico, Ireland, and Russia, all sub-jects of previous issues of the *Survey Graphic;* accordingly, Locke would pick up this line of reasoning in his introductory essay, "Enter the New Negro." The editorial voice concludes with a flourish that continues the theatrical metaphor: "a dramatic flowering of a new race-spirit is taking place close at home—among American Negroes, and the stage of that new episode is Harlem."

Locke's editorial work in connection with the New Negro movement won him great praise and recognition among many people. It was also work that required an amicable working relationship with Kellogg. The rela-tionship produced not only the issue of the journal that appeared in March 1925—known officially as "The *Survey Graphic* Harlem Number"—but also led to the book version, the anthology titled *The New Negro* that was published by Boni and Liveright several months later. The two publications vary in contents and editorial thrust, though what those differences signify, in terms of values and the struggle to shape them, can be differently inter-preted. Locke's reputation in the Renaissance rested on the anthology, but it was Kellogg's faith in Locke that made the journal issue a bright possibility. In any case, Kellogg and Locke made a well-functioning team, and both men remained friends throughout.[10]

Locke called on all his diplomatic skills in deciding what to include, what to leave out, and what to alter. He threw himself into the work with thorough relish and pent-up energy. Kellogg wrote to Locke in August 1923 to say that he was glad Locke was at Howard and added "we want much more of you in the Survey." Eight months later he again wrote Locke, this time to express regret that he had gotten nothing from him on the Sanhedrin conference in Chicago. But by May 1924—just after the face-to-face meeting arranged by Charles Johnson—Kellogg wrote at some length to tell Locke about the *Survey*'s editorial staff's approval of "the general scheme of the issue," which had met with "great enthusiasm." Locke went to work on the introduction and the section on the poems. The staff meanwhile had set out its reaction to the issue's general scheme, which had apparently been devised by Locke, though perhaps shaped in part by consultation with Kellogg. The staff ap-proved the first section in its entirety, had a small query about the second section, and said the third section was disproportionately long, as they were planning for the whole issue to run to eighty pages. The deadline of June 10 was suggested.[11]

Set to travel to Europe in the summer, as usual, Locke faced a considerable workload gathering the essays and communicating with the two dozen or so authors and Kellogg as well. But he completed the task by the deadline and before he sailed, and Kellogg was able to say: "You left everything in apple-pie shape and I can only wish you every success for the summer and thank you for all you have done." He added, in a handwritten note: "It's been a treat to work with you." The plans for the issue percolated in Locke's mind for at least several months prior to the June 10 deadline, so he was able to complete most of the work before he learned of his dismissal from Howard in the following spring, but some of the subsequent work, related to the conversion of the issue into the book, occurred even as Locke was fighting for his job.

In keeping with the editorial nature of the *Survey Graphic,* Locke intended to use some visual images in the issue. He turned to Winold Reiss to supply these, and he and Kellogg together approached Reiss. A Bavarian whose father had been a painter, Reiss came to America in 1913, already well trained in several forms of visual art. Most active as a magazine illustrator and before that as an interior decorator, he was also widely traveled to places such as Montana and Mexico, where his interest in folklore cross-fertilized his graphic style. Reiss's training had taken place in Munich, where he encountered not only Picasso's work but the theoretician Carl Einstein, whose *Negerplastik* (1915) was crucial in regarding African sculpture as more than fetishes. Even more than some French artists, Reiss absorbed many of the elements of modernism, but he concentrated on portraits rather than abstract paintings. His first show in America was mounted by the Anderson Galleries in New York in late 1922. Locke admired Reiss for his art, that "in idiom, technical treatment and objective social angle . . . [was] a bold iconoclastic break with the current traditions that have grown up about the Negro subject in America."[12]

Locke, with his customary erudition, further characterized the work of Reiss in the issue: "What Gauguin and his followers have done for the Far East and the work of Ufer and Blumenschein and the Taos school for the Pueblo and Indian, seems about to become for the Negro and Africa: in short, painting, the most local of the arts, in terms of its own limitation even, is achieving universality." In October 1924, Kellogg wrote to say that Reiss wanted to use Roland Hayes as a subject, and this would grace the cover of the issue. Hayes's great tenor voice had produced a sterling reputation for the artist, who was already in the midst of a concert career. Other artists were approached, and after the issue appeared it inspired Aaron Douglas, who contributed very important work for the book version; he later came to be recognized as one of the leading visual artists of the Renaissance. Locke's interest in African art, already quite developed through his contacts with German art historians and his friendship with Albert Barnes, would be transmitted to Douglas and thus amplified.[13]

Locke drafted a form letter to approach the contributors. It said in part: "The purpose is to get, if possible, a representative interpretation of our contemporary race development, and to use Harlem life both as setting and symbol." Symbolic representation was crucial for Locke, and it explains in large measure why he so admired Reiss's portraiture, for example, which had a certain abstract aspect that kept the idealizing elements from tipping over into sentimentality. Larger issues were present in the making of virtually every choice. What would count as "representative" in the literary works? How much attention would be paid to "setting"? By opening the issue with his essay titled simply, "Harlem," but also using the metaphor of "Harlem: The Mecca of the New Negro," Locke invoked a transnational context to help universalize the local details of the new American capital of the race.

Meanwhile, many pressing practical considerations caused delays in the actual publication. As early as November 11, 1924 Kellogg said a lack of funds meant the issue would be postponed until February, though he added that four-fifths of the articles were in hand and only six were still out or being revised. A month later there was another delay, this one explained as allowing for interest to build and advertising to be developed. Kellogg offered Locke a "free hand in the poetry section of Youth Speaks" and discussed the fee for the poems. Cullen's "Heritage" earned its author $40.00, since Cullen had planned to submit it in the *Opportunity* contest, where the first prize was that amount. Cullen also wanted extra for his other contributions, and Kellogg offered $10. This transaction led Locke to chastise Cullen, though the two men were able to maintain their friendship. Most important perhaps, Kellogg heard from the publisher Albert Boni about a republication agreement for the issue. In January 1925, Kellogg discussed plans for a gala dinner to launch the issue: "perhaps we could get poets and playwrights and others to contribute as you did at that little Civic Club dinner which set the ball rolling for this number." There was even some hope that Hayes would sing at the event. But three weeks later the plans were scrapped, partly because the dinner would have conflicted with the *Opportunity* awards dinner planned in April. Kellogg added another factor, however, which he also hoped was not decisive: the staff had questioned "what effect such an interracial dinner here in New York might have, especially in the South, on the fortunes of the *Survey* as a whole." Even now, the shadow of what Kallen fifteen years earlier had called the "cotton belters" was a consideration.

Throughout the months of early 1925 all sorts of problems, and some solutions, confronted Locke as the issue neared its publication date. Locke argued that the Reiss portrait of Hayes on the cover would double the sales. He also offered Kellogg "swift understanding in regard the dinner project," apparently disappointed but ready to acknowledge all the pressures at work. Locke was trying hard to persuade Eric Walrond to contribute but was meeting resistance. (Eventually, he was able to secure a short story for the book version.) Some people promised work, but only for later issues of the journal. Robert Moton, for example, whom Locke described as feeling "slighted," promised a piece on Tuskegee, and it too ended up in the book version only. In February, Kellogg relayed the news that Reiss would do portraits of Du Bois and Moton, and the issue would total one hundred pages, with thirty pages of ads. Hayes telegraphed his permission to have his portrait grace the cover. A portrait of a West African by Walter von Ruckterschell would simply be called "Young Africa," since, as Kellogg argued, most American blacks came from that part of the continent. Kellogg placed this portrait between Locke's essay and the sociological articles on Harlem. He also decided not to use the Moton portrait or any material on lynchings. The portrait by Reiss of Harold Jackman received his usual universalizing treatment; it was titled "A College Lad" and placed near the end of the issue. Kellogg asked Locke to sit for Reiss, which he did, and was rewarded with a handsome and flattering result that made him look quite young.

Shortly after the issue appeared, on 1 March, Kellogg wrote to tell Locke that the journal has received six hundred new subscriptions. Quickly a press run of twelve thousand copies was ordered. Albert Barnes took a thousand; another thousand went to George Peabody, who would distribute them to missionaries in Africa; and another thousand went to the Spingarns, activists who had help found the NAACP, to give away to students. All of this was Locke's idea. Eventually the issue sold more than thirty thousand copies. Locke clearly considered it a major statement about "race development," and he meant to use it in as much as an educational as a political context. The May issue of the journal contained two pages of "reviews," taken from a variety of prepublication responses. Marcus Garvey wrote that the "effort you have made to present partially the life of the race as it strikes you in Harlem is commendable"; this arrived by telegram from a penitentiary in Atlanta where Garvey was being held on federal charges. Clement Wood called the issue "a splendid thing." H. L. Mencken put in that it was "an excellent piece of work. It is full of valuable stuff." Waldo Frank called it "a most fertile, meaty, fascinating magazine," echoing the agricultural metaphor that lay behind much of his work. The *Nation* hailed it as "a notable contribution to the fact and philosophy of a democratic America." The success of the issue was striking, widespread, and quickly capitalized on in the form of a very successful book.

The changes from journal issue to trade book displayed positive and negative effects. Most positive was obviously the increase in the number of contributors, from just under two dozen to thirty-four, not counting the graphic artists. These in fact increased from but two to four, plus several photographs of African sculpture. One of the noticeable losses in the transformation was Locke's essay, "Harlem," which introduced the journal issue. It shows a striking familiarity with the locale, and as such testifies to his frequent visits there. A ripe sense of the socio-historical moment pervades the essay, which is only three pages long, but it shows Locke writing with considerable acuity. He attempts to reveal the secret that "distinguishes Harlem from the ghettos with which it is sometimes compared. The ghetto picture is that of a slowly dissolving mass, bound by ties of custom and culture and association, in the midst of a freer and more varied society. From the racial standpoint, our Harlems are themselves crucibles." Speaking of Harlem's diversity and its role as the "laboratory of a great-race welding," he added: "Each group has come with its own separate motives and for its own special ends, but their greatest experience has been the finding of one another. Proscription and prejudice have thrown these dissimilar elements into a common area of contact and interaction. Within this area, race sympathy and unity have determined a further fusing of sentiment and experience." Locke contends with the concept that animated much of his thought, namely, the quality and values of group experience, but he has also set this against the diasporic experience of black people and expounded the rudiments of a pluralistic sociological picture, so as to capture the "race contacts" explored earlier. His recourse to a semi-scientific vocabulary—"crucibles," "fusing," "laboratory"—invokes some of the modernist spirit in which he was operating.

Locke was aware of many issues that were being discussed in the black community at the time. One of the most discussed of these—perhaps the one that would last the longest, until the Renaissance had run its course and even beyond—was the issue of the "talented tenth," and moreover the question as to which forces resided in the masses and which were controlled by the "tenth." Locke and Du Bois held views in common on this issue, though there were nuanced differences as well. In particular, Locke believed in the social energies of the younger generation, the migrating peasant, and the "man furthest down." In another passage of the opening essay, Locke's picture of Harlem presents this mix in a populist vision:

> Harlem, I grant you, isn't typical—but it is significant, it is prophetic. No sane observer, however sympathetic to the new trend, would contend that the great masses are articulate as yet, but they stir, they move, they are more than physically restless. . . . But are we after all only reading into the stirrings of a sleeping giant the dreams of an agitator?

Locke then cites the "migrating peasant," the professionals, and the clergymen as showing in just what the movement of the "sleeping giant" consists. He concludes: "In a real sense it is the rank and file who are leading, and the leaders who are following. A transformed and transforming psychology permeates the masses." Some of this argument, and its democratic sentiment, survived, as it was incorporated into the later version of Locke's "Introduction," the long essay called "The New Negro," but it is not as brightly presented there, not as rife with expressive sentiment. In both the journal and the book version there is an essay by James Weldon Johnson, called "Harlem: The Culture Capital" that takes the place, so to speak, of Locke's version of "Harlem." Johnson's piece is filled with lively detail, but it lacks Locke's poetic, evocative quality.

———•—•———

The transformation of journal issue into book was fostered by Albert Boni, whose ideas about it Kellogg transmitted to Locke. "The scope of the book he [Boni] has in mind is not Harlem, but the cultural revival as a whole," Kellogg wrote. Locke answered quickly, favorably disposed, and offered to meet Boni and Kellogg for lunch in New York. The *Survey Graphic* meanwhile was paying Locke's expenses when he came to New York. Reiss, however, warned Kellogg that he had had experience with Boni and claimed "he was a difficult man to deal with and rather inclined to gouge." But Locke was ready to expand the scope—and the length—of the project. Boni wanted the book to sell for $4.50 and be double the length of the journal. Meanwhile Locke dealt with the issue of his dismissal from Howard. Kellogg wrote in July, from Quebec, to encourage Locke to keep fighting the administration but to consider locating in a city with a growing black population, such as Pittsburgh or Chicago, and work as an academic only part time. Locke spent time in the winter of 1925–26 traveling to various American cities, giving lectures and hearing the first responses to *The New Negro,* which appeared at the end of 1925.

The book version dropped three contributions from the journal; these were detailed sociological studies from Konrad Bercovici, Eunice Roberta Hunton, and Winthrop D. Lane, which probably originated from Kellogg's contacts. The Lane piece discussed prostitution and the numbers racket, so it may have been dropped because it did not speak to "race development" very effectively. Du Bois's "The Black Man Brings His Gifts," an ironic short story rather discordant in the context, was dropped, and for the book version, Locke substituted Du Bois's essay called "The Negro Mind Reaches Out," a broad internationally ranging essay reprinted from *Foreign Affairs.* Locke put this as the last essay of the volume, just before the bibliographies, and gave it the heading, "Worlds of Color." Making an emphatic point of reaching out beyond the locality of Harlem, it reflected Locke's interest in the broadest views of culture and its role in social and political advancement.

A notable expansion, in terms of emphasis and increased space, occurred between the two publications in the realm of cultural expression. Here Locke set up separate sections in the book version; fiction, poetry, drama, and music were given discrete headings under Part I. This part was titled "The Negro Renaissance" and also included Locke's long introductory essay and pieces by Barnes and Braithwaite, and a section called "The Negro Digs Up His Past." This section contained five items, most notably Locke's essay on "The Legacy of the Ancestral Arts" and Cullen's famous poem, "Heritage." Part II was called "The New Negro in a New World," a title that alluded both to America and to the putative society that was being born. All the material here represented a considerable increase over the journal issue, not only with Kellogg's essay and pieces by Locke's Howard colleague Kelly Miller and the sociologists E. Franklin Frazier and Elise McDougald but also with Melville Herskovits's expansion of his original offering. So the increase in cultural material was balanced by the additional socio-historical and political essays.

The emphasis on cultural expression testified to Locke's recent thinking as well as to his lifelong disposition toward a pluralistic approach to esthetic matters. The section on music, for example, included an essay on jazz by J. A. Rogers, carried over from the journal, along with two poems by Hughes that used jazz material and rhythms, as well as Claude McKay's "Negro Dancers." This balanced Locke's own essay on "The Negro Spirituals," which he described as "the most characteristic product of the race genius as yet in America," reproducing a few pages of sheet music in illustration for his argument. Locke was denigrated by many for his supposed elitist rejection of

DR. W. E. BURGHARDT DU BOIS

F I G . 6.1. Drawing of W. E. B. Du Bois by Winold Reiss. Locke used this in *The New Negro*. Moorland-Spingarn Research Center.

jazz, but it is clear from this section that his musical taste, though formed on classical lines and most gratified by the spirituals, appreciated other musical idioms. Indeed, Rogers, a journalist for the *Messenger*, began his essay by using one of Locke's favorite words, calling jazz a "marvel of paradox."

The visual arts were perhaps expanded most of all between the two versions. The book's border decorations were entrusted to Winold Reiss, the "Young Negro" portrait by Ruckterschell was retained, there was an illustration by Miguel Covarrubias, and there were also ten photographs from African art collections, seven from the Barnes alone. All this was greatly supplemented by the work of Aaron Douglas, who supplied almost a dozen illustrations and designs. Douglas came from Kansas City, at first on his way to study art in Paris, but he was convinced—by, among other things, his favorable impression of the *Survey Graphic* issue—to settle for a while in Harlem. There he wrote to Locke at Howard and said he would like to submit his work for Locke's judgment. His letter carried an emotional plea that echoed a figure from Booker T. Washington and probably appealed to Locke's idealism: "we must let down our buckets into our own souls where joy and pain, misery and sadness, still flows swift and deep and free, and drink until we are drunk as with an overpowering desire for expression." Influenced by Locke's preoccupation with the visual idioms of African art, Douglas contributed to the book's coherent stylistic tone. His decorative borders and abstract depictions of such subjects as "The Spirit of Africa" and "The Poet" were influenced by Locke's esthetics and also by Reiss, who served for a while as his mentor.

In Locke's *Survey Graphic* essay, "The Art of the Ancestors," which he expanded for the book as "The Legacy of the Ancestral Arts," he argued that African art "may very well be taken as the basis for a characteristic school of expression in the plastic and pictorial arts, and give to us again a renewed mastery of them. . . . Surely this art, once known and appreciated, can scarcely have less influence upon the blood descendants than upon those who inherit by tradition alone." Later readers would hear in this formulation an essentialism that had racialist overtones. But Locke was merely analogously applying his notion of race as a cultural construction rather than a scientific fact. Tradition was the word Locke used to establish a continuity of group experience and expression, though here it was modified to allow for historical interventions, negative and positive, such as the experience of centuries of slavery and the later "discovery" of African art by Europeans. By explicitly pointing to the book's graphic design with "The Legacy of the Ancestral Arts," which was one of his more important esthetic statements, Locke made one of his most prescriptive contributions to contemporary black culture. He presented the possibility partly in terms of cultural contact, partly in terms of a classical esthetic, and partly in terms of group expression and identity: "But what the Negro artist of today has most to gain from the arts of the forefathers is perhaps not cultural inspiration or technical innovations, but the lesson of a classic background, the lesson of discipline, of style, of technical control pushed to the limits of technical mastery." The "highly stylized art" of the African was an original endowment that "can be sufficiently augmented to express itself with equal power in more complex patterns and substance, [and] then the Negro may well become what some have predicted, the artist of American life" (NN, 256–58). Locke drew on the concepts of a Pan-African consciousness and was one of the first to argue that

African art, to be fully and correctly understood, must be seen in the context of its specific locale in Africa and in its role in the lives of those who produced it. But here he took the occasion of his editorship of *The New Negro,* and the pedagogic possibilities it offered, to advance a reconceptualization of how modern art worked when traditions could be made and remade by an act of the informed will. Locke built on his arguments here to develop his interest in the formative role of an African artistic spirit as a source of inspiration for contemporary African American art.

The fiction, poetry, and drama included in the book were also considerably richer and more polyvocal than that of the *Survey Graphic* issue. The drama was rather thin as a section, as Locke resorted to two essays—by Montgomery Gregory and Jessie Fauset—to bolster the single play, "Compromise," by Willis Richardson, who had had some of his earlier work produced by the Howard Players and was awarded the Amy Spingarn Prize earlier in the year. Gregory's piece was a well-informed history of black drama since Reconstruction. Fauset's essay was included at the insistence of Du Bois, who employed Fauset in the editorial office of the *Crisis;* he had told Charles Johnson that if she were not to be included in the book, he would withdraw his participation in the anthology. He also exchanged letters with Locke on the same point. Du Bois said: "[A] survey of Harlem would have many excuses for omitting any particular author; but a survey of the rise of the new Negro, particularly from the point of view of art and literature, which should omit Miss Fauset's work would be too glaring and would cause a great deal of criticism. Moreover, you must have a college bred woman there." Locke wrote on this letter: "Isn't this rich!! Confidential Locke"—but it is not clear to whom he showed it. He answered quite stiffly: "Evidently I did not sufficiently impress you in our last conversation of my agreement with your advice not to omit Miss Fauset from consideration. Your contingent reconsideration therefore offers no embarrassment further than that I cannot assure you quite definitely yet just what particular contribution of hers we shall request." If Locke were at all infuriated by Du Bois's high-handed approach, he appears to have sublimated his reaction into rather arch rhetoric.

In his reading of Fauset's essay, Locke displayed his editorial acumen as well as his frankness and esthetic positions. He and Fauset knew each other for years, dating back to their early life in Philadelphia. Jessie's brother, Arthur Huff Fauset, was one of Locke's closest friends and someone he constantly turned to for financial advice. Jessie, a very serious novelist and well connected with all of the Renaissance writers, prided herself on her role as Du Bois's editorial assistant at the *Crisis.* She worshipped Du Bois, and rumors circulated that they were involved in an affair. Fauset was of great help to Langston Hughes and others and was unstinting in her commitment to what she saw as talented writing. Her own work, in the tradition of the novel of manners, dealt with the black bourgeoisie and came in for a good deal of criticism from those who preferred the use of folk material or a gritty urban idiom. She and Locke treated each other with a mixture of wariness and overly stiff politeness. But when Locke received Fauset's essay he was unsparing in his reaction:

> The Gift of Laughter arrived,—and almost provoked tears. You certainly have been serious about it. Of course I could have given more of an idea of what I had in mind, but it was to be your essay. . . . You see a great many of us are joyous even if not socially happy, and even Dr. Du Bois regards this, rightly, I think,—and I apologize for the 'even'—it is only his reputation that is bitter, not his personality—as our great instrument of survival,—our emotional salvator—and perhaps one of our most valuable and conquering contributions.

Setting Du Bois's love of joyous laughter against Fauset's dour disposition rankled the novelist. Locke was not only chafing under Du Bois's insistence that Fauset be included in the anthology, there was also the question of the esthetic value and role of laughter in black art, since not only Du Bois but many others had identified it as one of the chief stylistic markers of black art. Here Locke talked to Fauset as more than her editor; he was in some way asserting his leadership in the Renaissance.[14]

Locke continued: "It almost seems as if you hadn't heard, seen, and enjoyed Shuffle Along, and Eliza, etc.," referring to the very popular musical revues of the day that had greatly expanded the audiences, black and white, for stage performances by blacks. "I shall never forget my first experience at seeing Bill Robinson dance, and I have followed dancing in Europe until I count myself a connoisseur," Locke went on, demonstrating his appreciation of both the high and popular forms of art. Referring to Bert Williams, he corrected Fauset by pointing out the way his art developed "the pantomimic resources of it all—talk about Bert as a pantomimic genius tied to the shack[l]es of the minstrel, if you wish—that is perfectly true, but the genius of pantomime was there." After making some specific suggestions about various edits, he asked Fauset to drop a negative paragraph about Reiss's drawings, as being "irrelevant to the subject under discussion." Then he concluded with this: "I didn't want to intrude a schoolmasterish note into the peace of your

FIG. 6.2. Jesse Fauset, Langston Hughes, and Zora Neale Hurston, Tuskegee, summer 1927, standing at the *Up From Slavery* memorial statue to Booker T. Washington. These three authors were often the subjects of Locke's public reviews and private reflections. Yale Collection of American Literature, Beinecke Rare Book and Manuscript Library.

vacation—I hope you enjoyed Great Barrington ever so, and I knew your carbons were in New York. But do give us a smile in the next <u>Gift of Laughter.</u> Just send additions—I will tack them on. And many thanks for the trouble." Even allowing for the difficulty of editing those one knows very well on a personal basis, such an approach to editorial control would often earn Locke a reputation as elitist and demanding. His opinions about all the arts, their histories of development and their esthetic values, were seldom equivocal.

Poetry was where Locke's knowledge of the talent and reputation of the younger poets, as well as his personal friendships, was most evident. Though some of the poets, still quite young, had already published in prominent journals, Locke displayed his commitment to the younger generation and his eye for talent. Eight poems by Cullen, nine by Hughes, and five by Claude McKay formed the bulk of the section. But there were poems by women, namely Anne Spencer, Angelina Grimke, and Georgia Johnson, whose Saturday night literary socials had probably entertained every poet represented in the collection. All this was rounded out by two poems by Toomer, an important James Weldon Johnson contribution, "The Creation," in the form of the sermon-poem he was to develop as one of the more striking examples of African American poetics, and a poem each by Arna Bontemps and Lewis Alexander, a student from Howard and an aspiring playwright. Cullen's lyrics were especially notable for their emphasis on sensuality, even though their graceful rhymes and controlled rhythms made them seem a bit placid to some readers. Hughes was represented by the poems he wrote before he completed his adaptation of jazz rhythms into his verse, but "The Negro Speaks of Rivers," "Dream Variation," and "I, Too" were all to become some of his most frequently quoted poems. Claude McKay's selection ranged over a wide spectrum of subjects and tones. His versification was as traditional as Cullen's, his attitudes as bracing as Hughes's.

One poem in particular became the subject of much commentary in later years, though less for its content than for its title. This was McKay's sonnet with a near Shakespearean rhyme scheme, bearing the original title of "White House." Locke felt the title too provocative, since the poem was built on barely controlled violent impulses:

> Oh I must search for wisdom every hour,
> Deep in my wrathful bosom sore and raw,
> And find it in the superhuman power
> To hold me to the letter of your law!
> Oh I must keep my heart inviolate
> Against the potent poison of your hate.

The speaker's urge to dissolve the social contract—to put it rather mildly—leads him to see himself as "sharp as steel with discontent," and the poem offers no apologies for its wrath nor extenuation for the poison of white supremacy. Directing this set of attitudes at the president was more than Locke felt would be acceptable. But by pluralizing the title, the anger would diffuse, to some extent; it would also invoke the whited sepulchers of the biblical metaphor. However, Locke made the change without notifying McKay ahead of time and ran the poem as "White Houses" in both the journal and the anthology. It proved to be an explosive decision.

Locke and McKay had known each other for a few years before the *Survey Graphic* issue and *The New Negro* appeared. Their friendship was fairly solid prior to the incident with "White Houses" and was able to continue even afterwards. But at the moment, McKay was incensed. He barked at Locke in a letter of August 1, 1926 that the change in title changed the meaning of the poem and made it read as if the speaker envied bourgeois respectability. McKay insisted that with the change, "the poem immediately becomes cheap, flat Afro-American propaganda." This overstates the case, yet to tighten the screw even more he told Locke that he dropped "Black Dancer"— one of the other poems Locke had chosen for the anthology—from his collection, *Harlem Shadows,* because it was not up to the level of his best work. Clearly the mercurial McKay was giving free rein to his temper. In another letter ten months later, he picked up the cudgel again. The incident, he told Locke, had "destroy[ed] every vestige of intellectual and fraternal understanding that may have existed between us." He went on to aver that he "did not want to splash about in the hog-water of Negro journalism," and that as far as Locke went, he could "keep [his] opinion and, forgive me but, I don't care a damn for it." The irony is that "White Houses," regardless of its title, is perhaps the most outspoken piece in the anthology, though not perhaps as fierce as "If We Must Die" ("Like men we'll face the murderous, cowardly pack,/ Pressed to the wall, dying, but fighting back"), which was written by McKay in the heat of the lynchings of 1919.[15]

McKay's friendship with Locke began in the spring of 1924. They shared an interest in high art, and both had become familiar with the homosexual community in Berlin. He once remarked to Locke that he had gone "around to all sorts of places" there, but "had fewer affairs than you imagine." In March 1925, writing from a Mediterranean port, he told Locke about visiting a "sordid" place in Paris, worse than any place they knew in Berlin. "I have small rough commonplace hangouts like these around here in Toulon," he added. He also asked Locke to "Give him [Langston] my fraternal and professional love." Sharing with Locke that he was undergoing treatment for venereal disease, he spoke of how he "must take treatment at intervals for about a year or two for the germs in the blood." McKay thus began their friendship on a note that was both brusque and intimate, saying that "we have so much in common." They were to discuss, or perhaps to argue over, questions of esthetic values and black leadership for fifteen years, though with decreasing frequency.

Born in 1889 in Jamaica and educated there, McKay was much traveled, and he liked the world of seamen and working-class neighborhoods. He often expressed the feeling that he was not African American, stressing instead his Caribbean roots. At the same time he cultivated many friends in white literary circles, working for a time with Max Eastman on the *Masses* and constantly involving himself with left-wing causes and personalities. His esthetic, which produced some of the best poetry of the Renaissance and several novels as well, was a fluctuating balance between a defense of pure estheticism and an impulse to speak with satiric bile. He tried to keep this tension under control; he once told Locke: "Although I have strong social opinion I cannot mix up art and racial propaganda." In May 1924, shortly after they first met, he wrote to ask Locke "why I never heard from you," though apparently their letters crossed in the mail. But immediately he offered his opinion on matters artistic and social: chiding Locke for "diffuse emotion," he attacked all those who have lost "the taste for any rich morsel of life's sensations." Any call for total hedonism, however, must be kept in check; "I must not forget that emotionally the artist is a self-protective animal." He often opined about the role and status of the artist. In complaining to Locke that Jesse Fauset "made light of discrimination against Negroes in America," he claimed that "why, just a little prejudice has killed and enervated artists among the white races. The nerves of Negroes are not made of wire." In a letter of September 22, 1924 advising Locke to seek psychoanalysis for his "neurasthenia," he said of his friends that "the best sort are the casual aristocrats of the world."[16]

By October 1924, he first heard about Locke's selection of his poems for the *Survey Graphic* issue and especially about Locke's reluctance to publish "Mulatto," and he was willing to show Locke his aggressive side: "I am suicidally frank. . . . [Y]our letter has angered me—[it shows] a playing safe attitude—the ultimate reward of which are dry husks and ashes! . . . It isn't the 'Survey' that hasn't guts enough. It is you." Then, as usual, McKay broadens the attack: "No wonder [Marcus] Garvey remains strong despite his glaring defects. When Negro intellectuals like you take such a weak line! . . . And if you do publish any of the other poems and leave out 'Mulatto' after this protest you may count upon me as your intellectual enemy for life!" McKay finished off by calling Locke a "dyed-in-the-wool pussy footing professor." Locke replied coolly: "Glad to accept your ultimatum favorably after conference with Mr. Kellogg," and he indicated that the poem would be published in *Survey Graphic* along with two others. However, "Mulatto" did not appear, in either the journal or book version. When, writing from Europe in March 1925, McKay first heard that "Mulatto" had been dropped for certain, he told Locke: "But how can I fight you from way over here? . . . better let it be as it is." McKay would always impress his friends as combative, and his touchiness was in evidence when matters of art or politics were concerned. He and Locke could seem at times antipodal.

The two men may be quaintly described as agreeing to disagree, though McKay's vituperation and Locke's stagy gentility showed through in their correspondence. In a much later, undated letter McKay told Locke that he "liked extremely [Locke's] critique of A Long Way From Home," McKay's autobiography, which appeared in 1937, "even though it roasted me, because you kept it where it belongs—on the intellectual level." He also added that he himself always kept the personal and intellectual levels separate, and that is why "so many friends do not understand me." But McKay did not always escape from a stereotyped view of Locke, or at least Locke's writing about literature. For, as Locke's introduction to the *Survey Graphic*'s selection of poems, later printed as "Negro Youth Speaks" in *The New Negro*, put it:

> Not all the new art is in the field of pure art values. There is poetry of sturdy social protest, and fiction of calm dispassionate social analysis. But reason and realism have cured us of sentimentality: instead of the wail and appeal, there is challenge and indictment. Satire is just beneath the surface of our latest prose, and tonic irony has come into our poetic wells. These are good medicines for the common mind, for us they are necessary antidotes against social poison.

This passage shows that Locke, though committed to discipline and high standards, did not favor an art of completely otherworldly themes or subjects.

When he came to the fiction in his anthology, Locke chose again with an eye to the variety that characterized his inclusive taste. The two selections from Toomer's *Cane* were obviously full of the evocation of the place and soil of the American South, whereas Bruce Nugent's story, "Sahdji," was written in a very experimental stream of consciousness technique and treated of an African locale. Rudolph Fisher's two stories traced the collision of the folk mentality and modern chaos and did much to add to the urban myths of Harlem. John Matthews's "Fog" won first prize in *Opportunity*'s contest in 1925; it used straightforward realism. "Spunk," which won the second prize, was Zora Neale Hurston's contribution, drawing on the folkloric tradition which she would soon encounter in her studies at Columbia with Franz Boas and would later explore in her own ethnographic studies. She had previously been Locke's student at Howard, and he was one of her early supporters, seeing that her work was published in the university's literary magazine. Eric

Walrond, then the business manager at *Opportunity,* used his origins in British Guiana to craft a story set in the tropics that mixed realism and poetic prose to fresh effect. All in all, the fiction section represented a talented and impressive collection of narrative voices, and one that Locke presumably appreciated for its authors' "calm dispassionate social analysis" as well as their artistic skill.

The social and political essays in *The New Negro* evidenced the same variety of viewpoint and style as did the sections on cultural and artistic matters. The sociology of James Weldon Johnson's "Harlem," carried over from the *Survey Graphic,* was extended into pieces on Durham, North Carolina, by E. Franklin Frazier and the tropics by W. A. Domingo. Kellogg and Charles S. Johnson contributed historically inflected studies of recent developments in black societies. Two pieces on black universities, one by Kelly Miller on Howard and the other on Hampton-Tuskegee by Robert Moton, gave the anthology an educational direction that clearly reflected Locke's pedagogic predilections. Locke grouped three essays in a subsection called "The Negro and American Tradition": these were by Melville Herskovits, Walter White, and Elise Johnson McDougald, the latter focused on "Negro Womanhood." The anthology was rounded off with Du Bois's contribution, set in its own subsection, titled "Worlds of Color." Called "The Negro Mind Reaches Out," it ended with the famous claim that the problem of the "20th century [is] the Problem of the Color Line." Du Bois indicated this was a claim he first made in 1899; Locke felt the piece, reprinted from *Foreign Affairs,* where it had appeared a few years earlier, was warmed-over material. But its scope and its powerful Pan-African viewpoint gave to the Harlem Renaissance the largest context imaginable and demonstrated how different from the *Survey Graphic* issue was *The New Negro,* a difference Locke had crafted in just a matter of months.

Du Bois's essay rehearsed his arguments that the problem of the color line and the problem of labor were eventually the same. Giving a detailed account of his travels in Africa, he set out a damning picture of how imperialism—of the French, Belgian, German, and English varieties—was now facing a "new group of groups," as millions of black people throughout the world were moving toward a unified vision. Du Bois reached his conclusions as his thought in the middle 1920s turned more and more in a Marxist direction, seeing the exploitation of people through wage slavery as the root of all of the modern world's ills. It was with the critique of imperialism as a lens that this truth could be viewed in the sharpest focus. Locke was not of the same mind, or rather, though he had opposed imperialism as early as his Oxford years and pointed to its depredations in his lectures on race, he never accepted the type of radical social solutions Du Bois increasingly favored.

The two men had started on a friendly basis, and Du Bois invited Locke to attend with him the Pan-African Congress in London in 1924 or the one in Lisbon in 1925, though Locke declined. At this time Du Bois dedicated a great deal of time and energy organizing these congresses and building the Pan-African movement. He offered to read a paper of Locke's at one of the meetings if he could not attend. Locke did not attend, but a year later, in November 1924, Du Bois told Locke that "Claude McKay writes . . . that you had an interview with Ras Tafari. Would you like to write an account of it for the CRISIS." Perhaps it was Locke's failure to give Du Bois a paper for the movement that led him to complain in confidence to Roscoe Conkling Bruce that Locke "has shown repeatedly a nasty attitude towards The Crisis, and I am through." Perhaps Locke felt his first obligation was to *Opportunity* and Charles S. Johnson, with whom he got on much better. Du Bois never allowed his discomfort with Locke to obliterate his awareness of the younger man's values, however. In 1927, Du Bois wrote to Jesse Moorland, apparently in response to a request for a recommendation about Locke: "While I have known Mr. Locke for sometime, he is not a particularly close friend. I have not always agreed with him. . . . Locke is by long odds the best trained man among the younger American Negroes." Though Du Bois co-authored a piece with Locke about the "younger" generation, it was clear in different and subtle ways that there was a generational divide between the two men; Du Bois was born almost twenty years before Locke. That divide had other causes as well as a difference in age, and its breadth shifted from time to time, and for a variety of reasons, but it never ceased to be.[17]

———•———

Locke's contribution to the Renaissance extended beyond his critical eye and editorial discipline, for he included his own introduction to the anthology that many saw as the herald of the movement. This introduction was the eponymous essay, "The New Negro," and it is perhaps Locke's finest piece of writing, combining the polished style of an essay and the forceful argument of a manifesto. Using the tutelary spirit of an unfolding of the human spirit, the sort of unbridled faith Locke frequently expressed in the human spirit to move toward the universal, and calling on his own immensely broad reading, Locke was able to capture a tone that was at once celebratory, sober, a bit homiletic, and finally self-aware and self-critical in a way that character-ized his best talents. Most great political writing is optative, and it is finally this mood that dominates in the essay. Locke balances the energy of the im-mediate past with the horizon-scanning eye of the future to depict a complex sense of "race development." His voice is by turns subtle and direct, and at times it has an edge, even an urgency, as he sets about replacing one kind of discourse with another: "The popular melodrama has about played itself out, and it is time to scrap the fictions, garret the bogeys and settle down to a realistic facing of facts."

The opening paragraph sets the terms by which Locke will accomplish his reading of the moment and his vision for the future. The social phenom-enon of the New Negro, by virtue of its newness, is not subject to easy catego-rization; it "simply cannot be swathed in . . . formulae." An unbridled hope is sounded, and what had been identified as the "Negro problem," by which the people so referred to were "more of a formula than . . . human being[s]," has been transformed, and their spirit is enlivened. "For the younger genera-tion is vibrant with a new psychology; the new spirit is awake in the masses, and under the very eyes of the professional observers is transforming what has been a perennial problem into the progressive phases of contemporary Negro life" (NN, 3). The vocabulary here—of unseen spirit being revealed and transformed—allows Locke to conceptualize the movement that he is both describing and attempting to call into existence. To further this argu-ment, he steps into the streams of recent history and tells of the "Old Ne-gro" and that group's slow progress toward "self-understanding," the state that matters most to Locke and to the essay. The burgeoning reality of self-respecting, assertive African Americans was a concomitant manifestation of, or at least a pleasing expression of, Locke's ethics of self-realization.[18]

Locke draws on Du Bois's idea of the "talented tenth," though he re-phrases it as "the thinking few," to explain the forward movement of the group. But this elite notion gains force because it operates inside the causal phenomena of mass migration, the Ku Klux Klan, and the boll-weevil, all important factors, but not sufficient to explain the changes that are occur-ring. That explanation needs to add "a new vision of opportunity, of social and economic freedom, of a spirit to seize, even in the face of an extortion-ate and heavy toll, a chance for the improvement of conditions." Locke then uses much of his essay on Harlem from the *Survey Graphic* to give material evidence for these "conditions" and their improvement. Shifting to the use of a "civilization type," such as he worked out in his race lectures, drawing on

the sociology of Simmel, satisfies the need to draw the conjoining lines between individual and group expression. "The American mind must reckon
with a fundamentally changed Negro." These changes involve a new group
consciousness and even a new way of being conscious of one's place and function within the group. "The Negro too, for his part, has idols of the tribe to
smash . . . the Negro . . . has too often unnecessarily excused himself because
of the way he has been treated. The intelligent Negro of to-day is resolved not
to make discrimination an extenuation of his shortcomings in performance,
individual or collective; he is trying to hold himself at par, neither inflated by
sentimental allowances nor depreciated by current social discounts." Locke
then sounds the urgent call: "For this he must know himself and be known
for precisely what he is . . . " (NN, 8). Self-knowledge shapes and is shaped
by a knowledge of one's group. The sort of knowledge Locke refers to in this
passage arises from the self-expression that culture allows and shapes. The
keys sounded in the essay's hymn to possibility are both social and esthetic.
Locke changes the social key into another, national frame of harmony.

For Locke, the responsiveness of the New Negro to his own situation is
"an augury of a new democracy in American culture." Locke does not refer
to the group of white writers, such as Van Wyck Brooks, Lewis Mumford,
Waldo Frank, and the then deceased Randolph Bourne, and their consuming
interest in establishing an indigenous national culture, freed at last from the
Old World values, but clearly Locke knew of their existence and was at least
distantly sympathetic to their goals. The larger, containing frame of modern
American culture, and its then current interest in artistic self-assertiveness,
had its role to play in the destiny of the New Negro. Not only is American
democracy a context for the New Negro but so is the "increasing group who
affiliate with radical and liberal movements." Here he rather covertly refers
to Garvey's movement, among others, and sees it as more of a warning than
a solution. "Harlem's quixotic radicalisms call for their ounce of democracy
to-day lest to-morrow they be beyond cure." Reaching back to his essay on
the American temperament, Locke pursues the framework of American
nationalism, but as with the example of Garvey, he does not see "quixotic"
panaceas, even through the lens of American exceptionalism: "The Negro
mind reaches out as yet to nothing but American wants, American ideas. But
this forced attempt to build his Americanism on race values is a unique social
experiment, and its ultimate success is impossible except through the fullest
sharing of American culture and institutions. There should be no delusion
about this. . . . " The New Negro consciousness leads to a "constructive effort
to build the obstructions in the stream of his progress into an efficient dam

of social energy and power." But not every movement is efficient, as "Democracy itself is obstructed and stagnated to the extent that any of its channels are closed. Indeed they cannot be selectively closed. So the choice is not between one way for the Negro and another way for the rest, but between American institutions frustrated on the one hand and American ideals progressively fulfilled and realized on the other" (NN, 11–12). Locke joins a long line of prophetic commentators on American idealism, calling the nation back to its highest values. What he adds to that line in this particular essay is an ironic—but altogether serious—revisioning of the New Negro's embrace of racialism and a conversion of it into a way to gather "social energy and power." Locke's fondness for paradox is here melded with one of the central ideas of his philosophy. Difference need not be a cause of ostracism or weakness; it can serve to create a pluralistic strength.

Locke never blinks at the "great discrepancy between the American social creed and the American social practice," identifying one strategy of combating this discrepancy as "the simple expedient of fighting prejudice by mental passive resistance, in other words by trying to ignore it." This sounds like Locke speaking out of personal experience, but it is important that he goes on to say "this manna may perhaps be effective, but the masses cannot thrive upon it." For the masses Locke offers something else. It is a recognition, an optative one to be sure, that Negroes can "act . . . as the advance-guard of the African peoples in their contact with Twentieth Century civilization." Balancing American nationalism with an international, Pan-African, context, Locke greatly complicates his vision. "As a world phenomenon this wider race consciousness is a different thing from the much asserted rising tide of color." Here he refers to the virulent theories of men like Lothrop Stoddard, whose book *The Rising Tide of Color,* was part of an outpouring of alarmist racist tracts in the 1920s. Having decided to expand the focus from the *Survey Graphic* issue to the anthology, from Harlem to the development of the entire racial group, Locke readjusts his thoughts to consider a mass movement and a worldwide scale.

Having earlier evoked the parallel between Harlem and the role of Dublin and Prague in the New Ireland and New Czechoslovakia movements, respectively, Locke builds on the imagery of nineteenth-century romantic nationalism—strongly motivated by the right of self-determination and Herder's concept of the role of folk culture in the shaping of national consciousness—to counteract this racist literature. By pointing to a different tide, Locke reaches back to his earlier interest in the cosmopolitan ideal that at once grounds identity in a group existence and reaches beyond national boundaries to a more universal perspective. "Harlem . . . is the home of the Negro's 'Zionism.' . . . In terms of the race question as a world problem, the Negro mind has leapt, so to speak, upon the parapets of prejudice and extended its cramped horizons" (NN, 14). Merging an image of romantic nationalism with the American concept of the pluralistic gathering of voices and values, Locke points to the power of an informed, well-read body politic and its foundation in the Enlightenment's trust in the corrective power of reason as advanced through the printed word.

Then, drawing upon his experience with the opening of Tut-ankh-amen's tomb and his recently developed work in the field of African art, Locke enlarges the frame of his thought: "Garveyism may be a transient, if spectacular phenomenon, but the possible role of the American Negro in the future development of Africa is one of the most constructive and universally helpful missions that any modern people can lay claim to." Locke's Pan-African interest thus rounds out his essay, but only once it has been given a cultural cast. "The especially cultural recognition they [talented Negro artists] win should in turn prove the key to that revaluation of the Negro which must precede or accompany any considerable further betterment of race relationships." Then the essay concludes with high, but conditional, optimism:

> No one who understandingly faces the situation with its substantial accomplishment or views the new scene with its still more abundant promise can be entirely without hope. And certainly, if in our lifetime the Negro should not be able to celebrate his full initiation into American democracy, he can at least, on the warrant of these things, celebrate the attainment of a significant and satisfying new phase of group development, and with it a spiritual Coming of Age. (NN, 16)

The note of pragmatic caution conditions, but does not obscure, the faith Locke had in his project. The warranty here is, of course, embodied in these "things" of culture and thought, the very contents of *The New Negro*.

When Locke sent off the manuscript for *The New Negro* to Albert Boni at the end of August 1925, he said: "I feel a very great responsibility about this book—it isn't as if it were a personal matter. Being racial, it is more delicate and difficult." Also around this time he was prevented from coming to New

York because of the difficulties in his position at Howard. He explained to Boni that this had caused some errors in the bibliography of *The New Negro,* which seemed to be entirely the work of Locke's own hand. Boni, ever the salesman, wanted Locke to be interviewed by New York City newspapers, but apparently this did not happen. Boni also saw to it that the anthology was accompanied with a brochure, with several blurbs included. One from Du Bois, perhaps reflecting his somewhat clenched participation in the project, read: "A certain tolerance and oneness of general aim among us . . . makes this book possible." Another, less equivocal, came from James Weldon Johnson: "Because it shatters traditions and smashes stereotypes, it comes in the nature of a flashing revelation. . . . There is not a more vitally important book for Americans now offered to the public." By the end of 1930, the book had sold over 4,300 copies, at a retail price of $5.00.

The Modern Quarterly ran a review by Howard Odum in its February 1926 issue. It was perhaps one of the best evaluations: "I know of no better approach to a newer outlook for the rediscovery of the Negro than such a volume. . . . It is a work of art." In the same issue, Charles S. Johnson, while identifying himself as one of the volume's contributors, said: "It is . . . a cultural symphony. This integration has been accomplished by Dr. Alain Locke, versatile, scholarly, and altogether charming . . . expressing himself in a language beautifully limpid and almost epigrammatic in its phraseology." An anonymous note in *The Dial* said the book was "well edited and superbly produced." H. L. Mencken, hardly a liberal voice, opined in the *American Mercury* that "this book . . . is a phenomenon of immense significance." He then went on, with some surprise, to characterize the contributors: "They show no sign of being sorry that they are Negroes; they take a fierce sort of pride in it." Carl Van Vechten, who had rejected an offer to contribute, conveyed by Langston Hughes from Locke, claimed in the *New York Herald Tribune* that it was "indeed a remarkable book." The *New York Times Book Review* noted, somewhat cryptically: "It is a book of surprises."

While the reviews of *The New Negro* were generally positive, there were also some exceptions. Ernest Boyd in the *Independent* offered an assessment that claimed, "as a revelation of a great renaissance of negro art and literature it is no more convincing than the momentary vogue of the 'Charleston.'" Herbert Seligman, in the *New York Sun,* complained that Locke "writes with more facility than authority." Though the anthology's major measure of success was the amount of interest it created in the Renaissance, that interest in turn did not always elicit a positive note. Sometimes the charge was that the

Renaissance was out of touch with ordinary people; sometimes that it was too disrespectful of the past. Langston Hughes, in *The Big Sea,* retrospectively quipped: "The ordinary Negroes hadn't heard of the Negro Renaissance. And if they had, it hadn't raised their wages any." The *Pittsburgh Courier,* a pivotal African American newspaper for disseminating community news, ran a front-page piece in March 1927 in which Hubert Harrison attacked not so much *The New Negro* as the entire Renaissance:

> This "Negro literary renaissance" has its existence at present only in the noxious night life of the Greenwich village neurotics who invented it, not for the black brothers' profit but for their own. Nor do their darker dupes stand on any safer ground. If anyone, in public, should care to pick an decade between 1850 and 1910 I will undertake to present from the Negroes of that decade as many writers and (with Schomburg to back me) as many lines of literary and artistic endeavor as he can show for this decade.

Locke, of course, was aware of the relation between high culture and the masses, as his introductory essay showed, and he certainly believed in the values of preserving, and learning from, the Negro writers of preceding decades. But the *New York World* could say, with some loosely founded optimism, that "art is slowly but surely knitting a close kinship between white and colored America." The debate was not always on a high philosophical level.

However, Paul Kellogg was especially exercised by one review and told Locke about what "Dr. Du Bois wrote [in the *Crisis*] of the New Negro, in which he dug up a cat, 13 years dead, to throw at me. His version of the same was thoroughly distorted; but I am sorry that your book got some of the missile he aimed at me." The reference here is to an incident in 1914, related by Du Bois in his January 1926 *Crisis* review, when A. G. Dill, the business manager of the *Crisis,* was at a dinner with Kellogg, who told him that the idea of full social rights for the Negro was not something the *Survey* could advocate. But Du Bois went on in the review to argue about *The New Negro:*

> With one point alone do I differ with the Editor. Mr. Locke has newly been seized with the idea that Beauty rather than Propaganda should be the object of Negro literature and art. His book proves the falseness of this thesis. . . . [I]f Mr. Locke's thesis is insisted on too much it is going to turn the Negro renaissance into decadence.

In this review Du Bois announced his views on art and the privileged realm of the esthetic, views that would eventually be sharply opposed by Locke, and others, in one of the central debates of the Renaissance.

In the case of Du Bois's criticism, the debate took on a somewhat more philosophical cast. He decided, after his own review of *The New Negro,* to continue with the questions of propaganda and decadence, which were awkwardly parallel terms for didactic and autotelic art. The best way to explore this, Du Bois felt, was to run a symposium in several consecutive issues of the *Crisis* that would allow people to air their views. The symposium began in March 1926 and ended with a capstone essay, setting out Du Bois's own opinions, that appeared in the October issue. This essay was entitled "Criteria of Negro Art," and its strident oratory—he had delivered the essay as a speech at the NAACP conference in Chicago in June 1926—was to serve as a watershed in the development of Du Bois's esthetic philosophy.[19] Somewhat ironically, the questions for the symposium were framed by Carl Van Vechten, whose own novel *Nigger Heaven* (1926) scandalized many and would be very negatively assessed by Du Bois himself in the December *Crisis.* The symposium contained virtually every position that could be held about the central question: should literature produced by Negroes be devoted to racial uplift or should it proceed to present all aspects of Negro life in any way the individual writer chose?

This central question was cast into several topics in the symposium—such as the obligations of publishers to do more than reflect stereotypes and the need for black fiction to include stories about all the classes—and this may have led to the great variety of responses. Some respondents, however, put a very subjective spin on the issues. Hughes, for example, was brief and said little beyond why bother, since artists would do what they felt they must do. (His landmark essay, "The Negro Artist and the Racial Mountain," made a similar point more eloquently.) Van Vechten was waggish, urging black writers to take up decadent or jazzy material before white writers beat them to it. Mencken suggested sardonically that black writers should put aside their sensitivity in the face of white portrayals of their race and turn the tables by satirizing whites. Vachel Lindsay chided white publishers for rejecting black fiction about the educated classes, but Benjamin Brawley a bit too soberly said that publishing had to be run on commercial principles.

Du Bois's essay contained several claims, and it has been read largely as a clarion call for the propaganda role in art. While it contains a great deal of anger at the prevailing and persistent racism of the society, it also has a commitment to a high and disinterested esthetic at its core. While admitting that he may be "naturally too suspicious," he goes on to give instances of where racial prejudice has caused Negro writing to be undervalued and even unpublished. It is his strong sense of the need for equity that comes across in the main point of the essay:

> Thus all art is propaganda and ever must be, despite the wailing of the purists. I stand in utter shamelessness and say that whatever art I have for writing has been used always for propaganda for gaining the right of black folk to love and enjoy. I do not care a damn for any art that is not used for propaganda. But I do care when propaganda is confined to one side while the other side is stripped and silent.

So intense is Du Bois's tone that the last image here evokes memories of lynching, and Du Bois is not about to stop and make fine distinctions between his nonfiction prose and his novels, which had a didactic aspect in any case. Later he says the same thing about the two sides more clearly: "[I]t is not the positive propaganda of people who believe white blood is divine, infallible and holy to which I object. It is the denial of a similar right of propaganda to those who believe black blood human, lovable, and inspired with new ideals for the world." The polemic tends to suggest all writing by whites is based on racial supremacy, while all that by blacks is built out of an idealizing humanism. Locke would differ from the implications here, but he felt that he had to answer Du Bois on the question of "propaganda."

It was not until late in 1928 that Locke responded fully to the issue, in an essay entitled "Art or Propaganda?" Two other essays took up the issue closer in time to the *Crisis* symposium: "Our Little Renaissance," printed in a collection of pieces edited by Charles S. Johnson in 1927, and "Beauty Instead of Ashes," which appeared in the *Nation* in April 1928.[20] The three taken together form a coherent poetics. In the *Nation* piece Locke argued that "most Negro artists would repudiate their own art program if it were presented as a reformer's duty or a prophet's mission, and to the extent that they were true artists be quite justified." White writers were portraying Negro subjects, and "we are glad that Negro life is an artistic province free to everyone." Not content to proffer a generalization, Locke names both those white and Negro writers who have "at last dug down to richer treasure" beneath the earlier forms of folk and genre depictions. Van Vechten's *Nigger Heaven* is praised as "a studied but brilliant novel of manners," and the radically experimental work in *FIRE!!* is singled out as the work of "Negro artists

[who] as modernists have the same slant and interest" in the "contemporary love for strong local color." One image of Locke, based on rumor and second-hand impressions, charged him with being unable to appreciate the more experimental literature of the Renaissance period, but this essay alone corrects that view.

"Beauty Instead of Ashes" is one of Locke's fullest and most advanced statements of his esthetics. He and Du Bois were separated by a generation and by temperament, and Locke often wrote his cultural criticism out of a fuller commitment to the principles of modernism than those embraced by Du Bois. Directly invoking the historical context of modernist art, Locke not only introduces such standard modernist topics as the "modern recoil from the machine" and the "reaction against oversophistication" but also reaches back to a Romantic understanding of how folk culture gives vitality to modern art, though modern art "may not perpetuate [it] in readily recognizable form." Central to his esthetic at this time is his belief that "the folk temperament raised to the levels of conscious art promises more originality and beauty than any assumed or imitated class or national or clique psychology available." The folk spirit provides art with its universality. Locke sees the use of folk temperament as something that can be tied to the modernist spirit by the artistic work of the race temperament, thus strengthening all three elements. He says of the latter: "It stands today . . . in the position of the German temperament in Herder's day. There is only one way for it to get any further—to find genius of the first order to give it final definiteness of outline and animate it with creative universality." Locke's idea of esthetic experience is a dynamic culmination or, in Dewey's terms, a consummatory experience.

In his 1927 essay, "Our Little Renaissance," Locke proposed that "the time has come for some sort of critical appraisal" of the movement that he described as already "much-heralded." He continued to have Du Bois and the *Crisis* symposium in mind when he argued: "Overt propaganda now is as exceptional as it used to be typical. The acceptance of race is steadily becoming less rhetorical, and more instinctively taken for granted." In "Art and Propaganda" he even more directly addressed Du Bois : "Art in the best sense is rooted in self-expression and whether naive or sophisticated is self-contained. In our spiritual growth genius and talent must more and more choose the role of group expression, or even at times the role of free individualistic expression,—in a word must choose art and put aside propaganda." This essay launched and defined the artistic goals of a new magazine, *Harlem,* which did not survive for very long. Locke wanted to make sure that his "espousal of art thus becomes no mere idle acceptance of 'art-for-art's sake' or cultivation of the last decadences of the overcivilized, but rather a deep realization of the fundamental purpose of art and of its function as a tap root of vigorous, flourishing living." This formulation led Locke to say what he felt should take the place of propaganda: "We need, I suppose in addition to art, some substitute for propaganda. . . . Surely we must take some cognizance of the fact that we live at the center of a social problem. Propaganda . . . nurtured some form of serious social discussion. . . . [But] the difficulty and shortcoming of propaganda is its partisanship. It is one-sided and often pre-judging" (CTAL, 27–28). He goes on to say that we need skepticism and dissent and criticism to escape the threat of conformity. Concluding this brief manifesto, he says he does not want to "remain at [a] negative pole" and imagines that after Beauty, Truth can enter the Renaissance. Such a hope may not be premature, "for eventually it [Truth] must come and if we can accomplish that, instead of having to hang our prophets, we can silence them or change their lamentations to song with a Great Fulfillment." The image of silence here may reach back to the passage of Du Bois in which he pictured the Negro artist as "stripped and silent." For Locke the silencing of the prophets could be transformed into the singing of the poets.

These essays on the role of race temperament and the folk spirit in modern art were direct responses to Du Bois's rather stern and authoritarian views. Locke's bid to be a race leader in this period of his life was obviously grounded on his editing of *The New Negro,* and he acted as if his success with this book gave him authority as a critic in terms he had not previously enjoyed. The edited volume not only spoke to his intellectual breadth, but it showed that his pluralistic approach to cultural questions was an avenue that might lead to a deeper understanding of how to address the race "problem." Though an anthology, *The New Negro* helped establish Locke at or near the center of African American culture and esthetics. His own commitment to diversity and polyvocalism would not allow anyone to claim that his or her trajectory or stance epitomized all of African American experience. Still, his vision and his cultural criticism involved many of the major strains and issues awakened by the Renaissance. Part of his new stance rested on the belief that the race issue could best be faced by assuming that it had ceased to be a problem, or at least was not a problem in the older terms. Instead of seeing the Negro as a "problem," Locke's cultural work was meant to grant the individuals of the group a measure of agency, that is, the means and will to achieve their own identities and purposes. Instead of being the end product of someone else's social beliefs, or existing only through identification according to a fixed list of characteristics, the New Negro would be able to achieve autonomy. Such a redefining of the racial experience would allow Negroes greater scope and authority. But there remained much to be done with Locke's own newly acquired scope and authority. The time away from Howard was energetically put to use, and the latter half of the 1920s was to be one of the most productive of Locke's long career.

CHAPTER SEVEN

After *The New Negro*

The Renaissance saw the flourishing of many talents, creative and critical, among black writers. With this flourishing came ambition and disputes, and the questions of group values often took on a personal cast. The personal politics of the Renaissance deeply involved Locke; indeed, many felt he was exacerbating the situation, and not just with Du Bois. Some black leaders, in what would be seen as the older generation—people such as Charles Johnson, Walter White, James Weldon Johnson, and others—had established friendships with people in the white publishing world. Some guarded this access closely, while others used it generously. The Renaissance is often discussed as a history of publication, for it impressed many simply because of the rise in the number of books published during the latter 1920s. Also, the awards given by *Opportunity* and the *Crisis* both generated publicity for the younger generation and kept the older generation apprised of what was being done by way of sponsoring younger writers. After the appearance of *The New Negro*, Locke's reputation was solidly established, and so he shared in the authority of the older group of men, but at the same time he was close to Hughes and Cullen, less because of age than because of temperament and tastes. At times this would be a distinct advantage; at other times, his views, because of generational forces, would be at odds with both groups.

Walter White, one of the most important figures of the Renaissance, was occasionally competitive with Locke. White enjoyed access to white publishers, because his own novel, *The Fire in the Flint*, had been brought out by Knopf in 1924 and then had garnered the enthusiastic support of Carl Van Vechten. White busily exercised his influence by showing Countee Cullen's poems to Boni and Liveright and then to Harper Brothers, who published them in 1925. Locke, limited by the amount of time he had to devote to his duties at Howard, lacked the sorts of contacts in the white world that the younger writers wanted for their books. White had earlier served as the Assistant Secretary of the NAACP and was greatly admired among many figures in the Renaissance. Perhaps because of his past experience as an insurance salesman in Atlanta, he was able to convince publishers and literary figures—Sinclair Lewis and Carl Van Vechten, as well as Horace Liveright and Albert Knopf—that Negro writers were worth publishing and that their books could be successfully marketed. He also used his connections with a newspaper, the *Pittsburgh Courier,* to write about the Renaissance in the first half of 1926.[1]

White's interest in African art also brought him into contact with Locke, though in a complicated way. White had decided that African art could be used in an argument to claim that "artistically, the world would probably be much further advanced if Negroes had been the masters and whites the slaves in the South," as he told Carl Van Doren in December 1923. Locke would have rejected this stand as being racially chauvinistic and at odds with his commitment to pluralism. Exchanging one hierarchy for another was not the way to solve a problem based on false metaphysics in the first place. At the dinner in March 1924 that launched the idea for the *Survey Graphic* number, White met Albert Barnes, whose collection of African art was already extensive, and which Barnes wanted to use in his own theories about African American culture. Eventually Barnes and White fell out, because Barnes felt White was a "personal pusher," as he said to Locke, and because he felt White had tried to steal his ideas. Barnes was cranky, especially when promulgating his ideas about how formalist art theory could be used as a part of general education.

Meanwhile Locke wanted to publish an essay, "Color Lines," that White had submitted for the *Survey Graphic* number. But he felt White's essay should take account of the recent work of Melville Herskovits, whose work on ethnicity and culture Locke respected. Herskovits doubted whether any definite traces of African culture had survived the middle passage or the generations of slavery that followed; the Negro spirit was best expressed by its adaptability to modern urban life. Though White balked at this—"I have read his article and, frankly, I don't see anything in it which would improve my Survey article," White complained to Locke—Locke decided to use Herskovits's article in the *Survey Graphic* and included it in *The New Negro* as well. As an editor, Locke was willing to publish arguments that contradicted his own. Many issues inflamed the personal politics of the time, and the question of the proper understanding of African art and its role in the further development of African American culture was especially heated. Locke's positions on these issues and his temperament were difficult to disentangle, for he could often be seen as taking both sides of an argument. Barnes was often harsh and blunt in the exercise of his power as an authority on culture. Just after the dinner where he met White, Barnes wrote to tell Locke his opinion of the man, as well as the essay White had sent him for critique: "if babes like him [White] are to be entrusted with the presentation of [N]egro essentials to an educated public, I fear the cause will be a hard one to push to its right end. I saw the other night that he was a lightweight but his manuscript has revealed a cheapness which I hardly suspected." Barnes was so negative because he knew Locke shared his stance about African art, and especially about its educative role and the need to see that its reception by contemporary viewers was handled rigorously. Even though Locke's views on the uses of African art were born in a contentious context, they remained with him for years after and largely shaped his esthetics about visual art in general. The personal politics could be as prickly as it was because most of the partisans held their beliefs with considerable fervor.[2]

———————————

The years immediately after the appearance of *The New Negro* were unsettled ones for Locke, but he was at the same time amazingly productive. Because he had a paid leave the academic year 1925–26, and because the following academic year saw him without any permanent position—he had a visiting professorship with Fisk University in 1926–27—he had ample time for travel. But he also further developed his ideas about African Americans and Africa itself. His commitment to African art was fostered by his relation with Barnes, but it also grew because of the growing importance of Pan-Africanism. Other interests drove Locke as well: his sense that African art supplied contemporary African American writers with a sense of tradition; his intrinsic interest in Africa because of his long-term interest in internationalism and "cultural contact"; and his engagement with the African Mandates system, which he explored through his association with the Foreign Policy Institute. As with his manifold skills in the editing of *The New Negro,* Locke dealt with African art in a variety of contexts. His first writing about African art in fact preceded the appearance of *The New Negro.* But it was largely in the years between 1926 and 1930 that his activities in this regard crested.

Locke's views on African art were intertwined with his friendship with two men—Albert Barnes and Paul Guillaume—who had already done much to introduce African art into the discussion of modernist painting and sculpture. Locke met Barnes and Guillaume in early 1924, when he first gave Langston Hughes an introduction to both. Barnes, a self-made millionaire, was already an important collector of modern and African art, and Paul Guillaume, a Parisian art dealer and collector, was well known as one of the leading commentators on African art. The two collectors entered the Renaissance discussion of the visual arts by way of their articles in *Opportunity*. Guillaume wrote an article about the African art at Barnes's collection for the May 1924 issue, which also included a piece by Barnes, and Guillaume added another piece two years later. Locke may have been instrumental in placing the pieces in the magazine. Barnes had started collecting as early as 1912; his distinctive pedagogical approach was solidified when he attended a series of lectures by John Dewey in 1917. After he chartered his foundation, located in Merion, Pennsylvania, in 1922, he appointed Guillaume the foreign secretary of the foundation in 1926. As a dealer, Guillaume was unusual. He not only wanted to be an author so as to advance his views of modern art, but he also cultivated relationships with the artists he represented in an innovative manner, treating the artists more as their equal than their patron. The Frenchman had had eighteen pieces of his African sculpture collection exhibited at Alfred Stieglitz's "291" gallery in New York City in 1914, and his "Fête Nègre" of 1918 introduced the Parisian art world to the idea of using so-called primitive objects in the remaking of modern art. Guillaume and Barnes, formalists in their appreciation of African art, shared many interests. Guillaume's book, *Primitive African Sculpture,* was later included by Locke in his course on African art and culture. Locke quickly realized that what Barnes and Guillaume were proposing for white European sculptors and painters could be adapted to African American artists. Locke appreciated the pedagogic function of esthetic experience that Barnes promoted, and he knew the writers he would review and critique, just as Guillaume knew the contemporary Parisian artists.[3]

In the May 1924 *Opportunity* Locke contributed an important piece of his own, "A Note on African Art." The essay shows considerable erudition in its references and a clear sense of the possibilities of the "field" of African sculpture. It ends tentatively when it speculates on how this material can be adapted by African American artists. Locke was not a supporter of mere "primitivism," which held that modernist art needed to reinvigorate itself by pursuing esthetic possibilities outside of those offered by an industrialized, urban culture. Instead, his plans for African American art and its use of African material rested on different assumptions. Locke separates the sculpture's cultural and esthetic meanings and argues that its esthetic meaning is bound up with the ability of its creators to freely explore three-dimensional form—"complete plastic freedom," as Roger Fry, the English esthetician, described it. Locke further draws on Guillaume and Fry, yet goes far beyond both to claim for African examples a "classic" status equal to that of ancient Greece and Rome. This bold claim comes about for several reasons: there is a historical moment of exhaustion in European art and a consequent looking for new forms; this interest, Locke quotes Guillaume as saying, was "first technical, then substantive, and finally, theoretical." At the same time the cultural interest was bound up with the ethnographical study of the sculpture, and Locke cites *Early Civilization,* by A. A. Goldenweiser, arguing that sculpture has both mimetic and abstract forms. By arriving at this conclusion men like Goldenweiser were putting the study of African art on a more scientific footing, and this in turn leads to a consideration of the work in comparative terms, and such study will "supply the most reliable clues and tests for African values." Locke insisted on distinguishing the scientific or ethnographical aspect of African art from its esthetic qualities; eventually he would try to make use of both, but with a special emphasis on the esthetic.

Locke ends the essay as he turns to his own cultural setting: "it becomes finally a natural and important question as to what artistic and cultural effect it [African art] can or will have upon the life of the American Negro." Because of "Europeanized conventions" the contemporary appreciation of African art must pass through the lens of French postimpressionist and modern art. But "we must believe that there still slumbers in the blood something which once stirred and will react with peculiar emotional intensity towards it." The vague metaphor of blood consciousness here invokes a deterministic, even a racial, framework that Locke almost never employed and that is at first glance contrary to his views on the nature of race. Drawing back from this metaphor, he goes on to qualify the blood argument, substituting for it a culturally rooted, and universal, form of recognition, thereby reducing the mystical component: "If by nothing more mystical than the sense of being ethnically related, some of us will feel its influence at least as keenly as those who have already made it recognized and famous. Nothing is more galvanizing than the sense of a cultural past. This at least the intelligent presentation of African art will supply to us" (CTAL, 135). Unlike the theorists of "primitivism," Locke sees in African art a connection as well as a disruption of an ages-long continuity. Contemporary French painters—and their dealers—

could see the important formal qualities and esthetic uses of African art, and so surely the contemporary Renaissance painters and sculptors could enrich their practice with this discovery. Locke characteristically adds the proviso that the work must be "intelligently" presented.

Locke put his interest in African art in the forefront of much of his activity in the years after he met Barnes and Guillaume. His essay in *The New Negro*, "The Legacy of the Ancestral Arts," with illustrations drawn from the Barnes collection of African sculpture, attempted to reorient the discussion of folk material and its role in the "higher arts." This attempt was ambitious, for it recognized the intrinsic esthetic value of African art even as it appropriated it for other purposes. But Locke carefully entered caveats. For example, he made it clear that "to the individual talent in art one must never dictate." And the example of European modernists' adaptation of African motifs and forms could possibly inspire his own contemporaries in America to "move in the direction of a racial school of art." After all, the legacy from Africa was not a specific or essential consciousness but a "deep seated aesthetic endowment," although one that was "the acquired and not the original artistic temperament." Locke argued optatively but was willing to advance a bold rhetorical question: "If the forefathers could so adroitly master these mediums, why not we?"[4]

What Locke advanced rhetorically he worked on in practical terms. In February 1927, Locke was part of a meeting, held at the New Art Circle, at 35 West 57th Street in New York, that would form the core of a later Harlem Museum devoted to African art. Locke served as the secretary for the group, and Charlotte Osgood Mason, whom he first met at this time, was the vice chairperson. A "selection committee" was set up as well, which included Locke, Amy Spingarn, and Walter Pach, an American artist who had helped to organize the Armory Show in 1913. Edith Isaacs, a wealthy patroness and editor of *Theatre Arts Magazine,* was to be a main benefactor, and a fund totaling $2,500.00 was subscribed. This provided the acquisition of the Blondiau-Theatre Arts Collection, which Locke had first seen in Europe in the summer of 1926, when he traveled to Egypt and Jerusalem as well as Paris. This important collection included 400 or more pieces, assembled over twenty-five years, by a Belgian, M. Raoul Blondiau, during his travels in Ghana and the Belgian Congo. The group included works from many tribes: Bushongo, Basonge, Bambala, and Kasai, among others. Locke wrote the catalogue essay for the New York exhibit, which eventually traveled to Chicago, Rochester, and Buffalo.

Locke soon broadened the audience for his arguments about African art.

Responding to a review of the exhibit by Thomas Munro, in the March 2, 1927 issue of the *Nation,* which claimed that "this collection as a whole is not good Negro art, but consists chiefly of debased modern examples," Locke defended the enterprise. His letter to the editor amounted to an editorial, arguing that African art should be seen not merely as some handmaiden to modernist experimentalism but as having its own esthetic value. Locke said that "the Blondiau Collection [is] more representative of its [African art's] range and types than any other ever exhibited in America." Anticipating a notion that would be developed later in Dewey's *Art as Experience,* Locke rejected any clear separation between the fine arts and handicraft, since the distinction would only produce a "vicious misinterpretation" of African art. The obvious ethnological use of the collection was as good a use as would be promoting it "as a side exhibit to modernist painting and . . . [using] it as a stalking horse for a particular school of aesthetics." Locke was not contradictory here, for his enlisting African art in the furtherance of the artistic inspiration of the Renaissance was always balanced by his respect for the integrity of African experience and culture.

Locke's plans for a Harlem Museum of African Art were never fully realized. Eventually many of the works he sought to collect for this project, especially those of the Blondiau Collection, ended up in the 135th Street branch of the New York Public Library, later to be known as the Schomburg Center. Locke also contributed his personal pieces of African sculpture to Howard, where they formed the core of the university's collection. They can still be seen there today, and several goldweights form an especially striking part of this collection. Locke spent much of his own money on the collection and did most of the curatorial work in terms of describing and logging in the various pieces. In June 1928 he arranged "An Exhibition of African Sculpture and Handicraft" at Howard; the program described it as from the "Traveling Collection of Harlem Museum of African Art of New York City." Lois Mailou Jones, the painter who joined the Howard faculty in 1930, spoke of how Locke stopped her on campus one day and personally encouraged her to use African motifs in her paintings.[5]

Locke's interest as a cultural critic extended beyond literature, music, and the plastic arts to the stage. As a thoroughly avid theatergoer, he pursued a lifelong interest in dramatic productions and perceptively described the special esthetics involved in the performing arts. Appearing in the *Theatre Arts Monthly* for February 1926, his essay "The Negro and the American Stage" set out a strong case for the emerging importance of Negro actors.[6] Though not at all understating the importance of Negro drama—both by Negro dra-

matists and about Negro life—he chose to stress "the deep and unemanci-
pated resources of the Negro actor, and the folk arts of which he is as yet
only a blind and hampered exponent." Having "to struggle up out of the
shambles of minstrelsy and make slow headway against very fixed limitations
of popular taste," Negro actors were especially victims of racial prejudice.
What should have been accounted their great strength—"the free use of the
body and voice as direct instruments of feeling"—and what could thereby
regenerate the dramatic arts was instead seen in stereotypical terms, and the
phrase "natural-born actor" was usually "intended as a disparaging estimate
of the Negro's limitations." Locke referred in the essay to an interview he and
Charles S. Johnson conducted with Max Reinhardt, who praised the early
stage work in *Shuffle Along* and *Runnin' Wild*. The famous director at first
earned only polite demurs from Locke and his friend, until he made it clear
he was talking about the promise shown by the Negro performers in these
productions and was not condescending to them in the context of serious
drama. This clearly impressed Locke, who took up the point and argued it
even more forcefully.

In the essay Locke also reverted to two issues that were present throughout *The New Negro:* the use of folk material and the importance of Africa as a
source of esthetic interest. Locke wanted Negro drama to be "creatively experimental" but to "seek its materials in the rich native soil of Negro life." He
suggested that "the surest sign of a folk renascence seems to be a dramatic
flowering." Meanwhile, the drama had to move beyond its present state and
become "genuinely representative of the folk spirit which it is now forced to
travesty." Equally strong in his stress on the role of Africa, he insisted that
"one can scarcely think of a complete development of dramatic art by the
Negro without some significant artistic reexpression of African life, and the
traditions associated with it." Within a few years, he attempted to inaugurate
a tradition of African American ballet, using material drawn from his knowledge of African tribal lore, when he approached William Grant Still to write
the music for Bruce Nugent's "Sahdji." But in the period immediately following *The New Negro* he found little to convince him that a renascence of drama
was underway, though in the year-end reviews he wrote during the next two
decades he tracked Negro drama with keen interest and high standards.

In addition to the esthetic theory he set out in "The Legacy of the Ancestral Arts" and the practical and pedagogic work of arranging for the exhibit
of the Blondiau Collection, Locke's interest in Africa took a political turn as
well. In June 1927 Locke ambitiously applied to the Social Sciences Research
Council for a grant of $5,000.00 per year for two years, in order to fund what

he called a "Study Project in African Art and Culture," but this application was unsuccessful. Only a month earlier he had applied to the Foreign Policy Association for a different project, at the suggestion of a Mrs. Moorhead; this was to serve as a credited observer at the League of Nations during its meeting in Geneva in 1927. In a sense, both of these projects were versions of the plan he had submitted years earlier for a Khan traveling scholarship. But it was the League of Nations, and the question of the African Mandates, that occupied a considerable investment of his attention and energy.[7]

The League had set up the Mandates through Article 22 of its charter, in order to deal with the territories which were earlier under the control of Germany and the Ottoman Empire. The article set out the governing principles in idealized terms:

> To those colonies and territories which as a consequence of the late war have ceased to be under the sovereignty of the States which formerly governed them and which are inhabited by peoples not yet able to stand by themselves under the strenuous conditions of the modern world, there should be applied the principle that the well-being and development of such peoples form a sacred trust of civilization. . . .
>
> The best method of giving practical effect to this principle is that the tutelage of such peoples should be entrusted to advanced nations . . . and that this tutelage should be exercised by them as Mandatories on behalf of the League.

Various nations had states or territories assigned to them; for example, Syria and Lebanon were assigned to France, while Iraq and Palestine were under the control of Britain; these were Class A Mandates (of the three classes, A, B, and C). After 1945 the Mandates became United Nations Trust Territories. In the meantime, the Mandates were little more than colonies of the nations to which they were assigned. Each Mandate was governed according to its special circumstances, but for those in Central Africa, placed in Class B, no fortifications could be constructed nor any army raised. There also had to be an annual report to the League.

The Foreign Policy Association produced a press release that said that Locke would sail to Geneva on July 2 (presumably 1927) to study the Mandates and their functioning under the League of Nations, a trip financed in part by a grant from the association's McCabe Memorial Fund. In his application Locke stressed that American Negroes did not know of the Mandates, but that they should, as their problems were similar to those faced by the postwar efforts of the League. As Locke explained, the administration of the Mandates was designed to guard the rights of undeveloped peoples and to insure their participation in government and their "constructive self-adjustment." But the more Locke came to know about the Mandates, in part through his trip to Geneva, the more he saw what a compromised situation had developed. When Raymond Leslie Buell, research director of the association, wrote to Locke in Paris in 1927 and asked him to check on some statistics—specifically if those showing the death rate of six hundred men per thousand during the building of the Brazzaville Ocean Railway were accurate—Locke wrote a long report on what he discovered about this, and other aspects of the treatment of Africans under the Mandate system.

Locke's discovery of the continuing horrendous treatment of native Africans by European powers would have recalled for him the history of the Congo Free State. King Leopold II, operating with the authorization rendered him by the Berlin Conference in 1884–85, plundered the natural wealth of the Congo basin. Diamonds, gold, and especially rubber—which enjoyed a worldwide boom after the invention of the inflatable tire—were wrested from the native population by forced labor. Leopold's mercenary army held women and children captive in order to coerce the men into the brutal work of mining and of gathering rubber from the dense forest. A revolt of the labor force brought a massacre in its wake, only compounding the repressive policies. Laborers were shot in order to enforce control, and their right hands were amputated to show that the soldiers had indeed killed their victims. Leopold's bureaucratic administration insisted that bullets not be wasted, and records were kept to show that the number of amputated hands was equal to the bullets fired. Eventually an extensive public outcry, which included anti-imperialist voices such as those of Mark Twain and Roger Casement, and the shifting politics of the various European states, brought the worst of the suffering to a close. But forced labor continued to be used even after the death of Leopold. In the "Free" State of 900,000 square miles there were estimated to live thirty million people; the estimates of those killed as a direct result of the savagery range from four to as many as twenty million.

The Foreign Policy Association was in some ways an extension of the anti-imperialist leagues that had agitated for the last several decades. At the executive board meeting of the association in November 1927, Locke reported on his trip to Geneva and presented an oral version to the board members. In the written version, he spoke frankly of the deficiencies of the Mandate system, chiefly the forced labor and the overall failure to allow anything like "self-adjustment." He was, however, prevented from making the report public without the prior approval of the association; in fact, Paul Kellogg wrote him in December 1927 to remind him that the report would remain the property of the Foreign Policy Association. Kellogg had been urged by Mrs. Moorhead to send this reminder. This might indicate some squeamishness on the part of the association. Yet in another press release of April 1928, Buell attacked the Firestone Tire Company's million-acre concession in Liberia, which involved forced labor at the rate of one penny per man per day. Buell himself became the president of the association in 1935, so his views were obviously broadly representative of the association. But Locke apparently had great difficulty spelling out what he wanted to say. Throughout the early fall of 1928, Buell had to write Locke twice to ask about the progress of his writing of the report. In October 1928, Locke submitted a memorandum explaining his delay; he had gone back to Geneva, at his own expense, to do further research. In January 1929 Buell was able to tell Locke that the report as submitted has satisfied the obligation incurred by the grant. However, Buell added that the association wanted a revision before any publication could take place. In the end, no report by Locke was made public.

As with the lecture series on race relations, Locke did not publish a work to which he clearly devoted a great deal of time and intelligence. Mrs. Moorhead had told Locke at the end of 1927 that she would eventually arrange for the work to be published, in pamphlet form, in an edition of nine thousand copies, which would be given away for free. Perhaps Locke balked at the point in January where Buell had accepted the report as complete except for revisions. In any case, his relations with Buell continued in a friendly manner. At Howard it was the conservative administration that had made it difficult to deliver the lectures on race in 1915, but the Foreign Policy Association was not like the Howard administration. Indeed, Buell, in his capacity at the association, consulted Locke throughout the late 1920s on a number of issues. Locke in 1928 declined an invitation, offered through Buell's good graces, to speak on Africa at Williams College and also declined to recommend Du Bois in his place. Later, in December 1929, however, he was able to recommend Du Bois for a luncheon program in connection with the Haiti Commission being organized by the association, while at the same time insisting that "no cheap Negro politician" be added. Locke wanted Buell to come to Howard and address the students, presumably on the Haiti Commission issue, and he was also approaching Walter White about it.

Locke was drawn to the Mandate question, as his application made clear, because of the way it paralleled the situation of African Americans. Seeing such a parallel formulates the situation in political terms, terms that were also informed by Locke's internationalist perspective. Though he was faulted in years to come for privileging the cultural context over the political one, Locke was able to see the political ramifications of his social and racial experience. Since the prior-approval restriction on publication was evidently set even before Locke went to make his study, he apparently felt obliged to honor it. But in terms of the race question of the day, and the international context in which Locke was thinking on a number of topics, it is not altogether clear why he was not able—or willing—to turn his efforts on the Mandate question into something instructive for a larger audience.

The Renaissance saw the appearance of a number of novels, by Fauset, Thurman, Hurston, McKay, and Hughes, among others. Locke reviewed almost all of them in one venue or another, and some he dealt with—or was involved in—in more immediate ways. Two of the novels especially caught his attention, forming a frame on the Renaissance, since they were published six years apart: *Nigger Heaven* (1926) by Carl Van Vechten, and *Infants of the Spring* (1932) by Wallace Thurman. The former enjoyed a reception that made it a bestseller, but also a *succès de scandale,* while the latter was a roman à clef in which Locke himself made a brief disguised appearance. Both books raised the esthetic questions that Locke and most of the other participants in the Renaissance had been debating publicly and privately: was there a distinctive Negro subject matter or style? Should art be used for racial uplift or for purely esthetic ends?

Obviously Van Vechten meant to shock with his title, even though when the word first appears in the novel, it is accompanied with a footnote explaining the conventions in which it can—and should not—be used. More than a touch of scandal accompanied Thurman's tale. People read it for the inside sense of what was really going on at the parties attended by what Hurston had dubbed the "Niggerati," her archly witty term that combined "nigger" and "literati" in a way that seemed to discredit both. Locke's commitment to combat what he repeatedly referred to as the Puritanism of American culture led him to avoid expressing shock, at least in print, when he took up the issues that the novels entertained. But his reactions to both books ended up with a fair degree of complex judgment.[8]

Locke often visited Van Vechten's apartment on West 55th Street when he came to New York during the late 1920s, and Locke shared many of Van

Vechten's tastes. In September 1926, he told Van Vechten that *Nigger Heaven* was "a good corrective sketch for the white reader who takes Negro life under-seriously." He remarked that "the society approach is at least made for the first time . . . and the novel of manners is the acid test." Locke said he wanted to write a review of the novel, but he never did, though he did mention it briefly in "Beauty Instead of Ashes.." He probably saw the genre of the novel of manners as bestowing a certain degree of normalcy on depictions of the Negro; the novel was generally considered the first written by a white author about the world of urban blacks. But later opinions expressed by Locke on a number of works suggest that the sensationalistic elements that Van Vechten employed so casually may have, upon reflection, dissipated his enthusiasm. Other figures expressed sharply opposing judgments about the book; Du Bois recommended to his readers that they "drop it gently into the grate," while Hughes said he was "at a loss to understand the yelps of colored critics and the reason for their ill-mannered onslaught against Mr. Van Vechten."[9]

With a background as a photographer and a society editor for the *Chicago American*, Van Vechten arrived in New York in 1906, bringing with him a family tradition of devotion to aiding Negro causes. Friends with many Renaissance writers, he was instrumental in aiding the careers of many African Americans, especially Hughes, Hurston, Cullen, and Nella Larsen. His photographic record of the Harlem artistic world remains as valuable as his social evenings were dazzling. He used his journalistic skills to present his experience of African American culture to a white readership in the pages of *Vanity Fair* and the *New York Herald Tribune*. As a gay white man, Van Vechten was obviously closer to some of the Renaissance figures than others, and many blacks resented his use of material they felt was sensationalistic and too readily exploited.[10]

Nigger Heaven offers only a thin, melodramatic plot, and its structure is rather simplified—a brief prologue, one part devoted to Mary Love, the central female character, and another to Byron Kasson, the main male character. Their affair is first made unsteady by her reserve and then by her jealousy. Byron is a failed novelist, easily insulted whenever he feels condescended to, and yet the truest snob of all. The book introduces but hardly resolves the standard issues of the day: the question of how to use "low" material, passing the color line, and color consciousness within the black community. The phenomenon of the New Negro is referred to glancingly, as Byron assumes that he should be a part of the movement. Though all the action takes place in Harlem, referred to as the "Mecca" of the New Negro, there is also

a brief reference to some difficulty at Howard University. Literary and cultural images abound, as Hughes supplied Van Vechten with the song lyrics quoted throughout the story. Toomer's *Cane* is mentioned, and Mary
quotes a Wallace Stevens poem from memory. Locke's concerns are also alluded to, as Mary has installed an exhibit of African sculpture at the branch
library where she works. All of these references to the cultural activities of
the day flow from Van Vechten's esthetic, based largely on his desire for con-
temporaneity, but they are not especially well integrated into the narrative;
certainly they form no serious analysis or critique of Locke's esthetic. The
book ends with a stream-of-consciousness phantasmagoria that borrows
from James Joyce, though otherwise there is not much of lasting artistic innovation in the book.

Thurman's *Infants of the Spring* does discuss Locke's views on art and the
use of cultural expression, but not altogether seriously. The novel, however,
involved the issues raised by the Renaissance in ways that were more substantive and without the extremely exaggerated and dehumanizing characters of
Nigger Heaven. Wallace Thurman was a complex, and often contradictory,
personality. Langston Hughes described him as "a strange kind of fellow,
who liked to drink gin, but didn't like to drink gin; who liked being a Negro,
but felt it a great handicap; who adored Bohemianism, but thought it wrong
to be bohemian." Born in Salt Lake City, Utah, he spent time on the West
Coast as a journalist before coming to Harlem. He became known for editing
two short-lived magazines: *FIRE!!* (1926) and *Harlem: A Forum of Negro Life*
(1928). Locke helped fund the former and contributed to the latter. *FIRE!!* set
out an editorial policy directly counter to Du Bois's call for propaganda, arguing for an approach purely "artistic in intent and conception." Thurman sent
Locke a letter soliciting his support for *FIRE!!* Later, in 1928, asking Locke
for a contribution to *Harlem,* Thurman characterized his efforts by saying
that the *Messenger* was dead, and "Crisis is dying. Voila here comes Harlem,
independent, fearless and general, trying to appeal to all." Locke responded
by sending Thurman the essay "Art or Propaganda?," a clear response to Du
Bois's symposium, and approving "especially a journal that will recognize
that there is more than one side to most issues." Almost constantly the center
of gossip and controversy, Thurman, in one of his novels, *The Blacker the
Berry,* addressed the problem of color prejudice among blacks. His marriage
to Louise Thompson dissolved quickly, and afterwards she spread the rumor that their divorce was necessary because he was gay. His success was
always compromised by what seemed his unfailing bad luck. His play, *Harlem, a Melodrama of Negro Life in Harlem,* which Locke did not approve of,

ran for almost one hundred performances in 1929, even though he was for a while denied admission to it because of his color. At the end of 1934 he died of tuberculosis; he was thirty-two years old.[11]

It is fair to say that all the contradictions Hughes saw in Thurman are expressed in *The Infants of the Spring.* Though the idea and experience of racial values are seldom absent from the novel's dialogue, the book offers no consistent view. Its narrative expresses the fundamental notion that claims about the essence of race are false yet unavoidable. Thurman's characters, both black and white, hold diverse opinions about race and about the Renaissance, and their behavior is frequently irresolute and seldom guided by their views. Thurman had some ambitions to write for the movies, and the novel is structured largely as a series of set scenes in which the characters argue out their ideals and values, or rather their failure to hold them steadily and clearly. The Renaissance is the immediate backdrop to the action, but there is no possibility that a cultural movement might flourish. The main character, Ray, expressing the cultural skepticism at the heart of the book, wonders "what accounted for the fact that most Negroes of talent were wont to make one splurge, then sink into oblivion." Questions of creativity are constantly discussed by all the characters, but no finished artistic products command anyone's attention.

Ray sees himself as a struggling novelist whose desire is to fulfill his personality through art and friendship. His friends spend a great deal of time drinking gin and discussing their fates. Steve, a white Swede, comes to know Ray well and moves in with him, though he eventually abandons the house where the friends congregate. Paul, a bisexual black, exudes irony and bitterness and eventually commits suicide in the novel's closing pages. In a sense what is referred to as Ray's "complex" is the center of the novel, an allegorized version of the social malaise generated by racial consciousness. Locke enters the novel as the character Dr. Parkes, a professor from a northern college. His first appearance, far from flattering, is cast in language clearly coded as referring to Locke's homosexuality. "He was a mother hen clucking at her chicks. Small, dapper, with sensitive features, graying hair, a dominating head, and restless hands and feet, he smiled benevolently at his brood. Then, in his best continental manner, which he had acquired during four years at European universities, he began to speak." Parkes expounds his theory that contemporary African American artists would greatly profit from "going back to [their] racial roots and cultivating a healthy paganism based on African traditions." At the same time Parkes admits to the "salon" that has assembled one evening that he is "somewhat fearful of the decadent strain which seems to have filtered into most of your work."[12]

The salon is Parkes's idea, but this salon occurs after an especially drunken party, as a result of which Ray experiences something like a nervous breakdown. The narrative thus presents the salon as a futile attempt to revive through artistic and intellectual discussion a social group that has generally exhausted itself. Thurman uses the occasion of the salon not only to introduce Locke as Parkes but also to show Hughes, Hurston, and Cullen, among others, in less than attractive terms. Even Du Bois comes in for some stinging satire, as his views are ridiculed when presented by a character named Allen Fenderson, who "taught school and had ambitions to become a crusader" in the style of the editor of the *Crisis*. The description of the melee that ends the salon suggests that the high ideals of the Renaissance were already on the wane by the time the novel appeared in 1932, as the Depression is a felt but unwritten presence in the novel.

The salon passage satirizes Locke and his views, but commentators who stress this often fail to point out that everyone in the novel is satirized in one way or another. As a comedy of manners, *Infants* is not especially successful, though some of its period details have an enjoyable flavor. But in any case the novel shaped the public view of Locke in incalculable but extensive ways. His views on African art are presented without nuance, and he is described as "clucking" when he attempts to energize the discussion and later when he tries unsuccessfully to restore order after the group's opinions turn contentious and chaotic. Locke's reputation as elitist, and hence out of touch, and his desire to use culture as a force for social betterment led him to be censorious. Yet the charge that Locke accused the "Niggerati" of being decadent is no more—or less—than what Thurman's novel suggests to its readers was the case. In February 1932, Hurston wrote to Locke to say that she had "a copy of Wallace Thurman's 'INFANTS OF THE SPRING.' You and I are in it in a small way. Not a bad book at all." But her tolerance for being satirized was proportionate to her own spontaneous and mocking spirit. Locke may very well have felt differently. He reviewed the novel for *Opportunity* in 1933 and had this to say about what he called "the first picture of the younger Negro intelligentsia":

The trouble with the set he [Thurman] delineates, and with the author's own literary philosophy and outlook, is that the attitude and foibles of Nordic decadence have been carried into the buds of racial expression, and the healthy elemental simplicity of the Negro folk spirit and its native tradition forgotten or ignored by many who nevertheless have traded on the popularity for Negro art. As the novel of this spiritual failure and perversion, Mr. Thurman's book will have real documentary value, even though it represents only the lost wing of the younger generation movement.

Clearly Locke had little taste for the satire in the novel, and yet his appeal to a "healthy elemental simplicity" is, frankly, misplaced since Thurman had no intention at all to invoke such a value, committed as he was to a thoroughly urbanized sensibility.

Locke's own social rounds were even more frenetic and urbane than those depicted in *Infants,* as his efforts in advancing the agenda of the Renaissance brought him into relations with many people, especially in New York City. One such friend, almost twenty years younger than Locke, was C. Glenn Carrington, whose career was devoted to social work. He left a large collection of letters and memorabilia to Howard, a collection which included correspondence with Van Vechten, Du Bois, Hughes, and many others. Locke first met him in 1925, and they maintained a warm friendship for the next two and a half decades. They often met when Locke passed through New York on his way to Europe, and they shared a great love of the theater and dance, as well as a network of gay friends. Locke served as an advisor to Carrington in matters of the heart. In an undated letter, but apparently from the late 1920s, Locke increases his intimacy with Carrington even as he answers the younger man's concerns about having to chose between two lovers, to both of whom Locke had recently been introduced. "I think both friendships mean much to you," Locke says, but then turns to more direct remarks to Carrington, while sketching out his own social world:

> I do appreciate the spiritual development and enfranchisement you have undergone—and am really grateful to have you attribute some of it to my influence. . . . I shall be glad—especially now that your inhibitions are broken through and that it is really profitable to chat,—to make special effort to see you when next in New York. Of course, I have to spread myself around: I have many friends and a multitude of diverse interests.

In the same letter Locke spells out his own sense of how friendships were to be maintained:

As you know, I incline to an appreciation of all types each on their separate level—and I hold to no proprietary notion about human relationships. Jealousy and the monopoly it implies, corporeal or spiritual, I hold essentially vulgar. I make sharp discriminations about reservations or mercenary motives, but barring these, one is completely possessed for the time being—(as an atom chemically is) but that is all—nature and life are always shifting the combinations.

Locke's recourse here to a mechanistic sense of human attraction combines with an attitude that is at once antisentimental and elitist, yet marked by striking self-awareness. Clearly his work on value theory was not a mere academic exercise, for with his gay friends as well as with his other social and artistic circles Locke sought to approach his desires on a rational basis, while realizing the protean nature of human desire, the shifting combinations and the "multitude of diverse interests."[13]

Of his many interests, Locke remained especially devoted to the fostering of lyric poets. In 1927 Simon and Schuster brought out a collection called simply *Four Negro Poets,* edited and with a brief introduction by Locke. The four—McKay, Cullen, Toomer, and Hughes—were already well known to both black and white readers, and Locke's ability to find a publisher as established as Simon and Schuster resulted from the rising interest in black writers in the Renaissance period. His introduction pointed out that "the Negro poet becomes as much an expression of his age as of his folk." But Locke was defining what was racially characteristic about the four lyric poets, and he said of his principle of selection: "Though their poetry ranges through all possible themes, it is . . . no spiritual distortion or misrepresentation that their more racially distinctive poems have been selected for this little anthology." The matter was hardly settled, however. Toomer would object to his inclusion, for by this time he had already begun to cast off his racial identity. Cullen meanwhile had professed a desire to be known more simply as a poet than a black poet. And to this attitude Hughes had responded with his 1926 essay, "The Negro Artist and the Racial Mountain." In that well-known essay Hughes would argue that "this is the mountain standing in the way of any true Negro art in America—this urge within the race towards whiteness, the desire to pour racial individuality into the mold of American standardization, and to be as little Negro and as much American as possible." Locke would close his introduction by saying: "In the chorus of American singing [these poets] have registered distinctive notes whose characteristic timbre we would never lose or willingly let lapse; however more and more they

become orchestrated into our national art and culture." Locke is clearly trying to finesse—or complexify—the question of racially characteristic cultural
expression by joining it with the national version of the esthetic argument.[14]

The questions surrounding the issue of just what general or group characteristics lyric poetry can or should express would remain ones that Locke
continued to explore. Race was not the only subject where these questions
were joined; they were involved in poetry that had a basis in gendered experience. Though Locke was often rumored to be misogynistic, he was close to
several women artists, chief among them the poet and playwright Georgia
Douglas Johnson. A frequent visitor at her salon in Washington, Locke introduced and met people there, helping make it one of the centers of cultural
life for blacks in the capital. Johnson was an accomplished poet who wrote
about unrequited love in a style that mixed Victorian high sentiment with
more modern psychology, though her versification remained traditional. She
was one of Du Bois's lovers, having begun an affair with him around the time
of her husband's death in 1926. With an ancestry that included Cherokee and
English forebears, she was born into a wealthy family and graduated from
Oberlin with a desire to study music before she turned to poetry. After her
husband's death she supported herself with a patronage job in the Department of Labor and maintained a steady calendar of tea parties and evenings
full of literary discussion. There was a rumor that the idea for the Civic Club
dinner that supposedly launched the Renaissance originated at her salon.

In 1928 Locke wrote an introduction to her third book of poems, *An
Autumn Love Cycle*. He said that "the task which she has set herself is the
documenting of the feminine heart." He praised her poetry for the way it
worked toward a balance of esthetic attributes even while it refused to "make
a sphinx of woman, who herself now yearns to throw off along with the mystery, the psychological vestments of disguise." Johnson manages "candid
self-expression," and "she succeeds where others more doctrinally feminist
than she have failed; for they in oversophistication, in terror of platitudes and
the commonplace, have stressed the bizarre, the exceptional, in one way or
another have overintellectualized their message and overleapt the common
elemental experience they would nevertheless express." Locke's predilection for balance and control in esthetic matters is set against what he foresees
in her future growth as a poet, and he attempts to point the way for her art,
just as he often did for the other writers whom he championed. "In a deeper
and somewhat more individual message, upon which she only verges, and
which we believe will later be her most mature and valuable contribution,
Mrs. Johnson probes under the experiences of love to the underlying forces

of natural instinct which so fatalistically control our lives." Here the idea of fatalistic control echoes the observation he made to Carrington about how being possessed, even if only momentarily, in matters of the heart resembles the atom being chemically caught. By her willingness to go beneath the accepted views and expression of love poetry, Johnson created an "individual message" that nevertheless was at once fully female and universal. She wrote a poetry that, for Locke, had a "candor that shows she brings to the poetic field what it lacks most—the gift of the elemental touch." Locke's residual Romantic temperament would resort to the language of "elemental" and "fatalistic" in discussing lyric poetry, while he reserved the vocabularies of historical development and group values for his reflections on the novel. This distinction, between the large genres of fiction and poetry, was a traditional, even a hallowed, one in literary criticism, and Locke fit his own criticism into it quite comfortably.[15]

Another development in Locke's life and career that came about after the publication of *The New Negro* was one of the most formative of all. This was his meeting Charlotte Osgood Mason, which involved him in a relationship where the questions of race and culture would take on decidedly different accents. He and Mason shared and articulated between them a major part of his work as a cultural critic for almost two decades. Mason acted as a patron to a number of African American artists, Hughes and Hurston chief among them, but also Aaron Douglas, Claude McKay, and others. She dispensed money to them, but also advice, and exercised a stringent control over their artistic endeavors and demanded a close accounting of how they spent their funds. Locke, who introduced some of these artists to Mason, and was so close to Mason as to appear to be her personal executor, was thereby closely involved with the question of patronage, which often met with divided opinion as to its long-term usefulness. Some felt strongly that the system was inherently racist, despite the ostensible benefits, while others realized its practical benefits. Locke's relationship with Mason was one of the most complex of his life, involving not only his role as mediator in Mason's patronage, but a years' long form of self-analysis motivated, and in part directed, by Mason's idiosyncratic ideals. His mediating role caused his reputation to be cast often in a negative light, and his self-analysis complicated what he saw as his vocation as a writer and race leader. Mason was inordinately secretive—one of the rare times when she scolded Locke came about because he revealed their plans to Aaron Douglas—and yet the public roles Locke continued to play from 1927 until Mason's death in 1946, at the age of ninety-two, were shaped by his dealings with her.[16]

When Locke first met Mason she had been a widow for twenty five years, and her psychological situation, in large measure a mixture of prolonged mourning and idealistic piety, was determined by the memories of her husband. Rufus Osgood Mason graduated from Dartmouth College in the class of 1854, having studied for the ministry. He switched to medicine, however, and earned an M.D. from Columbia College in 1859, where he was the class valedictorian. His interests began to focus on hypnotism and psychic experience, and he studied the idea and phenomenon of genius. There were other interests as well; the *National Cyclopedia of American Biography* would list them as "primitive forms of life, . . . the affinity of chemicals, and the building, migratory and homing faculties of birds and animals." All in all, Osgood was a recognizable nineteenth-century type, combining features of the autodidact, the spiritualist, and the scientific quester. He managed to bequeath to his wife a handsome fortune and a commitment to an exploration of the higher dimensions of human existence.

Charlotte Mason's character can be amply displayed by the way she memorialized her husband in an extraordinary essay, a copy of which she gave to Locke, called "The Passing of a Prophet." Published in the *North American Review* in 1907, the piece never mentions her husband by name. It begins with a vaporous disquisition on death as a state of transformation to the spiritual dimension. A mélange of Christian sentiment, *Lebensphilosophie*, nineteenth-century psychic sciences, and heavy moralism, Mason's essay is perhaps best read as an attempt, common enough for her time, to meld the languages of science and of faith into a higher form of expression and knowledge. So with images and metaphors of force, vibration, and channels, the world of nobility and spiritual ideals is brought into a set of protocols:

> Again, death and failure are of one blood—children of the same parent thought. Yet each exists that something finer may be born in us of our grief. A complete failure in the eyes of the world is often a glowing success in the universe of God; and even if the failure be in the essentials of life, it will have vibrations powerful enough to sweep the experience into the realm of victory if the soul so wills. The force that produces the failure is ours to distribute into other channels. Such victories mean the death of the ignoble; they are victories wholly of the spirit,

and until manifested in the flesh, in a man's face or in his deeds, we of the world still treat the soul as if it had not been reborn.

Introducing a cloudy narrative near the end—"The hearth of the home was cold. Strong winds had threatened its fires, and the embers gave forth neither warmth nor light."—the essay relates the death and burial and mystic transfiguration of a man. The "prophet" of the essay's title obviously serves as the center of this tale, and just as clearly the prophet is Dr. Mason. When the speaker of the essay spreads the prophet's ashes "out upon the winds," an "Infinite Spirit" is invoked to help us "to live so in touch with the Eternal and Infinite that we may give out all that we see of truth," truth being what the prophet lived for. Thus the prophet's death becomes a form of rebirth.

The correspondence between Mason and Locke strongly suggests that she used a similar vocabulary and set of ideas when discussing her goals for the writers for whom she acted as patron. Before she met Locke, Mason was under the influence of *The Indians' Book* (1907), a compilation of tales, music, and other ethnographic lore that was the work of Natalie Curtis. Curtis, a self-taught folklorist, used her influence with Theodore Roosevelt to improve the efforts of the federal government in the study and preservation of Native American culture. She believed that this culture was "of great value to the history of the Human Race as well as the history of America." Mason absorbed Curtis's spiritual interpretation of what she considered a primitive but more vital civilization, one that could redeem and revivify a decadent urban and industrialized world. By the time she met Locke, Mason had wholly transferred her spiritual attention to African Americans, and she felt that their culture was as strong and vital as that of Native Americans and with as much redemptive power. However, her interest in African Americans accompanied a strong and willful sense that there was a constant danger that the culture of white people remained corrupting, if only because it had been so deeply implanted.[17]

Mason met Locke on February 6, 1927, a day the two would celebrate each year thereafter. It was a Sunday and Locke gave a lecture to mark the opening of the African Art Exhibit, drawn from the Blondiau Collection, on West 57th Street. They were introduced by Edith Isaacs, who was serving on the board of directors for the planned Museum of African Art. According to a notebook Locke kept at the time, he and Mason immediately established a "tremendous" rapport. He invited himself to come and visit her. A few days later he telephoned her to arrange the meeting, and when he arrived, she sat him in her great-great-grandfather's chair. Within a week he had given her a copy of Hughes's poetry, and shortly thereafter he brought the poet to meet her. A round of visits and teas and dinners followed in March and April. He talked to her more about his museum lecture and "met her with open arms and a brush of the spirit." She gave him a check for $500.00 to aid the board in the formation of the African Art project. Advice and opinions poured freely from Mason: a series of physical exercises; the ideal of emptying one's bowels two hours after each meal; "lying still opens your door to unseen psychic forces—never do that"; slavery had turned the Negroes' sexual imagination toward vulgarity; her ancestors had freed their slaves before the Revolution, and so none of her inheritance was from slavery. By May Locke was telling Mason about his childhood, about his forthcoming *Four Negro Poets,* and his work on the Mandate question. Thus began a relationship in which all their private thoughts and ideals were constantly and freely shared.

Mason resided at 399 Park Avenue, and Locke visited there whenever he came to New York. He wrote Mason often, both when he was in Europe and when teaching at Howard. In the summer of 1927, just months after they met, she told him that "African Art stands as a Sentinel a Champion for the Negro Race." Locke, for his part, described his possible reinstatement at Howard and mentioned his spending the winter term of 1927 at Fisk; he also shared the news that a Mr. Nelson had become his assistant in the philosophy department at Howard, and he kept Mason informed about successive assistants. By the end of the year, Locke was planning to speak on African art in Chicago, and Mason was already referring to him as "My precious Brown Boy." Mason was often called the "Godmother" by all who knew her; for Locke, she clearly took on a maternal role. He apparently tried to interest Mason in underwriting a film about African art, but she demurred, claiming "I do not know African primitive life." However, she added: "All Negroes are after all the children of the sun and I know you cannot be well without it."

Her support for African American writers was already underway. After Locke introduced Hughes to her, she told Locke that "Langston has been a most precious child so far in keeping me posted of his whereabouts and what he is doing—and here and there nourishing flights of his beautiful spirit." Hughes, for his part, mentioned Locke favorably in all his letters to Mason. Locke had sailed to Europe in the summer of 1927 and was hoping to rendezvous with Toomer at Fontainebleau, concerned that Toomer had been more and more reluctant to be identified as a Negro writer. The meeting, however, seems not to have happened. Mason had formed a high opinion of Toomer, perhaps in response to Locke's advocacy of his work, though she was apparently aware of his racial theorizing: "I realize that a flaming spirit like that can burn to ashes the things that push upon him and hide his miraculous power from his own vision."

By February 1928, Locke had gone to Fisk, where he was giving lectures on "The Negro in American Literature" and a course in philosophy. He described his situation to Mason; he found Nashville horrible, full of fog and coal dust. "Remaining here is of course out of the question, but I am glad I came," he told her, as he would mention other offers and possible relocations in the years to come. He also updated her about Hurston, whom he had introduced to Mason. Locke was concerned that Zora might give some of her recently collected folklore material to a white professor at Fisk; he and Mason would spend much time and energy advising Hurston how best to protect and maximize her anthropological efforts, paying particular attention to the conditions under which they might be published. Locke suggested that he would not allow the collection of African art to be displayed in Philadelphia if the Museum of Art there could not dedicate a secure room for the purpose. At the same time he was reading the proofs of McKay's new novel, *Home to Harlem,* which he characterized as "only removed from Nigger Heaven by its deeper poetry of language." Neither novel would appeal to Mason, Locke knew, and his comment about McKay's language was an instance of how his own esthetic judgments were mediated when he presented them to her.

Locke reported to his patron constantly on all his cultural and personal projects and relied on her for a large measure of emotional comfort, and they gossiped constantly. He was trying hard to finish his report on the Mandates for the Foreign Policy Association, but even by the end of the year he was not sure exactly what he wanted to say on the subject. Charles S. Johnson left *Opportunity* in March to take a position at Fisk, and Locke remarked that part of the reason had to do with what he called the "incompetency" of Countee Cullen, who was serving as an assistant editor at the magazine. Locke, who felt he should have been offered Cullen's position several months earlier, would on several occasions denigrate him to Mason. At the same time, however, he maintained a cordial correspondence with Cullen. He told Mason that his own lectures at Fisk would make "two perfectly good books eventually," though they did not; he also said that his essay, "The Message of the Negro Poets," which appeared in *Carolina Magazine* in May, was the best thing he had written that year.

By the end of 1928, Locke was offering Mason his opinion on a wide range of contemporary subjects. He had recently heard Roland Hayes in concert, and he said that Hayes sang like a white man and "not at all with his old reverent spirit." As for the journal that had published so much of his work, he exclaimed: "How white and flat Opportunity is under this management." Mason reciprocated with strong opinions, claiming that Thurman's play *Harlem* was "far worse than anything I have ever seen on a stage. A Judas act on Thurman's part." She clearly saw the treatment of lower-class subjects as demeaning to the whole project of racial uplift. Later Locke would be equally negative: "I knew the quality of Wallace Thurman's play and book from what I know of him. If only one could see some way of sidetracking these traitors. Would you approve of an open attack in the press?" No such attack appeared, though perhaps it was only Mason's persistent desire to avoid all negative publicity that prevented it. But they approved of some artistic efforts; Locke gave Mason a Christmas gift of Richmond Barthé's sculpture *Jubilee Singer.* In early 1929, Locke presented a lecture, which he shared in part with Mason, in which he argued that the "younger generation was interested in finding a point of view within themselves that could afford to ignore the white man's attitude toward them; but they have not yet discovered it."

Locke wrote to Mason that, in other lectures he gave in March 1929, he felt that he had learned to better gauge his audience and "change a tune to their ears." Mason wanted him to do this, and he in fact desired her to hear him, for the sake of "close-up criticism and inspiration." In an undated letter, Mason spells out just how thoroughly she served as a superego figure for Locke: "This means dear boy that the old battle we have been fighting for your freedom from worship of culture and education (and all those numerous things that 'Godmother' came into your life to put to sleep, that you might really live) has been deeply worthwhile." In April, Mason told him, in a contradictory message: "There are so many beautiful things Alain that I believe you are going to be able to do as you slough off this weight of white culture— using it only to clarify the thoughts that sing in your being." In March he decided to cut back on his speaking schedule and expressed a desire to spend a great deal of time in the coming summer with Hughes, whom he described as "gaining in power." He was also happy to report that he had heard from Hurston, who seemed confident and enthusiastic. His management of the patronage at this time seemed generally efficacious, but his overall schedule was quite heavy, and there were periods of considerable strain.

Locke was at this time medicating himself, largely in an attempt to recover from the stress of his heavy schedule. Among the preparations he took were Nux vomica, Red Bone marrow, and neurophosphates, all quite untraditional preparations thought to be helpful in digestion. In July Mason expressed concern about Locke's health and insisted that her nurse check his blood. She fretted about Locke's arrangements to go to Africa and asked him to change his plans, which he did, unfortunately. He would do more good in America, according to her intuition, which, however, she admitted might be wrong. She continued to mother him, often using the language of spirituality and rebirth: "[W]hat can I do to help you in your growth, your health and your message for your people if I let you submerge the Alain whom I believe can be born, and be a unit, with my other godchildren to transfigure before the white race, what lies in the real Negro." Acting in some ways as an analyst for Locke, Mason was attentive to his emotional life:

> Dear Alain, you say, "I wonder if Godmother quite realizes how little solitude I really get as someone is always on my back." Of course I have always, from the beginning realized that you didn't have a life that gave you enough solitude. The reason you have not had it is because you have not had the right attitude towards yourself, hoping to create, and therefore things do not live within your being silently, to be well born. You know I have talked to you about this ever since I have known you. Alain, it is the silent men upon whom no one dares intrude.

However well intentioned such advice may have been, Locke would always choose a public role for himself over any thoroughgoing silence.

Despite Mason's concerns about his health, Locke was told by his physician that he had seen a "decided improvement." There were also treatments at the spa in Bad Neuheim, Germany, part of his travels in Europe in the summer of 1929, where he met McKay, whom he found "young and fresh." In August he took time to write a letter to Cullen, using the stationery from the Hotel "Europaischer Hof":

> I am finding time both for rest and some writing. The cure is excellent. I am in the Kurheim section of the hotel—nurses, laboratories for Xray treatments, doctors office, etc right in the same building. The physician is a wizard—and almost promises me life everlasting. And what joy! He says Eat what you like for pleasure—I'll feed you the food you need chemically—and so by way of my mouth sometimes and my shoulder veins every other day I'm being fed what I hope will be elixir vitae. Certainly I feel renewed even after a week—and I think I'll remain three weeks longer, if I'm not sent for to come home early.

On at least one occasion Mason gave Locke the money needed to pay for such treatments, and it is probably unlikely that he could have enjoyed such luxury in those summers abroad without her monetary support.

There were more artists of the younger generation to encounter. Later in the year he met the painter William Johnson and visited his studio; he bought one of Johnson's paintings and also tried to persuade Duncan Phillips, an important collector in Washington, to buy some of the others. Johnson would later be a Harmon Award winner, due in part to Locke's support. The stock market crash apparently had little immediate effect on Mason. In early 1930, she was especially pleased with Hurston's work: "There is no end to the preservation in Zora's soul of the Divine gifts that are an open book to her, because she never soils either her way of life or her character in relation to the Almighty, by going down into that devilish hole, egotism." But Mason was not blind to the creation of an audience, for she urged "that Conjure book [of Hurston] must be pushed as rapidly as possible. The whole public has gone mad on Negro things since the appearance of Green Pastures," referring to the Pulitzer Prize-winning play by Marc Connelly which appeared in 1930. Mason also followed the career of Gandhi and announced that his example was a manifestation of what she called "Divine Power," which was "the only thing that will fling white man's Christianity under foot and put Christ's suffering (and all great souls who have followed him) in a Holy light before the people of the world."

Locke suffered a bout of depression in early 1930, though his physical condition had improved. His new assistant in the philosophy department had been admitted to a sanitarium and was so ill that even his wife was allowed to visit only once a week. The pressures of academic and esthetic judgment remained high. Locke did not see Hurston's gift at first, according to Mason, but he took up her enthusiasm for Hurston's work and urged Zora to send her manuscript to the publishing house of Covici-Friede. Meanwhile, James Weldon Johnson retired from the NAACP and was seeking a position at Howard. There was also talk of Charles Johnson coming to Howard, after fulfilling a five-year term at Fisk. Locke took the time to scuttle a Howard appointment for Louise Thompson, whom he felt had been disloyal to Mason. In April Locke sent Mason a memo, which he did from time to time, to keep her abreast of all his activities. In it he mentioned he was applying to foundations for support for a joint endowment that would serve the Harlem Museum of African Art and the Howard University African collection; that he would again visit Neuheim for treatment; that he had arranged to visit Geneva in the coming summer months and would interview Ras Tafari; that he hoped to

secure some ecclesiastical manuscripts from Abyssinian churches for Howard; and that Hurston's manuscript would be ready by the end of May. Whatever of his projects did not originate with Mason, the others were discussed
with her in order to gain her approval. Locke had evolved a dual role, for he
served as mediator with the younger generation of writers and artists, even as
he drew on Mason's wealth to fund the projects that mattered most to him.

By this point in their relationship, however, Locke was adept at mediating
between Mason and those for whom she was a patron. As difficult as it was
for Locke to manage the relations between Mason and Zora Neale Hurston,
it was even more difficult for Hurston herself. She was at least of two minds
about Locke and his role as mediator, for it meant that the protection of Mason's good graces had to be won twice over. Hurston first knew Locke when
she was briefly a student at Howard, where she had won membership in the
literary club and published in the campus magazine, the *Stylus*. "Dr. Alain
Leroy Locke was the presiding genius and we had very interesting meetings," she recalled years later. Locke published one of her stories in *The
New Negro* and may have introduced her to other leaders of the Renaissance.
Having formed a sense of his role as mediator between Mason and black artists, Locke had to decide who would be the ones to benefit. He was aware of
Hurston's lack of discipline, which many of her contemporaries commented
on, and Hurston never concealed her sense of wanting to defy convention,
except perhaps from Mason. She said of herself to Countee Cullen that the
regular grind of college work was "beginning to drive me lopsided. Dont be
surprised to hear that I have suddenly taken to the woods. I hate routine."[18]

   But Hurston had plenty of drive of her own. She managed to arrive in New
York with only $1.50 in her pocket in January 1925. Always in need of finan-
cial assistance throughout the 1920s and 1930s, she worked as a secretary and
driver for Fannie Hurst, the bestselling author of novels such as *Imitation
of Life*, while studying at Columbia as a scholarship student. Further support came from Annie Nathan Meyer, a wealthy benefactress and activist
who wrote a number of plays and served on the Board of Trustees of Barnard
College, which she had helped found. Shortly after beginning at Columbia,
Hurston became an admiring and dedicated student of Franz Boas; she referred to him as the "king of kings." He taught her anthropological and ethnographic techniques, and her impressive talent as a writer was both diverted
and enriched by her field studies in collecting folklore. She spent a great deal

of time in the Renaissance period traveling throughout the South collecting songs and stories and interviewing conjurers and voodoo doctors. Her relations with Mason were complicated by the need to turn these activities—which were to an important extent supported by Mason's patronage—into artistic literary and dramatic works that would be publishable, commercially viable (in part to repay the patronage), and acceptable to Mason's high-minded sense of spirituality. Though Locke's own esthetic appreciated and even encouraged the conversion of folk material into high art, it is not apparent that he fully appreciated the pressures under which Hurston operated. There were few ready-at-hand genres or models for this conversion. All of this, joined with Hurston's at times frail health and volatile personality, made for many misunderstandings and tense explanations.

Hurston, however, enjoyed her relation with Locke as her teacher in artistic matters. She shared with Hughes an affinity for the "low down" members of the community, but she had lofty ambitions to improve her talent. Willing to be tutored by Locke at a distance, she complimented him in ways that were sincere, at least in part. In October 1927 she wrote him from New York, lamenting the demise of *FIRE!!* and at the same time trying to rally the spirit that provoked that experimental magazine's attitude:

> The way I look at it, "The Crisis" is the house org. of the N.A.A.C.P. and "Opportunity["] is the same to the Urban League. They are in literature on the side, as it were. Mr. Johnson is an excellent man and full of zeal but he has a great deal on his hands. The same is true of Dr. Du Bois. Dont you think too that it is not good that there should be only two outlets for Negro fire? Your work in Philosophy is less confining than either of the others, why can't our triangle—Locke—Hughes—Hurston do something with you at the apex? Besides I am certain that you can bind groups with more ease than any other man in America. Will you think it over?

This letter was illustrated with a small triangle, with the initials, "L," "L.H." and "Z.H" at the three points. Hurston appealed to Locke's desire for race leadership, comparing him favorably with two of the most renowned African Americans of the day, suggesting his philosophical training gave him an edge the others lacked. Locke had cautiously but favorably reviewed *FIRE!!* in the *Survey*, arguing that its "strong sex radicalism . . . will shock many well-wishers and elate some of our adversaries; but the young Negro evidently

repudiates any special moral burden of proof along with any of the other social disabilities that public opinion saddled upon his fathers." Hughes and
Hurston both would have appreciated the professor's support of the young
against the fathers.

From December 1927, when she first met Mason through Locke's intercession, until September 1932, when Mason stopped her monetary support,
Hurston went through many cycles of despair and energetic composition.
All the while telling the Godmother how much she owed her, she continually protested that she desired her friendship even if she were ultimately unable to produce the sort of uplifting work that Mason had in mind. The first
meeting had about it a sense of destiny and high spiritual calling: "It was
decreed in the beginning that I should meet Mrs. R. Osgood Mason. She
had been in the last of my prophetic visions from the first coming of them . . .
the moment I walked into the room, I knew that this was the end." Her letters to Mason were sometimes obsequious—"Flowers to you—the true conceptual Mother—not a biological accident. To you of the immaculate conception where everything is conceived in beauty and every child is hovered
in truth"—but apparently Mason received such adulation without a blush.
Shortly after the payments stopped, Hurston could refer to Mason as "the
dragon on Park Avenue."

Such conflicted emotions were paralleled in Hurston's friendship with
Locke. She often praised him to Mason, saying that he was "too valuable a
man for the world to lose and particularly for the Negro world to lose," but
apparently she did this knowing that Locke was the patron's favorite, so she
dare not speak against him to her. To others she could be acidulous about
Locke. When he had published a partly critical review of her novel, *Their
Eyes Were Watching God*, she told James Weldon Johnson that Locke was
"a malicious, spiteful little snot that thinks he ought to be the leading Negro
because of his degrees." She did not stop there:

> Foiled in that, he spends his time trying to cut the ground from under
> everybody else. So far as the young writers are concerned, he runs a
> mental pawnshop. He lends out his patronage and takes in ideas which
> he soon passes off as his own. And God help you if you get on without
> letting him "represent" you! His interest in Sterling Brown makes him
> see Claude McKay as a rival to Sterling. Hence his snide remarks about
> Claude. I sent the original of this to OPPORTUNITY. I hope they
> print it.

The magazine did not print it, but clearly the diatribe reflected the complex of negative feelings that Hurston had toward Mason as well as Locke.

Locke helped Hurston in her writing, in part because of Mason's urging. But he knew when to stay away as well. He never publicly entered into the questions raised over *Mule Bone,* the play on which Hurston and Hughes collaborated and the copyright and authorship of which led to a very nasty dispute. In January 1932, Hurston was able to have *The Great Day,* which she referred to as her concert, made up of songs and dances based on her folklore studies, successfully performed in a number of New York venues, and Locke wrote the program notes for the production. Mason, such was her controlling eye, evidently objected to the quality of the paper stock on which the program was printed. But Locke presumably advised Hurston on some points of dramatic structure and devices. Later that year, when the work was performed at the New School for Social Research, Hurston wrote Mason that her "meeting with Alain on Sunday was very, very happy. I have been sing-ing ever since. I shall ask him to make the announcement about one or two minor changes in the program. I hope he wont refuse. Also I want him to say a few words about the type of material in the concert." Mason financed the concert, but despite quite favorable press notices, it never enjoyed a sus-tained run and so the work returned no profit. Locke and Mason had wor-ried together that Hurston would betray the "primitive" spirit of the material she had collected—this concern operated in all of the patronage that Mason distributed—so clearly Locke was acting as the Godmother's surrogate in staying close to the production. By this time Mason was too sickly to attend any performances despite Hurston's repeated invitations. The relationships among the three were thus further complicated, since many communications came second hand.

In the early and middle 1930s Hurston was finally able to achieve a fair level of economic independence. Asked to teach at Rollins College in Florida, near her home town of Eatonville, she was increasingly devoted to the idea of a Negro drama. Her first novel, *Jonah's Gourd Vine,* appeared from Lippin-cott in 1934, and she was able to secure advance contracts for other works. She wrote asking Locke to come and visit in March 1933, promising that the dramatic work she was doing would produce "a wonderful chance for Negro playwrights and young actors to grow." Over a year later Locke wrote to ask her to send a copy of *Jonah's Gourd Vine* to Mason, which she did. Near the end of 1934 she asked Locke his advice on whether to dedicate her newest book, *Mules and Men,* to Mason. She also took the occasion of this letter to launch a jibe—"they tell a lurid tale of his brazen tactics"—at Hughes, whose book tour in 1932 had earned him scorn when he spoke out against racism. A month later she told Locke that she had written to ask Mason for permission to dedicate the book to her, but she ended up dedicating it to someone else, perhaps because of Mason's desire to operate out of public view. Still, she took time to appeal in idealizing terms to the relationship that Locke had done much to nurture: "I would like very much to have you tell the audience [at her concert] what godmother has meant to Negro literature and art. She is where she can do no more, but before she passes I think there ought to be some acknowledgment to the world, from at least one of the people she has saved or tried to save, and what she has meant to America." The vexed matter of white patronage for black writers was seldom more complicated than it was between Mason as patron and Hurston and Hughes as recipients. Locke's part in it was inevitably seen in negative terms by some of his contemporaries and by later generations as well. In some ways his role in the patronage arrangement overlapped with his role as critic and teacher; such overlap, however, did not clarify his motives and actions but rather added to them the self-consciousness and sense of paradox that he carried with him constantly.

In the summer of 1930 Locke was consoled and chided by Mason, who wrote from her idyllic retreat in Maine, ostensibly concerned about a book that Paul Robeson's wife, Eslanda, had written in which she revealed her marital troubles with the great actor and singer. Locke himself was made the focus of Godmother's anxiety:

> It is a shame that on all hands you are being so badly represented, but really Alain, in every case, it harks back to the stupidity and vanity of your own people. . . . What is the use of building all these radiant possibilities for a group that seems to have no recognition either of these possibilities or the sum of their effort on the present need and condition of the world! . . . The flaming call, Alain, to great leadership is sounding, sounding everywhere.

Three weeks later her tone was more positive, but there were still reasons to be anxious. "You began to grow after you were 35 years old the things you should have had at the beginning of your life, and I believe you can attain a realization of the possibility of your people in relation to other countries that no other educated Negro is able to do at this moment." Mason's high-minded compliments were part of Locke's emotional bargain with his patron, even though they may have contributed to his penchant for treating others with disdain. Meanwhile Hurston's financial troubles were increasing, and publishers were not especially interested in her work. Locke had learned that an Abyssinian friend, known as Amoah, whom Locke had earlier tried to support in his efforts to start a bank in Abyssinia, had been duped in his business dealings and was now in an asylum suffering from a breakdown. Mason told Locke that she was feeling weak, and in the coming years she would be virtually housebound because of her medical condition. Locke's assistant in the philosophy department continued to be ill, and though he was supposed to return in the fall, he had not been able to. Just around the corner was the dispute over *Mule Bone* that set Hughes and Hurston at odds. So 1930 ended on an unsteady note, and there would be yet more occasions on which Locke's personal diplomacy and race leadership would be sternly tested.

CHAPTER EIGHT

New Horizons:
Sahdji to the Bronze Booklets

In the early 1930s Locke energetically pursued a number of different interests and projects, most of them dealing with cultural and philosophic issues. He remained steadily committed to exercising a leadership role, but he shifted some of his interests from the esthetic to the pedagogical realm. How much of this shift resulted from his dialogue with Mason is hard to determine precisely. Their relationship flourished as it did because Mason's sense of the need for spiritual growth answered to Locke's lifelong commitment to the notion of *Bildung,* or self-development. He never showed any reluctance to take Godmother's values to heart, and her advice to him plainly served to replace the counsel he had long received from his mother. Mason's ideas about morality—and propriety—also increased Locke's sense that the younger generation of artists involved in the Renaissance had fallen into a decadence of style and, perhaps, of spirit as well. Though he often looked to achieve a sense of balance—of hearing the full force of all sides—in any philosophical or cultural debate, he so favored development over decadence that he would have little interest in exploring the latter. Instead, he turned to the many forms of education as the extension of the cultural invigoration he hoped would flow from the Renaissance. In this sense, education was the form that Locke's political hopes took after the years of the New Negro. At the same time he returned again and again to strictly esthetic issues, for he could never imagine his life without them.

In 1931 Locke brought to fruition a dream he had had for a long time, namely the staging of a Negro ballet. He had long felt that African American artists could make intelligent and beautiful use not only of material from

FIG. 8.1. William Grant Still, photographed by Carl Van Vechten, 1949. Still and Locke worked closely together on *Sahdji*. Still also composed the music for the choral work, "And They Lynched Him on a Tree," based on a poem by Katherine Garrison Chapin, whom Locke introduced to Still. Library of Congress.

African sources but of forms and media hallowed by the Western tradition. On May 22, at the Rochester Music festival, *Sahdji* was performed, and Locke's role in this production was central. He began working on it as early as 1927, when, in a letter to William Grant Still, he proposed that Still undertake the composition of a ballet based on the short story, running to less than a page, by Bruce Nugent. By the time of the premiere, Locke had helped Nugent rewrite the story and contributed to the stage production in the form of African proverbs sung by the chorus and the "Chanter." In between these efforts, he worked hard to keep the project alive, and it meant a great deal to him to see it through to completion. His experience as a "midwife" for Renaissance literary and visual artists was extended onto the musical stage.

The narrative of *Sahdji,* which Locke published in both *The New Negro* as a short story and in *Plays of Negro Life* as a one-act drama, uses the form of a folk tale. An African king, Konombju, loves Sahdji, though she is in love with Mrabo, a member of the tribe and heir to the king. When the king is killed in a hunting accident, Sahdji reveals to the elders her adulterous love, but she is spurned by Mrabo, who cannot face the ostracism that his liaison would surely cause. Sahdji then throws herself into a passionate dance that ends with her suicide, seemingly in accordance with tradition. Throughout the ballet, a narrator stands at the side of the stage and comments on the action, using the various adages that Locke discovered by researching African folklore, in order to shape the thematics of the story. The dancing involved a large chorus that beat out a rhythm with their bare feet. Very little dialogue was used, and it appears that the narrative was conveyed largely by pantomime. The total time of the piece was a little over twenty minutes, a considerable portion of it spent on the dance parts.[1]

Olin Downes, well-known music critic for the *New York Times,* attended the premier on May 22, 1931 and wrote a positive review that appeared two days later. He reported that the festival had drawn an audience of thousands, and Mr. Still was "a composer of marked talents" who had "reason to be gratified with [his] reception." He went on: "The work is cast in an unusual form which has enough relation to the narrator of old mystery plays and dramas and might even be said to have an artistic kinship with the Grecian conception of commentary upon the events which pass upon the stage." Downes acknowledged the "experimental" nature of the work, while adding that Still demonstrated a "rapidly growing but not complete mastery, as yet, of the [theatrical] medium." The issue of the racial basis of esthetic experience, so important to the Renaissance, was brought to the fore, as Downes cryptically remarked: "It is not Negro music diluted with conventions of the white, nor yet is it cast in the forms of negroid [*sic*] expression which has also become conventional." Downes clarified his reaction somewhat by adding: "Mr. Still does not indulge in Harlem jazz, but harks back to more primitive sources, for brutal, persistent and barbaric rhythms." Unfortunately this remark reinforced racist stereotypes about African Americans and their musical traditions and shows a misunderstanding of Locke's artistic goals. This misunderstanding differed from that shown by artists and others when Locke spoke of the usefulness of an "ancestral legacy," but in both cases Locke held his own.

Sahdji was built on African materials, but it became a virtually forgotten predecessor of later efforts by African American artists to utilize fully the great storehouse of African motifs, images, and cultural significance. Locke suggested that Nugent employ African chants to lend the theatrical piece authenticity, even going so far as to supply him with fifty or so examples of African proverbs, which Nugent would later interweave into the work's third version, as a ballet with chorus. Nugent, a precocious nineteen-year-old when he first sketched out the story of Sahdji "on odd pieces of scrap paper," was the grandson of Locke's mother's classmate, Norrie Nugent. He was known in the middle-class black community of Washington, D.C., as "a much misunderstood and persecuted ne'er-do-well." Locke, however, instantly recognized Nugent's talents and included him in the pages of *The New Negro.* Nugent was launched on his career, until, as Locke put it, "he got to New York and the hazardous circles of Harlem life of 1926–27." But Locke was able not only to recognize Nugent's talent but to imagine it in combination with an important musical composition.[2] At Van Vechten's request for a history of the ballet and the location of its original manuscript, Nugent wrote to Van Vechten and credited Locke for *Sahdji*'s development and informed Van Vechten that Locke was the person to contact regarding *Sahdji*'s history. In response to the same prompting from Van Vechten, Locke wrote a brief history of the play's development: "My decision to include myself as co-owner of the copyright was not so much this editorial sharing of the revised version as a desire to protect the royalties in case the ballet would be set to music by a Negro musician rather than any of the white musicians who at that time were haunting Harlem for new finds and leads in the suddenly popular Negro materials." Locke's wish for an African American cast and music by a Negro composer was at least partially fulfilled by the much abridged student production, albeit without Still's music or credit to himself.[3]

When Locke set out to remake *Sahdji* as a ballet, he needed a composer, and so he turned to William Grant Still, known today as one of the formative musical talents of African American classical music. Having earlier in his musical career played clarinet in Eubie Blake's "Shuffle Along" orchestra, Still decided on a career as a composer devoted to music in the African American tradition. His best known work, *African American Symphony,* premiered in 1931, and he enjoyed the distinction of being the composer of the first black opera, *The Troubled Island* (1938), with a libretto by Langston Hughes (though this was not performed until 1949), as well as the first black to lead a symphony orchestra, the Los Angeles Philharmonic, at the Holly- wood Bowl in 1936. Locke, personally familiar with almost everyone in the African American community, had not yet met Still in 1927, despite being an avid follower of his music. He wrote Still in his usual gracious way to say: "I have been following your work on every possible occasion and have heard two of the International Composers' League programs. You will notice your work listed in the music bibliography of The New Negro—and comment in passing in the essay on Negro Spirituals." Still responded positively and first approached the work on an epic scale. This, however, resulted in defeat, causing a "failure" that dismayed him and that took Locke by surprise. But he remained patient and persistent; several weeks later he again approached Still, "with a sympathetic note and plea that he go through with it." This time it took. Eventually Still completed the work and told Locke that "in spite of its technical difficulties and huge cast, [Howard] Hanson was going to put it in for the [University of] Rochester May Festival."[4]

Locke sensed Still was best equipped to move African American music from its preoccupation with folk material into a higher stage where complex harmonies and developed structures could be made available to the black au- dience. Locke reasoned out the poetics of the visual arts and their reliance on an "ancestral legacy," and he saw a direct parallel with the musical and theatrical work he was keen to foster. Doing what he could to insure that the African aspects of the ballet were authentic, Locke conducted his typically thorough research. As early as May 1928, "cheered . . . to know that [Still was] actively working on the score for the ballet," he sent him a list of names and terms he had discovered were part of the language of the Azande tribe, from the southern reaches of the Sudan.

Despite his efforts, research, and personal dedication to the project, Locke did not attend the premiere of the ballet. This would not be the only perfor- mance of the ballet, and Locke had such high hopes for it that he assumed he could see it at a later date or in a different production. However, he made a genuine effort to attend the premiere, and to bring Nugent as well. He "went to New York to find Bruce, but he was in one of his homeless periods and I could not trace him until too late to get him up to Rochester," as he would later tell Van Vechten in recounting the history of the ballet. To Still, he sup- plied a different account as his excuse for not attending: an important mat- ter at Howard University (probably a Depression-induced fiscal crisis), and the illness of his assistant were to blame. As for Nugent, he "was also pretty busy with rehearsals for a role he is to play in The Golem, produced by the New School." Locke later told Van Vechten that the performance of *Sahdji* was "too studied," but "it was none the less one of the first indications of the serious use of African background and idiom, and I take it, was an early step toward Negro ballet." Locke, however, felt that "a Negro chanter and chorus would have given it warmth and more contagious rhythm." His original hope was to have the piece be the first ballet performed by a black cast. As it turned out, it was scored for "chorus, orchestra, bass soloist, [and] corps de ballet," and the all-white cast—wearing full body make-up—numbered about eighty dancers and actors. Sixty-five orchestral players and two dozen musical instruments were used, with a full range of percussion. Still excitedly wrote Locke five months before the performance to say that the bass soloist "will be engaged from the personnel of the Metropolitan Opera Co.," and he had hopes that the ballet might eventually be performed by that company. Howard Hanson was the conductor, and Still dedicated the music to him.

Writing to Still shortly after the premiere of *Sahdji,* Locke excitedly proposed future projects, looking to extend his collaborative activities with the man he considered the most accomplished African American composer. "[D]ont you think the next move should be an opera?" Locke said, and went on, tantalizingly, to sketch a project which unfortunately never came to fruition. "Already I have a wonderful scenario idea, with an African and American background. I started to work it out in conjunction with a local musician and we have registered the title and outline scenario, under the name 'Atlantis.'" Preoccupation with the subject of Africa did not prevent Locke from turning to something with an "American background." Several suggestions about the possibility of support followed, showing Locke's ambition to shape a role for himself in the African American theater: he would ask Hanson to "sponsor" the project, and he hoped to "get a subsidy from Mr. Eastman." Still went on to enjoy several commissions as his career flourished, aided by the ministrations of his second wife Verna Arvey, herself a concert pianist. But he was unable to take up Locke's suggestions as to "Atlantis."

Obviously a black producer in the 1930s and 1940s could not assemble the sort of cast and orchestra that Hanson made available in the Rochester festival. This alone accounts for the failure of *Sahdji* to enjoy many further performances, though it was staged twice more in Rochester, in 1936 and 1950. Eventually, through the talents of people like Katherine Dunham and her troupe, black Americans would bring African-inspired material into the traditions of American dance and music. From his college days scraping together the money for piano lessons, Locke regarded music as one of the sup-

FIG. 8.2. *Sahdji*, performed at the Rochester Music Festival. William G. Still and Locke worked on the score from as early as 1927; the Eastman School of Music played and performed *Sahdji* in blackface in January 1931. William Grant Still Estate.

FIG. 8.3. *Sahdji*, performed at the University of Illinois, Urbana-Champaign. On Saturday, March 24, 1934, Cenacle, a Negro student theater group at the University of Illinois, Urbana-Champaign, staged *Sahdji* as a Negro folk play with a much smaller cast than its Rochester Music Festival performance and full score, but without blackface parody. Moorland-Spingarn Research Center.

porting columns in the temple of culture. To be lifted by music, especially music that arose out of and gave spiritual clarity to a group experience, was long one of the chief ideas Locke adopted from the traditions of high German culture. Yet music's greater importance in reinterpreting its legacy through the frame of African culture—and the African American experience—drove Locke's participation in the founding of one of the important strains in our national culture. Locke aspired to recreate and extend his triumph, though *Sahdji* stands as one of his unique, though neglected, personal achievements. As Locke, ever the believer in the possibility of culture, wrote to Still after "their" work was first performed, "At any rate, my dear friend, you can climb the heights—all future success to you."

Locke's wish for an all-black cast for the staging of *Sahdji* as a ballet with Still's music was, at best, partially accomplished when it was staged as an one-act folk drama with black actors. Less than three years after the Rochester performance, on Saturday, March 24, 1934, Cenacle, a Negro student theater group at the University of Illinois, Urbana-Champaign, staged *Sahdji* as a Negro folk play. This *Sahdji,* however, was a student production and a far cry smaller than the full performance Locke had diligently promoted, using only eighteen players. The parodic image of Africans, by white actors in painted faces with a veneer of primitive exoticism, was absent in the performance by black actors. Nugent, ironically credited as Richard Bruce, was the sole author, described as "the young writer born in Washington D.C., 1905." The program used a quote from Eugene O'Neil to introduce the play: "The gifts the Negro can and will bring to our native American drama are invaluable, and to a dramatist, they open up new and intriguing possibilities." The play was directed by Miss Ione Johnson and Mr. Wesley Swanson, with the setting designed by Mr. Olaf Fjelde. The role of Sahdji was played by Helen Payne, and two of the actors, Kathryn Ashby and Helen Payne, had their pictures published by the *Daily Illini. Sahdji* as a one-act play would possibly have been performed more frequently if Locke had been able to involve himself with its promotion.[5]

Another realm where esthetic issues were conjoined with questions of patronage, itself a form of pedagogy, was the work Locke did with the Harmon Foundation. Established in 1922, it resulted from the philanthropy of its founder, William Harmon, a highly successful real estate developer, who in his childhood came to know the black soldiers that served in his father's Civil War regiment. This formed "his sympathy for the colored people and his desire for stimulating creative work," as the announcement of the beginning of the foundation's award program in the pages of *Opportunity* put it in 1926.

Harmon himself spoke in *Opportunity* of the motivation behind his charity, by relating a story of how black workmen restored his plantation house in South Carolina. The moral he drew was clear: "No one has a greater appreciation of the definite line of demarcation between the servant and the master than my family and I, nor a greater distaste for trespass on either side, but we interpret that relationship as did Jesus, and make it a beautiful thing rather than a vulgar one." Since for him, "The result is love, obedience and cheerfulness on one side, and gentleness and equal love on the other," he turned to philanthropy. Such was the philanthropy of the time, however, that it tended to add obedience—on the side of the servant—to the combination of love and tenderness. Harmon was nevertheless genuine in his tenderness. He funded different projects: playgrounds for inner city youth, loans for college students, awards in the creative arts, and a series of juried prizes and exhibitions in the visual arts. The latter area involved Locke. The foundation's director, Mary Beattie Brady, a stern, energetic manager, drew on Locke's critical expertise in exercising her care of the Division of Awards for Constructive and Creative Achievement. This included awards in literature, music, science and invention, and other fields. Brady was director until the foundation ceased operations in 1967.[6]

For a trial period of five years, from 1927 to 1930, the foundation, in conjunction with the Federal Council of Churches, sponsored a juried show for all African American visual artists, painters, photographers, and sculptors who cared to apply. In 1931 and 1933 the foundation sponsored two more shows on its own; there was no show in 1932, as the foundation was reevaluating all its programs. The juries consisted of established artists, and the shows were held at the foundation's headquarters in lower Manhattan, on Nassau Street, or in the International House associated with Rockefeller University, on the upper East Side. They also traveled to other cities, providing many black artists their first broad exposure. The original awards included a gold medal, with an honorarium of $400.00; a bronze medal, with no cash award; and an honorarium of $100. Later there were smaller cash prizes for second and third place. The press took notice of the exhibits, and over the five years the number and quality of the submissions grew appreciably. In 1931, for example, the exhibit was divided into two parts of forty-six works each and traveled to a total of twenty-six cities. Brady decided in 1928 to add a catalogue with essays on the issues which the works raised, and Locke contributed essays in both the 1931 and 1933 catalogues. This put him in the position of mediator of funds and recognition, a role his relationship with Mason had brought to a high finish.

The Harmon Foundation, relying on the jury system of selection, was always careful to have established artists serve in making the selections. This did not solve all problems, however, since juries were often divided as to the standards to be applied, with some favoring a high level of technical skill, while others leaned in the direction of more racially expressive motifs and manners. These differences in judgment reflected the larger issues in the Renaissance, and so some artists, out of a strong sense of how art should establish its audience, rejected the assumptions behind the foundation's shows. Romare Bearden, in a 1934 article in *Opportunity,* protested that the foundation's attitude "from the beginning had been of a coddling and patronizing nature." Though the public reception of the shows was often positive, the arguments returned: Should Negro artists look to their own heritage and social situation? Should they try to adopt, and adapt to, European standards? Was there some distinctive set of qualities or subject matter that gave Negro art authenticity? No easy answers to these questions appeared, and unlike the writers in the Renaissance, the painters and sculptors had to face them in the context of a public that was thoroughly socialized by European models in the plastic arts.

Locke and Brady did not always agree on the esthetic principles that the foundation's exhibits attempted to embody. Locke used both of his catalogue essays to further his notions about the use of African art by contemporary African Americans. Brady felt that this stance, especially if adhered to too closely, would produce an art lacking broad appeal. She maintained that the main purpose of the foundation was to teach people about art—this belief only strengthened as the foundation, in the later 1930s and 1940s, devoted more of its resources to schools and art centers—and her taste in art was more conservative and Eurocentric than Locke's.

In Locke's Harmon catalogues he furthered his views about the role of African art in contemporary African American painting and sculpture, and he addressed the overall context of American art as well. In the 1933 catalogue he argued that "the share of Negro subject material in the field of American fine art was negligible; little if anything, was being done for the encouragement of the Negro artist in the program of Negro art as 'racial self-expression.'" The 1931 catalogue, however, became an essay addressed to a national audience, in the *American Magazine of Art;* entitled "The American Negro as Artist," it was Locke's fullest and most nuanced presentation of his views on visual art until his later book-length study, *Negro Art: Past and Present.* Some of the points in the essay echoed Mason's ideas; some were clearly post-Renaissance thoughts applied to the younger artists he had met since the early 1920s. As with the phrase "racial self-expression," Locke spoke to the styles of the individual artists and their intersection with the larger group's sense of cultural identity.[7]

This essay presents the fruit of Locke's thinking about issues in the visual arts which he had expounded for several years. Typifying his skills as a critic, it combines a historical framework with an esthetic argument, illustrated with several examples of individual artists. Locke begins with "an historical reason" explaining why in Africa the characteristic cultural expressions of black people were decorative and craft arts, whereas in America they were music, dance, and folk poetry. The historical reason arises from a materialist base. Cut off from their cultural roots, the African American artists faced "the hardships of cotton and rice-field labor, the crudities of the hoe, the axe, and the plow." This "reduced the typical Negro hand to a gnarled stump, incapable of fine craftsmanship." The expression then flowed into the "only channels left open—those of song, movement, and speech." Locke divides recent history into three periods, 1860–90, 1890–1915, and 1915 to the present, and illustrates each with a number of examples. The third period, that of the younger generation, shows a "new social background and another art creed," as it "aims to express the race spirit and background as well as the individual skill and temperament of the artist." This generation has three groups: Traditionalists, Modernists, and Africanists or Neo-Primitives. Again, examples are provided; Hale Woodruff and James Lesesne Wells are modernists, and Richmond Barthé and Sargent Johnson are Africanists. Locke demonstrates the nuances of his argument by adding that Wells is a modernist, but his black-and-white work uses design and decorative motifs in a way that makes him Africanist.

Locke indulges his habit of pointing to emergent trends. He claims the younger talents who leave behind the "academic and imitative vein" will become "more particularistic and racial" and thus "wider and more spontaneous" in their appeal. From this emergence comes a clear direction: "And so, the immediate future seems to be with the racialists, both by virtue of their talent and their creed." This sounds a distinctly Lockean note of how new categories, meanings, and values emerge from incongruous cultural elements. Assured of his historical scheme and his esthetic theory, Locke concludes with a triumphalist note instead of his usual argumentative balance:

One of the advances evident in a comparison of the five successful annual shows of the works of Negro artists, sponsored by the Harmon Foundation, along with a marked improvement in the average technical quality, has been the steadily increasing emphasis on racial themes and types in the work submitted. Thus the best available gauge records not only a new vitality and maturity among American Negro artists, but a pronounced trend towards racialism in both style and subject. In this downfall of classic models and Caucasian idols, one may see the passing of the childhood period of the young Negro artists, the advancement of a representative school of expression, and an important new contribution, therefore, to the whole body of American art.

Locke took advantage of the fact that this essay appeared in a national magazine, one whose audience would include white readers in greater numbers than black. His reference to "the whole body of American art" uses the nationalist framework that had guided some of his reflections in *The New Negro*. In the future, with his attention on questions of adult education, among other things, his focus would sharpen on the black audience whose group expression he was keen to enhance.

Locke and Mason shared opinions on any number of topics, often mixed with gossip about scores of people. The Harmon Foundation demonstrated its debt to Locke by having a prize named in his honor, and in 1931, it was awarded to Edward Harleston for his portrait of an elderly woman. Locke, ever the discriminator, told Mason he felt it should have gone instead to Sargent Johnson's *Chester*. He added that Richmond Barthé's work "has fallen down quite decidedly." In February 1931, Locke visited Braithwaite in Cambridge and listened to his troubles, which were largely financial, and Locke tried to get him a position at Fisk but failed. He told Mason of how Braithwaite was starving while James Weldon Johnson was flourishing, even though the idea for Johnson's anthology of Negro poetry was originally proposed by Braithwaite. Mason, in response to this, replied that "Johnson can never recover from the stupid blunder he made in regard to 'God's Trombones.'" This referred to the poems that used a folk idiom based on sermons and biblical motifs, which probably jarred Mason's piety. A few weeks later, Locke enjoyed a visit from Arthur Fauset, Jessie's half-brother, and they reminisced about the old days in Philadelphia. Fauset was preparing to marry Crystal Byrd, whom Locke referred to as "that hawk-woman," and so he was "lost" to Locke and Mason. Meanwhile Johnson, in revising his anthology, planned to omit Toomer, which disgusted Locke, though Toomer did not in fact want to be considered a Negro poet.

During the years 1931–32, Locke published only a half dozen articles or so, rather below his average. Clearly "The American Negro as Artist" was the most important of these. Two others were the annual retrospective reviews he did of African American books for *Opportunity*. His focus remained on two problems, one personal, the other professional, that kept him in a state of anxiety. The professional issue had to do with Mordecai Johnson, whose presidency at Howard had started quite well but had run into opposition. The atmosphere at the university became "thick with suspicion, intrigue and pretense." The main cause was the rumor—which refused to be dispelled— that Johnson was a bolshevist. By April, the Washington papers were onto the story, and an investigative committee was formed to protect the university's reputation. Locke was a member, and he spent many hours trying to control events and appearances. In the middle of the month, the faculty coalesced in a vote of confidence, which might have settled the matter, but the board of trustees insisted on further investigation. Locke entered the fray with strong feelings. To him Emmet Scott, the university secretary, was a "crook if ever there was one," and Locke felt he was out to get Johnson, who refused to cave in in order to insure the school's appropriations from Congress. Locke surely remembered Scott's nonsupportive role during Locke's dismissal six years earlier. Meanwhile, Locke's time at Howard was made more pleasant when he became a colleague and close friend with Ralph Bunche, the future undersecretary to the United Nations and Nobel Laureate, and even helped him arrive at his thesis topic, on a comparison of the French colonial government and the French Togoland Mandate. Bunche was one of Johnson's chief supporters. The president weathered this particular storm, but the remainder of his administration saw a sharp division between his supporters and detractors.[8]

The personal issue that preoccupied Locke was a murky one. Though many details are lacking, Locke was named as a partial heir in the will of Thomas Charles Clark, presumably a friend from his Oxford days. Clark, a partner in an engineering firm as well as a tea importer, left an estate of one million pounds. A codicil, apparently the one naming Locke, was not duly witnessed, and indeed Clark's sanity was in dispute. He was killed in a car crash in Bournemouth on September 15, 1930, and the coroner ruled the death an accident, though Locke, mysteriously, expressed his doubts. Clarke made out his will on September 9th, had a revelation on the 13th— which was Locke's birthday—wrote a memo the following day, and was killed two days later. The codicil read in part: "It is the Divine Will that the World God's missionary shall be Dr. Alain L. Locke of Harvard University [*sic*] in the United States of America, and that Dr. Locke shall appoint Lord God's missionaries under him." The will was subject to probate in England.

In April 1931, Locke mentioned to Mason the possibility that he might secure enough money from this situation to enable him to teach only part-time at Howard, where he imagined he could have "a special post as lecturer on Negro Art and African Culture." Freed from the hassles of academic politics, he could devote considerably more energy to his cultural work. He hired a firm of English lawyers, Savage, Cooper, and Wright, to defend his interests and perhaps work out a "consent settlement." He told Mason: "I must follow up that crazy legacy."

The probate, scheduled for July 6, 1931, gave Locke little hope that the proceeding would rule in his favor, and he dreaded the size of the lawyers' bill. Convinced they only wanted their fees, Locke remarked: "That's English—and it makes me mad to realize now how much of their psychology got into me at a plastic stage of my development." This was said for Mason's sake, to assure her he was still working against his overcultivation. Having gone to London for the proceeding, he sought relaxation by seeing Josephine Baker and opined that "really the woman has genius," and later at the bar where she and her entourage went for drinks he observed that she was "simple and unspoiled." He spent part of the next day napping in Green Park, in one of "those sling canvas chairs," just opposite the Park Lane Hotel. He met Paul Robeson for tea and sent back the gossip that the singer lacked the courage to get a legal separation from his wife. He wryly observed: "One great advantage of the depression is the relative absence of Americans in the usual droves." As expected, nothing came of the probate actions for Locke, and Mason offered to pay his legal fees of $120. By August he was brooding over his "lost" fortune and telling Mason: "The old egotism has about gone, at last, and I really am on fire to do things for others and release forces that will live long after me."[9]

This new resolution motivated his eventual commitment to adult education and, perhaps, his renewed interest in philosophy. His summer sojourn proceeded as usual, however. Shortly after leaving London, he went on to Bad Neuheim, only to discover that his doctor there had been ruined by the crash of the market. A student friend from his Berlin days, named von Veltheim, invited him to his lush estate, and then it was on to Bayreuth, where he heard *Parsifal* and *Tristan,* conducted by Toscanini and Furtwängler. He worked fitfully at a never-to-be-finished translation of Maran's *Batouala* and then decided to take the "cure" at Bad Gastern, with its regimen of baths and electric treatments. He "walked up on the footpaths under the pines and sent spirit greetings out to my two mothers—Mary and dear Godmother." Later that summer he saw an exhibit of African art in Munich and said: "The crazy way they see it is that Egyptian civilization has influenced the African Negro—really of course it is the other way round." With education on his mind, and a sharp sense of social responsibility, he remarked on a science fair he visited: "Really when one thinks that every good-sized city might have one of these great educational toys for the price of two battleships, the idea comes home of how far off the track civilization really is—even on its own real values and achievements."

Extending his stay in Europe as long as he could, he visited another spa, at Franzenbad, in Czechoslovakia, and listened to Lehar and Strauss operettas at night. His weight—a mere ninety-seven pounds—dropped, though he felt his treatments were going well. Vowing to settle down and start "writing that book on the Negro in America which I have so often spoken to you [Mason] about," he also voiced his desire to write the story of his family and its influence on him. He would call it "the story of a mulatto who became a Negro" and cast it in the third person, perhaps imitating *The Education of Henry Adams.* Sharing some of his memories with Mason, he recalled from Berlin how in 1914 he and Mary were in Hamburg on mobilization day, but then they had gone on to Berlin to see some of his friends. Nostalgically relating it all to Mason, he recalled how he once hoped to "finish out my study here [in Berlin] for the degree I eventually took at Harvard in 1917." It was his mother's first year of retirement, and they celebrated her birthday at the Pschorr Brau Haus, in Charlottenburg. Only by circumstance was the border briefly reopened back in 1914, and they were able to leave Germany hastily, before the war began. He made a point in 1931 of returning to the table in the Brau Haus just opposite the one he and Mary had used, and there he again enjoyed a dinner.

The remark about the "mulatto who became a Negro" was addressed to Mason because it would be the sort of narrative core that she would approve. Locke often wrote from Europe, and from Washington, in a smooth, even unctuous, manner in his correspondence with Mason, expressing attitudes—about race and spirituality, among other issues—that did not always find expression in his work and writings. He would frequently portray himself in a subservient role, utterly dependent on Mason's largesse of spirit and mind. This contrasted sharply with the self-assurance he manifested in his personal and professional dealings. His self-presentation as someone who only "became" a Negro overstates—or melodramatizes, for Mason's sake—his maturation at Harvard and Oxford as he slowly but surely defined his identity as a race leader and cultural critic. This aspect of his relation with Mason and her maternal attributes suggests that his mourning for his mother was being protracted and displaced into a friendship that he saw as unique and very private.

When Locke returned to Howard for the fall term in 1931, he told President Johnson that he needed to do more creative work, doubtlessly energized by the success of *Sahdji*. Often occupied with mediating Hurston's needs and accomplishments with Mason, he knew their relationship was greatly troubled by the dispute over *Mule Bone*, the dramatic work on which Hughes and Hurston had collaborated. The two writers disagreed as to whom should get the credit of authorship and also the monetary reward they both hoped would come from a successful Broadway production. Based on an idea by Hughes, the play was built up by the use of Hurston's folklore. Through an elaborate series of misunderstandings and false assumptions, the play was presented to a theatrical company in Cleveland as solely the work of Hurston, though without her direct knowledge. When Hughes discovered this, he felt deceived and objected strongly, claiming he had contributed substantial amounts of dialogue and the play was at the least a joint effort. Hurston retaliated, saying Hughes had done virtually nothing on any aspect of the play. The presence of Louise Thompson, serving as the typist for the two collaborators and being paid for it by Mason, raised the temperature of Hurston's jealousy. She felt Hughes was being deceitful when he suggested Thompson share in the profits from the play. Attempts by Van Vechten and Arthur Spingarn, acting as Hughes's legal representative, to work out some settlement were at first successful, but eventually Hurston decided to withdraw all her cooperation and claim the play as her own.[10]

The controversy meant that the play was never produced in either Hurston's or Hughes's lifetime. Though some slight reconciliation occurred later on, both bore strong grudges against the other. Given Hurston's volatility and Hughes's penchant for being retrospectively self-serving, the task of reconstructing just who said and did what, and with what intention, remains dauntingly complex. Locke was inevitably involved in giving advice to both writers and in interpreting events for Mason. When he first heard of the dispute in January 1931, Locke too quickly suggested to Mason that Hughes was trying to "blackmail" Hurston. Hughes telegraphed Locke to ask for his "slant" on things, but Locke, according to Hughes's account, offered no help or consolation. A few months later, Hughes sailed off for the West Indies, an act which Locke described as "shameless," especially since he was using money from the Harmon Award (for which Locke had nominated him) as well as Mason's patronage. Locke simmered about it all, and in April he wrote "sharply" to the poet and then told Mason that "I think he [Hughes] owes something to the pedestal on which he has stood, and that to pick it down completely may not leave him or anyone else anything to stand on."

The *Mule Bone* controversy has never been cleared up in a way that satisfies everyone. But Mason and Locke still kept faith with Hurston, whose work they continued to support throughout the early 1930s, while generally Hughes fell from favor. After the beginning of 1931, Mason no longer offered Hughes any financial support. A poem he had written about the Waldorf-Astoria Hotel, which attacked upper-class indifference to poverty, ignited her strong objections. Locke's reactions to this development went unrecorded, though he felt, as did many others, that Hughes's recent poetry was weaker than his best. Even Van Vechten advised him not to publish the manuscript he had recently prepared for submission. Mason concluded he was not writing diligently enough; this last attitude was especially repugnant to Hughes. He tells in his autobiography how the whole situation upset him so much that his health suffered.

Locke all the while reported frequently to Mason how often he called Hurston, or had or had not heard from her. When Mason heard the publishers would not accept Hurston's book, called "Barracoon" at the time, she commanded Locke: "Break the stone heads of these publishers and throw them into the debris heap!" Locke thought the book was a "strong true piece of work" and sent it off to an editor at Viking. This manuscript, which was never published, dealt in part with a fable called "Cudjo's Own Story of the Last African Slaver." Locke urged Hurston to get a steady job, since her support was beginning to weigh on Mason. This was not meant as a criticism of Hurston's talent, for Locke vouched to Mason that she was "simply and consistently responsive," the most productive of all of Mason's "godchildren." As to the controversy over *Mule Bone,* Locke told Hurston: "Although I am myself very bewildered and disappointed by this muddle, I hope you can manage somehow to get your feet on the ground and in a straight track." By January 1932 Locke decided that the order of presentation of Hurston's material in a stage version had spoiled it. Later Hurston herself would blame this on the show's director, who insisted on adding Panamanian dances, in part because Hurston's southern folk material was not ready. Hurston meanwhile continued to ingratiate herself with Mason, and Locke continued in his role as mediator, even trying to help Hurston get a teaching job at a college. The three-party relationship often swayed from steady to turbulent and back again.

Locke's own concerns with the situation at Howard, and his health and personal relations, were occasionally troubled. At Howard, he learned to his dismay that his leave for the spring 1932 term was canceled because of budgetary problems at the university, exacerbated by the continuing investigation of Johnson and by the Depression. The enrollment shrank by 250 students, and the $1.9 million request for the yearly Congressional appropriation was cut to $1.1 million, while the endowment's annual income fell over $50,000. Racial insults were unavoidable. At the end of January, while at a performance in Baltimore of *Lysistrata,* the usher asked him "Are you colored?" "Yes," Locke replied, "I wouldn't be anything else." After a brief confrontation with the manager, he was shown to his seat. Seeking her approval for his manners, he told Mason he was not complaining, only describing the incident. An infected tooth hospitalized him for four days in February, and in May he suffered a mild heart attack and was ordered to bed for two days, suffering from palpitations and severe vertigo. This was one of several similar episodes, brought on by overwork, that would increase in frequency over the years. Meanwhile he kept up with the progress of several writers. He characterized Hughes as using the "old shyster's trick, of moving on to fresh fields before being found out." Will Marion Cook was unhappy with Cullen's play, *God Sends Sunday,* for which he had supplied the music, and he wanted Sterling Brown to rewrite the dialogue. He asked Locke to intercede, and he agreed. Locke sent Mason a copy of Brown's book of poems, apologizing for the introduction by James Weldon Johnson, who had forced his way into the book; he and Johnson held each other in low regard. Around this time he told Mason that he kept his mother's ashes on his table, "the place of the ancestors for me," as he piously put it. He also kept Curtis's *The Indians' Book* there, "now that I have learned how to worship the ancestors—and not have their dead weight on my shoulders—but the fire of their unrealized ambitions in my heart—."

Locke's deep consciousness of his ancestors animated him to engage in an important project in the early 1930s. This was a biographical essay on Frederick Douglass. He finished a draft of it but never managed to publish it, though it occupied considerable time and energy. As early as 1915, Locke had taken his students to Douglass's home in Anacostia. Clearly the figure of an escaped slave who became a magnificent race leader attracted Locke for several reasons, not least his gift of oratory. But his admiration was tempered when he presented the project to Mason in the spring of 1932. "The weather has been too bad for me to go down to the Frederick Douglass place; but I have been weighing the moral issues of his life and have nearly come in sight of the weakness you bade me watch for in his character. It will strengthen the book to know this. He was a great man in spite of it, though." By April he was at work on what he called the "Douglass manuscript." In May he shifted his attention to the pamphlet called *The Negro in America,* for the American Library Association; it was "put as straight from the shoulder as writing for such an organization would permit—remember it had to go South, North, and West and to fit the White and Negro reader." He sailed for Europe in June, but a month later he told Mason that he was "trying to dig in now on the Frederick Douglass material (I mean the records) . . . if I should succeed, his life-story will live again, and be influential in this and the next generation. For we need manly Negroes above all else, and F.D. did set a standard of manliness." He added that Douglass's vanity and egotism only appeared after the Emancipation. In October he resolved to "get seriously down to the . . . manuscript," and in November he was nearly finished with it. Despite a few scattered subsequent references, however, the project faded from his correspondence with Mason. Some of his effort survives in an introduction he contributed to a memorial edition of Douglass's autobiography.

Locke's sailing to Europe in the summer of 1932 proved especially eventful, as he confronted his bumpy relationship with Hughes. Bunche had decided to sail with Locke and traveled with him as far as Paris, where Locke then went on to Germany. Locke learned that Hughes and Louise Thompson had booked transatlantic passage around the same time. They were bound for Russia with an entourage in order to make a film under the auspices of the Soviet government. Locke managed to change his booking in order to avoid them, and then discovered, to his dismay, that the whole entourage had shifted their plans and they all ended up on the same boat. Encountering Hughes on board, and, without any handshake, Locke was offered a casual greeting, with "a mock jaunty tone." A Howard student was a member of the entourage, and he told Locke that Hughes behaved "mighty uppity, except when Louise is around—she makes him do anything she wants." Bunche asked Locke to introduce him to Hughes, but Langston cut the conversation short; Bunche opined that the group was largely deluded and did not know what communism was. In Locke's eyes Hughes had "coarsened and aged considerably," and Thompson was bloated with drink.[11]

The group was divided amongst itself politically and artistically, and eventually its project foundered when the Soviet hosts celebrated Hughes's arrival but failed to work out the production details for the film. The excuse was that the Russians feared inflaming public opinion in America; for his part, Locke ascribed the failure to the group's dissension and lack of talent. A few years later Hughes, in a newspaper interview, claimed the cancellation resulted from a failure to agree on the scenario. The Howard student later sent Locke other tidbits: the group suffered from the poor Russian food, and Thompson "has definitely showed herself to be very selfish and cheap, and we see very little of her. . . . Langston remains in the background very mysteriously." Mason chimed in with a negative thought: "I only hope L— was not weaving some of Zora's play that she took to Cleveland into this Negro film from Russia." She and Locke never restored Hughes to his former level of approval.

In Paris Locke enjoyed a concert by Paderewski, "an inspired titan," playing Chopin. Faced with the nationalistic spirit of the composer, Locke, thinking of his investment in *Sahdji,* lamented that he "thought the time will come when a Negro musician will make his patriotism flow into his art like that! I'll be dead, I suppose, but it will and must come." He delayed leaving Paris because of a bout of food poisoning. When he recovered, he visited Percy Philip, his old Oxford friend, and went to Aaron Douglas's garret, where he found the painter arty and affected in his manner. There was also the usual exchange of gossip; Robeson was involved with the daughter of an English lord, and Hughes, along with Loren Miller, a young poet, had gone Communist and was supporting the Party's slate in the presidential election. By the middle of July he reached Bad Neuheim, his favorite spa, but the larger scene was far from peaceful.

Demonstrations were taking place throughout Germany, and "Somebody's head gets cracked nightly," Locke observed. Percy Philip was a friend of Ramsay MacDonald, and he relayed to Locke in Paris the inside story of the Lausanne conference. Locke said that years ago bargaining would have produced a demand of Germany that it disarm and pledge to have no secret treaties. But current foreign relations were based more on belligerent force. Locke felt the Germans were "using Hitler as an international bogeyman— and that they will use the possibility of his coming to power to bargain with France and America." Later Locke opined that "Hitler was the clown juggled in front to amuse the world, while things went on behind the scenes." When he heard of the dictator's famous "beer hall" putsch in September, he said: "It is really alarming unless it is all part of a pre-arranged trick." As bad as things appeared at the moment, his next trip to Germany would reveal even more ominous forces.

The fall semester back at Howard was filled with disputes and tensions, since the campaign to remove President Johnson was still underway. Sterling Brown was especially unhappy at the university and felt he was poorly treated. Locke was "now on the look-out for a way out of Washington and Howard," and it would happen if he could "concentrate and have sufficient courage." Within months of this hope, fifteen faculty members were fired from Howard, though the philosophy department was spared. In November he wondered if he might not sound the president of Atlanta University about a job. He complained that Herbert Hoover's commencement address the previous spring, in which "as usual [he] said nothing," was "just a chance to placate Negro opinion just before election time after three years of contemptuous neglect." His anticlerical anger also boiled over on a religious topic: "When I think of the warped and narrow beliefs and teachings Christianity rammed down our Negro throats, I really feel like burning the churches. Because no absence of church or dogma could make the Negro irreligious—while the white man even with his churches is really at bottom irreligious—I suppose that's why he has to have so many churches!" In December he mused that "I'll someday have to write out for my own satisfaction—and absolution—the inside story of 'the Negro renaissance' and how it was scuttled from within." Continuing to reflect on the political actions of black people, he observed, shifting from a cultural to a political register, that in Washington "Negroes here are scrambling now to try to get the ear of the incoming administration; largely for jobs, of course—when they really ought to ask for big measures— like the change of disenfranchisement in the South," but he was convinced that no Negro leader would take up this charge.

In 1933 the spring brought Locke his "usual March slump," but this year it came earlier. At the start of the year he heard from Jessie Fauset, who had recently published her novel about passing, *Comedy, American Style,* which Locke reviewed in *Opportunity.* Having referred to the book's style as "too mid-Victorian for moving power today, and the point of view falls into the sentimental hazard," Locke bore the brunt of ten years of repressed anger: "I have always disliked your attitude toward my work" she fumed, "dating from the time years ago when you went out of your way to tell my brother that the dinner given at the Civic Club for 'There is Confusion' wasn't for me. . . . [Your articles in *The New Negro*] are stuffed with a pedantry which fails to conceal their poverty of thought. . . . [I recall] the adage that a critic is a self-acknowledged failure as a writer." Fauset then saw fit to throw at Locke the highest of insults: "You have shown yourself so clearly as a subscriber to that purely Negroid school whose motto is 'whatever is white is right.'" She asks that he never review another book of hers, and then changes her mind, insisting that she does not care. "Your malice, your lack of true discrimination and above all your tendency to play safe with the grand white folks renders you anything but a reliable critic." The letter is signed, Jessie F. Harris, her married name. Locke's response to Fauset, if any, is not recorded, but both of them probably remembered the sharp criticism of her essay on Negro humor that Locke had sent her in 1925. His reputation among some in the African-American community, especially posthumously, derived from feelings similar to those of Fauset, though not always so personally generated.[12]

That spring Wylie, the secretary of the Rhodes committee, paid a visit to Washington; "He was reasonably decent to me—at least in comparison with the other Rhodes people," Locke recalled. This visit may have led Locke to mull over his discriminatory treatment at Oxford and his strategy for dealing with it. On an undated card, he wrote about those years in England as part of his autobiographical musings that were never gathered or published. He reflected on "the strategy of covering up a controversy which even should it have vindicated me personally would certainly have jeopardized the chances of other Negro youth for the Rhodes scholarship competitions. I shall explain completely but only posthumously in a chapter in my autobiography—already written."[13]

The chapter referred to does not exist or at least is not labeled as such. But on another undated manuscript, titled "Race Problem," Locke has recorded a different strategy: "I had it figured out in 1916—30 years before it broke—and put it down for the record. But as to any general acceptance of it then, I knew it was impossible—Negroes were too busy indulging their self-pity by thinking theirs was the only race question[. T]he white man was totally averse to any suggestion that he, his civilization and its supremacy would die of the racism question—so, I just wrapped it up in polysyllables and sat tight." The date of 1916 suggests that Locke was thinking of his lectures on race, and the wry reference to "polysyllables" could mean his Harvard dissertation, or even the entire body of his writings on culture, value, and race. In any case, his defense against such charges as those leveled by Fauset and others would be parried by his own way of dealing with the racism he had often directly confronted. Whether he saw it as repression or discipline, Locke's strategy took into account the way his actions would ramify throughout the community, and at the same time he never lost sight of the tenacity and immorality of theories of racial supremacy. He felt confident that his part in the struggles of antiracism had more than sufficient justification.

Later that spring, the catalogue essay for the Harmon exhibit offered a bright spot in his cultural work. But troubles persisted, and some grew ominously. Mason was taken ill, and Locke addressed one letter to her as "Dear Guardian Angel Godmother." In June he sailed for Europe, but obviously the international situation had developed in increasingly negative ways, and things were already disturbingly different: "I notice a certain coolness on the ship—and think it reflects the new barbarism—or rather the old barbarism come to the surface—but I must wait till I land to be certain." Two summers before he had witnessed street rioting in a National Socialist demonstration against Jews. He opined that "it [was] a tryout for the revolution which will actually happen in Berlin sometime this winter." The situation had worsened, as the fascist forces became increasingly dominant. First impressions focused on how tourists were "in a sort of glass bell," even though he saw Nazi salutes everywhere, even in small and middle-sized towns. In Germany he cautiously kept his notes in code. In Austria the Nazification program was jamming radio broadcasts and interrupting music programs. A psychologist from New York, who told him that Goering's medical history was that of a psychopath, and that Hitler and Goebbels were insane as well, led Locke to remark sardonically: "In these uncertain times one perhaps ought to be thankful for bed and board in Hades." He celebrated his forty-seventh birthday in September and was still planning to write his life story, "as soon as it ripens."

Back home, Locke witnessed a different growing political activity. A boycott of a grocery store in Washington successfully led the A&P to hire Negroes, and Locke was touched to find out that the strikers had used as part of their slogan the phrase "The New Negro." He attended one of their meetings but did not address the group; the activists had succeeded in preventing a white school in Alexandria, Virginia, from getting WPA funds unless a Negro school got them as well. He heard a Roosevelt speech, which condemned lynching, at the twenty-fifth anniversary of the Federal Council of Churches. A lecture trip to the South, Locke's first in six years, left him feeling a "new sense of being truly Negro and part of the real folk." Remarking on his audiences, he said "they all have a genuine joy in living and a direct simplicity and sincerity. If only that could be kept along with education—and maybe that will in time be possible." Meanwhile, as the year drew to a close, he began helping William Marion Cook write his memoirs, which he had undertaken in part to answer what Cook felt were misrepresentations in James Weldon Johnson's autobiography.

In January 1934, Locke's assistant in the philosophy department, suffering what Locke called a "paranoiac breakdown," attacked him physically. The

assistant was diagnosed as having "dementia praecox," forcing Locke to replace him. Locke heard that McKay returned to America and had spoken in
Harlem; Locke was eager to see him and wrote to his publisher in order to reestablish contact. McKay was penniless and living with Arthur Schomburg,
having relied on Max Eastman to pay his passage back to New York. Hurston's novel, *Jonah's Gourd Vine,* drawn form her folkloric work, appeared
in April, and Locke sent Mason the *New York Times* review of it. "I somehow
think and hope that in the long run Zora will come through, and justify what
you have done for her. Even now, it is somewhat of an atonement." Locke
expressed the cautious judgment that the novel was "not flaming—but it does
flicker." He continued teaching courses in philosophy and the question of
value, lecturing his students on the necessity of self-discipline and personal
growth. But he also lamented his lot at Howard and what he considered its
insufficiently high academic standards, while nonetheless maintaining his
faith in education: "I never thought . . . that I would ever think of my work
as just a 'job'—and daily my resentment grows against those forces that have
made it so. . . . but what couldn't be done in a real school!" In May he decided
not to go to Germany, fearing any improvement in his health would be more
than offset by the spiritual dismay provoked by further evidence of the rise
of fascism. Instead, he cruised the Mediterranean past Constantinople and
visited Russia as well.

Before he left, he remarked on a newspaper picture of Mrs. Roosevelt posing with a young black boy, her hand on his shoulder. He wrote Mason that
"small things like that tell." When the cruise operators discovered he was
a Negro they refused to book any onshore excursions for him. On board in
July, he was seated at a table by himself and saw the steward erasing names;
he knew instinctively what that meant. Eventually, however, he was joined by
two white women, a New York City schoolteacher and a nurse from Florida,
and then two more guests. He remarked "the boat has been divided into two
camps and . . . they are re-fighting the Civil War with the North winning as
before." He drew his lesson from this: "I do think we Negroes ought more
and more to venture forth and by quiet dignified stands force the contradictions of these things home." This recalls the need to "controvert" the social
standards, as he had argued in his race lectures. Able to see Greece for the
first time, he was disturbed by being chased out of the museum in Athens by
a bell and a police whistle at closing time; he groused, "the modern Greeks
aren't the Greeks." But truly amazed by what he saw, he insisted: "No really
deep vices could have produced such beauty," reflecting a pagan streak that
he never abandoned.

Visits to Sicily, Lebanon, and Cairo put him into a mood where he felt the West had a lot to learn from the East. The uncovering of some mosaics in an Istanbul church older than St. Sophia's led him to judge, against the received opinions: "From these pictures you can see that Giotto was a gloomy morbid imitator of the early glories of Byzantine art." He revisited Tut-ankh-amen's tomb and saw the pyramids under a full moon. In Russia, the beauty of the children struck him, but he deplored the Soviet system, which he felt had produced "an indirect extermination of whole classes." To his mind "the original vision must have been a great one—but somehow class vengeance came in and fogged this vision." His resistance to any thorough Marxist analysis in the coming years was strengthened by these observations, and his instinctive trust in pluralism would mitigate any desire for a classless society. Back in Rome, he was offered a 70 percent reduction in rail fare if one was willing to pass through fourteen rooms of fascist propaganda. Locke took the offer, but said he sardonically shut his eyes and occasionally kept his hat on. Twice the guards requested he remove it, and he felt the third request might be fatal.

Back in America, he faced new developments and a number of valedictory notes as the year drew to a close. Staying briefly in Harlem, he noted how the living conditions for many were now "wretched." This shaped his views as reflected in the 1935 issue of the *Survey Graphic* called "Harlem: Dark Weather-Vane," which would soon be one of his major projects. Visiting Mason in the hospital, he deplored the new play by Kenneth Perkins, *Dance with Your Gods.* Marred by sensationalism in Locke's view, it was nevertheless successful with the audience, especially as it featured the Broadway debut of Lena Horne in the role of an octoroon. Roland Hayes, who was coming out of retirement, planned an upcoming Carnegie Hall concert, but Locke did not think "he [could] recover lost ground." In November, a trip to Chicago to help elect a black Democratic congressman, Arthur Mitchell, provoked the observation that "the pet argument that the Negro is a hand-tied Republican will have to go to the discard." While there, Locke saw William Marion Cook, who was planning a radio series on "Black Master Music." When he returned to Washington he heard the apparently dubious news that Hughes was in Reno getting a divorce from the white woman to whom he was briefly married, and he said "this is all news to me since Langston and I had our differences, or rather since Langston repudiated a loyalty to something we once had in common, I had no idea of his marriage, but I'm not so surprised after all." The end of the year brought sad news: "Just this week two squandered talents have flickered out—Wallace Thurman and Rudolph Fisher (who wrote those fine short stories but got dazzled with attention and got singed in the flame of Van Vechten's trap-lights)." Planning a retrospective article on a subject that would cause him considerable rumination over the years, he would call it "Why the Negro Renaissance Failed." On an almost sermonizing note, he said: "The deaths of Fisher and Thurman, and the bankruptcy of L. H. and Cullen make a good text." He thought "it is impossible to keep completely still, having been so intimately involved." The article never appeared in this journal or with this title, but it was revised and would appear in part as "Spiritual Truancy" in 1937.

Locke's skills as a writer remained prominently in evidence in the format of the annual survey of Negro literature that he produced over seventeen times. Starting in 1928 and running off and on through 1952, in the pages of *Opportunity* and later in *Phylon,* he chronicled the year's work in books of all sorts—poetry, fiction, and drama, but also history, folklore, sociology, African studies, and so forth. He missed 1930, and 1941 to 1946, when the continuing effects of the Depression and the war on black authors created serious obstacles. These reviews exhibited remarkable style and judgment in arriving at an informed esthetic assessment, but also used a keen critical eye in framing and discussing the contemporary social and political background, and what Locke called the Zeitgeist. The review essays were highly appropriate vehicles for blending Locke's literary judgments and his sense of the need to have race leadership be constant and thorough. Nimble in the transitions between paragraphs, inventive and playful with his imagery, and always sure-handed in his rhetoric of mixing praise and blame, these essays are among Locke's more skillful expressions of his values and beliefs. He could be blunt in his summary of a book's features, yet he never used the space simply to even scores, though often the books under review were by people he knew well, such as Hughes and Hurston, and his Howard colleagues, like Sterling Brown and E. Franklin Frazier. Serving the community as the chronicler of its self-expression, Locke gracefully shaped the emerging trends and extended his teacherly impulses to the broadest possible audience.[14]

Clearly taking the format of the annual review seriously, Locke titled them with phrases that captured the main organizing idea. The review for 1934 was one of the longest and appeared in two parts in the January and February 1935 issues of *Opportunity.* Locke began by reflecting at length and seriously on the format and by setting high standards for what many would consider only an ephemeral effort:

A retrospective review must needs ask the question: what have been the dominant trends in the literature of the year? I make no apology for presenting my conclusions first, although I vouch for their being conclusions and not preconceptions. Only toward the end of a long list of reading was there any semblance of dominant notes and outstanding trends. But in retrospect they were unmistakably clear; each writer somewhere along the road, no matter what his mission, creed or race had met the Zeitgeist, had been confronted with the same hard riddle, and had not been allowed to pass on without some answer. . . . [T]he artist is concerned with his own specific theme and knows first hand only the problems of his own personality. But the Zeitgeist is inescapable as that goblin of chatter-box days that wormed himself as tape through the key-hole of a bolted door to become a real ogre again as soon as he had twisted through. . . . [T]he dominant question of the day relentlessly comes in sooner or later. It is the small-souled artist who runs and cringes; the great artist goes out to meet the Zeitgeist. (CTAL, 228)

The artistic and cultural tension between self-expression and a larger group experience reasserts itself here, as it often does when Locke steps back to look at esthetics in general terms. Commingled with his belief in art's ability to reach a universal truth, the artist's burden of living in a world of socially and historically causative forces led Locke to respect that tension. Though always present, these themes received added attention in Locke's post-Depression reviews. His year-end reviews, though thoroughly professional, read like an esthetic autobiography in which his many complex feelings about African American life and culture are expounded.

The annual reviews display different aspects. The first, for 1928 (which appeared, as they all did, in the first month or so of the following year), Locke presented as a "flood tide of the present Negrophile movement." By using the term "Negrophile" Locke signaled that the Renaissance had turned into a different cultural phenomenon. Though many books were being published by Negro authors, Locke worried that stereotypes and fads and "fluctuating experimentalism" led to a situation where excessive material of less than lasting quality was being produced. "[T]he water will need to be squeezed out of much inflated stock and many bubbles must burst." However, he managed to find value in the fiction that had appeared, though poetry has seen "subsidence" after years of "extraordinary productiveness." Locke hailed as the "most significant of all recent developments . . . the new interest in Negro origins." A half-dozen books were praised, chief among them J. W. Vander-cook's *Black Majesty*, as Locke argued that "a reevaluation of the Negro without an equivalent restatement of the Negro background could easily sag back to old points of view."

The second review, "This Year of Grace," dealt with the books that appeared in 1930. The overall note was rather negative, as the Depression was making itself felt even as Locke's sense of the cultural force of the Renaissance was fading. He complained that the "much exploited Negro renaissance was after all a product of the expansive period we are now willing to call the period of expansion and overproduction; perhaps there was much in it that was unsound, and perhaps our aesthetic gods are turning their backs only a little more gracefully than the gods of the market place." A "second and truly sound phase of the cultural development of the Negro in American literature and art cannot begin without a collapse of the boom," he insisted, using his sense of historical progress to wring some optimism out of the moment. Referring to Marc Connelly's *Green Pastures*, he quipped: "In spite of a heaven of jasper walls, golden wings and crowns and harps, the true Negro peasant spirit would stop to tilt a halo and to scratch an itch." A spate of Negro biographies, often afflicted by false piety, was "pitiably fettered . . . to the missionary mode." A near-exception was produced by Robeson's wife, Eslanda, who wrote a "boldly intimate but too worshipful biography of her great and versatile husband." It almost broke the mold, though the total effect was of "a great statue half spoiled by an over-elaborate pedestal." Sociological works earned merit for Locke if they did not swamp the reader with facts and statistics without any interpretive framework. He especially disliked Negro sociology that did not relate its findings to the larger social and historical environment. Locke concluded with the claim that "the constructive gains . . . have been in . . . criticism and interpretation rather than in the literature of creative expression."

"We Turn To Prose," the title of the review for 1931, signaled that Negro and white authors were "obsessed nowadays with the social seriousness of the racial situation, and seem convinced of an imperative need for sober inventory, analysis, and appraisal." Such optimism would not dominate the review, however. Though poetry was scant, Locke mentioned the work of Sterling Brown, whom he would praise throughout the coming years. As for Hughes, his new work "deserts his poetic platform of folk-poetry for the dubious plane of entertainment and propaganda"; Locke had used the latter term as one of disvalue since his early argument against Du Bois. James Weldon Johnson's reissue of the *Book of American Negro Poetry* allowed the younger generation space, but Locke worried, somewhat ambiguously, that "it is sometimes regrettable that the racial themes are not preferentially stressed, though it is quite possible to make too much of the differences and too little of the common lyric motives of the Negro poets." The most notable books were historical studies, about the slave trade and Toussaint L'Ouverture, among other topics. Seven books of Africana, among which Locke heralded *Africa View* by Julian Huxley, were described as casting light on the continent's "tragic conflict, uncertainty and dilemma." Locke formed his closing observation: "[T]here is an interest deeper than superficial curiosity and more universal than mere ethnologic or sociological interest." His commitment to the esthetic possibilities—and legacy—of African culture, such a vital part of his imagination from the 1920s, never flagged throughout the rest of his life.

Locke named Sterling Brown's *The Southern Road* as his choice for "the outstanding literary event of the year" in 1932. Its "difficult combination of intimacy and detachment" introduces "a new dimension into Negro folk portraiture," combining features into the sort of paradox he often praised. Locke's taste for folk culture and artistic expression, clearly evident in his writing though missing from his reputation as an elitist, delights in the balances, as Brown shows us a "Negro peasant humble but epic, care-free but cynical, sensual but stoical, and as he himself says, 'illiterate, but somehow very wise.'" The next year's review, entitled "The Saving Grace of Realism," omits poetry as a category and concentrates on history and sociology. The typical Negro author, in Locke's characteristic view of counterbalancing viewpoints, is now "no longer propagandist on the one hand or exhibitionist on the other." Different dominant keynotes are sounded; they are "sobriety, poise and dignity." This change results from a turn to what Locke calls "realism," by which he means not the high-nineteenth-century fictional style so much as a levelheaded dismissal of stereotypes. Novels by Julia Peterkin and Roark Bradford embody this, as does the autobiography of James Weldon Johnson. McKay's *Banana Bottom* and Jessie Fauset's *Comedy, American Style* are praised, though the latter author felt condescension directed at her work being regarded as "persevering and slowly maturing." As for the sociology and history, Locke inveighs against the "modern plague called 'research.'" This reflects his mistrust of pure empiricism and the scientific method, which he saw as draining the human values from the mere collection of data. He ends by saying that "a year of material stress and depression has not adversely affected the literature of the Negro," a too-hopeful conclusion, perhaps, since the pauperizing effects of the Depression lasted for several more years.

For 1934 Locke wrote a long essay entitled "The Eleventh Hour of Nordicism," which he published in two installments. Clearly influenced by his firsthand experiences in Germany the previous summer, the essay signaled Locke's concern with the current international situation and its rapidly approaching crisis. Locke probably chose the word "Nordicism," rather than, say, racism or white supremacy, in order to focus on the German fascists, but the essay stays on a general level of analysis. Locke praises the recent fiction of Hughes, *The Ways of White Folks,* and Hurston, *Jonah's Gourd Vine,* despite his strained relations with both writers. "Avowedly propagandist, and motivated by radical social philosophy, we have here the beginnings of the revolutionary school of Negro fiction," he says, speaking of Hughes's book of short stories. Locke's flexible esthetics stand out in this instance as he puts aside his distaste for propaganda. He also says that "for pure folk quality . . . even the sort that a proletarian school of Negro fiction must think of achieving," Hurston's first novel had the "genuine strain." He willingly adapts his years'-long commitment to folk expression in order to include a sense of proletarian solidarity. Along with many others, he responded to the fiction writer's critique of American capitalism and approved speaking out against the mores of a market economy that had obviously failed the African American community.

In the second part of the essay, Locke turns his attention more directly to sociology, Africana, and education. The interest in books on education, first reviewed in this year's essay, was prompted by his newly energized commitment to adult education, an interest he would pursue for the next two decades. Cheered by the output, he suggested that in education "we may anticipate a new development in this numerous but somewhat stagnated and stultified profession." As for the sociology, Locke reiterated his abiding mistrust of any social science that was blinded by a too-strong worship of mere facts, which he bitingly refers to as a "fetich." He realizes, however, that the stringent values of science are necessary in certain cases and areas, and he praises Boas and his "scientific school" for daring "to bring the citadel of Nordicism into range of scientific encirclement and bombardment." He singles out a book by W. O. Brown, *Culture Contact and Race Conflict,* for its theoretical boldness in formulating a six-step process of cultural contact that would end in the liquidation of conflict and produce "racial fusion of the peoples in contact." The strong echoes between this book's title and Locke's lecture series of two decades earlier obviously drew his attention to the work, which he called "the most significant sociological item of the year." From the Africana books he draws what is for him the familiar but important lesson that "there are ele-

ments of permanent value in African cultures and their tradition, and that the
complete displacement of these cultures would be an irreparable loss."

His sense of balance was Locke's chief attribute as a critic, and this balance applies in the esthetic field alongside his pragmatic values of wide-
ranging curiosity and informed skepticism. In this particular year's review
he obviously felt the building pressure of the international conflict, and he
expressed rather unchecked enthusiasm for a play by Paul Peters and George
Sklar, called *Stevedore,* that concerns the struggles of a black New Orleans
dockworker to protect his rights. Now nearly forgotten, the play was favorably
reviewed by Mike Gold in the *Masses.* Resembling other proletarian plays
such as Odets's *Waiting for Lefty,* which appeared the following year, the
play called forth Locke's praise in challenging terms: "Coming into the thick
of the race problem by the unusual route of the class struggle and its radical
formulae, this vehicle . . . has harnessed the theater to propaganda more successfully than has been done in this generation. Its clock, so to speak, strikes
eleven for capitalism and Nordicism by the same pounding realistic strokes."
He proclaimed "there is no denying the force and effect of 'Stevedore,'"
naming it a "synthesis of race and class as a new type of problem drama."
Locke's antipathy to propaganda, firmly consistent throughout the middle
1920s, here gives way in the face of his deep unease with fascism. Adding the
sentiment of anticapitalism to his antiracism also reflects the economic stress
of the Depression; this portion of the review clearly demonstrates his move
toward a left-wing stance in his political outlook. Locke experienced similar
strong feelings when he first confronted the onset of the Great War, only to
have his patriotism reassert itself, along with that of many others, once America entered the war. Throughout the remainder of the 1930s, however, Locke
would unwaveringly be occupied with addressing the problems of economic
injustice. His social activism, at the same time, would focus on developing a
better system of education for adults rather than on any extended socioeco-
nomic analysis. His year's-end reviews closely trace his social consciousness
throughout the decades.

Locke worked as an educator for his entire adult life, inspired in large part by
his parents, especially his mother, whose commitment to Felix Adler meant
there was always and chiefly a moral element in pedagogy. The example of
Mason and her spiritual concerns also led him into reflections on the importance of transmitting culture as a transcendent commitment. The daily round

of abrasions and disappointments at Howard had sometimes dulled his commitment, but they did not extinguish it. Furthermore, there was the more pragmatic work of Dewey on education, of which Locke was likely aware, especially since both always linked education and democratic values. In the middle of the 1930s he began increasingly to focus his attention on adult education. This focus involved a deepening friendship with Arthur Schomburg, someone Locke first met during his early days at Howard. Schomburg, ten years older than Locke, was a Puerto Rican who held the militant view that blacks should know their own history as a way to combat prejudice. Lacking in formal advanced education, he became a self-taught historian and bibliophile. During the Renaissance his activities as a book collector made him an important source for many writers and intellectuals who turned to him for facts and historical understanding. He had been active in the Negro Society for Historical Research, founded by John Edward Bruce in 1911; the two men had invited Locke to give a lecture to the society in its early years. Schomburg greatly admired Locke's erudition, though he also felt that Locke was less than successful in addressing blacks who were hampered with little education.[15]

Locke and Schomburg, however, shared an interest in learning and the culture of books, and they joined together to help advance each other's careers. In 1924 Schomburg had written Stanley Durkee at Howard to recommend Locke for the expedition to Luxor for the opening of the tomb of Tutankh-amen. Throughout their close friendship, Schomburg told Locke of his luck in finding rare books by black authors, and Locke frequently helped out by tracking down such items during his various travels. Locke happily possessed the collector's temperament, and he devoted himself to collecting not only African and African American art but also the classics of the Negro tradition. Schomburg, grateful for Locke's practical assistance, also valued his intellectual guidance. Using his own collection as the core, Schomburg set up a study center at the 135th Street Branch of the New York Public Library as a hub of black study and historical scholarship. So, in 1932, when Schomburg felt the need to reassert the branch's role in the education of the community, he turned to Locke.

Schomburg, for several years active in the field of adult education, had originated the Harlem Project in Community Adult Education, with help from grants supplied by the Carnegie Foundation and the American Association for Adult Education (AAAE). In 1934 Locke, at the suggestion of Schomburg, was enlisted to write a report for the American Association of Adult Education on the Harlem Project and on a similar undertaking, the Atlanta

Project. Locke's report thoroughly examined the strengths and weaknesses of the two projects and concluded, among other things, that adult education for Negroes should focus on Negro culture. This idea was one of Locke's central contributions in his work in adult education. Locke arrived at this conclusion from looking at the interests demonstrated by people in the two projects, and, like Dewey, he felt education should always begin by taking into account the immediate situation of the learner. Shortly after this report was completed, however, the AAAE decided not to spend any extra effort on adult Negro education. As a result, Schomburg and others decided to form a new organization, which was called the Associates in Negro Folk Education, which would remain affiliated with AAAE but have its autonomous projects. Locke became the first president of the associates, and Schomburg was listed as a "founding member" along with Charles Johnson, Mary McLeod Bethune, and others. Schomburg took up his role with enthusiasm, and during the early 1930s lectured to community groups and instructed them in the use of the research materials in the library.[16]

The associates devoted themselves to the major project of publishing the Bronze Booklet Series, a group of paperbound titles on Negro topics that appeared between 1936 and 1938. Locke played a decisive role in this, selecting and editing virtually all the titles in the series. Early on, he asked Carter Woodson to write a volume for the series on Negro history, but Woodson, after giving Locke the impression that he accepted the offer, decided to produce a volume on the subject with his own Washington-based firm. Locke then turned to Schomburg, who agreed to undertake the task. Schomburg worked diligently on the book, with Locke serving as editor. Locke held that his work editing the manuscript was "a labor of love ... [since] my good loyal friend Schomburg who can gather facts ... cannot write. He was trained in Porto Rico on florid Spanish and his English is impossible." Before Locke could complete the needed revisions, Schomburg died in 1938, at the age of sixty-four. The volume unfortunately never appeared.

Locke took very seriously the problems confronting those who would seek to improve the field of adult education. Too often the activities were of a merely recreational sort, and Locke longed for a way to structure a program with genuine intellectual content and cognitive development. A further problem was that of coordination, as many institutions, such as the YMCA and church groups, were involved but in ways that were detrimentally diffuse. In his report on the Harlem and Atlanta Projects he spelt out the benefits of using Negro culture as an organizing subject that would speak to the problems of adult life, and at the same time proceed with "information and discussion of an intellectual, informative, and non-propagandist character." He set out his definitive views:

> The task of adult educationists . . . lies in discovering and using ways to generate serious and sustained interests. For the Negro, the one word "race," with all its mental association, is a tragically magic charm that instantly evokes dead serious thought. Provided we do not overwork the appeal of this charm, this special interest of the Negro, I believe that we have in it a positive focusing point for mass adult education.

This would provide the keynote for the Bronze Booklet series in which Locke himself would provide two volumes, the books on Negro music and Negro art. The cautionary note, about overworking the appeal, was typical of Locke's approach to problems, which to his eye always needed a sense of balance and circumspection.[17]

Though 1935 was in some ways a sobering year for Locke—as he looked back on the Renaissance and saw mostly failure, and witnessed the threatening omens of fascism and international strife—he was able to inaugurate a number of writing projects that would carry his thoughts forward and greatly increase his productivity. His future work would include perhaps most prominently the Bronze Booklets, and he would also edit another very significant issue of the *Survey Graphic,* this one on the sociology of Harlem in the Depression, in part a response to a race riot that rocked the black community in 1935. The issue would be markedly less well known than *The New Negro,* but it reflects equally the web of Locke's values and thoughts about questions of race and culture. The year also saw the appearance of his single most important philosophical essay, "Values and Imperatives." This essay was the last one he would publish in his role as a professional philosopher, but he would carry his philosophical training and beliefs with him as he ventured further into the field of adult education. The remainder of the grim decade of the 1930s proved, against considerable odds, a surprisingly fertile time for Locke.

CHAPTER NINE

The Educator at Work and at Large

Locke continually pursued his vocation as a race leader in many ways and many contexts throughout the last two decades of his life. The appearance of fascist dictatorships, which heralded a yet more vicious form of race superiority, would turn his attention to the fundamental countering values of democracy and cultural reciprocity. Among the roles he sought for himself, three were aspects of each other: educator, editor, and author. He published a number of essays every year on education, culture, and racial issues, as well as continuing his review of the year's books by African American writers. At Howard he continued to teach courses in philosophy, but also to speak to students there, and audiences throughout the country, about the purposes of education. Though self-admittedly elitist in his esthetic and intellectual standards, his teacherly impulses remained democratic, most obviously in his editorial work on the Bronze Booklets. His political and social awareness never flagged, and he sought to intervene in several issues through the agency of the printed word. Maintaining a national audience also meant lecturing in many states, mainly at black universities and annual meetings of various associations, most of them concerned with improving the status of African Americans. His hectic social and cultural calendar remained brim full, as he still traveled to New York City on a regular basis. Deadlines for his work as author and editor made demands that must have seemed unbearable at times, but, if he complained, he seldom refused a request for another essay, another lecture.

The second half of the 1930s presented Locke with not only an increased vocational commitment to adult education but also with the culmination of two of his longstanding efforts: his esthetic commitments and writings that formed around the issues of the New Negro, and his work as a professional philosopher. The latter came to fruition in his publication of "Values and Imperatives," and the former was to a large extent encapsulated in his publication of "Spiritual Truancy," a short review that can be read as a virtual valediction to the New Negro movement. The philosophical essay, "Values and Imperatives," had its origins in a lecture Locke gave to the Harvard Philosophical Club in 1930, and further back, of course, in his doctoral thesis. It was published in 1935 in a collection of essays called *American Philosophy Today and Tomorrow,* edited by Horace Kallen, Locke's friend from his early days at Harvard, and Sidney Hook, one of Dewey's chief followers at the time.

Locke's brief contributor's note to "Values and Imperatives," perhaps his most succinct self-portrait, described himself as "more of a philosophical mid-wife to a generation of younger Negro poets, writers and artists than a professional philosopher." This remark contains a measure of waggish self-deprecation—given its appearance in a collection of essays by professional philosophers—as well as some self-regard and an attempt to explain his purposes and values. The opening sentence of the essay is consonant with this mix of tones and intentions, since it advances one of the chief claims in Locke's personal philosophy:

> All philosophies, it seems to me, are in ultimate derivation philosophies of life and not of abstract, disembodied "objective" reality; products of time, place and situation, and thus systems of timed history rather than timeless eternity. (PAL, 31)

The mix of tones—"seems" and "ultimate" indicating the intuitive balanced with the inevitable—guides the claims of personal testament into a framework where eternal considerations are mentioned, if only to be put aside. The essay's nuanced argument, solidly in the Deweyan tradition of pragmatism, avoids ending with a single or absolute moral imperative, while it still faces squarely the fundamental aspects of moral values, moral choice, and moral behavior. Axiology, the philosophical study of values, balances a concern for judgment with the need for analysis, and is in many ways the ideal discourse for a thinker like Locke.

The opening briefly sets out the argument for an anti-foundationalist position, which holds that there can be no absolute metaphysical truth that transcends all time-bound human consciousness. However, the argument quickly introduces its main qualification: "no conception of philosophy, however relativistic, however opposed to absolutism, can afford to ignore the question of ultimates or abandon what has been so aptly though skeptically termed 'the quest for certainty.'" Citing the title of one of Dewey's chief works, Locke announces his philosophical commitment even as he challenges one of the main popular understandings of pragmatism and relativism. The absence of metaphysical certainty cannot be an end of philosophy; there is still much to be discussed and discovered, and certainty in matters of belief and valuation will likely remain a constant desideratum. By introducing the phrase "philosophies of life" Locke points toward the understanding of philosophy as experiential as well as, if not more than, analytical. In the improbable event that all metaphysical issues were to be resolved, there would still be the business of living. As such, we still need to have some understanding of the springs of our actions, the "imperatives" that guide us in our choices, either on an everyday, even a moment-to-moment, basis or in our long-range plans and ineffable desires. Locke says, "pragmatism has only transposed the question from the traditional one of what ends should govern life to the more provocative one of how and why activity creates them."

That our actions generate our values rather than the other way around is a tenet of pragmatism. What makes this investigation provocative, however, is that we cannot live at the extremes of "the sheerest nominalism or the most colorlessly objective behaviorism." Locke here continues to object to the rampant authority of scientism and looks instead for a non-absolute ground for human meaning. In part he finds it in what had been a main thrust of his thinking for the past two decades: group identity and the individual expression. Riding alongside this problem is another, namely why do both personal and group identity look to impose "imperatives" of universal import? Locke invokes the "characteristically American repudiation of 'ultimates,'" which does away with universalism and absolutes, but he points out that this translates into a "common sense" that seeks a "universal fundamentalism of values in action." This is an example of how all people tend to set up "personal and private and group norms as standards and principles, and rightly or wrongly hypostasize . . . them as universals for all conditions, all times and all men." So even the nationalistic spirit, with its considerable stake in an opposition to absolutism, ends by forming universal imperatives. Locke seems to echo the Nietzschean claim that our values are always rooted in our self interest, rationalize them as we will.

Locke then adapts this paradoxical argument—a version of the law of unintended consequences—to indicate that the same problems apply even if we avoid the muddled thoughts of either the common man or the philosopher. He again invokes the Deweyan phrase to build the argument:

> Our quest for certainty, motivated from the same urge [to proceed in "the name of eternal ends and deified ultimates"] leads to similar dilemmas. The blind practicality of the common man and the disinterested impracticality of the philosopher yield similar results and rationalizations. Moreover, such transvaluations of value as from time to time we have, lead neither to a truce of values nor to an effective devaluation; they merely resolve one dilemma and set up another. (PAL, 35-36)

He pointedly summarizes the dilemma: "And so, the conflict of irreconcilables goes on as the divisive and competitive forces of our practical imperatives parallel the incompatibilities of our formal absolutes." As is fairly common in philosophical arguments, the author paints a picture in which all our practical solutions and abstract formulations end up questing for a certainty that is always beyond our means, thus generating endless strife. This amounts to a counsel of despair.

Locke avoids this analytic dead end by rejecting the two extremes, "value-anarchism" and the "mere descriptive analysis of interests." Instead he argues for a "functional analysis of value modes," which demonstrates how our schemes of valuation work inside the complex creation of imperatives. Our value modes—that is, the way we create and assess values in the different aspects of our experience, whether esthetic, moral, religious, or logical—posit "end-values." These have a stereotypical function, using stereotypical in the nonpejorative sense; each act of valuation aims at and is guided by an "end-value" specific to that form of valuation. (In esthetics it would be the beautiful or artistic, in morals the good or noble, etc.) Functional analysis of valuation shows us that the reinforcement of our value judgments by reason is secondary, and it offers a "practical understanding of the operative mechanisms of valuation and of the grounds for our agreements and conflicts over values." In short, by seeing how valuation works, we can better adapt it—and adapt to it—the imperatives that we live by. Clearly based on Enlightenment principles, Locke's argument looks at valuation as a human experience that has hidden causes of action that can eventually be uncovered, and such revelations show us not only how our values function but how we can use their understandable functionality to arrive at greater self-knowledge and comity in and between groups.

Meaning to put value at the heart of philosophical knowledge and analysis,

Locke emphasized the necessity of realizing that truth, along with "the confirmation of fact," may also "sometimes be the sustaining of an attitude, the satisfaction of a way of feeling, the corroboration of a value." Again, Locke does not want to invalidate or reject the scientific method; rather, he wants to balance it with the fuller understanding of the valuative aspects of experience. He saw this problem in nationalist terms, and, reaching back to his early essay on "The American Temperament," saw part of the problem, and part of the solution as well, in American traits and habits of mind. "[W]e are saying that but for a certain blindness, value theory might easily have been an American forte, and may still become so if our predominantly functionalist doctrines ever shed their arbitrary objectivism and extend themselves beyond their present concentrations on theories of truth and knowledge into a balanced analysis of values generally" (PAL, 37). By insisting on "the experimental-instrumental aspects of thought," philosophy has "disabled itself" for the pursuit of a "fundamental interpretation" of value in its many different modes. The split between fact and value, one of the hallmarks of modernity, is a split Locke argues his way past, into a full realization that "[v]alue reactions guided by emotional preferences and affinities are as potent in the determination of attitudes as pragmatic consequences are in the determinations of actions."

Feeling sure that the functional criteria of values must lie somewhere between "the atomistic relativism of a pleasure-pain scale and the colorless, uniformitarian criterion of logic," Locke wends his way between the various extreme formulations that axiology had offered in the past half-century or so. Each value-mode "establishes for itself, directly through feeling, a qualitative category"; people discriminate in this value category (e.g., holy/unholy or good/evil in the religious mode) by an appropriate feeling-quality. Most important, Locke realized that value therefore begins in emotion and ends by mediating it. Locke postulates that the attitude engendered by our feelings shapes the value-mode (in effect, letting us know whether we are experiencing esthetic, moral, logical, or religious values), and, by leaning on the results of Gestalt theory in psychology, he adds that there is an appropriate form for each value mode. Value modes, however, are porous: the logic of a mathematical proof can be "beautiful," or creative esthetic expression can be felt as a "duty." Furthermore, in the esthetic mode, which Locke posits as the form that can exist in or support the other modes, anything can be felt as beautiful. The porosity of feeling modes means values shift and change, and even bring about new values. Values, both old and new, maintain a solid form in Locke's view, however, and this causes them to be recuperated, as it were, under the aegis of the "standard" functions of valuation, namely the making of claims and differentiations. The form of the valuation guides us in determining what the new value entails and how it can generate an imperative. Feeling plays a role in the origin, change, and eventually even the understanding of values. Values are corroborated by feelings, as Locke said, and, by taking feeling into account, we can see how values function.

Locke secures the analytic framework by setting out four kinds of feeling: exaltation, tension, acceptance, and repose. He illustrates the wide range of valuational activities and forms by means of a table, adapted from his doctoral thesis, with the feeling qualities (exaltation, tension, acceptance, and repose) along one axis, and the value types (esthetic, moral, religious and logical), with their predicates and polarities, along the other. Thus values can be placed within an analytic context and examined as to their function— that is, how and why they take the shape they do. The central part of the essay, and almost half of its length, is occupied with various examples that are illustrated by reference back to the table. It is, then, the "field of the genetics and dynamics of values" that the table can illuminate, and thus enable us to "apply a common principle of explanation to value mergings, transfers, and conflicts." Examples supplied by Locke show how logical proofs can become esthetic, moral reflections become "detached appreciation[s]," and religious rituals resemble art works, with their "reposeful, equilibrated projection." The examples illustrate how the esthetic mode, given pride of place and function, can absorb and transvalue the moral, logical, and religious modes.

An analytic framework shows us that each value has a function and a form and is not an insight into any absolute but rather a result of individual or limited group experience. The "only peace a scientific view of value can sanction between [such antinomies] is one based not upon priority and precedence but upon parity and reciprocity." Reciprocity, grounded not only in empathy but in the porousness of feeling and value modes, becomes one of the cornerstones of Locke's philosophy and his writings on education and world peace during the final decades of his life. Since we ourselves can and do shift from one value mode to another and experience a range of feelings with each mode and each shift, we should be able to apply this realization to the conflict between groups. "The effective antidote to value absolutism lies in a systematic and realistic demonstration that values are rooted in attitudes, not in reality, and pertain to ourselves, not to the world." Here Locke verges into the moral of his essay, and one can feel that he is drawing on his knowledge of Simmel on group relations, Perry on value, and Royce on loyalty, as well as his own lived experience as a member of a community blocked and discriminated against on grounds that lack any rational or scientific basis.

His sense of paradox, however, leads Locke to prescribe a strong dose of caution to supplement his moral urgency. He says, "no one can sensibly expect a sudden or complete change in our value behavior from any transformation, however radical, in our value theory." Reform is possible, however, though it will be neither swift nor clear. Faced in the middle of the 1930s with the rise of fascism and communism, Locke saw that revolution might occur as a result of the Depression and also that even some form of classless utopia, as envisioned by the Marxists, might be possible. But questions of value would persist:

> One way of reform undoubtedly is to combat the monopolistic traditions of most of our institutions. This sounds Marxian, and is to an extent. But the curtailing of the struggle over the means and instrumentalities of values will not eliminate our quarrels and conflicts about ends, and long after the possible elimination of the profit motive, our varied imperatives will persist. Economic classes may be absorbed, but our psychological tribes will not thereby be dissolved. (PAL, 49)

Implicitly addressing Du Bois and others who were insisting that racism could be eliminated only through economic struggle based in class consciousness, Locke takes a meliorist view. In concluding his essay, he proposed a "non-Marxian principle of maximizing values." This was the idea of "loyalty to loyalty," the notion first advanced by Royce when Locke was still a student at Harvard. Locke summarizes Royce's argument: "In its larger outlines and implications it proclaimed a relativism of values and a principle of reciprocity." If "transposed to all the fundamental value orders," the notion of a loyalty to loyalty meant "reverence for reverence, toleration between moral systems, reciprocity in art, and had so good a metaphysician been able to conceive it, relativism in philosophy."

Locke concludes by imagining a religion, a morality, an art, and a philosophy that would all be able to see that values were forms of feeling, but this did not mean values were phantasms or self-indulgences. Rather, they formed a set of truths that could be changed, tested by experience, and made into a way of corroborating ourselves and the allegiances that lie behind our common humanity. Locke's philosophy and his experience as a black man in the first third of the twentieth century were co-assertive, so to speak. As with his notion of the "civilization type" in the lectures on race contacts, Locke structured his analysis so as to end with an idealized formulation, but one that kept clear the direction of rigorous thought and did not lose itself in the clouds of wishful thinking. Though he formulated no elaborate version of social psychology, he never ceased considering the ways in which the individual and the group were intertwined, their shared destinies tied up with their shared values. When he speculated on social and political questions, he often concluded by reverting to the optative mode, not only because he wanted to see past the end of racism and other social depredations but also because his meliorism was as dear to him as his elitism. As both a midwife to poets and as a sometime professional philosopher, Locke's values were rooted in his feeling for cultural expression and what he would come to call the "third dimension" of culture, a sense of self-awareness that made pluralism and reciprocity possible.

His esthetic sense clearly engaged with his philosophical reflections, as Locke attempted to clarify his theory of value. Meanwhile he was also sorting out his feelings about the Negro Renaissance and in particular about the increasing sense, shared by many, that the movement had faltered if not failed completely. The Depression accounted for some of the frustration of the writers who failed to find an audience and who consequently were unable to devote a career-long set of energies to their art. But there were other reasons, and Locke felt some of them in personal terms as well as in the difficulties that faced the larger black community. In conversations with Mason and in his yearly review of books by black authors, Locke fitfully commented on the Renaissance. However, he wanted to say something definitive about what looked to be a hardening estimation of the art the Renaissance produced and even more about the values and forces that drove it and that eventually failed to sustain it.

An occasion presented itself with "Spiritual Truancy," an essay largely taken up with a review of Claude McKay's autobiography.[1] Though this appeared in 1937, Locke had been mulling over his feelings about the issues it raised for several years. These feelings were intertwined with his long and frequently troubled friendship with Claude McKay, whose own situation in the later 1930s was anything but comfortable. In 1934 McKay had returned to Harlem from a number of years abroad, in Soviet Russia and North Africa as well as Europe, where his health and finances were often precarious. His views on race, as expressed in his autobiography, *A Long Way from Home*, were often conflicted, swerving between a desire for universalism and racial pride, but often marked by strong resentments.

FIG. 9.1. Arthur Schomburg. Bibliophile and educator, he and Locke shared many interests and together were active in forming the African-American Associates in Adult Education. Moorland-Spingarn Research Center.

FIG. 9.2. Claude McKay, signed photograph. McKay's friendship with Locke was contentious at times. Moorland-Spingarn Research Center.

Surprisingly, McKay's views began to resemble those of Du Bois, for whom he had often expressed disdain. In the early years of the Depression both men confronted the necessity for economic independence and group self-definition. Also, McKay was firmly convinced of his class analysis of oppression, but by the last half of the 1930s he was growing increasingly anticommunist. Contradictorily, his political and social views were both firmly held and mercurial. In at least one context, this tension took the form of a debate over whether and how black writers should form guilds and what the policies of admission to them should be. In early 1937 he left the Federal Writers' Project, a group sponsored as part of the government's New Deal, because he felt it was insufficiently activist. He responded by forming a similar group, called the Negro Writers' Guild, which would limit membership to blacks only. Some of its members, such as Jessie Fauset, attended few of the meetings, while others, such as James Weldon Johnson, who acted as its president, chose not to involve themselves in the workaday details. Eventually McKay argued with others in the group and before long the guild failed. He was unhappy with any program directed by writers that did not embody ideals of social justice, yet at the same time he argued against propagandistic writing and any pressure to adhere to a strict ideological line.[2]

Locke considered McKay's attitudes about restricted membership in an artistic guild as a form of racial chauvinism. Toward such attitudes Locke felt only repugnance. Moreover, he had added reason to deliver harsh judgments against McKay. The 1937 publication of *A Long Way from Home* featured some of the most caustic observations about Locke to appear in print during his lifetime, and they no doubt played a considerable part in the hardening of the negative aspects of Locke's reputation. McKay betrayed his once close relation with Locke by revealing things that were available to him only because Locke had trusted in their friendship. Clearly, a sense of loyalty had been breached. In the chapter of his autobiography called "The New Negro in Paris," McKay sets the scene by describing a lunch at "one of the most expensive restaurants in the *grands boulevards*," probably in 1930, with Locke and President Hope of Atlanta University. Then he shifts the context to recount his first meeting with Locke in 1923, when they had visited the Tiergarten in Berlin and shared remarks on the classical statuary there. Locke admired the statues greatly, representing as they did a high-water mark of German art, though McKay counterposed the drawings of George Grosz, equally German, but which Locke recoiled from because of their "brutal realism." McKay went further and dismissed Locke's expertise in African art, expressing a general disdain and a total dismissal: "from the indication of his

[Locke's] appreciations it was evident that he could not lead a Negro renaissance." McKay's attitude toward the Renaissance was complicated; by virtue of his expatriated status, he likely felt left out of many of its activities in the 1920s. There was as well the prejudice he felt as a West Indian in dealing with African Americans, a sore point that fed his resentments against privilege, especially if based in class or color. So the subject of Locke's place in the Renaissance was bound to be a point of contention with him.[3]

It was not so much Locke's role in the Renaissance, for which McKay grudgingly gave him some limited credit, but Locke's often criticized sense of elitism that McKay focused on. He turned this criticism into an acerbic attack on Locke's character. McKay took the occasion to rehearse the details of the publication of "White Houses" in *The New Negro*, but before he did that he presented a passage that was quite acidulously *ad hominem*:

> Yet I must admit that although Dr. Locke seemed a perfect symbol of the Aframerican rococo in his personality as much as in his prose style, he was doing his utmost to appreciate the new Negro that he had uncovered. He had brought the best examples of their work together in a pioneer book. But . . . [h]is introductory remarks were all so weakly winding round and round and getting nowhere. Probably this results from a kink in Dr. Locke's artistic outlook, perhaps due to its effete European academic quality.

The use of coded words such as "effete" and "kink," combined with McKay's not mentioning his own homosexual experiences in the autobiography, suggests, if not a homophobic reaction on McKay's part, at lest a subtle effort at character defamation. He mentions Locke once more, near the end of the book, when he says of "The New Negro" that "Dr. Locke's essay is a remarkable chocolate soufflé of art and politics, with not an ingredient of information inside." The attack was clearly undertaken without remorse.

Locke and McKay shared many things: a taste for discipline in art, a continuing fascination with group identity, a desire to eliminate the social and personal costs of racism, and a homosexual lifestyle built in part on a pattern of concealment and furtive recognitions. Yet their differences seemed to weigh more heavily in the long run. He knew of McKay's temper from the incident with "White Houses." Though eager to speak with McKay when he had heard of his return to America, the passages in *A Long Way from Home* must have seemed like an unforgivable insult. Locke took his very measured revenge on McKay's acidic portrait when he had the chance to review the book. The review was also a valediction of sorts, laying to rest, more or less finally, all the ghosts of esthetic idealism associated with the Renaissance.

Locke used the pages of the *New Challenge,* a journal edited by Dorothy West, to answer McKay.[4] Ironically, according to one of its editorials, the journal was not interested in "attempting to re-stage the 'revolt' and 'renaissance' which grew unsteadily and upon false foundations ten years ago." Since McKay's autobiography was a work of nonfiction, Locke's negative estimation of it in "Spiritual Truancy" did not bother with esthetic values but instead focused on the author's attitudes. Taking up a line of McKay's description of himself as a "truant," Locke's unrelieved attack turned McKay's attitudes toward life and art, and especially group identity, back against him. He acknowledged that McKay was "a prose and verse writer of stellar talent," but "spiritually unmoored," he had become "the unabashed 'playboy of the Negro renaissance.'" An example of "chronic and perverse truancy," there were at least half a dozen movements to which he could have given his loyalty, but, by his own account, he had withheld his full commitment from them all. His autobiography presented a lonely uncorrupted skeptic, who saw through the Soviet experiment and all the bourgeoisie, white and black. Locke turned this valuation on its head, and, reaching back to his early admiration for Josiah Royce, used the concept of loyalty—and McKay's lack of it—to condemn McKay. "Even a fascinating style and the naivest egotism cannot cloak such inconsistency or condone such lack of common loyalty," Locke averred, disallowing any esthetic excuse for McKay's behavior and attitudes. McKay had deserted the Renaissance by his disregard for all the values of the community. Locke was certain that the balance between the individual and the community was completely off center in this case.

This hostile review served ironically as an occasion for Locke to develop his friendship with Richard Wright, who was on the editorial board of the *New Challenge.* Locke responded to Wright's request for a review of the book by saying he had turned down two other requests but was willing to do one for the new journal. "I didn't want to wash our linen in the wrong wash-tub," he wrote, "but in the privacy of our own kitchen, [I] will welcome a chance to do so. And hope it will not be too out of line; I shall try, of course, to be fair. I think I can hit a note that will have significance for the departure you are trying to make in the New Challenge." Sending the review to Wright, Locke commented: "I tried not to vent a personal grudge, but nevertheless to flay the gentleman quite honestly. I think he deserves this—but if you don't care to print it, O.K. with me." Locke expressed strongly—and paradoxically— one of his esthetic principles when he told Wright, "Though an aesthete myself, I have no patience with arty posing and inappropriate aestheticism." He went on to support Wright's application for a grant and to review favorably his novel, *Native Son*. He made other efforts to advance Wright's career, clearly recognizing his talents and welcoming the element of realism that his fiction brought into African American literature.[5]

But Locke had more to say in the *New Challenge* on the subject of McKay, or rather some of the issues that his autobiography had raised. Having dispensed with the author and his book, he turned in the review's last paragraph to his reflections on the Renaissance. Aggressively defensive, and more than a bit revisionist, he set out to define what had been the movement's aims. "The program of the Negro Renaissance was to interpret the folk to itself, to vitalize it from within; it was a wholesome, vigorous, assertive racialism, even if not explicitly proletarian in conception and justification. McKay himself yearns for some such thing, no doubt, when he speaks in his last chapter of the Negro's need to discover his 'group soul.'" Locke refers to that "group soul" and offers his formula for its fate and those who look for it with faulty means. "A main aim of the New Negro movement will be unrealized so long as that [the "group soul"] remains undiscovered and dormant; and it is still the task of the Negro writer to be a main agent in evoking it, even if the added formula of proletarian art be necessary to cure this literary anemia and make our art the nourishing life blood of the people rather than the caviar and cake of the artists themselves." Ending with a prescriptive flair, he says: "Negro writers must become truer sons of the people, more loyal providers of spiritual bread and less aesthetic wastrels and truants of the streets."

In using the image of "the nourishing life blood of the people" Locke flirts with a biologism he normally rejected, and in his allowance for the possibility—though not the necessity—of a proletarian art, he beckons to a propaganda that he often argued against. Apparently Locke needed to seize the high ground against McKay by claiming a commitment to the spirit of the folk while relegating McKay's sensibility to the status of a lumpen proletarian. He may simply be responding to McKay's charge against his idealizing elitism. But as often happened in disputes between Negro intellectuals and artists during the Renaissance, as well as before and after, the claim to speak for the folk, the people, the masses, was a necessary entailment of any claim of race leadership. For Locke, this need uneasily combined with his Romantic understanding of the role of the true artist, whose art ideally combined, even if paradoxically, the truest personal expression with the most pressing group experience.

McKay was not the only person with whom Locke experienced a conflict that involved larger issues of group identity and personal authority in the middle 1930s. Locke engaged many black intellectuals in a dialogue about pressing issues such as the purposes of black education, but it was in some ways with Du Bois that the engagement had the most at stake. As with their dialogue about esthetic issues in the middle 1920s, the two men often failed to agree on basic principles, and Du Bois's mistrust of Locke was to a large extent reciprocated. Mutual wariness, mixed with less than laudable judgments about each other's professional role as cultural and political leader, simmered beneath the incident that most irrevocably demonstrated their differences and made any future cooperation nearly impossible. This was Locke's rejection of Du Bois's manuscript, "The Negro and Social Reconstruction," in 1936. The idea of the manuscript came about in part because Locke and Du Bois were trying separately to develop an aggressive and efficient program for black education. Locke was almost certainly aware of Du Bois's views, as the elder spokesman gave the Howard commencement address in 1930, in which he set them out with characteristic force. That address, a rather dour assessment of the state of black education, had Du Bois claiming that both the assimilationist ideas of Booker T. Washington and his own more activist stance had failed to achieve the desired results. Struggling against the "growing mass of stupidity and indifference" at the leading black colleges, Du Bois pleaded for recognition of the "tremendous organization of industry, commerce, capital, and credit which today forms a superorganization, dominating and ruling the universe, subordinating to its ends government, democracy, religion, and education." Only if black college students were informed about, and prepared to challenge, such a superorganization, would their education be accorded any value.[6]

These stringent views on education accompanied Du Bois's gradually shifting attitude toward the necessity for a form of economic separatism and activist electoral politics. Du Bois was looked at warily by several black leaders, who felt his politics were becoming too radical. At the same time, Du Bois left his editorial position at the *Crisis* in 1934, after many years of strife with the NAACP board of directors, and turned increasingly to international arenas while still acting in a leadership role at home. Locke gave Du Bois a wide berth, and while he himself had developed more leftist views in the 1930s, he would never adopt Du Bois's political stances nor operate at his rhetorical temperature. Locke, however, did not publicly voice the opinion, shared by a number of black leaders, that Du Bois's program, with its call for economic independence and a concentration on industrial unionizing, among other features, meant that Du Bois had distanced himself from more conservative civil rights activists who focused less on the class divide and more on racial uplift. Locke never ignored the economic aspects of the lower social positions created by racist attitudes, but his temperament was more suited for academic instruction than for mass organizing.

In the spring of 1935 Locke organized a lecture series on the problems of minorities at Howard University. The series included a number of notable professors from Ivy League colleges, as well as Sidney Hook, then a disciple of Dewey who later became a well-known anti-Marxist, Raymond Buell, E. Franklin Frazier, Ralph Bunche, and Mordecai Johnson, among others. Dewey, invited to be the keynote speaker, could not attend. The conference expressed Locke's attitude toward the use of academic structures and educational approaches to combat racism. That same year he had led the way in reorganizing the social sciences at Howard, seeing to it that his own philosophy department was to be included in the new division. Acting as a chief force in the remaking of the liberal arts curriculum, he suggested changes similar to those at the University of Chicago and Columbia University, which stressed the Great Books approach of Robert Maynard Hutchins and others. Locke taught Dewey's *How We Think* and *Freedom and Culture* for a number of years, and he wanted critical thinking, especially about value and culture, to be the core of undergraduate education. Du Bois was added to the list of speakers and was to speak on the topic of "Negro Group Alternatives Today." In a letter asking Du Bois to speak twice during the conference, Locke raised the issue of a booklet which would be "a little more concretely remunerative," since Howard was unable to cover all of Du Bois's expenses. The Bronze Booklets, supported by the Rosenwald Fund and the Carnegie Corporation, could give Du Bois two hundred dollars as an honorarium plus another fifty dollars for stenographic help. At breakfast one morning during the lecture series, Locke and Du Bois discussed the project, and Du Bois was inclined to participate. On April 17, Locke wrote with the details of the offer and asked that Du Bois submit the manuscript at his earliest convenience. Du Bois accepted, asking only that the title be changed from "Social Reconstruction and the Negro" to "The Negro and Social Reconstruction," a change Du Bois said made "a slight difference in the point of view."

As slight as that change seemed, it augured for a significant difference in outlook and values. By the end of May Du Bois mailed Locke the completed manuscript, with the acknowledgment that it was long and would need editing. Locke thought that it was "very interesting and adequate" and said he would set to work editing it, adding that half of the honorarium would follow. But by February 1936 Du Bois, having heard nothing about his work, had to

ask: "What on earth has become of our booklets?" Locke answered by plead-
ing special circumstances; in order to minimize printing costs, the booklets
were to be done four at a time, but the other manuscripts had been delayed.
On March 6, he explained further to Du Bois: "I quite sympathize with your
inquiry and your legitimate impatience about the booklets. But we are dealing with 'our ain folks,' and you ought to know them." In a postscript Locke
recounted hearing a speech in which Hans Kohn, generalizing from the Jewish experience and the treatment of minorities in the Soviet Union, addressed
the question of nationalism in a way that agreed with Du Bois's views. In May
Du Bois sent Locke a revision of the manuscript, guided largely by Locke's
editing. Then on May 30 Locke wrote Du Bois with a promise "of reasonably prompt printing now." Locke had a caveat, though, and said "it would
be unwise to print the basic American Negro creed, especially in view of the
vigorous defense in the last chapter of the underlying point of view." What
Locke objected to was the programmatic and polemical spelling out of Du
Bois's political and economic plans for ending the second-class citizenship of
Negroes. "Of course, if you have the time to prepare it, we would welcome a
page and a half of general summary," Locke added, hinting that the booklets
were meant to be used as introductory texts and not agitate for a specific plan
of action.

The "Basic American Negro Creed," which Du Bois likely added to his
revised version, mounted a set of vigorous arguments for economic independence, political activism, and antiracist measures that summarized his
changed views on the issues he had been dealing with for three decades or
more. Locke almost surely saw in the arguments an implicit attack on the policies of the New Deal. In 1936 Locke had given a speech called "The Negro
Vote and the New Deal," arguing strongly that black voters should no longer
feel any loyalty to the Republican Party, which had "little to offer out of its
long reign of power and responsibility but broken promises and betrayed loyalties; except a paltry mess of political porridge to a few self-seeking, hireling
politicians. No thinking Negro can believe that the Republican Party and its
leadership believe in the Constitution except for some people sometimes."
Locke ended by implicitly calling for support of the New Deal policies of the
Roosevelt administration: "the Negro knows best what the whole country
needs,—not a constitutional charter of property and privilege with dead-
letter human rights, but a flexible, fearless humanized executive program of
progressive social action . . . regardless of race or creed, but not regardless of
condition." Locke's political views were clearly moving leftward, as he faced
not only the continuing deprivations of the Depression but was aware of the

rising tide of fascist sentiments that appeared during his summer trips to Europe. However, he could not support or argue for the promulgation of Du Bois's more strident opinions and analysis.

In a report that Locke wrote with L. Eugene Jones, dated October 22, the board of the Association for Negro Folk Education was informed: "Doubt over the controversial character and tone of at least one of the manuscripts early completed also caused a postponement of possible publication of an initial group of pamphlets last June." Then, on November 30, 1936 Locke wrote Du Bois with some discomfiting news. "[A]fter full Committee discussion at its last meeting, November 13th, it was decided that it would be inadvisable to publish your manuscript: 'Social Reconstruction and the Negro' in its present form," citing as the reason, "its frequent references to specific situations of public program and policy which in the regrettable interim of delay since the manuscript was written have changed very materially." It is impossible to tell just what "specific situations" Locke was referring to, but the phrase about "public program and policy" suggested that the committee, too, felt the booklet would be seen as an attack on the New Deal. Waves of reactionary feelings had settled upon the directors and staff of various philanthropic organizations in the 1930s and had softened the resolve of the Carnegie Corporation. In February 1937, after his return from his trip around the world, Du Bois finally read Locke's letter of rejection, and asked that the manuscript be returned at the earliest convenience. Du Bois briefly related the episode in his biography, *Dusk of Dawn,* and he summarized it with the cryptic remark, "Just who pronounced the veto I do not know." The manuscript of "The Negro and Social Reorganization" was never published.[7]

Locke survived the unenviable duty of having to write Du Bois a letter of rejection. In 1936 he was especially active, lecturing at Smith College and Lincoln University, where the students asked about their famous alumnus, Langston Hughes. He also visited Berea College, where he met Robert Maynard Hutchins of the University of Chicago, who was visiting his father, then the president of the college. During the spring he learned that Hughes's play, *Mulatto,* was becoming the source of another controversy similar to the one that plagued *Mule Bone.* The play's producer, Martin Jones, claimed authorship of the work and threatened to sue Hughes over the issue. Locke thought Jones probably had cheated Hughes and reflected to Mason: "How the logic of justice works! Here he was trying to cheat Zora out of her play—and now he is in the same quicksand himself." (Six months later, while visiting Hughes in Cleveland, Hughes told Locke, "That's not really my play—Jones rewrote it.") By July, on board the Cunard's *Queen Mary,* he was bound for Russia and the Black Sea Coast. He spent two weeks there, struck by "a wonderful sense of social unity" and remarking on the two-foot wide hats worn by the Cossack peasants. He had trouble getting fresh news but heard about the Civil War in Spain, which troubled him as a further portent of fascism. He fretted to Mason: "I suspect there is heavy aid being given the militarists by Germany and Italy. It looks like the prelude to Armageddon, sure enough, doesn't it?"[8]

Russia, uniquely in his eyes, treated its racial and national minorities honestly. A Moscow drama festival demonstrated that there was "no theater like it in the world." In a speech he delivered on Russian radio, he lamented that the Negroes in America had no such opportunity to present their own folk drama. Another radio speech, broadcast from Leningrad, featured one of his favorite arguments, that ethnic and national art can be universal and can lay a foundation for world art. This recalled the argument for cultural reciprocity that he had developed in recent years. Back home in October he heard Franklin D. Roosevelt give a speech at the dedication of the chemistry building at Howard. Around Thanksgiving, he busily prepared for lectures in Indianapolis and Chicago, where he would rendezvous with Professor T. V. Smith, the editor of the *International Journal of Ethics,* whom he had met earlier and much admired, remarking that he was "almost too human to be a regular philosopher." Smith, a student of Dewey and George Herbert Mead, taught in the philosophy department at the University of Chicago and also served in the Illinois legislature from 1935 to 1938, and in the United States Congress from 1939 to 1941. His debates with Senator Robert Taft were broadcast on the radio and then published in 1939 as *Foundations of Democracy,* a book that Locke would later add to his syllabus when he taught a course on the theory and values of democracy at the New School. Locke lent Smith support when he was running for elective office, and they shared interests in social ethics, poetry, and philosophy.[9]

Locke soon turned his full attention to the Bronze Booklets, including his own, but before he did so he produced one of his more sociological essays as he set out his description of the conditions in Harlem in 1935. These conditions had led to a riot in March of that year, and that became the starting focus of the essay "Harlem: Dark Weather Vane," which appeared in a special issue of the *Survey Graphic* in August 1936. The riot—in Locke's account—had started in March when a young boy was erroneously charged with stealing a pocket knife from Kresge's department store on 125th Street, a store that refused to hire Negroes. An earlier picketing campaign had forced Kresge's to relent, but the blacks they hired were quickly relegated to serving at the store's lunch counter. On the day the riot started, a crowd believed that the boy had been harmed, and the presence of an ambulance at the store fed this rumor. There were a small number of deaths, and "many injuries to police and citizens, destruction of property, and a serious aftermath of public grievance and anger." In May, Paul Kellogg wrote to ask Locke for an article focusing on the Mayor's Investigation Report, drafted by a commission appointed by Fiorello La Guardia to examine the causes of the riot. The commission's report described conditions so shocking that the mayor exercised what amounted to a "pocket veto" of the report. However, Locke obtained some knowledge of the report through his Howard colleague, E. Franklin Frazier, who was in charge of assembling its various sections. Locke himself did further research by corresponding with the hospital administrators in Harlem, and his essay is especially telling about the lack of health care available in Harlem. The riot itself was less a matter of racial animosity than a protest against deep and prolonged economic injustice, what Locke termed "a swelling sense of grievance over past civic neglect and proscription." Locke argued that the cause was not "the unfortunate rumors, but the state of mind on which they fell." He sent the essay to the managing editor of the *Survey Graphic* on June 28, 1936, with a somewhat defensive note: "I only want it [the essay] considered for publication on its merits and will not be at all disappointed to have it scrapped." Two days later the editor replied that the fact that the report of the commission had to be vetted by the mayor's office and the heads of various involved departments need not deter the publication of Locke's essay. Shortly after the essay was submitted, the editor telephoned Locke and pronounced it "splendid."[10]

Locke's essay, carefully and gracefully written, can be read as a substitute for the commission report on which it was partially based. It contrasts the "thrill and ferment of sudden progress and prosperity" of the Harlem Renaissance with the situation in 1936, when the community was "prostrate in the grip of the depression and throes of social unrest." But Locke takes little comfort in the nostalgia for the Renaissance; in fact he sets it in a stark context that does not flinch at the necessity for improving what the radicals of the 1930s call "the material base":

[N]o cultural advance is safe without some sound economic underpinning, the foundation of a decent and reasonably secure average standard of living; and no emerging elite—artistic, professional or mercantile—can suspend itself in thin air over the abyss of the unemployed stranded in an over-expensive, disease- and crime-ridden slum.

It is easier to dally over black Bohemia or revel in the hardy survivals of Negro art and culture than to contemplate this dark Harlem of semi-starvation, mass exploitation and seething unrest. But turn we must. For there is no cure or saving magic in poetry and art, an emerging generation of talent, or in international prestige and interracial recognition, for unemployment or precarious marginal employment, for high rents, high mortality rates, civic neglect, capitalistic exploitation on the one hand and radical exploitation on the other.

This passage, and the spirit of the essay in general, impressively qualifies and balances the emphasis on cultural progress at the center of *The New Negro*. Locke here addressed not only the white liberal audience of the *Survey Graphic* but also other black leaders such as Du Bois and McKay, whose political views had moved in a more radical direction in the 1930s. The essay, though little known when compared to *The New Negro,* could go a long way toward balancing the view that Locke felt cultural progress would always trump political and social conditions.

Some recent improvements in services and institutions had been accomplished or at least undertaken since the riot. These included the women's hospital pavilion, a Harlem River housing project, "which will afford model housing for 574 low income families," and a Public Works Administration health clinic. Boldly setting out all aspects of the problems, Locke criticizes the "apathy and lack of public mindedness on the part of Harlem's Negro politicians and many professional leaders who either did not know or care about the condition of the masses." Locke's sense of social justice dominates the essay, but it is always expressed in moderate tones and with nuanced demands. Long an opponent of what he called race chauvinism, Locke would in this context modify his attitudes to take into account the immediacy of the situation. "Negroes are often accused of race chauvinism in their almost fanatical insistence upon race representatives on executive boards and in councils of policy, but the principle of this vital safeguard is of manifest importance. Especially in situations of accumulated wrong and distrust, mere practical expediency requires public assurance and reassurance."

The second half of the essay deals with unemployment, "Harlem's most acute problem," as well as housing and health. Using a mix of statistics, accounts of recent events, and pronouncements by city administrators and politicians, Locke paints a detailed picture with sociological accuracy and compelling argument.

One of Locke's hopes was that "Harlem: Dark Weather Vane" would convince the mayor to build an art and recreation center in Harlem with Public Works Administration funds. Perhaps he remembered the failure to establish a Harlem Museum for African Art, and perhaps he was dreaming that his sociology might produce results in the esthetic realm. When in Paris in the summer of 1936 he commented on the international scene: "Our last days of feudal capitalism in America have not yet come. But in Europe, the reaction is playing its last desperate trumps against the rising wrath of the exploited people." His sense of social injustice was seldom stronger than it was in the late 1930s. So he might have been quite surprised to see the editorial in the April 1937 issue of the *Crisis*. As that journal unfairly saw it, Locke had "accept[ed] the excuse of the administration that it is doing all it can." The commission's report had still not been made public, yet the editorial went on to say that "it is also true that what the present administration has done to correct the most glaring of the evils since it was apprised of them is nothing to go shouting about in the *Survey Graphic* or any other magazine." Locke's meliorism, even when combined with a genuine sense of outrage and a calm description of the oppressing forces, would not satisfy some members of the community, but meanwhile he continued to look for ways to contribute what he could.

In the early months of 1937 he was already correcting proofs for both of his own Bronze Booklets, *The Negro and His Music* and *Negro Art: Past and Present*. Describing them to Mason as "simply written," he felt he had left "that old psychological shell back down the road," meaning, perhaps, that he composed them without his usual self-consciousness. The first four booklets in the series, printed all at once, were "an experiment," and he hoped the next four would be better produced. The booklets sum up a great deal of Locke's learning in music and the visual arts, and compared to much of the material produced for adult education, they are strikingly comprehensive and sophisticated. Both of Locke's titles include questions for discussion and suggestions for further reading. They also achieve a remarkable tone of rigor without being condescending or overly didactic. In fact, they successfully exemplify Locke's attitude toward adult education specifically, but his often repeated call for historical and value-oriented knowledge as well.

The Negro and His Music displays Locke's critical skills in full flower. The book sketches a short but sweeping background about the role of music in American culture. Believing as he did in the value of folk music, Locke wryly argued that Negroes supplied this in America because of special historical reasons, among them the fate of the Native Americans: "If American civilization had absorbed instead of exterminating the American Indian, his music would be the folk music of this country." Locke advanced his beliefs and critical standards uncompromisingly, as when he said:

> But the Negro is American as well as Negro. He has his musical shortcomings. If Negro music is to fulfill its best possibilities, Negroes must become musical by nurture and not rest content with being musical by nature. They must build upon two things essential for the highest musical success;—a class of trained musicians who know and love the folk music and are able to develop it into great classical music, and a class of trained music lovers who will support by appreciation the best in the Negro's musical heritage and not allow it to be prostituted by the vaudeville stage or Tin Pan Alley, or to be cut off at its roots by lack of appreciation of its humble but gifted peasant creators. (NMNA, 4)

This reflects Locke's full appreciation of "popular" music, as did his enjoyment of Noble Sissle and Eubie Blake and many other black musicians of the 1920s, yet he realized that commercial interests would always be at work, with the potential result that the genuine folk spirit would be disvalued or altogether lost.

Locke's presentation of Negro music features his three categories: folk, popular, and classical. Characterizing the first of these, Locke uses a series of balanced attributes, referring to the spirituals as "sad but not somber, intense but buoyant, tragic but ecstatic." He defines the second category, popular music, as reacting to these attributes with qualities of its own: "light, mock-sentimental, and full of pagan humor and pungent irony." As for the third category, Locke claims it is "classical jazz" that "is an important part of our present-day typical or national American music, and . . . is reckoned as one of the Negro's major cultural contributions." In each category Locke is able to demonstrate the social roots of the music as well as its relation to national and historical frameworks; this often calls for subtle qualifications. In the area of jazz, for example, he argues that the threat of commercialism is always there in popular music, and so classical jazz, an outgrowth of popular forms like marches and ragtime, is also threatened by such forces. But the development of jazz is a story of triumph. Here is a typical passage of analysis and history:

> But in addition to jazz rhythm and harmony, jazz improvisation came rocketing out of the blues. It grew out of the improvised musical "filling-in" of the gap between the short measure of the blues and the longer eight bar line, the break interval in the original folk-form of the

three line blues. Such filling in and compounding of the basic rhythm are characteristic of Negro music everywhere, from deepest Africa to the streets of Charleston, from the unaccompanied hand-clapping of the street corner "hoe-down" to the interpolations of shouts, amens and exclamations in Negro church revivals. (NMNA, 77)

Locke's three categories avoid a static sense of music as something with fixed levels of high and low, or fixed forms. While he drew on many books and articles in preparing his history and analysis, his own musical skills and his universal taste for the great diversity of musical experiences, as well as his respect for the Negro musical spirit, drove him in writing out his account of a major cultural expression. He composed as a critic very close to his subject.

Though many people would later mistakenly decide that Locke denigrated jazz, because of his elitist sense of cultural standards, the approach to this form in *The Negro and His Music* is not only positive but laudatory. And his value judgments throughout the book are often rooted in precise examples. Pointing to the nature of a true folk spirit he says:

There is no truer test of what is genuine folk quality in Negro folk music than . . . to contrast, for example, the melodramatic sentimentality of a manufactured spiritual like "De Glory Road" with the heroic simplicity of "Go Down Moses" or "My Lord, What a Mornin'," or again the contrast of the slapstick comedy of "It Ain't Goin' Rain No More" with the true folk humor of "Oh, Didn't It Rain." (NMNA, 8-9)

In writing his criticism of various art forms, Locke's own feeling for his esthetic experiences led him to willingly declare what counted as a "true" artistic quality.

The Negro and His Music is filled with many names, and Locke clearly wanted to shine a light on a vast range of talents while at the same time keeping a sense of history and judgment active in the book. He brought in examples frequently and usually placed them in a context that conferred singularity. For example, the use of the symphonic form by African American composers commanded his attention, and he singled out William Grant Still's *Afro-American Symphony* (1935) for its "approach to pure music," even though rooted in a folk theme. But he also mentioned William Dawson's *Negro Folk Symphony,* which had been performed by the Philadelphia Symphony Orchestra in 1931, and Florence Price's *Symphony in E Minor,* which won the Wanamaker Prize and was performed at the 1932 Chicago World's

F I G . 9.3. Locke and Paul Robeson. Locke supported Robeson's singing career, though he objected to the communist politics he and his wife Eslanda practiced in their later years. Moorland-Spingarn Research Center.

Fair. In this context he spoke of the "Negro composer's right" to "go up Parnassus by the broad high road of classicism, rather than the narrower, more hazardous, but often more rewarding path of racialism," though at "the pinnacle, the paths converge."[11]

In the chapter on individual black vocal artists he mentions both Roland Hayes and Paul Robeson and designs a similar balanced judgment: "For Robeson sings the Negro folk songs in their flesh and blood reality; Hayes in their disembodied spirit and mystical inner meaning. Our musical tradition is richer and better understood for both interpretations, however different." In the book's final chapter, "The Future of Negro Music," Locke reports that the feud between the folk idiom and classical forms was fading as a force, and this opens the way for a fusion of the two traditions. Locke is sanguine here, and he also anticipates his interest in the African diaspora, which would flourish with his trip to Haiti in 1943, when he recounts the recent developments in Afro-Cuban music, and mentions "the serious music of Central and South America, but particularly Cuba, Mexico, Haiti, and Brazil, are saturated with African idioms and survivals, which only need further study to stimulate and nourish the Negro elements in the North American musical tradition." Locke adds these sources are especially valuable because they were "free of the cultural distortions of the plantation tradition; that is, they have no minstrel taint." Locke ends by discussing the possible uses of African music, contrasting its antiphonal quality to the polyphonic nature of European music. Concluding with a playful extension of the culturing metaphor, Locke returns to the importance of rhythm and says: "From a kernel of rhythm, African music has sprouted in strange lands, spread out a rootage of folk-dance and folk song, and then gone through the whole cycle of complete musical expression as far as soil and cultural conditions have permitted." For Locke, the future of Negro music was as bright as the support of its audience was solid, and as long as there was sufficient "cultural opportunity and appreciation," the truly creative musician would thrive.[12]

Written in the same series as the book on Negro music, Locke's *Negro Art: Past and Present* (1936), can readily be seen as its companion volume. But Locke approaches the plastic arts differently, responding to the specific conditions that surround the cultural forms of painting and sculpture. He posits no historically developmental scheme, since for many, especially African Americans, modern forms of the plastic arts do not derive as traceably as does music out of its folk forms. Locke does not abandon history, however. What he offers in the art book is the story of the break in history caused by the African diaspora and the history of slavery. In the middle passage blacks sang but they could not paint or sculpt. Yet modernist art had made striking use of motifs from African art, so Locke circles back, as it were, to talk about how connections operated in the plastic arts. First he treats the early American colonial period, in which there was virtually no African American painting, and casts it as an "apprenticeship," which was then followed by a period of "journeyman work," between 1865 and 1890 (paralleling Reconstruction). Eventually he moves into the assessment of the work of his own contemporaries, working with a tripartite structure. This enables him to begin at the apprenticeship period by seeing painting and sculpture as rooted in the manual arts, such as woodcarving, metalwork, and so forth. As for his understanding of cultural expression, Locke kept the material conditions in mind, even as he sought to understand the larger historical and social forces that operated in both the production and consumption of art works.

Though intent on connecting African American art with the arts of Africa, Locke makes telling distinctions, usually derived from his sense of history.

For example, referring to the African American's love of color, he points out that the arts of Africa are generally somber in visual tones and then suggests that African Americans turned to bright coloration only after the end of slavery. This turn occurred after a long stretch when Negro slaves were unable to create any visual arts of their own. This theory of severe breaks and tenuous connections spelt out in detail the idea that Locke advanced a decade earlier, in essays such as "The Legacy of the Ancestral Arts." There he argued that an important artistic and even spiritual tie could be reestablished between African and African American arts. In this book, however, Locke faces more directly the gaps in space and time caused by the slave trade. The theory also entails reflecting on the role European artists played in the development of the contemporary situation and tracing as well the different ways in which Negroes were depicted as subjects by European painters and sculptors.

Turning to the well-known historical trope in Negro history, of identifying the "first" to achieve some notable level of distinction, Locke cites Edward M. Bannister as the first Negro painter and Edmonia Lewis as the pioneer sculptor. Using the short biographical sketch when moving on to the next historical period, he praises Henry Ossawa Tanner, his development and his emigration to Paris. Locke says that Tanner "found an interest that made his fame, which, although apparently remote from any racial association, was spiritually close after all." Close, that is, to the concern with Negro experience from the vantage point of someone who was an agent in such experience as well as a recorder of it. Tanner, however, became "embittered" as his fame was tied up in the minds of many with his being a Negro. Locke arranges this dilemma in a clear frame: Tanner "resented the sensational publicity of this emphasis on his race instead of his art; rightfully,—but with little appreciation of how inevitable it was." This concern—whether art made by Negroes is automatically Negro art, and if it is not, what would determine what is?—serves as one of the main subjects of the book. Locke had written on this subject in his introduction to *Four Negro Poets* and had observed a parallel case with Jean Toomer.

After sketching the careers of Tanner and others, such as Meta Warrick and May Howard Jackson, Locke turned to "Negro Artists Today" in order to appraise and inventory a new generation of successful artists, introducing another three-part scheme, of Traditionalist, Modernist, and Racialist. These categories are determined by how artists are trained, and whether or not they accept new principles of representation, as well as how they relate to the use of Negro subject matter and the deployment of obvious racial attitudes. Before placing the living artists into the respective categories, Locke returns to the question raised by Tanner's career and sets out his thoughts on the question of Negro art and what defines it. As he would also do in the year-end reviews of the late 1930s and 1940s, Locke turned the argument in the direction of the national context:

[E]xcept for closer psychological contact and understanding, the relation of the Negro artist to racial subject matter is not so very different from that of his white fellow artist to the same material. To both it is important local color material, racial to one, national to the other. We are now able to see that a white artist can be a notable exponent of Negro art if he portrays this material with power and insight, and also to realize that Negro art does not restrict the Negro artist to a ghetto province, but only urges him to sustain his share in its interpretation, with no obligation but the universal one of a duty to express himself in originality and unhampered sincerity. On the whole the Negro subject has come into its own as an integral part of the development of the native element in American art. (NMNA, 61)

The passage aims to address the agency of Negro painters and sculptors and to support them if they can commit themselves to "originality and unhampered sincerity." He knew as well as anyone how manifold and persistent the hampering effects of living in a racist society were, yet he was willing to measure the artistic impulse by seeing it on the level of a universal obligation.

Locke moves in the book's penultimate chapter to the subject of African art proper. Displaying a wide range of references, he composes a survey of African tribes and their different artistic materials and media—from Benin bronzes to the polychrome beading of the Cameroons—and urged that such a broad and plentiful field can be of direct use and inspiration to contemporary African American artists. He allows himself a prediction, one that has indeed come true: "African art can count on . . . sustained interest and permanent significance even after the modernist vogue of abstract art and the contemporary cult of primitivism pass out in a new artistic style and philosophy, which they sooner or later must do." The book's brief final chapter suggests that blacks will continue to produce works of distinction in the plastic arts, and that "the younger Negro artist is now nearly abreast of his generation in modernism of style and subject." Locke's closing chapters were about matters very dear to him, of course, as he had spent much time and resources on his own collection of African art, and he was constantly eager to learn about and foster the talents of artists from a generation younger than his.

Three years after the appearance of *Negro Art: Past and Present,* Locke was able to enter his ideas into a different form of circulation. He wrote the foreword for an exhibit, Contemporary Negro Art, the first of its kind, mounted at the Baltimore Museum of Art in February 1939. The show included works by, among others, Archibald J. Motley Jr, Jacob Lawrence (his series on Toussaint L'Ouverture), Lois M. Jones (Locke's colleague at Howard), Sargent Johnson, Malvin Gray Johnson, Aaron Douglas, and Richmond Barthé (one of the pieces coming from Locke's own collection). The foreword in effect repeated the arguments of *Negro Art: Past and Present,* though it opened with a paragraph about art and democracy. "Art in a democracy should above all else be democratic, which is to say it must be truly representative," Locke proclaimed. He singled out the "progressive policy [that is] changing the role of museum from that of a treasure storehouse of the past to that of a clearing house for the contemporary artist." But he also took note of one of the legacies of the New Deal when he pointed to "the public patronage of the museum and the government," which meant "more segments of American life are apt to find expression than under the more traditional interests of a private patron class." Though brief, the foreword brought together in a direct way the concern for democratic values and recognition for the developing artistic achievements of Locke's contemporaries.

As to the business end of the Bronze Booklets, Locke was responsible for all of the negotiations with the printer. When the first shipment arrived, Locke noticed that the page alignment was faulty. He mused, "I am sure that if my agonies could have been foreseen, there would have been another editorial midwife," echoing the metaphor he applied to himself in connection with the Renaissance. He wanted "to have a striking rather modernistic cover, if possible." Remaining patient with all the details, he also explained to the printer that the delays resulted from the fact that "[o]ur authors are that strange sub-species of college professor; including myself, of course." But near the end of the process, in September 1938, the treasurer of the printing house wrote Locke to say: "Your own patience and courtesy have been a revelation to our people here—the average customer blows down the printer's roof under such circumstances." Librarians in Los Angeles and Chicago, among others, reviewed the series favorably. By the end of 1938, over eleven hundred copies had been sold, with Sterling Brown's volume on poetry and drama the leading seller, at two hundred and sixty four copies. A summary report in 1940 would record a total sales of over twelve thousand copies for the seven titles then available. An eighth title, *The Negro in the Caribbean,* by

Eric Williams, was published in 1942, and a planned tenth booklet on Negro history never appeared.

Busy attending a steady stream of musical concerts throughout the 1930s, Locke spent time with composers and singers, some of whom he knew as close friends. Will Marion Cook, the well-known African American composer, corresponded with Locke about his musical compositions, as Cook clearly valued Locke's musical knowledge. Cook, born in 1869, had his first great success with the 1898 production of *Chlorindy,* which he considered an opera. It featured lyrics by Paul Lawrence Dunbar, and cakewalk music and actors who danced and sang at the same time, clearly serving as a forerunner of the Broadway musical. Trained in a German conservatory, Cook had studied with Dvorak and was intent on using racial material in a way that incorporated classical esthetics. Throughout the 1930s Locke helped Cook, then in his seventies, with his memoirs, which the composer hoped would even the score with many of those who had pushed him aside in the musical world. Locke invited Cook to join him at a July 1937 concert by Marian Anderson, as he had been given two tickets by Mason. She promised Locke that she would "obliterate the color line forever" by having Anderson sing at the Metropolitan Opera, but weakness prevented the effort, as Mason grew increasingly housebound.[13]

Not only did Locke's musical tastes extend from jazz to classical music, he was interested in the relations between the two. His esthetic, which saw racially based art as forming a solid base for universal cultural appreciation, led him to see music along a continuum of forms and genres. His social life, however, definitely slanted in the direction of classical performances. He attended the famous free concert given by Anderson at the Lincoln Memorial in 1939, hoping she would sing "a memorial song like John Brown's Body." A few months later he went to Richmond, where Eleanor Roosevelt presented Anderson with the Spingarn Medal. He had first met Mrs. Roosevelt back in 1937, when he spoke before eight hundred guests at the Willard Hotel in Washington at the launching of a peace campaign by the Women's International League. For many years Locke was also close to Roland Hayes, having used an article in *Opportunity* in 1923 to praise Hayes's "fine rhapsodic flow . . . that [was] taken over from the primitive race gift." He worked in the 1930s and 1940s to arrange concerts for Hayes, as well as others, at the Library of Congress. In December of 1937, the two men visited in Washington, and Hayes shared with Locke the lecture he was soon to give at Boston University on the spirituality of lieder singing. As for Still, the leading African American composer of his generation, he, like Cook, corresponded with Locke, who commented on his musical projects and interests.

His heavy social calendar and concert-going never abated, unless there were medical problems. In March 1937 Locke was hospitalized for nine days for a "heart upset," as he described it to Mason. However serious the episode may have been, he continued to travel and lecture, and he worked at correcting the proofs for his two Bronze Booklet titles. Other projects were short of completion, though. His biography of Fredrick Douglass continued to languish, even as he promised Mason that he had all the materials he needed and would spend the summer working on it and devote time each following summer as well. There was talk of another project, too: "What We Can Learn From Africa," presumably intended for the Bronze Booklet series. This added another dimension to his sense of where adult education should be fixing its focus. A booking on the *Queen Mary,* set to sail on June 23, promised a return to Russia, but his plans changed, perhaps due to the international situation. For whatever reason, he failed to visit Europe for the first summer in thirteen years. Able to write only a few paragraphs on each project, he apparently developed little momentum. There was also editorial effort expended on Sterling Brown's two Bronze Booklets, *Negro Poetry and Drama* and *The Negro in American Fiction,* both of which Locke described as reflecting his own point of view. In the fall he enjoyed a visit to Central High School in Philadelphia for a class reunion—it would be his thirtieth— and while there he ran into a trustee of Howard. The man reported that Mordecai Johnson had spoken of how Locke had approved of one of his recent speeches. Locke retorted, "Certainly not—how could I?" Locke, having once been told he should be president of Howard, was no more able to get on with Johnson than he was with any of his predecessors. The relation between Locke and Johnson started smoothly but quickly turned, especially as Locke pushed hard for his curricular changes and general reforms in undergraduate courses. He felt strongly that his views on values, whether esthetic, social, or moral, and the critical thinking that had led to them, had to become part of the main objectives of a university education.

Literary criticism and book reviewing continued as two of Locke's main activities. The second half of the decade of the 1930s included five of Locke's year-end reviews of books by black authors; these would be the last four before a hiatus of seven years, due largely to the war. "Deep River, Deeper Sea" appeared in 1936, to be followed by "God Save Reality!" in 1937. "Deep River" begins with an extended metaphor about the promise of greater skill and interest in writing by black authors, only to lament that such improvement has not yet occurred; the depth of the river promised that the ocean was within view, but instead the critic—in this case Locke himself—was still navigating in shoals. He lectured his readers that only if one could see "indigenous criticism on the part of the creative and articulate Negro himself" could there be any "truly universal or even fully representative art." But in addition to his disappointment at the quality of black writing in the preceding twelve months, Locke pointed out the obvious "broadening of bases of Negro art in terms of the literature of class protest and proletarian realism." Separating himself from Marxists, whom he thought too doctrinaire, he asked for a grittier realism and a total rejection of sentimentalism and stereotyping. In mentioning Hurston's *Mules and Men,* he praised what he called her "great power of evoking atmosphere and character," but of Hughes's play *Mulatto* he could only say that "the magnificent potentialities of its theme . . . for the most part are amateurishly smothered in talk and naïve melodrama." As for Du Bois's *Black Reconstruction,* he mixed his praise—a "spirited and successful historical challenge"—with some qualification, referring to his rival's increasingly oppositional politics, but nevertheless he labeled it "one of the most challenging worthwhile books of the year."

In "God Save Reality!" Locke began by discussing the way Southern writers, mostly white (since there were no novels worthy of mention by black writers in 1936), treated the race problem. Claiming they largely failed to approach a real picture of the racial divide, he observed that "the South is a burning issue, and there are only two ways of reacting to it. There are novels that condone and those that condemn; emotional neutrality is almost impossible." He delightedly remarked on the seven books on Negro music, and singled out Maud Cuney Hare's *Negro Musicians and Their Music.* Its negative attitude toward jazz was criticized, and its contention that there was an antithesis between folk and art forms was misguided; he somewhat blandly referred to his own recent publication of *The Negro and His Music* as a refutation of this point of view. Citing the prediction in Louis Armstrong's *Swing That Music* that "swing is America's second big bid to bring forth a worthwhile music of its own," he exclaimed: "Let us hope Louis is as good a prophet as he is a musician!" The work of a new writer, C. L. R. James, later to achieve fame as one of the most important black writers of the century, Locke saw as coming from a "novelist and playwright of considerable power and much promise."

At the beginning of 1938, he reviewed Hurston's new novel, *Their Eyes Were Watching God,* in his *Opportunity* year-end survey, entitled "Jingo, Counter Jingo and Us." The novel challenged Locke, whose theories about folk art and a universal cultural expression allowed for the sort of black characters that Hurston favored, but in this instance he thought she had failed to "come to grips with motive fiction and social document fiction." Hurston's humorous rural characters were obviously inspired by her folklore studies, but they contained a dimension of irony and skepticism rooted in her singular personality. While praising Hurston's talent and her "gift for poetic phrase, for rare dialect, and folk humor," Locke complained that her characters were "pseudo-primitives." This angered Hurston considerably. She decided to respond by writing to *Opportunity*, but the vitriolic letter was never published. Despite her typical vehemence, Hurston eventually softened and years later approached Locke in a friendly way. In January 1943, she promised him that she had changed her attitude: "Really, Alain, I am through being a smart-aleck. You must forget that I ever was one." Six months later she even suggested they collaborate on the folklore thesis she was developing, which argued that universal patterns were to be found in Negro fables. Though their relationship had more than an abundant amount of strain and cross-purposes, it produced good things for both parties.

The year-end review that included the assessment of Hurston's work was one that Locke used for a nuanced argument about a topic that especially interested him: jingoism. Given his commitment to value pluralism, Locke found all forms of jingoism offensive. Taking into account his temperamental commitment to balance and even paradox, he would not, however, reject jingoism in simplistic terms. So the review called "Jingo, Counter Jingo and Us" contains one of the longest introductions written for any of the year-end pieces. The length is necessary because Locke was responding to a 1937 article called "Minority Jingo," by Benjamin Stolberg. A widely published journalist and historian of the American labor movement, who served on the committee to investigate Trotsky and the Moscow trials, Stolberg had reviewed a book by Benjamin Brawley, called *Negro Builders and Heroes*.

Extremely negative, this review accuses Brawley of resorting to a "colored jingoism, like that of all career men in the oppressed minorities, [which] is the usual solution of racial self-pity in racial vain-glory." Stolberg even stops to ask the reader if he is "wondering why all this heavy artillery [is] blasting a Mr. Brawley." Proceeding relentlessly, Stolberg argues that such men as Brawley—who exist in other minority groups, but less egregiously so—"are forever appealing to enlightened opinion to protect them in their minority rights, by which they mean primarily freedom from radical criticism." This criticism is launched in the context of Stolberg's own ideological orientation, namely as someone who wants the oppressed groups in society to mobilize and assert their political and civil rights in the terms of the organized labor movement. But Locke would not view the criticism as altogether fraternal.

What makes the Stolberg response of special interest is that in attacking "minority jingoism," not only from Brawley but from Kelly Miller and others, Stolberg mentions Locke as someone who agrees with his negative assessment. Near the end of the review Stolberg compliments the "most significant intellectual leadership" in the Negro community, by which he means some of the faculty at Howard. After mentioning E. Franklin Frazier, Ralph Bunche, and others, Stolberg comes to Locke. "Dr. Alain Locke, head of the Philosophy Department—who some time ago wrote me that he bitterly regretted having started the New Negro fad in the mid-twenties—is a man of great culture and influence." In the context of Stolberg's polemic, this otherwise high praise would serve to condemn Locke in the eyes of black readers. Not only would Locke be seen as someone who reversed his own support of the Renaissance but also as a critic of men like Brawley and Miller who produced what was admittedly the literature of racial uplift. Locke had no option but to respond, and to respond in a way that patiently but firmly avoided any further overstatements and polemicizing.

In the opening pages Locke spells out the limitations—but also the occasional necessity—of combating one absolutist position with another. "Minority-jingo is counter-jingo; the real jingo is majority jingo and there lies the original sin. Minority jingo is the defensive reaction, sadly inevitable as an antidote, and even science has had to learn to fight poison with poison." Locke at the same time insisted that "for cure and compensation, it must be the right poison and in the right amount." Locke here takes into account what provokes "minority jingoism" in the first place, and, just as important, what its uses and effects are. In advancing a set of claims laden with value judgments, Locke calls on his sense of history and temporal development when it comes to understanding more clearly and efficaciously how political and social values originate and eventuate. As he says, "revolution is successful treason and treason is unsuccessful revolution." But after exploring some of the ways in which social and political ideas and opinions get expressed, he brings the essay back to the books at hand: "Transposing back to our main theme, which is literary, this would mean corrective criticism rather than general excommunication, intelligent refereeing instead of ex-cathedra outlawing. For there can be proletarian jingo as well as bourgeois and capitalist jingo and class jingoism as well as the creedal and racial varieties." For Locke values could be transposed, and what applied in the political realm would be consonant with that in the literary world. Using such religious metaphors as "excommunication" and "ex cathedra," he also signals his own predilection to see absolutist opinions as derived from, or closely similar to, forms of religious prejudice; both must be rejected.

Near the end of 1938, Locke complained to Mason that he was amused and hurt by the obituaries for James Weldon Johnson, which gave Johnson credit for starting the New Negro movement. The questions about race leadership were never far from Locke's mind, and he wrote to Mason with a candor that he could not have displayed otherwise. He recalled how Johnson and Du Bois had to be begged to participate, and then "eagerly . . . claimed credit after the thing got under way." This memory provoked another one, as he recalled his uneasy relation with Du Bois. "[His] article in *The New Negro* I rewrote for him from two old articles of his that he contemptuously tossed over his desk top to me, saying if you can find anything to use in either of these, go ahead and use it. He refused to write anything fresh." Though he had resolved to make "Spiritual Truancy" his last public commentary on the Renaissance, personal echoes continued to resonate, and public opinions were never stilled.

Work for the betterment of the race and a general lifting of educational standards continued to occupy Locke's thoughts and shape his activities. In the fall Locke attended a conference on "Adult Education and the Negro," held at Hampton Institute in Virginia, under the joint auspices of the Association for Negro Folk Education and the AAAE. Over the next decade or so he wrote several essays on the issues of adult education, raising the subject in his mind to an importance shared with race and value questions. But of course not all his projects came to fruition. In September 1938 he responded to Benjamin Brawley, who was heading a Committee on the National Negro Library and Museum. Locke insisted that the project include a "comprehensive critical bibliography of Africana and Negro Americana." He took the occasion to remind Brawley that back in 1914 he had signed a petition, along with Kelly Miller, to the president and the board of trustees at Howard, for just such a plan. But, like Du Bois's attempt to assemble an encyclopedia on the Negro, Brawley's project came to naught, yet another casualty of the reduced philanthropy in the wake of the Depression.

The year-end review published at the start of 1939 was called "The Negro: 'New' or Newer," and the following year the title was "Dry Fields and Green Pastures." In the earlier of these two reviews, Locke opens with comments on the newer generation of Negro writers, but his thoughts are mainly directed at revisiting the New Negro movement. There is some nostalgia in what he says, but there is also some positive hope that Negro writing will have matured, though this is mixed with unmistakable bitterness ("they did not read carefully what was written carefully") about what he sees as the misunderstanding and betrayal of the ideals he had advanced fifteen years earlier. He reminds his readers that he never claimed prejudice was ending or would soon disappear, and he never argued that culture could replace the work of politics ("a philosophy of cultural isolation from the folk . . . and of cultural separatism was expressly repudiated"). At the same time he denigrates any belief in a "one-formula diagnosis" such as "economic exploitation" or "class action." Making his case even stronger, he quotes his own words from "Enter the New Negro." Calling the attempt by the Negro to build his Americanism on race values "a unique social experiment," Locke stresses that success in this effort is "impossible except through the fullest sharing of American culture and institutions. There should be no delusion about this." Obviously by referring to "the fullest sharing of . . . institutions" Locke meant nothing short of complete racial and social equality.

The essay is not consumed with polemics or setting the record straight, however. He finds time and space to praise Richard Wright especially. Locke had long wanted black fiction to deal more directly with all the aspects of the group's experience, whether uplifting or not. Just as he felt that racism could not be cured if not addressed in the context of the entirety of American life, so he felt Negro art would flourish only if it took broad and deep views. Referring to the then recent appearance of *Uncle Tom's Children,* and some of Wright's short stories as well, he says that "our Negro fiction of social interpretation comes of age." Picking up on a note from an earlier essay, he praises C. L. R. James's *The Black Jacobins.* And in the Africana section, which he made a point of including each year, he singles out George Padmore's *Africa and World Peace:* "[O]ne of the sharpest critiques of imperialism in a decade of increasing anti-imperialist attack, this book vividly expounds the close connection between fascism and imperialism, on the one hand, and fascism and African interests and issues on the other." To round out a review that included, typically, remarks on over five dozen volumes plus a section on juvenile books, he highly recommended the book of photographs by Hoyningen Huene, *African Mirage,* as "one of the most understandingly observed and beautifully written volumes" in its field, one that would help achieve "an anointing of the eyes."

Marked by the deprivations of the economic collapse of American capitalism, the decade of the 1930s induced Locke to increase his concern about the limits of artistic representation. In the ten year-end reviews he did up to 1940, he addressed many different esthetic issues, but it was clear that his ideas were definitely involved in coordinating the artistic, social, and political issues of his time. In "Dry Fields and Green Pastures" Locke's beginning paragraphs differentiate between realist and romantic approaches to Negro expression, making it explicit that he prefers the former. Facing up to the fact that readers favor the sentimental approach, he admits: "There is a legitimate appetite for the picturesque, the naïve, the zestful and the exuberantly imaginative," but this does not mean one must capitulate to popular taste. As he puts it, "folk life, as poetically picturesque, enjoys a more than ten-to-one advantage over folk life prosaically pictorial." What can be done to correct this esthetic weakness? For Locke, the answer is "poetic realism," an art that does not avoid the unpleasant aspects of experience but is able to combine "beauty with truth, and reconcile . . . the dilemma of having to have one at the expense of the other." This is no easy formula, despite the allusion to Keats, for Locke knows that to achieve it an artist must have "worked long and hard and deeply with Negro material."

Locke stresses throughout every section of his year-end reviews the need for artistic honesty, in fiction and drama especially, knowing that all the fields of the social sciences and the humanities can only advance if they provide a "more informative and less escapist literature and art." However, Locke did not favor or encourage only the sort of hard and bitter naturalism that flourished during the Depression years. In the 1939 year-end review, for example, he praised the drama of Owen Dodson, who would join the Howard faculty the following year, just after completing a M.F.A. degree at Yale. Locke described Dodson's play, *The Divine Comedy*, as a "somewhat overambitious expressionistic rendition of Negro cult religion." Then in the next year's review he cited Dodson's *The Garden of Time*, which used the juxtaposition of the Jason and Medea legend and a contemporary interracial romance, as being "the most complex piece of playwriting that any of our young authors has yet turned out."

In the 1939 year-end review Locke glowingly praised Arthur Fauset's new biography of Sojourner Truth, calling it "beyond doubt the prize biography of the year and one of the best Negro biographies ever done." To Mason he described it as "a real Negro book—clean, clear and true." Locke told Mason about how Fauset had joined the Communist Party but quit when he discovered their "bigotry and hatred." When he was divorcing Crystal Bird he told Locke he was sorry he had ignored his warnings about the marriage. Bird later became the first black woman elected to a state legislature, representing Philadelphia's largely white 13th district. She had been active in the American Friends' Service Committee, speaking constantly to groups about the deleterious effects of racial prejudice. Arthur Fauset, a close friend of Locke for many years, was born in 1899, the son of an AME preacher, Redmon Fauset, who died when Arthur was four years old, and Bella Huff, a white widow who had three children from a previous marriage. Redmon had earlier been married to Annie Seamon Fauset, who was the mother of Jessie Fauset. As Arthur's half-sister, Jessie always tried to advance his career, asking Locke at one point to mention their being related, as such recognition might help Arthur's literary ambitions. Arthur graduated from Central High in Philadelphia and took an M.A. degree in English from the University of Pennsylvania in 1924. During the Renaissance years he published a short story in *Opportunity* and an essay in *FIRE!!* The latter is entitled "Intelligentsia," and it attacks this class with such vehemence that it borders on anti-intellectualism. Having absorbed a full dose of *FIRE!!*'s dismissive attitude toward the older generation, Fauset pulls no punches: "Of all the doughty societies that have sprung up in this age of Kluxers and Beavers the one known by that unpronounceable word, 'Intelligentsia' is among the most benighted. The war seems to have given it birth, the press nurtured it, which should have been warning enough, then the public accepted it, and now we all suffer." But despite this attitude toward the intelligentsia, Fauset was dedicated to higher learning, and throughout his life was a student and educator.

Fauset's most important contribution came with his important anthropological work, *Black Gods of the Metropolis: Negro Religious Cults in the Urban North,* published in 1944. A classic study based on a project he began in 1939, it demonstrated how Negroes adapted their religious impulses to urban life. The book was a revision of the dissertation that he presented for his anthropology degree, a field of study he entered only in the middle 1930s. Studying the role of black churches was a relatively new phenomenon, and Fauset's formulations about how the churches fostered the community's ability to deal with business and political issues reach back to the urban sociology of Robert Park and Charles Johnson. Interested also in the phenomenon of mixed-blood marriages, Fauset collected oral folklore on this subject in Canada. Working as a teacher in the Philadelphia public school system, he became the vice-president of the teachers' union. Locke served as his mentor and made sure that he always aspired to more and more education. The two men together bought real estate, and they discussed business details at length. Even on his way to Reno to get his divorce from Bird in 1938, he sent Locke details about their contracts and arrangements, telling Locke that the houses they had purchased together would generate $150.00 a month for him upon retirement. In their correspondence Locke treats Fauset brusquely, but the younger man seemed to accept Locke's advice, and their friendship remained close for three decades.[14]

Meanwhile, the international situation continued to occupy Locke's thoughts. He attended a meeting on the Spanish Civil War in January 1939 and listened to a speech by a Mr. Donawa, a dentist from Howard who had joined the Loyalist side; he reported that at least three hundred Negro volunteers had gone to fight in Spain. Locke encountered Paul Robeson at a July 1939 meeting in New York City to discuss the problem of refugees from the Spanish Civil War, and there the two enjoyed a long talk. Locke gladly observed to Mason that Robeson "really has changed front completely," and that he wanted only roles that would do credit to his race, though his blacklisting continued to stunt his career. The singer, however, said he must continue to keep a distance from his wife, whose political influence over Robeson Locke had always lamented. A month later Locke was hard at work on his summer school assignments, perhaps especially burdensome since they were a constant reminder that for a second summer he was unable to visit Europe. For the moment the war was impending, but yet at a distance. On August 22, he wrote to Mason: "But now come the war clouds—and really I feel like a son of Noah. Suppose we must just build a private ark and weather it through dark and brooding isolation." Hitler's invasion of Poland came a week later. Ten days later Mason answered Locke, deploring the Munich pact: "To my mind England is waiting for small countries to revolt, that is the thing that would checkmate Hitler, because he can't understand anything that crosses his purposes. Chamberlaine [*sic*] is not a diplomat. He is a county manufacturer, therefore he was ideot [*sic*] enough to call a consultation with Hitler." A week later Locke alluded to the German-Russian Non-Aggression pact, expressing considerable gloom: "As much as I hate Hitler, I cannot like England nor respect Chamberlain's belated and hypocritical moralisms. And then—this Russian enigma—it is all too terrible. . . . [T]he only sensible thought is that a civilization that isn't civilized has no right to be saved." Mason's class-based condescension toward Chamberlain was echoed by Locke's increasing Anglophobia, even as he expressed sentiments that echoed his early reaction to World War I.

The remainder of 1939 did not completely sink in gloom. Locke did, however, observe that his new assistant failed to compliment him on the opening lecture in his philosophy course at Howard, something that Locke never would have done with his "elders." The students themselves nevertheless gave Locke pleasure, and he remarked how the freshmen, participating in a new course of his meant to serve as an orientation to higher learning, "stimulated [him] by their eagerness and open curiosity." A few months later he observed, with the nostalgia often felt by senior professors: "Once in a grand while—especially as I show visitors around, I realize that the human contacts with students have been the thing that has made it all worth while." In November a major effort began to take shape, though it would be three years until it was completed. Through his friendship with a Columbia sociologist, Bernhard Stern, Locke planned a collaboration on a "project . . . on race and minority situations." This was to be Locke's last major writing and editorial work, *When Peoples Meet*. The book, a gathering of essays by eighty-five major scholars from many different fields, would not appear until 1942, and a second edition was published in 1946, with a reprinting in 1949. Meanwhile the two men planned to begin work together at Stern's farm in Connecticut, but illness in Stern's family forced a change, and Locke worked alone in Washington throughout the next several months.

Continuously interested in music of all kinds, Locke was equally occupied with the question of how to turn musical compositions into a form of cultural expression that would have definite social and political purposes. These preoccupations apparently increased as the coming war seemed more inevitable, and he also thought about the problem of an esthetic that would have universalized import. The choral ballet of *Sahdji* was one instance of how Locke had explored the theatrical possibility of using African material in a way that displayed its universal meanings. On another occasion almost a decade later, at the end of the 1930s, Still and Locke entered into a second collaboration, though this time Locke's part was indirect. Locke met Katherine Biddle—she used the pen name Katherine Garrison Chapin—through Mason, who was her aunt. Chapin, the wife of Francis Biddle, the United States Solicitor General, was a widely published poet and author, and an active philanthropist, and Locke cultivated and enjoyed their friendship. Her play on Sojourner Truth, written in part through Locke's encouragement, was produced by the American Negro Theatre in 1948. In 1938 Chapin had had a piece of her writing set to music by Harl McDonald. Locke felt the piece, called "Lament for the Stolen," about the Lindberg kidnapping, failed to match the words with the music; he suggested to Chapin that, though unorthodox, putting the sopranos in the rear of the stage would improve the effect. Locke believed in Chapin's poetic talents, and in July 1939 he introduced Still to a poem written by Chapin, called "And They Lynched Him on a Tree." Eventually Still and Chapin met in person and were encouraged by Locke to collaborate, and he was eager to see a major work as the outcome.[15]

Working under the auspices of a Rosenwald Fellowship, Still composed an elaborate setting of the poem, featuring a full orchestra, a white chorus, a black chorus, and a contralto soloist and male narrator. Though the subject matter was a lynching, the poem was felt by the *New York Times* critic, Verna Arvey, who had recently become Still's second wife, to be free of propaganda and was instead "created purely as a human document." This was certainly an opinion shared by Locke. The piece bore a "spiritual" dedication to Charlotte Osgood Mason, "whose efforts for the betterment of Negro people are well known," as Arvey put it. She remarked of the May 26, 1940 performance in Los Angeles, where Still was living at the time: "There are tremendously exciting moments. Thematic material depicting the Negro mother and the colored onlookers is as poignant and noble as any to be found in Still's symphonies."

The New York Philharmonic performed it on June 25, 1940, on an outdoor program that included songs sung by Robeson and other American works. Locke hoped that Marian Anderson might be enlisted for the part of the contralto, but her schedule was too busy. Much work and planning went into arranging for the choruses, and there were last minute changes in the ending of the poem, which offered a more general view of the lynching's impact. Some felt it was too critical of America and should be softened. Critics praised the work, however, and Locke was especially enthusiastic about it, feeling that it would become a permanent part of the American musical canon. In a review in the August 1940 issue of *Opportunity*, Locke claimed that "it universalizes its particular theme and expands a Negro tragedy into a purging and inspiring plea for justice and a fuller democracy." Taking the occasion to make an observation of the political state of the country, he said that "democracy today needs sober criticism, even courageous chastising." Earlier that spring Congress had failed to pass an antilynching bill. The continuing racism in America, only worsened by the effects of the Depression, led Locke in the 1940s to assert, like Dewey in *The Public and Its Problems*, that the only cure for the shortcomings of democracy is more democracy. This theme dominated Locke's political and social writings for the remainder of his life.

Anticipating the fuller development of this theme, Locke contributed to the second congress of the League of American Writers, which was held in 1939. This congress included a broad array of writers—from Kenneth Burke to Dorothy Parker—and several panels devoted to various topics, such as Hollywood screenwriting and radio. Donald Ogden Stewart edited the speeches and discussion of the congress into a book called *Fighting Words*, published in 1940. The congress, organized around the theme of "War Aims," and Stewart's compilation were both left-leaning and were generally directed to combating fascism; indeed, Stewart, in later years, would be blacklisted in Hollywood for his association with the Communist Party. Locke contributed a talk to a panel on Negro writers, which also included contributions from Langston Hughes and Melville Herskovits. Hughes spoke about the need for black writers to have fairer treatment from white publishers and about the limitations on the size of the Negro readership. Herskovits recounted some of his argument about the vestiges of West African culture in the slaves who were brought to America, the essential frame of which he had explored in *The Myth of the Negro Past.*

Locke spoke next and began by referring back to the Renaissance and the need for "the development of an historical sense, a knowledge, adequate and accurate, of the Negro's past." He argued that the absence of such a sense had caused most representations of Negroes to suffer from the twin ills of sentimentality and stereotyping. Focusing on the role of Negro writers themselves, he suggested they must use their advantage of "psychological intimacy" in order to combat both their own situation and the counter-stereotypes to which they often resorted. Referring back to Herskovits's historical and anthropological argument, he said: "[A]s creative writers we owe to the contemporary public the truth, and the full truth, about Negro life. Now I think the truth is something which, being objective and being sound, everyone must eventually accept, even the section of the American public which is most reactionary and most conservative and most committed to prejudices." He urged the formation of "our own front for democracy," and fighting stereotypes is "a work that can only be done in close collaboration between the white and the Negro artist." The idea that democracy could serve as a cure for racism was more than a figure of speech for Locke, and this speech first raised the idea of collaboration between white and black writers, something which Locke himself would engage in more and more frequently in the next decade or so. The League of American Writers presented Locke and others with a forum that included a diverse audience, one engaged in immediate political and social struggles, and Locke addressed it forthrightly.

Locke had for decades struggled against racism using the tools of cultural criticism, artistic expression, philosophical analysis, and academic and adult educational institutions. But he increased his commitment, which seldom flagged in any case, when faced with the world situation at the beginning of the 1940s. Seeing fascism up close in Germany, combined with his work on values and his attempts to replace absolutist thinking, meant that Locke would face a new battle on the levels of cultural ideas and action, a battle which led him to reevaluate the meaning of democracy. The League of

American Writers speech was a harbinger of yet more serious thought on his part, and he would even go beyond the nationalist concerns in his earlier efforts at cultural work to embrace an internationalism that served as the main arena of his efforts in the last active years of his life. Committed as he was to the need to respect the changeability of values, along with their firm supporting grounds, he refused to rest on any laurels and instead eagerly set himself new tasks.

Sometime in the 1940s Locke read Freud. There is no record of what prompted this. But whatever he was looking for, and whatever he found, he set down some brief reflections on the subject of group psychology and individual psychological conflict. These thoughts were related to his philosophical formulations on values, and just as clearly they were shaped by his thoughts about race. In a manuscript entitled "Freud and Scientific Morality," possibly a talk given to the Ethical Culture Society in New York, Locke advanced the following: "While offering no panacea, undoubtedly objective analysis of the unconscious unstated assumptions of various societies and cultures, and of our own particularly, offers the first realistic step in the solution of . . . conflict dilemmas. . . . " Turning to the pragmatic need to undo absolutes, he added: "What has been man or history-made can certainly be more rationally considered both as needing explanation and as subject to possible change. . . . [Scientific morality] disestablished the old illusions of inevitability and self-righteousness." Again, the mix of tones—"no panacea" is claimed, even as the problem can "certainly" be rationally considered—characterizes his way of approaching value questions, even as the familiar result, the need to deny absolutist claims, guides the conclusion of the argument.

Another incomplete and undated manuscript supplements the Freudian musings, though it also addresses the concerns of Horace Kallen and the national discussion of how to understand ethnic and racial diversity. "But what if instead of a melting pot America should turn out to be a crucible where instead of amalgamation of tradition a crystallization of latent racial traits and characteristics was in process?" Locke envisions the latency of social and cultural features turning into something like a hardened set of "conflict dilemmas." From the pluralism of the melting pot to the crucible of racial antagonism was a transformation devoutly to be avoided. All of his efforts in the 1930s, indeed most of his work since *The New Negro*, aimed at a transvaluation of American attitudes about race, a transvaluation to be accomplished largely by cultural work and educational reform. Locke accepted the proposition that there was always more work to be done in the field of race relations, yet, as he saw the rise of fascism and the beginning of another world war, he felt that the social order was corrupt in ways that could seem limitless. His comments on the onset of the war often used apocalyptic images, yet his faith in the possible and even steady improvement in the status of Negroes served to support his sense of vocation. At his most hopeful, he could even imagine a new universal order in which values could serve not so much to divide peoples but to enable them to meet on a new and different level of understanding. In his closing years at Howard, he set out again to help bring about such understanding, by redrawing his sense of scale with a global measure.[16]

CHAPTER TEN

Theorizing Democracy

In the last decade of his life, Locke continued to be above all an educator. Remarkably, his dedication never visibly wavered and his schedule was never empty. Despite the persistent weakness of his heart and the occasions on which he needed hospitalization or a strict period of total rest, he kept an unremitting pace in his public life: teaching and lecturing, planning and attending conferences, writing and editing. The appearance of *When Peoples Meet* in 1942 offered an occasion for him once more to display his erudition and broaden his audience. He extended his interest in African culture and the black diaspora with a lecture tour in Haiti in the spring of 1943. The grand theme of the need for broader social democracy and the prospects for world peace gave him a transcendent purpose and the context for fuller thought and argument. As Mason's health slowly declined, Locke turned to others for the social and cultural conversation on which he thrived. The adult education movement took more and more of his time, and his place there increased in visibility and recognition. His leadership in the black community was secure. He continued to teach at Howard throughout the war, crafting his faculty obligations in a way that left time for travel and writing, which led to his participating in a broader circle of intellectuals. Various forms of national recognition came his way, but before any laurels were to be worn, he still had work to do.

Locke's vision deepened considerably during the first half of the 1940s. This had two major manifestations: his work on democracy and world peace, and his writings on cultural reciprocity, both of which drew heavily on his value theory. The former was concentrated when he delivered papers on three occasions, at the Conference on Science, Philosophy and Religion, in 1941, 1943, and 1950. Here he stressed the need for a purer sense of democracy's inclusiveness that would eventually aid in promoting the possibility of universal peace while at the same time serving to defeat the forces of fascism and racism. The second focus was evident in several places, but perhaps most notably during his lectures in Haiti in 1943. Cultural reciprocity supported the desired objective of increasing Pan-American understanding among the peoples of what he referred to as "the Three Americas." To the extent that both aspects of his vision drew on his value theory, they overlapped in many places. Conflicts between groups could be overcome by a better understanding of values. Democracy fostered a tentative but grounded hold on one's values, which in turn was strengthened by cultural self-knowledge and an appreciation of how the structure and function of the values of others were analogous to our own. These ideas and commitments had been growing in Locke's mind and directing his writing at least since the 1915 lectures on race contacts and interracial relations. But his lifelong efforts provided the foundation for yet further adaptations and developments.

Locke's views on democracy deserve fuller study than they have received. In general, Locke saw democracy as more a system of social values than a mechanism or procedure for mediating political power and interests. In the last decade and a half of his life he referred to democracy often, and he did so in a context of reasoned debate that implicitly affirmed it as the most inclusive and valuable of all political theories. Of course, democracy meant different things to different people. C. B. Macpherson has spelt out a major distinction between the ways it was understood by two different viewpoints. One group of thinkers treats democracy as a liberal form of society that "maximizes individual satisfactions or utilities." This view stresses things such as a free market and relies to a large extent on utilitarian values. Another group sees democracy as focused on maximizing human powers and on aiding citizens in "using and developing their uniquely human capacities." These include, among others, "the capacity for rational understanding, for moral judgment and action, for esthetic creation or contemplation, for the emotional activities of friendship and love, and, sometimes, for religious experience."[1] Locke clearly identified with the latter group. Because racism disallowed its victims the full development of their capacities, it was especially despicable to Locke, and he set all his own capacities to the service of eradicating it.

The Conference on Science, Philosophy, and Religion and Their Relation to the Democratic Way of Life, to use the full official title, originated in 1940 under the auspices of the Jewish Theological Seminary in New York City, with the seminary's chancellor, Louis Finkelstein, serving as its main organizer. Over the years that followed many of the country's leading intellectuals participated in the yearly gatherings, held at various colleges but most often at Columbia University. The roster included Albert Einstein, Franz Boas, Sidney Hook, Paul Tillich, Charles S. Johnson, Talcott Parsons, Margaret Mead, Van Wyck Brooks, and many others. A growing concern to promote the virtues of democracy in international affairs, and a desire to combat the rise of fascism, animated the participants. One of the members' most discussed points was the undesirable hegemony established by the dominance of scientific values, though the conference also dealt with issues of race, labor relations, and educational policy. The proceedings were frequently published—Locke, who was one of the founders of the conference, contributed to two of the volumes—but after 1943 the meetings were not open to the public, and in 1968 the conferences ceased. They had, however, formed an important part of a national dialogue about democratic values that was broadly exploratory before, during, and after the war.[2]

This dialogue was often more like a debate. One side invested a great deal of discussion and belief in the idea that science was itself an inherently democratic undertaking, because it opened itself to universal testing and operated without bias or prejudice. The other side resisted the claims of science, because of an antipathy to the overly empirical and technological developments in modern society, which were seen as dehumanizing; this group also thought democracy could only be achieved with a basis in a shared religious faith. The rise of Nazism, with its anti-Semitism and belief that only Nazi science deserved the name, combined a distortion of science's putative universalism with the political ideology of a viciously racist nationalism that flew in the face of all generally understood scientific values. As such, the need to combat Nazism on all fronts gave new impetus to those who would link science and democracy. But the Conference on Science, Philosophy, and Religion, especially in its first years, took a rather different approach and exhibited at least some skepticism about the claims of what came to be known as the culture of science. Locke on the whole sympathized with those who questioned science's exalted status, but, consonant with his temperament, he saw virtues on both sides.

At the 1941 conference, one of the more strident pieces, "God and the Professors," was written by Mortimer Adler, who was then one of the best-known philosophers in America. Though he did not speak for the entire conference, his views were set out as if they were the keynote address, and "God and the Professors" took a very broad and deeply polemical view. He claimed that the specialization of academic disciplines and the secularization of American culture were in danger of producing an irreligious society. Adler went even further to make the strong version of a culturalist argument when he said: "A culture dies of diseases which are themselves cultural. It may be born sick, as modern culture was . . . but . . . cultural disorder is a cause and not an effect of the political and economic disturbances which beset the world today." For Adler, this fear meant that John Dewey was a threat to America at least as grave as that of Nazism; "I say we have more to fear from our professors than from Hitler," he opined, with a clear reference to Dewey's secularism. Across town, so to speak, in 1943 another gathering of thinkers was advancing the idea that the qualities most valued by the scientific community—what Robert K. Merton identified as universalism, disinterestedness, communism, and skepticism—were congruent with and supportive of democratic and secular values. (By communism Merton meant that all advanced knowledge would be shared and equally available to all members of society.) This gathering was called the Conference on the Scientific Spirit and Democratic Faith. A number of years later a retrospective consideration about the split between the two conferences was offered by Sidney Hook. Writing in *Commentary,* he recalled: "By the time the third meeting of the Conference [on Science, Philosophy, and Religion] was convoked (at which an official statement emphasized the need of a knowledge that would bring men back to God), a sizable contingent of individuals who had supported the Conference departed." With Dewey as the leader of the dissidents, they "organized the Conference on the Scientific Spirit and the Democratic Faith, open to all irrespective of their theology or metaphysics, provided they were willing to explore the consequences of the democratic beliefs they shared in common." Locke resisted identifying wholly with either side in this debate, and his position occupied a middle ground. Indeed it is a measure of Locke's stature and his ability to approach problems openly and pragmatically that he eventually gave a paper at the second Conference on the Scientific Spirit and Democratic Faith in 1943, which he later published as "The Teaching of Dogmatic Religion in a Democratic Society," in the proceedings. In the battle of the conferences and their opposing values, Locke was a rare mediator.[3]

Locke's presentation at the 1941 Conference on Science, Philosophy, and Religion, "Pluralism and Intellectual Democracy," took sharp variance with the views of Adler. Setting the tone and context for most of his subsequent writings about democracy, the essay opens with three points: absolutist thinking has returned; in fighting absolutisms, we are in danger of creating our own uniformitarianism; and radical empiricism has become "arbitrary

and dogmatic." From these points, and a passage that resituates the traditional dispute over facts and values, he moves to an acknowledgement of the
importance of William James's emphasis on pluralism, but separates James
from his followers. For Locke, James proposed "giving up for good and all
the 'game of metaphysics' and the 'false' and categorical rationalizing of values, but he did not advocate sterilizing the 'will to believe' or abandoning the
search for pragmatic sanctions for our values." Locke uses this balancing act
to advance his own special sense of the way forward. Scientists must give up
their absolutist claims for empiricism, but at the same time he urges the ratio-
nalists to surrender their absolutisms:

> In a complementary concession, the value disciplines, it seems to me,
> should make the concession of relativism. Frankly, this asks that they
> dethrone their absolutes, not as values or even as preferred values, but
> nonetheless as arbitrary universals, whether they be "sole ways of sal-
> vation," "perfect forms of the state or society," or self-evident systems
> of interpretation. Difficult as this may be for our various traditional
> value systems, once they do so, they thereby make not only peace
> with one another, but also make an honorable peace with science.
> (PAL, 55–56)

Clearly derived from his thoughts in "Values and Imperatives"—and reaching back to his Harvard dissertation and its attempt to find some common
function between empirical and logical orders of meaning—this argument addresses the social and historical moment when some advocates of democracy
were claiming too much, just as scientists were also overreaching in placing
their culture at the center of a realm of transcendent truth. Though written in
the optative mode, the essay is not utopian but rather relies on Locke's deep
sense of the importance of finding the middle way through the constant and
strenuous application of the principle of reciprocity.

Invoking one of his Harvard teachers, Locke says wryly: "To intelligent
partisans, especially those who can come within hailing distance of Royce's
principle of 'loyalty to loyalty,' such value reciprocity might be acceptable
and welcome." Reciprocity extended the axiology that Locke had developed
in the two preceding decades, namely that values were plural and historically determined and yet functioned in cultural schemes as guides to action.
Locke knew that values could be treated as reciprocal, and this important
insight was fostered through his rational analysis of values. This analysis
showed that, though different cultures might have different values, in some

cases the values occupied, as it were, analogous places in the structure of the culture's overall formation. This meant that values performed similar functions in different cultures, or served as reciprocal terms, without necessarily being simply exchangeable or regarded as identical. What Royce had argued some years earlier—that every culture had different values to which they were loyal, but across all cultures people were committed to the notion that loyalty to one's values was itself a social good—served Locke as an example of how one could deal with values without essentializing them or treating them as unique. Scientists should see that the values of the humanist were important in guiding judgment, just as humanists should see that the analytic approach of the scientist was a useful instrument in establishing truth.

Obviously informed by his own experience and his analysis of the question of race, Locke's cautions about the failed promises of American democracy anticipated a slowly dawning recognition on the part of others. Asking for "a less bigoted national and cultural tradition," he argued: "Democratic liberalism, limited both by the viewpoint of its generation and by its close affiliation with doctrinal religious and philosophical traditions, modeled its rationale of democracy too closely to authoritarian patterns, and made a creed of democratic principles. For wide acceptance or easy assent it condoned or compromised with too much dogmatism and orthodoxy" (PAL, 59). This claim, skeptical about the virtues of religious belief, separates Locke from the position of Adler. It also anticipates the claim of what would become in two years one of the most famous books about the race issue. This was Gunnar Myrdal's *The American Dilemma,* which attained national and even international fame upon its publication in 1944. Written by a Swedish sociologist who worked for years with a team of six researchers, the book spelt out the depth and nature of America's racism as directed toward its black citizens. "From the point of view of the American Creed the status accorded the Negro in America represents nothing more and nothing less than a century-long lag of public morals. . . . The Negro in America has not yet been given the elemental civil and political rights of formal democracy, including a fair opportunity to earn his living, upon which a general accord was already won when the American Creed was first taking form." Though the word "creed" links Locke and Myrdal, for Locke the word also suggests his attitude toward religion, with its tendency to harden into dogmatism just as science stiffened into positivism.[4]

The two terms of Locke's title contained the cure for such calcified scientific or religious views. Locke means by "intellectual democracy" a version of pragmatism seen as a set of mental habits that would enable people to discover universal truths without wandering into the thickets of dogmatic thought. Drawing on "Values and Imperatives," Locke argues for a critical value pluralism that would lend a scientific—but not overly scientized—rigor to key questions:

> For if once this broader relativistic approach could discover beneath the expected cultural differentials of time and place such functional "universals" as actually may be there, these common-denominator values would stand out pragmatically confirmed by common human experience. . . . [They would have] status far beyond any "universals" merely asserted by orthodox dogmatisms. (PAL, 56)

Here Locke carefully refuses to claim too much, though his idea that values could be rationally studied was a commitment about which he grew more and more insistent. He pushed the point further when he said: "Value assertion would . . . be a tolerant assertion of preference, not an intolerant insistence on agreement or finality. Value disciplines would take on the tentative and revisionist procedure of natural science." Along with the pragmatic lineage of this sort of thinking, Locke invoked the spirit of democracy. He steadfastly believed that "our duty to democracy on the plane of ideas, especially in time of crisis, is the analysis" of value pluralism. Such pluralism should form "a sturdier intellectual base for democracy."

Locke called on the tradition of pragmatism for his support of democracy, and vice versa, and so entered an energized contemporary debate about the nature and role of democratic thought and practice as a means to combat fascism. Dewey, however, was one of his immediate sources. In books such as *The Public and Its Problems,* Dewey had shown how a democratic polity needed to rely on a scientific approach to any crisis, but the approach could not be modeled on the extreme specialized knowledge of experts alone. Still, a certain sort of social and political form needed, and would benefit from, a certain way of thinking. To this Deweyan combination of pragmatism in thought and democracy in social and political theory, Locke supplied a distinctive and valuable contribution when he added value as the key third term. His value theorizing had led him to the principle of reciprocity in values and culture as a guarantee against fanaticism. In fact, he had first used the phrase "cultural reciprocity" in an essay, "Internationalism: Friend or Foe?," published years earlier in the March 1925 issue of a journal called *The World Tomorrow.* There he argued: "We must uproot cultural partisanship and egotism, personal and professional, learn to produce art nationally or ra-

cially, or in vital localism, even, but to consume it humanly and universally."
His experience with racism in the 1910s and 1920s clearly continued to influence him, for the dogmatism of racial supremacists like Lothrop Stoddard
displayed all the faults of moral absolutism unenlightened by any "tentative
or revisionist" practices of natural science.

To avoid the temptation to fight one absolutism with another, Locke came
up with one of his boldest claims, and again used the word "creed" to indicate his orientation:

> Far too much of our present democratic creed and practice is cast in
> the mold of such blind loyalty and en bloc rationalization, with too
> many of our citizens the best of democrats for the worst of reasons—
> mere conformity. Apart from the theoretical absolutistic taint, it should
> be disconcerting to ponder that by the same token, if transported,
> these citizens would be "perfect" Nazis and the best of totalitarians.
> (PAL, 58)

To make this claim—really a charge—against Americans even as the war
against Nazism was being fought was a bold political utterance. In the First
World War Locke began by considering the struggle a battle of commercial
interests, and he saw it as a death drive among the civilized nations. Then his
patriotism reasserted itself. Here he was taking no explicit stand against the
war, but he clearly saw that going to war on a worldwide scale would never by
itself result in the triumph of democratic values. At a minimum, that triumph
waited upon education and critical thought.

Another of his claims dealt with some of the more important benefits of
what he termed critical relativism. Such thought "breaks down the worship
of the form," he argued, pointing to "that dangerous identification of the
symbol with the value [as] the prime psychological root of the fallacies and
errors we have been discussing." By putting the "premium upon equivalence
not upon identity" and by promoting "reciprocity instead of factional antagonism," a close look, skeptical and scientific, at the function of values would
have "high practical consequences for democratic living." A final paradox
typifies Locke's approach to the problem. Absolutism was invidious, and we
suffered from it unawares; we avoided it only by realizing democracy must
not be imposed by force or unthinking conformity. "Broadening our cultural values and tempering our orthodoxies is of infinitely more service to
enlarged democracy than direct praise and advocacy of democracy itself." As
early as "The New Negro," Locke felt that democracy only flourished when

its substance was available to everyone; leaving its symbols to some while denying full political expression to others never cured the ills of the state. "Considerable political and cultural dogmatism, in the form of culture bias, nation worship, and racism, still stands in the way and must be invalidated and abandoned." In Locke's prescriptive words, "The democratic mind needs clarifying for the better guidance of the democratic will." His intellectual struggle on this score arose from deep emotion, though he set it out calmly.

But his attention was not totally devoted to political issues, as his esthetic experiences continued to be enriched. He published two more year-end reviews in *Opportunity,* in 1941 and 1942: "Of Native Sons: Real and Otherwise," and "Who and What Is 'Negro'?" The first took up the most important novel of the preceding year and one of the most important novels by an African American. Certainly Locke felt that way about Richard Wright's *Native Son,* and his review did much to help the novel's entry into the canon. The review opens with an extended reflection on the constant problem of accurate artistic representations of group experience, specifically that of a minority group. In some sense this is the central problem for those who would address the question of the relations between art and politics, and Locke enters the discussion eagerly. He sensed that Wright had written a book that was "not just a plea for the Negro, but a challenge to the nation and its own enlightened self-interest." Invoking the Negro experience as part of the nation's problem, one of the most insistent of Locke's stances in the 1930s and 1940s, he also urged the black readership to face up to the necessity of an art that would not blink at uncomfortable facts. "Eventually . . . this must involve the clarifying recognition that there is no one type of Negro, and that Bigger's type has the right to its day in the literary calendar, not only for what it might add in his own right to Negro portraiture, but for what it could say about America" (CTAL, 299).

Those who insistently saw Locke as effete or overly cultured probably did not take into account the way his taste and judgment as a critic were expressed in the case of *Native Son.* For several years he had been speaking and writing about the need for a more realistic approach to Negro art and the necessity of seeing it in the framework of the entire national culture. Indeed, in his own mind these two principles were present at least as early as *The New Negro.* Locke's respect for Wright derived chiefly from his admiration for his skills as a writer. But the gritty realism of *Native Son* convinced Locke that his longstanding resistance to stereotyping and sentimentalism had finally paid off. The growing sense of social resistance in the post-Depression years contributed to Locke's feeling that the fate of fiction by Negroes, which he had chronicled for many years and would continue to do so, needed a special dose of realist detail that would render a "clarifying recognition" to the group experience. One of Locke's special skills as a critic was his bold commitment to the emerging talents, as he identified them, of the new generation and a belief that artists would always appear when needed. This belief drew him to Toomer, Cullen, and Hughes a decade earlier, but those three writers had proved, in various ways, disappointing to Locke, and so he was if anything quite eager to hear a new voice. The fervor of his praise for Wright was virtually unmatched in all of his year-end reviews, until Ellison's *Invisible Man* appeared a number of years later.

Wright was not the only author who engaged Locke's strong esthetic views in the year-end review. He took the occasion to criticize the autobiographical efforts of Hughes and Du Bois, and to further chastise McKay for his memoir, *Harlem*. Hughes's book, *The Big Sea*, contained a rather cautious portrait of Locke himself, and it was this note of caution that Locke especially objected to, saying that "broad areas of [Hughes's] life's wide wanderings . . . are not plumbed to any depth of analysis or understanding." Speculating on whether or not for Langston "righteous anger is the mainspring of an interest in social analysis," Locke quipped that "one wishes more of life had irked him." Echoes from Hughes's coy and distant flirtation with Locke a decade earlier registered just below the surface here. For Du Bois's *Dusk of Dawn*, Locke lamented: "This might easily have been one of the important biographic memoirs of the generation had there been greater psychological perspective on the issues and events." The failure, in Locke's eyes, was that "an egocentric predicament" refracted Du Bois's own "warrantably personal" observations, so they read as if "an historian . . . had objectively examined all sides of the evidence." There is more than a little irony, to be sure, in Locke asking both Hughes and Du Bois to have been more subjective and personally revelatory, since he himself was often more than guarded about his private life. His reading of Freud may have influenced him here, yet he was able to base his judgment of relative weakness on both men's failure to take full advantage of the genre of autobiography, with its central trope of the unblinking scrutiny of personal habits and values.

"Of Native Sons: Real and Otherwise" also rated McKay's *Harlem* negatively: a "pretentious analysis" that "outdoes *The Big Sea* for superficiality and lack of serious evaluation." Turning again to a psychological vocabulary, Locke said McKay had filled his book with "personalisms of under-and over-emphasis—according, of course, to personal whim." But with McKay, repeating charges similar to those he made against *A Long Way from Home,* he went a bit further than with Hughes and Du Bois, adding that "[i]f ever warrantable, this flippancy and egocentrism is not to be condoned in a time like this." Observing that "war clouds have almost grounded the scholarly flights of African studies," Locke celebrated the reprint of C. G. Seligman's *Races of Africa,* "one of the few anthropological analyses both readable and reliable at the same time." In sorting out the various books on social analysis and Negro history, Locke carried through his standard that called for a higher seriousness and greater forthrightness. He also made a passing reference to the as-yet-unpublished study of "the Carnegie Myrdal collaborative research," which would appear later as *An American Dilemma.*

Locke published relatively little in 1941, though he worked at preparing *When Peoples Meet* and his essay on intellectual democracy, both of which appeared in the following year. A new edition of the *Life and Times of Frederick Douglass* came out, and Locke's brief foreword represented the total of what he would publish from the work he had done on his planned biography of Douglass. By marking the centennial of the Abolition Platform passed at the Nantucket Anti-Slavery Convention of 1841, the new edition was part of a "mission of revitalizing Negro life today through the revival and rediscovery of its heroic past," as Locke put it. It was also the 102nd anniversary of Douglass's escape from slavery. Locke's plans for the Douglass biography were apparently pushed aside by other projects, most of them focusing on democracy, but it is clear that Locke kept the idea of race leadership in mind throughout his life, testing it against his knowledge of all the major black leaders.

Locke's foreword vividly pictures Douglass and makes clear how Locke would have treated his subject if he had written a full-length biography. Douglass had a "personality [that] even on its most human side never lacked the fibre of manhood and manliness." Contrasting him with Booker T. Washington and the accommodationist stance that valued economic progress over spiritual development, Locke pictured Douglass as a model for all time, not just for his own generation. His life rebuked the failed promises of democracy, because it was a life that, inversely as it were, "reflects the dominant psychology of a whole American generation of materialism and reaction which dimmed, along with Douglass and other crisis heroes, the glory and fervor of much early American idealism." Then, invoking a favorite word he often used to describe his own personality, Locke said that Douglass "was full of paradoxes, and on several issues he can be quoted against himself." Locke balanced the heroicizing tone common in biography when he stressed that with Douglass we needed to "read or re-read [his] career in his own crisp and graphic words, lest he be minimized or maximized by the biographers. . . . For he was no paragon, without flaw or contradiction, even though, on the whole the consistent champion of human rights and the ardent, ever-loyal advocate of the Negro's cause." It was "evident" that Douglass had grown in "stature and significance," not only because of the contrast with Booker T. Washington, but because of his "militant courage," which is why "he promises to become a paramount hero for Negro youth . . . today." Trying to capture Douglass in a summation, Locke regarded him as inspirational: "Perhaps [Douglass's] claim to greatness came from his ability to generalize the issues of the Negro cause and see them as basic principles of human freedom, everywhere and in every instance." As with his esthetics, Locke was here using the particularities of Negro experience to arrive at a revitalized sense of justice that could have the effect of a universal force.[5]

It was not until the February and March 1942 issues of *Opportunity* that Locke's year-end review, "Who and What Is 'Negro'?" appeared. The last one of his published in that journal, this review marked the start of a five-year hiatus from a format at which Locke had increasingly excelled. Locke began with his usual reflections on an important problem, one he addressed as early as 1920: how can one determine if there is a distinctively Negro culture and what defines 'Negro art' and 'Negro literature'? There was no point in "throwing the question back at the sociologist or the anthropologist, for they scarcely know themselves, having twin sphinxes in their own bailiwicks." Since the term was difficult to define, the door was left open for "blind partisans" and "traditional fanaticisms." Of one thing, though, Locke was certain: "There is, in brief, no 'The Negro.'" Having embraced pluralism in terms of values and eliminated any scientific basis for racial distinctions, Locke concluded that one could speak of Negro culture only as a composite of racial, national, and regional idioms. Such a composite or hybrid culture could have great variety in the amount of any one of these three elements. He reiterated his firm belief that such a composite would only be fully intelligible in a larger, national framework: "The position leads, if soundly developed, not to cultural separatism but to cultural pluralism. To be 'Negro' in the cultural sense . . . is not to be radically different, but only to be distinctively composite and idiomatic, though basically American." Sometimes the critic, like a chemist, had the job of breaking down the elements of this composite, and this meant deciding on the representativeness of any particular elements among the regional, racial, and national material. "Theme and idiom would bulk more significantly" than authorship in defining a work as distinctively

Negro (CTAL, 311). Negro culture and Negro literature both involved appreciating idioms and social traits and not a racial essence.

In the summer of 1942, obviously unable to visit Europe, Locke gave a series of lectures in various places around the Washington area. Visiting Campobello Island, at the invitation of Bernhard Stern, he met Loren MacIver, who was hosting a Summer Training Institute. A panel led by Jacques Barzun met during the third week of the institute, and Locke read a paper entitled "The Relation of Class, Caste, and Democracy in the United States." At the end of the summer he was back in New York, where the third Conference on Science, Philosophy, and Religion was held. Locke presided over a session on "The Meaning of Human Dignity and Human Civilization in Terms of Various Disciplines," which featured papers by MacIver and Gregory Bateson. This was the beginning of Locke's social and professional contacts with several white intellectuals, with many of whom Locke would confer and publish throughout the 1940s.

From all of his various conferences and the many intellectual contacts and friendships he made, Locke derived at least one palpable result: the publication of *When Peoples Meet*. If one were to take the introduction to the book, as well as all the extensive interchapter material, and present it as a monographic work, it might well be seen as one of Locke's major achievements. Not only was the idea of cultural contact between different peoples on Locke's mind for the preceding three decades, the book's spirit is infused with the importance of reciprocity. *The New Negro* stood as the clarion for cultural renaissance, the work on value theory led to the appreciation of cultural relativism, and *When Peoples Meet* put cultural reciprocity at the heart of Locke's project. Of course, it was not written as a monograph but rather a collection of essays by different scholars and experts in several fields. The format of the book embodies Locke's sense of intellectual and cultural work as a group experience, a harmonizing of various points of view that entails an increased sense of self-criticism and growth for all those assembled. But the breadth and depth of Locke's commentary remains impressive, though largely unnoticed, as the book did not receive the number of sales or classroom adoptions for which its editors had hoped.[6]

As with much of Locke's work, *When Peoples Meet* began as a proposal, submitted as early as 1939, to an institution that could grant it funding. The Progressive Education Association (PEA), and specifically its Committee on Intercultural Education, included among others the anthropologist Ruth Benedict. Locke and his co-editor, Bernhard Stern, a Columbia lecturer in sociology and colleague of Benedict, approached the PEA and secured a contract for $5,000.00 to cover payments for the contributors and secretarial fees. Stern's wife, Charlotte, bore many of the clerical duties, and Locke asked for his fees to be equivalent to half his teaching salary for two months, a total of $400.00. Earlier some discussion between Locke and others questioned what sort of audience the book might have, and if it should be a sourcebook for college courses. There was also the question of what sort of publisher to approach, and the PEA asked whether or not Knopf might consider the project, as this could likely have increased its audience. But Locke objected, saying that "Knopf do not push their books sufficiently, and besides Carl Van Vechten still is an influence there, and I am I believe persona non grata with him, and not ashamed of that." Some unknown breach had clearly put the two men at odds.

The first edition appeared under the imprint of the Progressive Education Association, and a second edition appeared in 1946 from Hines, Hayden & Eldredge. The reader's report for the first edition arrived in March 1940, saying that the book exhibited "remarkably good literary form" and was "brilliantly written." Virtually all of the credit belongs to Locke on this score, for the editorial matter bears the strong impression of his writing style. A memo from W. Carson Ryan, the book's publisher, confirms this: "In the event that this type of introductory and summary material is not used in the source book, Locke is free to make whatever use of it he may wish to." There was also a "Foreword" in the second edition that said: "The project was originally conceived by Alain Locke," and "Alain Locke is primarily responsible for the text commentary." Stern was largely responsible for selecting and documenting the "source materials." Locke was also given a title, as "Research Director" for the PEA project on Intercultural Relations.

Locke and Stern assembled essays and excerpts from over eighty diverse writers, including Benedict, Randolph Bourne, Margaret Mead, Arnold Toynbee, Charles S. Johnson, Jacques Barzun, and E. Franklin Frazier. The opening essays, by Benedict and Boas, along with Locke's commentary, advanced the book's overriding argument, namely that civilization had benefited from the cultural contact of neighboring peoples, and in fact there was a "close connection between culture contacts and the growth of civilization itself." In this context Locke formulated one of his key phrases, "intercultural reciprocity," and did so with the progressive attitude he had employed in *The New Negro*. Reciprocity may have been implicit in Locke's sense of cultural diversity and intellectual pluralism all along, but he made it explicit in this book as an important development in his thought. Intercultural reciprocity relies on the anthropological notion of cultural contact, but it goes far beyond it in putting values—rather than, say, customs or rituals –at the center of such contact.

Over eight hundred pages of the text were divided into five large categories: I. Cultural Contact and the Growth of Civilization; II. Varieties of Cultural Conflict; III. The Ways of Dominant Peoples: Devices of Power; IV. The Ways of Submerged Peoples: Tactics of Survival and Counter-Assertion; and V. The Contemporary Scene in International Relations. Locke astutely presented the material in the framework of power relationships and so confronted the many ways in which racism and cultural contact generally persist and shape the experience of the world at large. Racism and conflict were the too-frequent results of culture contact, and Locke wanted to frame these issues in the largest possible context. This meant returning to the question he had dealt with in his 1915 lectures and off and on since then: imperialism. Early in his commentary he set out one version of the controlling frame:

> Modern imperialism has bred, in addition to its half-castes, its hybrid and border line cultures. A number of complex cultural reactions have resulted, according to the variations in modern colonial contacts and the divergent degrees of cultural level and resistance encountered. But, despite its historic uniquenesses, Europeanization and its moving force of economic imperialism are best understood as an interesting and complex variant of the process which has basically underlain all historic culture contacts; a process which has been the primary cause of the growth of what we know as "civilization."

Locke here sees imperialism as a version of cultural contact, and this enables him to deal with its global dimensions without resorting to a Marxist vocabulary, though his position will remain firmly anti-imperialist.

Another feature of Locke's introductions and interchapter material is how full they are of thoughtful comments and observations, some based on one of the excerpts he is discussing, but others reflective of his decades of analysis and life experience around the issues of race and cultural contact. For example, in discussing the notion of "social cleavage," he ranges across such topics as skin color, the contradictoriness of caste distinctions—how they aim at assimilation and exclusion, or define the minority as either parasitic or alien—and the functions played by etiquette and economics in the maintenance of social domination. Indeed, his thoughts on sexual domination clearly draw on previous arguments about suffragism and abolitionism, and anticipate some of the points made by feminists starting in the later 1960s.

Locke also observes: "Language is another differential of importance in a re-view of group discrimination and culture conflict. No more accurate than the other arbitrary symbols, language is one of the most frequently used devices both for symbolizing and propagating cultural solidarity and in reverse use, for symbolizing group exclusion and hostility." Locke offered a similar warn-ing about the misuse of symbols in his essay on "Pluralism and Intellectual Democracy," citing the tendency to worship the forms of patriotism or dog-matic religion instead of rationally examining their values. His prescience in discussing feminist issues and "the linguistic turn" characterizes the depth of his work on this project.

Wanting to bring his work into direct involvement with the issues of the day, especially the World War, Locke devoted the last section of the book, "Problems of Contemporary Imperialism," to those new movements and de-velopments he had addressed in several fora and would spend much of his remaining days trying to illuminate. He allowed himself a broad sweep, fore-casting and analyzing in abstract terms, yet informed by his continuing ef-forts to combat racism and all the forms of cultural dogmatism at the roots of social and political conflict. Pointing out the increasing tension of the con-tradictions generated by the gap between principles and actions on the part of governing regimes and cliques, he saw how this tension was increasingly noticed by the people who were being dominated. The "submerged" peoples had begun to talk back to the "dominant" ones. "Non-European cultures and repressed minorities seize upon such justifications as the 'civilizing mis-sion' of European civilization and all the formulas and creeds of democracy professed by the dominant orders to implement their struggle for minority assertion and its mounting claims." Western civilization was not prepared for "such wholesale unmasking of its practical politics," and this led directly to "the dilemma of the present time and scene." Part of this rhetorical strat-egy came from Locke's meliorist stance, and part of it came from his sense of logic and fair play; in both cases he might be proved wrong in the future, but his analysis was unrelenting in its call to a higher justice.

This call induced Locke to depict as paradoxical the self-contradicting forces that were engaged in a divisive clash of civilizational forces, namely those of imperialism and ethnic nationalism. The first was contradictory be-cause it sought to expand continuously even as it rested on discrimination and exclusion. As for ethnic nationalism, it created ever larger units which "by that very process" made it "increasingly multi-racial." But these destruc-tive and contradictory forces pitched themselves against peacefully integra-tive forces that were moving in the opposite direction. Locke considered what was perhaps the most crucial element in modern political life, namely the question of scale:

> In contemporary Western civilization there are two sets of forces op-
> erating on an expanded and accelerated scale. One set is geared to
> increased technological and cultural interchange and is developing
> increased economic inter-dependence and cultural interpenetration.
> Along with this, however, has gone an extension and intensification
> of the forces of imperialism, ethnic nationalism and the accompany-
> ing rationalizations of this struggle and clash of interests in cultural
> separatism and sectarianism. The modern world holds a precarious
> balance between these two sets of forces, one of which must achieve or
> be given preponderance to determine the future fate and character of
> Western civilization.

This broad vision was in many ways Locke's ultimate formulation of the problems he first addressed as far back as his days in Oxford, when he wrote about cosmopolitanism, and in his lectures on race and culture contacts in 1915. Of course the world had changed greatly since then, but so had Locke's sense of what was at stake in the problems of racism and their underlying cause in the persistence of dogmatism and value absolutism.

He decided to end his contribution to *When Peoples Meet* by returning to a theme that he had introduced as early as *The New Negro,* namely the need to see the problems of black people as a problem for all of America. In the inter-chapter section titled "Minority Issues in American Democracy," he called for true racial integration, arguing that "this feeling that all who are here may have a hand in the destiny of America . . . will make for a finer spirit of inte-gration than any narrow 'Americanism' or forced chauvinism." If the force of "increased technological and cultural interchange" would prevail, then the war would have provided us—again, paradoxically—with a crucial lesson. Locke addresses the "latest" immigrants in trying to imagine a radically new form of American "nationalism":

> We must see if the lesson of the war has not been for hundreds of these
> later Americans a vivid realization of their transnationality, a new
> consciousness of what America means to them as a citizenship in the
> world. It is the vague historic idealisms which have provided the fuel
> for the European flame. Our American ideal can make no progress
> until we do away with this romantic gilding of the past.

In the middle of the Second World War Locke was able to formulate, using a term also in Randolph Bourne's key essay, another daring paradox by which a new nationalized identity would in fact become a transnational citizenship, but this would be possible only if American ideals could manage yet one more historic adaptation. In keeping with his pragmatic commitment, this adaptation for Locke would involve the elimination of error, the doing away with illusion.

By the early fall of 1942 Locke was hard at work on another special issue of the *Survey Graphic,* this one to be called "Color." Earlier in that spring, at the *Survey Graphic* editorial meeting for March 14, Locke presented his idea for the issue, and at the subsequent meeting in June he emphasized the need for maps and graphs. He explained to Mason what was behind the issue, expressing his internationalist views and his continued devotion to her. "In November another *Survey Graphic* issue comes out. It . . . will treat not merely the American but the world race question. I pray that it will be worthy of my additional experience in all these years and what I know you will expect of a 56 year old Alain. I know it will have your guardian thoughts and blessing." From her hospital bed, where she was being attended by her longtime physician, Mason replied with her customary sense of uplift, even mentioning the frontispiece of the issue, a photograph of Barthé's statue memorializing James Weldon Johnson, which was accompanied by two stanzas from one of Johnson's poems. "And this title, dear Boy, this flaming title 'Color, the Unfinished Business of Democracy.' Each word of the opening leaves no chance for misunderstanding, and to have had the wit to put this fine statue opposite your opening page is tremendously strong in its effect on the dullest brain that can survey it." Mason hoped someone would give a copy to the president. That may not have happened, but the print run was 45,000 copies, and the USO ordered 1,200 for distribution to American soldiers, while the first printing of the issue sold out within a month.[7]

Locke's two previous efforts for the *Survey Graphic*—"Harlem: Mecca of the New Negro" and the 1935 collection on "Harlem: Dark Weather Vane"— stood behind Locke's skill at assembling and coordinating timely material in a professional way. Winold Reiss designed the cover for "Color," and the issue included work by Walter White, Charles S. Johnson, Eric Williams, and Sterling Brown, all previous contributors from "The New Negro." Some new names appeared as well, most notably A. Philip Randolph, with an essay called "Why Should We March?," and Pearl Buck, already a Nobel Prize winner. Photographs of "New Skilled Workers for War Jobs," "Southern Negro Life" and "Change in Africa" accompanied maps and charts of the pre-1939 world, which showed with considerable graphic force the percentages of white people in populations around the world. Jacob Lawrence, then only twenty-six years old, was represented by some of his paintings, and Margaret Walker contributed one of her poems. Locke said of Lawrence's work, drawn from his "Migration Series," that the "four paintings were not planned as a unit; yet they flow together like the stanzas of a poem." One of the journal's sections was built around "The Negro and the War," while others dealt with "The Negro in American Life" and "The Challenge of Color," the latter divided into sections on the Old World and the New.

For the special issue's lead essay, "Color: The Unfinished Business of Democracy," Locke verges on the prophetic, especially in terms of the range of his arguments and the tone of his rhetoric. Now in his mid-fifties, he willingly adopted an ever broader frame of reference than the one he had used during the Renaissance, in part as a result of his speaking more often to white intellectuals such as those who formed the Conference on Science, Philosophy, and Religion. Repeating the tactic used with *The New Negro,* Locke took advantage of his position as editor to set out the terms of the debate and to infuse the subject with the possibility of pragmatic reflections and idealized values. At its core the essay claims that racism, often regarded as a "minority disability," has become a "general weakness." This intensification of the problem, however, has produced a clear solution: "Under the threat of a ruthless enemy, the minority status becomes the majority danger. We then begin to realize that if we would effectively stave off totalitarian tyranny, democracy itself must first be universalized." Locke does not resort to a universal level of argument casually. First he sets out a number of claims, and a number of sociological and historical observations, in support of his argument. He had already advanced some of these claims and arguments in "Pluralism and Intellectual Democracy" and in more embryonic form in a number of essays about values and race questions from previous decades.

Beginning with the sense of profound change in "the geography of our lives," Locke sees the war as a challenge not only to "the strength but the moral fitness of the democratic nations." The challenge has taken the form of a "planetary civil war between two incompatible principles, social no less than political." Either "most of the hitherto free and independent nations [will] become exploited underlings" or there will be "a world in which all peoples . . . shall be freed even from the inconsistent half-way democracy which . . . conferred freedom for some and subordination for others." Locke, in his universalizing voice, does not restrict his argument about subordinated peoples to African Americans. He mentions "a Jewry [that must be] free from cultural disdain and persecution," and a free India, an "Africa liberated from colonial exploitation," and "a federated, self-governing Caribbean." He repeatedly drew the readers' attention to the contradictions of promises unfulfilled, hoping to invoke those "very forces destined to clear our own democracy of its present undemocratic inconsistencies," and identified such forces as our own commitments in the effort to win the war. "The more we define this world position and policy," he said, "the more paradoxical our race attitudes and traditions will in contrast become. Dictates of expediency may reinforce, at long last, the dictates of conscience."

The peroration of the essay uses global terms, though the focus has shifted by returning to the lens of Locke's own experience as a black man. He also moves to a more forthright sense of ethical value.

> . . . a lynching in Mississippi, over and above its enemy echo on a Tokyo short-wave, has as much symbolic meaning in Chunking, Bombay, and Brazzaville as it has in tragic reality in the hearts of African Americans. Steps taken to abolish second-class citizenship in Florida or to democratize the American army or our war industry have, on the other hand, favorable repercussions almost to the ends of the earth. It helps build up not necessarily a democracy of extended political power and domain, but a much more needed democracy of full moral stature, world influence and world respect. It is such unfinished business, foreign and domestic, that waits on democracy's calendar today.

Locke had spent several years working toward this sense of "a much more needed democracy." And his reflections and urgings, which arose out of his views on World War II, finally provided him with the full measure of a visionary democracy. Locke enjoyed many occasions and venues that presented themselves for him to speak publicly about that democracy.

In March 1942, Locke was asked to deliver the Phi Delta Kappa address at Harvard, entitled "Democracy Faces a World Order."[8] His core ideas on this subject rested on a very bold claim: the current world crisis could actually provide improvements in American democracy. This form of the argument distinguished him from Du Bois, who would mount a somewhat different approach in *Color and Democracy* (1945), though both men keenly called democratic principles to account. Du Bois attacked the hypocrisy of those nations that formed the Dumbarton Oaks conference, a forerunner of the United Nations. The democratic states, he argued, were not truly so, since many of the countries involved in the conference still rested their power on

the imperialistic—or near-imperialistic—sway they held over others, especially peoples of color. Du Bois polemically cited a great many sociological
and historical facts in his attempt not only to uncover the hypocrisy behind
the nations' approach but to point to the unworkability of the solutions they
were advancing. *Color and Democracy* appeared as the war was ending, and
hence a few years after Locke's argument, and Du Bois was typically tren-
chant on several points, including an especially acute analysis of how Nazism came to flourish in Germany. He also mixed his polemical sociological
analysis with some exalted rhetoric, saying at the end of the book: "The day
has dawned when above a wounded, tired earth unselfish sacrifice, without
sin and hell, may join thorough technique, shorn of ruthless greed, and make
a new religion, one with new knowledge, to shout from old hills of heaven:
Go down, Moses!"

Locke, however, proceeded less along the sociological line that Du Bois
used and appealed on ethical grounds to the necessity of honoring one's abstract principles, and so the two men's antiracism can be seen as complemen-
tary. Locke began his Phi Delta Kappa talk by pointing to the parallel with
the situation after World War I. Americans, he said, were slow to realize how
the war created certain possibilities, and he suggested that the League of Nations was simply substituted for the old balance of power. Locke was unim-
pressed with the previous arrangements of the great powers and attacked the
persisting imperialism that he had first confronted in Oxford in 1909. He also
recalled his work on the Mandates, saying that they had become "clandes-
tine colonies and relatively closed spheres of economic influence." What the
world was facing was "A Pax Romana of irrepressible power politics rather
than a Pax Democratica of reciprocal international rights and responsibilities. . . . That most sacrosanct of all our secular concepts, the autonomous
sovereignty of the self-arbiter nation, must surely be modified and voluntarily
abridged." Locke's reasoning and his desire for a truly peaceful world order
led him to this urgent plea to redefine nationalism, "that most sacrosanct"
concept.

But he did not stop at this heavy charge against nationalism and instead
reminded his audience that "we must not forget that with our dollar diplomacy we have shared the practice of this system [of economic imperialism] as
actively and almost as culpably as the other industrial nations with their more
explicit imperialisms." Perhaps being back at his alma mater led him to state
his thoughts boldly. Perhaps he remembered the speech he gave during the
First World War, against what he saw as the strife between imperialist powers acting on nationalist pride. In any case, his thinking was now focused

on democracy and the idea of cultural reciprocity. The combination of these two thematic constants, along with his unwavering consideration of the way race was treated in national and international terms, served to inform virtually everything he published in the last decade of his career. The speech was printed in the *Harvard Educational Review* shortly after it was delivered.

In 1943 Locke received an invitation that was to give him an opportunity to address the questions of democracy and culture in a Pan-American context. From May 9 until May 23, his visit to Haiti took place under the auspices of the Committee for Inter-American Artistic and Intellectual Relations. He delivered six lectures, the first five at l'Ecole de Droit, and the final one in the Rex Theatre, all in Port-au-Prince. The Haitian Ministry of Education also sponsored the event, and it was clear from the beginning that Locke would be treated as a visiting dignitary. His outline for the project was ready in October 1941, but the trip was delayed for a year while Locke did the editorial work for the *Survey Graphic* issue on "Color." Each lecture was drawn up into a manuscript of approximately twenty pages, and included in the project was a plan to publish the lectures as a separate book. Locke arranged to be on leave from Howard for the spring quarter and completed his rather elaborate plans for the occasion.[9]

He secured a translation fee of $200.00, which would be earmarked for Louis Achille, a native of Martinique and a professor at Howard. However, Achille was unable to complete the task, and the translation was eventually done by Dr. Camille Lherission. Locke received payments for ninety days of general expenses and eventually an overall total of $1,100.00. Part of this covered the purchase of Locke's books, which he then donated to various libraries in Haiti. The French edition of the published lectures was dedicated to the President of Haiti, Elie Lescot, "*avec les voeux les plus fervents et les plus sinceres de bonheur et de prosperité.*" In 1942 Locke had contributed an "Editorial Foreword" to the Bronze Booklet by Eric Williams, *The Negro in the Caribbean,* so he was already occupied with thoughts about the African diaspora in the Americas. His readings in Caribbean and Latin American literature, as well as African American history, had always been extensive, and now he would have an opportunity to put his thoughts into permanent form.

The main arguments to come out of Locke's trip to Haiti can be found in his final lecture, which he published as an article, "The Negro in the Three Americas," in the *Journal of Negro Education* in late 1944. He imports the argument that he had made in "Color," about how the international situation had altered the perspective in which one might approach the problems of race, and concludes how "the practical efficiency and integrity of . . . [a]

country's democracy can be gauged and judged" by the "conspicuous index" of its treatment of the Negro. Then he makes his central point: "That the Negro's situation in this hemisphere has this constructive contribution to make to the enlargement of the practice of democracy has been the main conviction and contention of these discussions." In between Locke mentions dozens of writers, painters, and composers from all the Americas, characterizing each of them very briefly, but stressing how the "cultural traffic" that ran back and forth between America and Europe has "now swung around to a continental axis North and South." Few African American intellectuals had at this time reflected on the Negro Diaspora and its cultural legacy, and so the breadth of Locke's critical scrutiny was as impressive as the seriousness of his analysis.

Turning to the historical background, Locke insists that it is slavery and its legacy that remains a central problem for all the Americas: "[I]n one situation [it] has left us an undemocratic problem of class and in another, an even less democratic situation of color caste." The former referred to the social problems of North America, while the latter pointed to Latin America. Taking this insight from E. Franklin Frazier, his colleague at Howard, Locke converts the historical legacy into a possible solution. Because slavery "planted the Negro in the very core of the dominant white civilization," and because slavery also planted the Negro "at the moral and political core of a basically democratic society," it is for Locke inevitable that this "historical American ill should have, in the long run, a typical and American cure." Locke's democratic faith was seldom expressed with such unqualified trust, and such trust is necessarily entailed by his rhetorical aim—to show how the culture of Central and South America needs to be seen in "an inter-American perspective" that will fully honor and celebrate the "great Negro progress in our respective national areas."

Locke closes his lecture by talking of "the radiant prospects for inter-American cultural democracy." He must, however, first acknowledge that "unlike our cultural differences, which may even attract, our differences of social culture really do, in most instances, seriously divide." Looking for a way to regard the regional and national differences in a constructive perspective, he returns to a theme he had worried over for years, the relation of the individual and the group. Some "unintended democratic consequences" arise from the "hard code" of racism:

> The Latin-American code of race does more justice and offers less harm to the individual, but at the historical price of an unhappy divorce

of the elite from the masses. The Anglo-Saxon practice of race seri-ously handicaps the individual and his chances for immediate prog-ress, but forges, despite intentions to the contrary, a binding bond of group solidarity, an inevitable responsibility of the elite for the masses, a necessary though painful condition for mass progress.

The echoes of the "talented tenth" resonate in the phrase about the "binding bond of group solidarity," and there are even hints of the ethical strictures that Locke leveled against Claude McKay for what he called his "spiritual truancy" in abandoning a sense of group solidarity. Locke was led in this part of his argument by his desire to foster links between the northern and southern portions of the American hemisphere and so found a way to create a balance of opposites that would eventually produce a greater strength.

Locke shared details of his visit to Haiti with Arthur Wright, then a twenty-nine year old sociology professor, who was enrolled in the army at a military base in Greenville, Pennsylvania, during the time Locke was in Haiti. Locke told Wright how he had had to rewrite all of the lectures, "when [I] sensed the situation." He made them even more formal and elaborate, as it became clear that the president would create a grand fete honoring the oc-casion. At the first lecture, for example, attended by eight hundred people, Locke described the "dramatic entrance of the President and staff and a click heel presentation before and after the Ambassador and staff[;] it was enough to make me nervous, even outwardly so." In August 1943, after returning to Washington, Locke was debriefed by the Guggenheim Foundation and the State Department about the political situation in Haiti.[10]

As for Wright, he maintained a relatively long correspondence with Locke, who was at least infatuated with him. Locke wrote him in November of 1943: "I almost hate to feed your vanity by telling you how much you have been in mind on solitary walks; even at my age I can dream on occasion." Wright was sent to France in 1945 and then stationed briefly in Charleroi and Rouen. When the war was over, Locke was a visiting professor at the University of Wisconsin in the Spring 1946 term, and wrote to Wright about a change of mind: "I am not in a hurry to want to come to Europe again. Her day is really over, or shut out for a long while. My own thoughts turn to Mexico and such places nowadays." He regretted not going south the preceding summer, and especially so since he did not work on the book after all, probably a reference to preparing the Haiti lectures for publication. As for Wright, he would even-tually marry in 1951, and he taught at the University of Bridgeport after a long effort finishing his Ph.D. at New York University. His final letter to Locke, in 1953, told of his duties as the secretary of the Queens Branch of the Urban League.

Arthur Wright was involved with Locke's wide circle of New York City friends, among them Maurice Victor Russell, an aspiring playwright who lived for a time in Philadelphia. Locke acted as his mentor and confidant, and would stop off and visit him between trips to New York. In 1942, Locke offered Russell confidential advice about his, Russell's, sexual orientation, commending his "effort to understand yourself and reconcile after your own psychological inner law." On another occasion Locke said: "Now the constructive side of our friendship can really begin, and I can deliver what I promised you; counsel, guidance, spiritual help." It was a role Locke took to earnestly and repeatedly with male friends, clearly related to earlier explanations he offered Hughes about a Greek style of friendship. Russell and Locke shared a love of classical music, and at one point Locke had to excuse the fact that he could not ask Russell to accompany him to a Marian Anderson concert at Constitution Hall, since the tickets were so hard to obtain.[11]

During the Haiti trip, Locke also wrote frequently to Russell, supplying him with numerous details about the various dinners and lectures. Writing from the Hotel Oloffson, Locke revealed how nervous the ceremony made him: "[W]ith Haitian and American dignitaries present and all the critics keen for the occasion, you can imagine it isn't easy even for a veteran." Locke had earlier shared with Russell recollections of an incident at Central High School, where he had suffered a severe case of stage fright. He had become stuck on his first sentence, and turned and left the podium. One of his teachers, Ernest Lacy, took the matter in hand, made him return, and since that day Locke was able to speak in public, and in later years he could lecture without notes and "never halt for a word." On Palm Sunday in Haiti Locke enjoyed a lavish dinner and described his hotel room with its veranda balcony and fifteen-foot ceilings. As an added delight, he was flown by military plane to visit the citadel at Christophe, and gave a talk at Cap-Haïtien.

Russell faced the prospect of military conscription, and so Locke made arrangements to loan $450.00 to Russell's mother, to cover her rent in the event he was drafted. Locke covered this loan by writing a check to Arthur Fauset, who was obviously Mrs. Russell's landlord. After the war Russell tried unsuccessfully to obtain a Rosenwald scholarship, and eventually he was employed in a government job, working in a civil service post in the Navy Department. During the war, however, his relationship with Locke intensified. Russell confessed he hated his own sexual orientation, and Locke continued trying to help him accept it, sending him books by Edward Carpenter and Havelock Ellis. Years earlier he had sent Cullen some of the same literature, and it clearly served to set a tone for Locke's sense of intimacy. After spending a weekend together, Russell told Locke: "I can see the beauty in relationships that I never saw before. As far as the body sex pattern is concerned, I feel that I can make certain adjustments which should be satisfactory." Locke introduced Russell to Richmond Barthé, and the two apparently become good friends. Russell was living with his mother as late as 1946, and he faced scorn from his sister who felt he had not fully deserved his deferment from the draft. This Russell put down to the particular nature of Philadelphia mores, something Locke could easily recognize.

At the beginning of 1944 Locke told Russell that "I am turning a little left these days myself, tho not entirely—too Philadelphian for that! I have just written an article for The New Masses—corrected the proof New Year's Day as a matter of fact." This short article, entitled "The Negro in American Culture," clearly derived from the large work Locke was trying to finish during this period. He also mentioned attending a New Year's Eve party at the Manhattan apartment of Clinton Oliver, a Harvard graduate with a specialty in Henry James, who would teach for many years at Queens College in the City University of New York. Locke's homosexual friends formed circles in New York as well as Washington, and in both cities Locke mentored young men. In April Locke received an invitation to lecture on the West Coast, which he accepted, traveling there in June. He visited Berkeley and Seattle, which he greatly enjoyed. The Berkeley talk was on "Race in the Present World Crisis," which he repeated a few weeks later in Los Angeles. In Seattle he spoke at the Institute of International Relations, on a program run by the American Friends Service Committee. There his paper was entitled "A Philosophy of Human Brotherhood." Somehow he also found time to visit Cleveland in the fall, where he presided over a session at the National Council for the Social Studies, called "Broader Realization of Democratic Values." These many trips testified to Locke's national reputation as a public speaker and extended his teacherly scope far beyond Howard.[12]

Locke performed one version of his many recurrent editorial duties when he composed an introduction to several essays on the subject of educational programs for the improvement of race relations for the summer 1944 issue of the *Journal of Negro Education*. As he had done with his year-end reviews for *Opportunity,* he turned a fairly ordinary occasion into a chance to cast a broad look at the issue of race. Concerned less to summarize the articles (most of which he described as "concise and objective") than to give a cross-

FIG. 10.1. Locke, photographed by Gordon Parks, at the South Side Community Art Center, Chicago, 1940. Parks was perhaps the best-known portrait photographer of African Americans in the 20th century. The sculpture in the foreground is a bust of Harold Kreutzberg by Richmond Barthé. Moorland-Spingarn Research Center. © Gordon Parks.

section of attitudes and developments, he began with five generalizations: the war had worsened the race problem, but also provoked new activities to solve it; more such activities were "specialized and concrete"; Northern and Southern differences were melding so that the problems were now thought of as national; more rank and file Negroes were active; and racial problems were being addressed by and with "general reformist organizations and programs." Such views derived in part from Locke's generally optimistic temperament when confronting racial problems.

This did not mean, however, that he was in any way driven by false hopes. For example, he pointed out that many philanthropic foundations (he named the Phelps-Stokes, Rosenthal, and Harmon Foundations among others) were embarrassed by their "tacit alliance in many cases with the undemocratic principle of segregation." He urged that the newly formed American Council on Race Relations could, "[i]f democratically administered," perform a valuable service in coordinating "in loose clearing-house fashion all the main organizational efforts and programs with a definite bearing on the racial situation." Despite his praise for the New Deal, Locke described the "net effect of the Federal government in the race situation [as] far off democratic par." He finished by saying that intellectuals had to confront the race problem head-on, for the sake of democracy as much as for the sake of the Negro. Joining the intellectuals, Locke said, "with horizons widened beyond selfish or narrow racialism, are many intelligent, sober but militant and morally aroused Negroes, who see no sanity or safety in half-way solutions."

In 1943, Locke and Mrs. Biddle had made plans to visit Mexico together, which seemed "the most progressively democratic country of the hemisphere." But this trip never took place, and Locke expressed his frustration to Mason from Los Angeles, on his first trip there in 1944, telling her as well about his dinner with Anne Morrow Lindberg in Carmel. His attention to countries in the "other" Americas was focused by the trip to Haiti, of course, and he kept close to his heart certain incidents from that visit. He gently bragged to Mason about the affection the students in Haiti expressed to him, saying they "gave me private memoranda on color prejudice between the upper class mulattos and the black peasantry, which in my judgment was more of a tribute than the decoration which the President gave me." He made what might have been one of his last visits to the Godmother in December of 1943, when she arranged for a two hour midday appointment. She wrote after the visit to say: "I am very changed dear boy, as I have very little strength and my memory is not what it used to be nor the power to use my imagination which was so powerful." She was then ninety-one years old and had been dictating her letters for some time. But she did what she could to keep up the correspondence with her "dear boy," and for his part Locke reported to her on his projects and travels with continuing solicitude.

Mason died on April 15, 1946. She maintained her spiritualized language until the end. In the last letter she wrote to Locke, dated August 29, 1945, she told him: "It is well Alain to reach out into space and try for new effects

FIG. 10.2. Louis Finkelstein and Loren McIver with Locke. These men were part of the circle of white intellectuals with whom Locke attended symposia and published essays in the early 1940s. Left to right: Locke, Finkelstein, McIver, and two unidentified clergymen. Moorland-Spingarn Research Center.

if your growth corresponds. Few people live wisely enough to commit themselves to paper." Apparently Locke derived considerable emotional support from Mason, though her language and controlling attitudes might have struck others as overly high-minded and controlling. Locke often spoke or wrote to her in ways that echoed her formulations. During the war, for example, he told her that he hoped Franklin Roosevelt would be another Lincoln: "I hope the lesson will be learned to the extermination of imperialism and all forms of human exploitation." He presented his vocation to her—and perhaps to himself—in terms that echoed her sense of spiritual striving and duty. In 1940 he told Mason about some talented artists he had recently met, including Horace Pippin, "who has astounded the sophisticates." He wearily added: "I feel like the old weary watcher of the Nine divinities, for it is a case of living to see the salvation. But I feel that I have work to do—in helping—and make reservations to the matter of 'letting thy servant depart in peace.'" By referring to the nine divinities from Egyptian mythology Locke may have been subtly ironic in his tone. But his work as an encourager of black art and culture, unstinting as it was, doubtlessly took some of its energy from Mason and her spiritualism.

Locke's schedule seemed to grow fuller as he approached retirement. The pattern of weekend trips to New York City was more than supplemented by his participation in conferences, and these in turn were added to by frequent attendance at concerts and plays. At the start of 1945, for example, perhaps as a result of having been a contributor to the magazine, he was at an awards dinner sponsored by *The New Masses,* along with Lena Horne, Lillian Hellman, and Carl Van Doren. At the end of January he spoke on "The New Import of Africa," at the Bahá'í Center on West 57th Street. In May he attended a meeting at the Waldorf Astoria in New York for the American Association for the United Nations. In June he had an invitation from Louis Finkelstein and Talcott Parsons, both of whom were clearly impressed with his work at previous conferences, to be the opening speaker on the subject of "Racial Threats" at the Institute for Religious Studies in Boston. A month later Finkelstein asked him to speak on Booker T. Washington as a religious leader, but it turned out that Locke chose to speak on George Washington Carver instead. There was the sixth Conference on Science, Philosophy and Religion, for four days in August. This was not at all above average for his roster of social and professional meetings.

His numerous writings and public speeches, combined with his many editorial efforts, signaled that Locke had fully assumed the role of a public intellectual by the end of the war. This was not a role easily carved out, especially considering his Howard commitments, with the concern over underprepared and undermotivated students and an administration that could often be most unaccommodating. His efforts in adult education and his special issues of the *Survey Graphic* were exertions that he treated with gusto, adding as they did to his claim to be a race leader in the areas of culture and education. For decades his many quickly written notes to friends revealed a man who had abundant deadlines, but one who also kept up friendships, intimate and emotional in some cases, and polished and professional in others. After the war a number of years lay ahead in which he would reflect on his achievements and continue to nuance his views on many subjects. As he entered his seventh decade, he knew there was still—there was always—more to be done.

CHAPTER ELEVEN

The Final Years

Throughout the 1940s Locke actively worked toward broadening and deepening the understanding of adult education. His annual year-end review of books by black authors, though interrupted by the war, remained a mainstay of his cultural authority, and it appeared seven times after 1946, the last one in 1953, shortly before he died. These reviews continued to be an esthetic autobiography, as Locke developed with greater nuance his views on several literary and cultural themes. Using professional friendships he had formed, he enjoyed visiting appointments at three different institutions. His thoughts on a wide and diverse range of topics—democracy, the tradition of the African American novel, critical thinking and value theory, and the nature and role of culture in group experience—found new impetus because of his heavy schedule of lecturing and teaching. An inevitable slowing and draining of his energies took on unignorable physical and medical form as he suffered increasing heart trouble. But he maintained close friendships and attended concerts and plays with no apparent diminishment of interest or pleasure. The valedictory note was sounded, however, especially as he reflected on his role in the Renaissance.

The activities associated with adult education were central to the way in which he had adapted the skills developed as a university professor: forceful reasoning, a sense of history, and a feel for developing social forces. These skills obviously were recognized by the American Association of Adult Education when it elected Locke its president in 1945. In the same year, in the summer issue of the *Journal of Negro Education*, he expounded his ideas most directly. In the essay, "Areas of Extension and Improvement of Adult

Education among Negroes," he wrote that goals were important, and that "in the long run, we must measure effective adult education . . . by its social or mass results." In adult education the substantive part was the noun and the word "adult" was "merely the adjectival reference." Programs and organizations could not settle for merely being chauvinistic about Negro culture, nor could they settle for being biracial. Real education required a commitment to standards and systematic training; it could not be merely the "persuading, entertaining or propagandizing of adults," which tended to be the dominant form most programs took. Again, Locke's sense of democratic values shaped nearly everything he had to say on the subject: "[A] large part of our adult training stands in need of a sounder, broader democratic basis, as well as of a firmer, more systematic professional base." Government support remained essential, as education was the responsibility of the state, and the state needed to insure an end to segregated educational systems. Locke heartily approved of new developments in this area and praised the nongovernmental agencies such as labor unions, the interracial Y.W.C.A., and settlement houses for supplementing and even expanding their desegregationist efforts in the field of adult education. Locke seized on these "progressive instances and demonstrations," though not large in number, to reiterate the meliorist views he had often put forth: "For they have demonstrated the practicability of the democratic principle of integration and have proved that a common objective and interest is sufficiently strong, if effectively pushed, to bridge the segregation gap even in the South, for a considerable amount of the labor union experiments have been in the South." This was written almost ten years before the *Brown v. Board of Education* decision which argued that segregated schools were inherently unequal and thus unconstitutional. Locke ended with the claim that "the tide of educational segregation is ebbing; the tide of educational integration is slowly but surely on."

In February 1946 Locke expanded the scope of his lecturing when he broadcast a talk from the University of Rochester, New York, with an audience of 500, followed by a lively question and answer period. Locke was invited to be a visiting professor at the University of Wisconsin for the spring 1946 term, the invitation coming from Professor Max Otto, the head of the philosophy department. Locke, treated with deference, enjoyed his time away from Howard. During his stay in Madison he met the actress Uta Hagen, the daughter of a Wisconsin professor, and attended two concerts by his old friend Paul Robeson, who was staying with the Hagens while in town. Locke proved to be a popular draw, as his class in esthetics enrolled 173 students and twice had to be moved to a larger lecture hall. He also had twelve graduate students in his seminar in value theory. Locke's course on art presented the opportunity to consider in a large context the many questions he had dealt with in the area of esthetics. He called it "The Philosophy of the Arts," and it ranged over a large body of philosophical reflection and analysis. The first lecture was entitled "Psycho-analytic Theories; Freud's influence on modern art theory," for which he used the two-volume *Art and Freedom,* edited by Horace Kallen. His willingness to investigate Freud's theories, and to see how they might clarify esthetic issues, testifies to Locke's openness as well as suggesting that his constant self-analysis was taking on a new vocabulary. Skills developed many years earlier, when writing about the classification of values, were much in evidence in the class notes that survive. Locke considered it his teacherly duty to impart the synoptic view, and his course material always incorporated his commitment to pluralism.

While at Wisconsin Locke received a letter from his old friend, Horace Kallen. In it, Kallen offered Locke a visiting appointment at the New School in New York City, which Locke eagerly accepted. The situation at Howard had never really been completely to Locke's liking, especially considering the decades of strife with the administration. But there were other considerations, not the least of which was economic. An added complication, however, was that Howard remained on the quarter system while the New School was on the semester calendar. Locke spelt out a suggestion in his response to Kallen: "Since your course offerings are in the evening, I could with a Thursday or Friday or a double offering Friday evening combine it with my regular schedule at Howard, at least from February through March, and then take leave only for the Spring Quarter. . . . Wouldn't this be possible?" He added that he had taken a financial loss by accepting the Wisconsin position. Besides the obvious attraction of being able to spend more time in New York, Locke took a moment to reflect—in retrospect and in prospect—on his situation:

> . . . it has been more than worth while. And I am delighted to be able to tell you that things continue to go well out here at Madison. I think and hope dear Max [Otto] is satisfied, and have tried my darndest to have it so. The contrast in student reaction, colleague's friendliness, and of course, administrative attitude has been damning in Howard's disfavor. Still I will stick to my post and guns there, with only five more years before retirement and the possibility of working out from there as a base on such welcome assignments as these, which, incidentally increase my prestige and potential influence at Howard itself.

Locke suggested that he teach a course in the philosophy of the arts and another in social philosophy, to be subtitled "Minority Problems," or a repeat of his seminar on value theory.[1]

Locke and Kallen had not corresponded very frequently. But they were able to reestablish their professional ties in the mid-1940s, which brought about Locke's contribution to a 1947 festschrift devoted to Kallen. The volume included essays by John Dewey and Sidney Hook, and also by John Herman Randall Jr, Ernst Kris, and Ernest Nagel, among others. Locke addressed pluralism, the topic on which he and Kallen had spoken many years earlier. Kallen, devoted to adult education as was Locke, was instrumental in founding the New School for Social Research, and many of the essays in the volume celebrated that part of his work. But it was mainly the idea of pluralism as applied to cultures and group experience on which Locke focused. The essay, "Pluralism and Ideological Peace," echoes many of the themes and arguments of the papers he wrote for the Conferences on Science, Philosophy, and Religion. Indeed, three essays form an impressive triptych which portrays in nuanced detail Locke's fullest thought on the questions that unite democracy, pluralism, and human community. In addition to "Pluralism and Ideological Peace," these are "Pluralism and Intellectual Democracy" and "Cultural Relativism and Ideological Peace."[2] Not only do the terms of the titles form a set of permutations, but two of the essays begin by mentioning William James and two quote Horace Kallen. They are perhaps Locke's most significant contribution to—and broadening of the terms of—the tradition of American pragmatism.

As noted above, Locke suggested to Kallen that he teach three courses at the New School, on the philosophy of art, "Minority Group Relations," and a seminar on value theory. The revised edition of *When Peoples Meet* served as his text for the course on minority group relations. While at the New School he took part in a fifteen-week course called "The World View of the Negro Question," which included appearances by Du Bois and Walter White as well. Locke also gave a talk to the students and faculty, called "Semantic Factors in Race Prejudice." By the spring of 1947 he had moved into an apartment in a building at 12 Grove Street in New York's Greenwich Village, and so the teaching schedule at the New School was even less burdensome as far as travel was concerned. But as he had told Kallen, positions taken as a visiting professor increased his prestige, and they tended to follow one another in rather quick succession in the late 1940s. At the same time he continued to maintain a full schedule of guest lectures and attendance at conferences and musical and theatrical events.

FIG. 11.1. Locke, photographed by Glenn Carrington. Carrington was an intimate of Countee Cullen, as well as a member of Locke's group of New York City friends. Moorland-Spingarn Research Center.

In 1947, with the disruptions of the war having faded, Locke resumed the yearly labor of reviewing the work of black authors that had appeared in the preceding twelve months, but his efforts were somewhat reduced. How much of this was due to the space limitation imposed on him by the editors at his new outlet, *Phylon,* or simply due to the restricted publishing during the war, is hard to know. Medical problems related to his heart condition, and his approaching retirement, added to his need to husband his strength. The 1947 review included only twenty-two titles, and it omitted the Africana section altogether. Subsequent years would see the number of titles vary from thirty or so to as many as forty in 1949, but there was no bumper crop of five dozen as in previous years. Locke called the 1947 review "Reason and Race," and he was generally positive about the books he dealt with, occasionally mixing prescription and praise, which reflected his critical temperament. His colleague Owen Dodson's book of poems, *Powerful Long Ladder*, was "competent" and "respectable," but Dodson should choose between traditional and more experimental esthetics, "if for no other reason than to achieve proper fusion of style and integration of feeling." Ann Petry's novel, *The Street*, elicited his unqualified praise: its "quiet, courageous, unsentimental realism [was] a substantial contribution to the true and effective novel of race." Works on social issues garnered Locke's even stronger praise, however, for he felt they augured a new era of "pragmatic action and common sense" that might be to "a practical degree a solvent of the difficult American traditions and mores of race."

Dodson became Locke's colleague at Howard in the early 1940s. After Locke's death Dodson was interviewed by a scholar who was writing a biography of him. The interview itself and the biography based on it contain slightly different accounts of Locke's personal life. In the interview Dodson spoke of Locke's personal and sexual life in a way that became a matter of continuous gossip, and it helped shape the reputation of Locke as sexually perverse. According to Dodson, Locke on occasion invited young men to his apartment on R Street, and there asked them to remove all their clothes while he played classical records. During the music Locke would sprinkle coins onto the naked visitor, who sat on Locke's bed; Dodson himself was one such visitor. The ambiguous anecdote relates nothing specific about any sexual act that might have taken place, though in the interview Dodson appears shocked and slightly disoriented, while the account in the biography is more matter of fact. In any case, Locke certainly had close and presumably intimate physical relations with a number of men throughout the years, and these relationships are spoken of in his correspondence with them. Locke was living in the same city as Dodson and so seldom corresponded with him, and no other evidence besides Dodson's personal account clarifies the relationship. At best, Dodson's account is another installment in the urban myths about Locke which have been easily accepted for the purpose of sustaining stereotypes.[3]

Locke's relationships with younger men took on different forms, depending on many circumstances. Locke apparently met Jimmy Daniels in the late 1920s through his circle of friends in Harlem. On April 6, 1948, he wrote a parole board in California on behalf of Daniels, an aspiring writer. Daniels had taken journalism courses by correspondence from the University of Nebraska and wrote short stories, but he was unsuccessful in getting them published. Locke's letter to the parole board told of his having read "hundreds of pages of [Daniels's] manuscripts," and having known him for fifteen years, though in fact it was closer to twenty. Daniels found himself penniless in California during the 1930s, having earlier been released from prison in Represa, California; he was usually arrested for theft and vagrancy. Locke corresponded with him for many years, beginning at least as early as 1929, when Daniels was at the time jailed on a burglary charge in Salt Lake City. Indeed, on a few occasions Locke wrote to Daniels from his summer stays in Germany in the early 1930s. Locke was able to congratulate him on his release from prison in California in 1948. Daniels went on to get a job at a black newspaper, the *Los Angeles Sentinel,* and to supplement his income by selling a multivitamin, "Nutrilite," which he tried to interest Locke in buying. Locke said he would try it, but was already taking Rutin, a bioflavonoid useful for strengthening the capillaries and controlling hypertension, having forsaken the supplements recommended by Mason. Throughout their correspondence Locke supported Daniels and his attempts, often fitful, to find steady work and avoid a life of crime.[4]

In 1948 the City College of the City University of New York offered Locke a position as visiting professor. There for the spring semester of 1949, he maintained his position at Howard, repeating the arrangement he had had the year before with the New School. It was probably while teaching at City College that Locke drew up a reading list for a course he called "The Philosophy of Democracy." Its twenty-six titles offer a cross-section of his own reading and suggest the ways he approached the theory of democratic government. He included his own edited issue of *Survey Graphic,* "Color: The Unfinished Business of Democracy." One title, *The Unfinished Task* (1942), by Corey Lewis, argued for the key role of capitalism and the free market as important supports of democracy, while another was *Democracy in Crisis* (1933) by Harold Laski, a socialist and chairman of the Labour Party in Britain, whose work caused considerable controversy for its left-wing views. Examining race and democracy in terms of one another was one of Locke's central issues, so Franz Boas was represented by *Race and Democratic Society* (1945), and Du Bois's *Color and Democracy* (1945) was included, along with works by Pearl Buck and Adolf Augustus Berle Jr, the well-known statesman and ex-Ambassador to Brazil. Merle Curti, one of the founding lights of intellectual history and American Studies, and his book, *The Roots of American*

Loyalty (1946), invoked a Deweyan stress on instrumentalism and relativism. This work was perhaps first brought to Locke's attention at the University of Wisconsin, where Curti taught for many years. Locke added two titles by T. V. Smith, his good friend from the University of Chicago: *The American Philosophy of Equality* (1927) and *The Democratic Way of Life* (1938). All in all, the list was balanced in its approaches, though heavily weighted toward American democracy and attentive to the postwar moment.

While teaching at City College, Locke certainly made full use of the city, which had always been a kind of second home to him. He enjoyed many chances to socialize with his circles of friends, including Harold Jackman and Owen Dodson, though the work load exhausted him. By May, however, he was instructed by his doctor to start a "prolonged regimen of restricted activity." He told Louis Finkelstein that he had suffered a mild heart attack at the end of 1948 and wanted to cut down on his teaching then but was prevented from doing so by pressures in the philosophy department at Howard. The two years, 1948 and 1949, were among the scantiest of all in terms of Locke's publications, though the year-end reviews of books by black authors appeared in *Phylon*. Beyond these there was only a foreword to a book by Rebecca Barton and a one page article in *Harlem Quarterly*.

The 1948 year-end review lacked a thematic title. But Locke had an important idea to pursue and develop, one mentioned several times in previous reviews. This was the relationship between sociology and art, addressed by him as the issue of whether art and politics could mix effectively. For Locke this problem centered in the novel. "Our artists increasingly become social critics and reformers as our novelists are fast becoming strident sociologists and castigating prophets," he mused. Invoking Zola as a positive model, he felt social criticism and the art of the novel can, and should, be combined: "[T]hat conjunction of art and sociology will recur, and I predict it will be the novel of race which achieves it, and maybe a Negro writer. If so, we will then have produced our first Negro-American novelist or short story writer of first magnitude." Increasingly in the early 1940s Locke turned to white writers as a way of framing some—though by no means all—of the esthetic questions with which he was dealing. Locke continued with a white writer in order to explore the artistic possibilities of a socially focused fiction, as he analyzed Sinclair Lewis's *Kingsblood Royal*. Concluding that Lewis's art falls somewhat short by resorting to satire, Locke discussed several novels by black authors, with a mixture of praise and blame, and decided that their sociology need not cause worry. However, he hoped the "artistic power of penetration" might increase if more authors tried to find the right mixture of factual foundations and imaginative "projection." This mixture of sweeping survey and hopeful prescription typifies his critical method.

This review is also notable for the sad assessment of Countee Cullen's *On These I Stand,* essentially Cullen's selected poems, which Locke lamented as a representation of the poet's declining career. For Locke, "Cullen shrank from reality" and this affected his poetry, since "[n]o intellectual maturing replaced it [Cullen's 'widest social vision'] when it lost its youthful ardor." Two decades earlier Locke had argued that lyric poetry, which was after all Cullen's main concern, should be exempt from carrying a social burden, but the experience of the Depression and the Second World War obviously made social and political issues increasingly unignorable. Referring to the "fallow years for Negro poetry," Locke mentioned that "our poets of the virile school," such as Hughes and Brown, "speak only intermittently at present." Some books were noteworthy, however, such as John Hope Franklin's *From Slavery to Freedom,* lauded as "likely [to] be the definitive one-volume history of the Negro." Locke offered measured praise for Shirley Graham, who would become Du Bois's wife a few years later, for her "dynamic" biography of Frederick Douglass. A much more positive note sounds at the end of the review, where Locke praises Du Bois's *The World and Africa,* calling it a "most unusual combination of readability and competence, of scholarship and sound popularization . . . a marvel from a writer approaching his eightieth birthday." Locke and Du Bois never collaborated on African subjects, unfortunately, but this latter-day recognition very likely pleased the older man.

As in the 1948 review, where he used Zola to set out some of the problems and possibilities of a socially committed fiction, Locke in 1949 praised Alan Paton's novel, *Cry the Beloved Country.* He discussed it in detail, to illumine the elements of Paton's ability to communicate, an ability "that lifts this novel to the plane of great social vision, and, simultaneously, to the plane of great art." Locke devoted the opening paragraphs of the year-end review, called "Dawn Patrol," to expressing his hope for "optimistic hints of new sensitivities of social conscience, of radically enlarged outlooks of human understanding" that would eventually become true portents of a "crucially reconstructive" fictional art. With his usual acumen for spotting new talent, he singled out a short story by James Baldwin, referring to him as "in all probability a significant young Negro writer." Dorothy West's novel, *The Living is Easy,* was also highlighted by Locke for its "power of boldness" in treating "intra-race prejudice and snobbery," a subject too often avoided because of its "conflict of value loyalties in the middle-class Negro." On the other hand,

Locke withholds high praise from the "almost completely anecdotal character" of Hurston's *Seraph on the Sewanee:* "[T]here is too much of serious social import to be said today for mere story-spinning to be regarded as worthy of such indisputable talent." The late 1940s offered Locke several occasions to register his shifting and developing esthetic views, especially on the novel and its social obligations. He erected no overall theory on this particular subject but remained nimble and attentive in his critical practice.

Locke again refined and clarified his thoughts about one of his key subjects when he delivered a lecture, "Frontiers of Culture," in 1949 to his students at Howard. The essay recalls problems he dealt with two decades earlier, in 1923, in another lecture to his students called "The Ethics of Culture." The essays display how practical and nuanced Locke's concept of culture was, and how culture was a concept almost as potent for Locke as that of race, since he seldom thought deeply about one without also reflecting on the other. The 1923 lecture reads as a prelude to *The New Negro,* arguing that culture contains elements which must be balanced with each other in order to be effective. For Locke, culture, properly speaking, cannot be taught; it can only be learned. As it is inherently self-defining, it is fruitless to try and impose it by authority. Locke answers all the standard charges against culture (charges that were often launched against him as a person), namely that culture is selfish, elitist, impractical, over-refined, and so forth. "It is," he says to the college freshmen who were his audience, "more than your personal duty to be cultured—it is one of your most direct responsibilities to your fellows, one of your most effective opportunities for group service." While Locke saw culture as a necessary mediation between self- and group-expression, he also foresaw an unequal development in the proportion of art and culture that could be produced by a new generation of artists and the lack of a developed audience to appreciate it. "As a race group we are at the critical stage where we are releasing creative artistic talent in excess of our group ability to understand and support it. Those of us who have been concerned about our progress in the things of culture have now begun to fear as the greatest handicap the stultifying effect upon our artistic talent of lack of appreciation from the group which it represents."

The companion piece, so to speak, of his 1923 lecture is his 1949 lecture, "Frontiers of Culture," given less than four years before his death. This was also something like Locke's valediction to the university where he had taught for almost four decades. In it he reflects directly, self-critically, and a bit caustically on the Harlem Renaissance. Complex in content as well as tone, the essay expresses a weariness and wry humor about the "success" of the work with which Locke was most often identified. He confesses that "at one time of life [he] may have been guilty of thinking of culture as a cake contrasted with bread," but he goes on to argue that "essential culture is baked into our daily bread or else it isn't truly culture." Building on this quotidian sense of culture, he insists that *The New Negro* was meant to spark "a movement for folk culture and folk representation, eventually even folk participation." Hoping this movement would be "democratically open," he believed that "no considerable creative advance" was possible if it had to "carry the dead weight of those hangers-on whose participation was merely in keeping up with the Joneses." He offers a valedictory summary of his core political and cultural beliefs:

> I am to stand firmly on the side of the democratic rather than the aristocratic notion of culture and have so stood for many years, without having gotten full credit, however. I realize the inevitability of such misunderstanding; what price Harvard and Oxford and their traditional snobbisms! Culture is so precious that it is worth even this price, if we can have it only at the high cost of nurturing and conserving it on the upper levels of caste and privilege. But one should not have to pay that exorbitant price for it. (PAL, 231)

Locke returns to the basic notion of the earlier, 1923 lecture, always concerned that culture would become superficial, a matter of the merest social competition and faddish compromise, in short, that culture would be commodified. In 1923 Locke made it clear that "one must pay a moral as well as an intellectual price for culture," because it involved a rejection of mediocrity and the elimination of that penchant to turn cultural behavior into a specious imitation of the behavior of others. In the 1949 lecture, he gives himself high marks for rejecting separatism, and he says that "[it] is my greatest pride that I have never written or edited a book on a chauvinistically racialist basis." He adds: "We can afford to be culturally patriotic but never culturally jingoistic." One of the key moments in his lifelong array of self-presentations, Locke urgently wanted the record to show that his commitment to value pluralism, and to the transformative power of culture rightly acquired, was sincere and consistent throughout his entire career.

In 1950 Locke again took up the problems in education, this time with an essay called "The New Organon in Education." He published it in *Goals for American Education,* the proceedings of the Ninth Symposium of the Conference on Science, Philosophy, and Science. Referring to the other essays in the volume, Locke coordinated his views with the then current debate on how best to integrate knowledge and to reform methodology at the same time. He advanced strong views on the subject. "It surely is a patent fallacy to assume a change in the scope of thinking will change the way of thinking." This meant that recent expansions in curriculum at many colleges, in the direction of including global studies beyond the range of the "conventional Western hemispheric scope," would not of themselves bring about the new organon he envisioned. Locke desired an educational system that would find a way to "treat material . . . with critical and normative regard for values, but without becoming didactic or dogmatic." He pointed to how "the empirical method, with laboratory science as its embodiment, was suited to the characteristic problems and interests of the first scientific age." But that method, with its "fixation on fact to the exclusion of value," was no longer appropriate. Now, in the social science fields, "we stand in further need of some way of correlating significantly and realistically their factual and their value aspects."

Though the social sciences drew Locke's attention most urgently in this essay, he felt the humanities should be involved in the new organon as well. Invoking and modifying the older model of humanistic education, Locke tailored his thoughts to present a clear picture of the educational scheme that he himself had been practicing over the past several decades:

> This generally conceded goal of an "integrated" education is, of course, the old humanist ideal and objective of the best possible human and self-understanding. But it recurs in our age in a radically new context, and as something only realizable in an essentially scientific way. . . . [I]t rests on the concrete study of man in all his infinite variety. If it is to yield any effective integration, that must be derived from an objective appraisal and understanding of the particularities of difference, both cultural and ideological. (PAL, 271)

Locke was aware of the radically new context that saw the older ideal as in need of profound changes because he thought historically about such matters. He stressed that it was an ability to see educational material and issues in their historical context that was one of the main goals of education. This ability, what he called "critical relativism," would foster a form of thinking that could "trace value development and change as a dynamic process instead of in terms of unrealistic analytic categories, and so eliminate the traditional illusions produced by generalized value terms—viz., static values and

fixed value concepts and ideals." With this ability one could "invade the in-
nermost citadel of dogmatic thinking, the realm of values." This would be
Locke's final word on the largest questions concerning education and the
possibility of its reform. It was also one of the final places where he dealt with
values and the need to study them objectively, in order to strip them of their
tendency to generate or buttress dogmatic or absolutist formulations.

Locke, in addition to developing his ideas on literature and education,
took charge of arranging various aspects of a conference called by the White
House in 1950. President Truman announced the purpose of the gathering
of educators and experts: "It is in the hope that in the next half century we
may write a new chapter of history, different from the first half, with its wars
and injustices on an unparalleled scale, that I have proposed the Midcentury
White House Conference on Children and Youth to be held in December
1950." Locke saw to it that his former student, Kenneth Clark, was included
in the gathering. Clark had been an editor of the *Hilltop*, the Howard paper,
while an undergraduate in the early 1930s, when he also led protests against
the segregation that still plagued official Washington. When Clark and his
fellow protesters were arrested, Mordecai Johnson timidly disavowed their
behavior, and only through the efforts of Ralph Bunche and others on the
discipline committee were the students spared expulsion. This incident inevitably recalled many others, of course, not least of all Locke's own dismissal
in 1925. Locke knew Clark's study of the effects of racism on young children,
based on innovative psychological research that would be instrumental in
the renowned court case, *Brown v. Board of Education*, that launched the
civil rights movement. He asked Clark to join a panel at the Midcentury Conference to present his results, since there was no particular study of racism
that concentrated on minority children. Locke became thereby an important
agent in supporting Clark's *Prejudice and Your Child* (1955). Clark's psychological research—showing how preschool children reacted to imagery about
skin color—incorporated a questioning of values that pleased Locke and fit
with his sense of how empirical data should best be utilized. The research
also served as part of the forensic data used in the *Brown* decision.[5]

In 1950 Locke produced another year-end review for *Phylon*, entitled
"Wisdom De Profundis." The opening employed a positive tone, but one
that included more than a touch of darkness. Locke claimed that "the creative literature of 1949 dealing with Negro life and its problems is especially
enlightening, at the inevitable cost, though, of being quite sobering and dis-
quieting." This mixed tone recurred throughout the remaining year-end
reviews, as Locke's views on the racial questions continued to mix realism

and hope, a case of pessimism of the intellect and optimism of the will. As he had used Zola and Paton in previous year-end reviews, he turned here to Faulkner, using his *Intruder in the Dust,* "the greatest novel of the South yet written," to exemplify how a novelist might "thunder out the doomsday of racial injustice by the simple device of holding up, quietly but unflinchingly, a relentless mirror before the face of the characteristic South." For the books in the section called "The Social Literature," he cited Myrdal's *The American Dilemma* for its accent on "developmental trends and on the shortcomings and potentialities of democratic society." He took a moment to say that by considering the Negro "in the framework of American society at large," Myrdal's work resembled the "approach [that] was advocated vigorously and cogently by several earlier studies, among them *The New Negro,* it may now be said twenty-five years earlier." As blacks might learn from whites, so the reverse was also clearly true, for value pluralism and integrationist politics demanded nothing less. This remark demonstrates that Locke's estimation of the work he contributed to the Renaissance was for him a subject of constant reflection and evaluation. The review ended with a tone of sharp regret over the failure of "African studies and comparative research" to attract the financial resources and professional interest that they deserved, resulting in the "most meretricious and unrepresentative . . . interpretations."

In the next year's review, "Inventory at Mid-Century," Locke declared that fiction "seems on the march," as he found several good novels to praise. Among these were Owen Dodson's first novel, *Boy at the Window,* and William Russell's *A Wind Is Rising,* the latter of which held Locke's attention for its depiction of "the decaying feudal structure of the old agrarian South." For J. Saunders Redding, however, he urged that he avoid stereotyping, saying that his novel, *Stranger and Alone,* an expose of Negro education in the South, "evokes more horror than sympathy and rouses more indignation than understanding." Melvin Tolson's poetry impressed Locke, with its "language echoes of the Eliot-Pound tradition" (a rare reference on Locke's part to Anglo-American modernists). There was also an important moment in African American letters when Locke declared that the torch of illumination in Negro historiography had passed from the recently deceased Carter Woodson—calling his work "an heroic and constructive accomplishment not merely to the Negro cause but to American history as such"—to John Hope Franklin, with whom began "a new phase of fully integrated historical writing," as he was to become the dean of African American historians in the second half of the twentieth century.

The 1952 year-end review, "The High Price of Integration," included forty titles, and it contained one of Locke's more nuanced arguments. Drawing on his sense of meliorism but tinged with caution, the essay notes that Negro authors were entering the mainstream, even as white authors were coming to terms with various aspects of black experience: "Each of these trends is in itself as desirable as it was inevitable, but for the moment they raise between them considerable confusion, best considered, no doubt, as the temporary stresses and shortages involved in liquidating the double literary standard and the cultural color line." He mixed his judgment of Hughes's volume of poems, *Montage of a Dream Deferred,* pronouncing it marred by "an unevenness of artistic conception which careful self-criticism could easily have avoided." A striking comparison was set up when Locke juxtaposed the memoirs of Ethel Waters and J. Saunders Redding. The former surprised Locke by its deft warding off of the stereotypes that poison racial relations, while the latter was a convincing portrayal of the mind of an educated black—it possessed "a commendable candor and earnest integrity," setting up a "courageous precedent of saying how and what the intellectual Negro feels and thinks."

Throughout more than two decades Locke worked out what might be called a group spiritual autobiography in his year-end reviews. They contain several important themes, such as the need for the Negro novel to be more realistic, and they tried repeatedly to take the temperature of an increasingly varied and complex culture. A productive tension was coiled between the wide appraisal and the moment's pulse, and between the prescriptive urging and the willingness to acknowledge surprisingly new talent. Some of his claims, such as the notion that the integration of black and white writing would one day be more or less complete, were too optimistic by far. Other positions, like the need to see Negro culture as part and parcel of American culture, more likely found widespread approval. The range of books, from fiction and poetry through the social sciences to Africana, was perhaps the most impressive aspect of the work, though the unfailingly literate writing was equally noteworthy. Like the interchapter commentaries in *When Peoples Meet,* the total intellectual expression of the year-end reviews taken together forms one of the major achievements of Locke's public life.

Maurice Russell visited Locke in February 1952 and remarked: "I felt you looked well and was especially pleased to hear of the plan to have someone in to prepare meals for you." In April Locke, exhausted from a trip to Toronto, was able to work on *The Negro in American Life,* which would only appear in an unfinished form after his death, completed by Margaret Just Butcher. He even mustered the energy to make plans for a trip to Europe or Jamaica. That same year, in September, Locke faced a hospital stay, where his shortness of breath was serious enough to require attention and complete rest. Russell enthusiastically reported the return of the Katherine Dunham dance troupe from a very successful European tour, since one of dancers of the troupe, Lenwood Morris, was an adolescent friend of his. The troupe was largely African American, and Dunham was one of the first of her race to attend the University of Chicago, where she attained the Ph.D. in anthropology. Locke's keen interest in the Dunham dancers was esthetic and personal: Katherine's brother had been Locke's assistant at Howard. In May 1952, after another visit to Washington, Russell reassured Locke, perhaps with comforting exaggeration, that "I agree that your health strides are nothing short of miraculous. I think you look better now than I can remember for some years." But Locke's heart condition could not have been all that strong. In the same month, as Russell turned thirty years of age, Locke offered him solace and continued firmly to play the role of mentor: "I myself can't get over the intuitive feeling that all your situation needs is that most difficult of all things—physically and psychologically satisfying friendship."

Locke probably shared with Russell just how serious his health problems had grown by the end of the summer of 1952. There had been a series of heart attacks, of varying severity, all brought on by overwork in the 1940s, and all more or less downplayed after a period of rest and recovery. But the cause of the apparently worsened condition in 1952 was ironically a source of pleasure. Locke felt that the commencement exercises at Howard that spring were "the most significant in all my forty years here—Truman's excellent civil rights speech, the honorary degrees to Judge Waring the perfect weather and arrangements and incidentally my official emeritus exit." But just after the academic exercises he "came down with another recurrence of the heart trouble the next day," and he acknowledged that "[t]he old enemy has been in the saddle off and on since January first." Locke took the planning of the academic exercises seriously, always attuned to the formal and ceremonial side of education, but this meant he faced a very crowded schedule. He even had to miss the funeral of John Dewey, who passed away at the age of ninety-two, in part because the student committee had dedicated its yearbook to him and he felt the obligation to be the guest speaker at the presentation ceremony.

In July 1952 Locke was admitted to the Fort Valley Heart Hospital in Fairview Village, Pennsylvania; Kallen had recommended this, with a special referral to a Dr. Wolffe. After the end of the commencement exercises at Howard, Locke could not manage to lower his pulse rate below 130, and so faced the possibility of a debilitating stroke. "[M]y main anxiety, since I had always anticipated a quick end with a heart attack, was how on a retirement income to afford a wheel chair and an attendant," he stoically told Kallen. But Wolffe helped a great deal, and Locke felt the doctor was "one of the most humane persons I have ever met." He added: "[W]hat surprises me most is the psychological transformation that has taken place in my attitude. The old man anxiety that rode my back for years has gone, and I calmly and confidently contemplate ten years or so of leisurely writing, lecturing and travel."

In the midst of these medical concerns, one of Locke's more significant publications appeared in the 1952 issue of *New World Writing*, a paperbound volume drawn from a wide variety of authors and intended for a mass audience. The list of well-known writers included Tennessee Williams, Gore Vidal, and Flannery O'Connor, and poets such as Howard Nemerov, James Schuyler, and Frank O'Hara. An excellent opportunity for Locke to address one of his broadest audiences, his essay was the only one by a black author to be included; he titled his contribution "The Negro in American Literature." The author's note identified this as part of *The Negro in American Culture*, the book that appeared posthumously, without Locke being able to give it final shape. But the essay was in some ways both a compendium and a variation on essays Locke had published earlier, one as far back as 1928 and another in 1944. The material in these three essays, a chief part of Locke's contribution to America's literary history, had served as the content of virtually countless speeches and talks Locke gave over the course of three decades and more, mostly to black colleges, but in many different venues.[6]

The essay in *New World Writing*, the most comprehensive of the three, addresses the very broad sweep of Negro literature. Beginning with Phyllis Wheatley and Jupiter Hammon, it moves through the slave narratives, touches on representations of blacks by white writers, discusses the Renaissance, treats poetry, fiction, and drama, and ends by singling out Willard Motley and Gwendolyn Brooks. Though he repeats many of the assessments he made in his year-end reviews, Locke brings the material together with a forceful style and demonstrates several important organizing themes, such as the rise of realism in the Negro novel and the crucial importance of blacks attaining a maturity in their group expression. He concludes by saying that "the history of the Negro's strange and tortuous career in American literature may become also the story of America's hard-won but easily endured attainment of cultural democracy." The essay's sweep joins with it precise evaluations and placements to form a brief survey that is still accurate and germane.

One last year-end review appeared under Locke's name in the early months of 1953, a fitting coda to his efforts as a chronicler of African American writing. Called "From Native Son to Invisible Man," it dealt with only twenty-five titles yet amply demonstrated his keen understanding of the progress of African American fiction in the first half of the twentieth century. Formulating a nascent tradition in Negro fiction, Locke reiterated his praise for Toomer's *Cane* and then went on to speak of Wright's "skillful sociological realism" in *Native Son* and *Uncle's Tom's Children*. This forms the lineage amply extended by Ralph Ellison's *Invisible Man*, "a great novel, although also not without its artistic flaws." Locke recognized from the beginning the book's "great merit" and said with convincing eloquence that "here is a Negro writer capable of real and sustained irony. *Invisible Man*, evidently years in the making, must not be Ralph Ellison's last novel." Two decades later, in December 1973, Ellison returned the attention and recognition when, at a symposium honoring Locke, he told of how he first met Locke in 1935 on the Tuskegee campus, where Locke was visiting his friend, the pianist Hazel Harrison, "who sponsored and encouraged all sorts of artistic and intellectual activities within her classroom and outside it." Locke, according to Ellison, was an encompassing and broad-minded "guide," someone who "stood for a conscious approach to American culture."

Locke had some final remarks on the artistry of Langston Hughes, about whose work he had written for thirty years. Evaluating the collection of short stories, *Laughing to Keep from Crying*, he mixed blame and praise: "his vignettes are, with all their faults, worth dozens of so-called 'Harlem novels.'" But Locke went a step further and introduced an appropriately higher standard, saying that "with just a little more art, Hughes could be Harlem's Daumier, or to change to the right figure, its Maupassant." Chancing intensification to a yet more general level, Locke used this advice to urge "the right approach for all writing about this province of Negro life: to see, feel and show not its difference but its different way of being human." A quarter of a century had passed since Locke was first infatuated with Hughes, and if anything, their personal relations with each other had been wary for the last two decades. But of all the artists whom Locke came to know well, Hughes probably caused him the greatest pleasure and the greatest pain. Hughes was enigmatic to many, even most, of his friends, and both his personality and

FIG. 11.2. Locke and Eleanor Roosevelt with two unidentified men. Locke befriended Eleanor Roosevelt in the late 1930s, when he generally supported New
Deal politics.

his esthetics kept him from reciprocating Locke's affection, but for that brief
spell in Paris. Locke seemed to remember his friendship with the poet as an
intense encounter, "a different way of being human."

Locke concluded the review with an especially sweeping peroration, as he
discussed the latest books on Africana. Referring to a book by Ladislas Segy,
African Sculpture Speaks, and a collection of *African Folk Tales & Sculpture,*
edited by Paul Radin, James Johnson Sweeney, and Elinore Marvel, Locke
lamented that people didn't know what a rich store of cultural expression lay
unused in this material. At the same time he sounded one of his main themes,
the equivalence of all cultural values when seen in a light of reciprocity and
recognition, a light that could correct the failures of civilized peoples:

> One yearns for the time when such knowledge and its transforming
> evaluations will percolate down to the level of generally educated men
> and women. That they are not yet so disseminated, even among edu-
> cated American Negroes, is just to be put down to contemporary me-

dievalism or cultural lag. Consider the evidence objectively, especially since the Greeks and the Teutons were "pagan" and the Jews non- or at least pre-Christian: some African creation myths are as "good" or meaningful as any, Genesis included, and some African fables are, even in their moral values, equal to the parables of the New Testament. Considering the billions of dollars worth of psychological damage missionary and racist misconceptions of Africa and the African have wrought, on both countless Negro and Caucasian minds, books such as these, though relatively expensive, are cheap and welcome antidotes—good medicine for the mind diseased. (CTAL, 393)

Locke was seldom bolder or more prophetic than here, and all the tones and nuances—for example, urging us to think "objectively," including Caucasians as victims, and using the main sacred texts of the "Western" tradition as his frame of comparison—serve to cast the depredations of racism in an unflinching way.

F I G . 11.3. Locke and Ralph Bunche were colleagues at Howard and close friends for many years; April 8, 1953, taken at the induction ceremony for Gamma Chapter, Phi Beta Kappa. Reading from left to right: Robert Julian Robinson, Lena P. Beauregard, Tazewell Banks (hidden), Norman Bradford Davis, Lillian Victoria Tinsley Walker (hidden), John Henry Powell, Jeanne Francis Craig Sinkford (shaking hands with Dr. Bunche), Raymond Elmer Contee, Dr. Ralph J. Bunche, Dr. Alain Locke, Florence Mae Cawthorne, Annette P. Williams, Esmond McDonald Mapp, Lois Fraces Mack, Albino Hamilton Forde. Moorland-Spingarn Research Center.

Locke achieved real pleasure when, in the spring of 1953, his final term at Howard, he was able to establish a chapter of the Phi Beta Kappa Society there. A year earlier Locke thought that he "gave perhaps an unwise amount of nervous energy" to the work that led up to the securing of this honor, though again his love of ceremony led him to great exertions. This particular event represented an important milestone in his career at Howard, and it epitomized his belief in his students and his elite commitment to knowledge in its most rigorous and humane forms. The ceremony was held on April 8 in the Rankin Memorial Chapel, with Locke presiding. Ralph Bunche delivered the commemoration address, and Locke would later cite Bunche's urging that black people must "stand ready to liquidate promptly and cheerfully all our vested interests in a segregated social order, and willingly renounce and reconstruct the separate church, the separate school, and whatever else was once a justifiable shield against discrimination and ostracism." Mrs. Roosevelt, though offered a personal invitation from Locke, was unfortunately unable to attend.

Two months after the establishment of the Phi Beta Kappa chapter, Howard held its commencement, on June 5, and conferred an honorary degree on Locke. His acceptance speech summarized his long and committed service to the university. Describing teaching as "a family calling," he reflected on the pedagogic role of his paternal grandfather, and even more so on that of his father Pliny, whose life he related to the history of Howard. Of himself, he said he came to Howard "bringing a philosophy of the market place not of the cloister." By this he meant that philosophy was "a crucial necessity" for those who would have a "trained minority leadership." He further explained: "In saying this, I do not mean formal philosophy merely, but critical thinking in other areas and subject-matters as well. For forty years the educational objective of our department has been not to teach students what to think but how to think, and to do so with critical independence." He went on to argue that "as long as education is racially separate, training for . . . social intelligence must be a primary aim and special emphasis."[7]

This speech is remarkable, not only for its eloquence and lightness of touch but also for its look into the future. Locke worked with Ralph Bunche, Kenneth Clark, and others in helping to evolve the thinking that would eventually produce the monumental decision of *Brown v. Board of Education.* He knew that some of the hope and trust he placed in the American democratic ideal would be rewarded. "Let us hasten to add," he said, "now that educational and other forms of official segregation are facing before the Supreme Court what we hope is their final judicial doomsday," minority education "should lapse along with the situations of enforced separatism, and then be merged in one overall program of progressive and democratic social education." He looked back to the days of the New Negro, and quoted a paragraph from his own essay, written "from a philosopher's viewpoint twenty-seven years" earlier: "This forced attempt to build his [the Negro's] Americanism on race values is a unique social experiment, and its ultimate success is impossible except through the fullest sharing of American culture and its institutions. . . . The racialism of the Negro is no limitation or reservation with respect to American life; it is only a constructive effort to build the obstructions in the stream of his progress into an efficient dam of social energy and power." Converting obstacles into power was a formula for culture and democracy as well. Seeing the problems in this way, so close in time to the *Brown* decision, meant Locke also knew the future course of the deeper river.

Locke's health steadily worsened in the first months of 1954. He was, according to one friend, taken from one hospital to another, though "during this hard period he showed great patience and courage." Having moved from Washington into the apartment on Grove Street in Greenwich Village, he had anticipated using his period of retirement to complete a major work, *The Negro in America*. He had worked on it fitfully for years, but it would only appear posthumously, edited by Margaret Just Butcher. On May 17, 1954, the Supreme Court decided in favor of the plaintiffs in *Brown v. Board of Education*. On June 9, 1954 Alain Locke died. A memorial was held at Benta's Funeral Home, 157 West 132nd Street, New York City, on June 11.

The June 10 obituary in the *New York Times* said that Locke "died early yesterday morning in Mount Sinai Hospital after an illness of six weeks, at the age of 67." It accurately listed his accomplishments and referred to him as "one of the leading interpreters of the cultural achievements of the Negro, and . . . one of the wisest analysts of his race and its relation to other races." Only one quotation from Locke appeared in the obituary: "The fiction is that the life of the races is separate, and increasingly so. The fact is that they touch too closely at the unfavorable and too lightly at the favorable levels." Race relations in Locke's lifetime are too complex to be summarized, but this formulation rings unforgettably true.

A number of funeral orations by Locke's friends and colleagues were collected and published in *Phylon*. In his eulogy for Locke, Ralph Bunche said: "I visited him at the hospital only a short time ago. I knew then that he was on his deathbed, and so, I am sure, did he." Bunche went on to say tenderly that "his frail little body and very big heart are gone," and "too few . . . well understood or adequately appreciated Alain Locke." Du Bois nobly looked past their disagreements and praised Locke in the highest terms, though at the same time using a combative tone; however, the combat was directed at their common target, the need constantly to honor and increase the standards of culture and the intellectual life:

> Alain Locke was a man who deliberately chose the intellectual life; not as a desirable relief from reality, but as a vocation compared with which all else is of little account. In a land like America and among a group as inexperienced as American Negroes this was simply not understandable. That a man in the midst of money-making or gambling should at intervals devote some time to thought itself or to the bases of human reason, is to our day possible if not profitable. But to give a life to thinking and its meaning, that is to most Americans quite inexplicable. So that to many this lonely figure, who spoke quietly and smiled with restraint, became often an object of pity if not evil gossip and ridicule.
>
> Yet in truth Alain Locke stood singular in a stupid land as a rare soul.

Locke's commitment to a pluralism of values and a rejection of absolutism will of necessity mean that his legacy is multifaceted. Such a legacy will be usefully multifaceted, to be sure, especially if it partakes of the many kinds of learning to which Locke added. He said of culture, that it could not be taught, but it could be learned. Throughout his life, he learned as well as he taught.[8]

CHAPTER TWELVE

Locke's Legacy

Because Locke's achievements as a cultural leader were reflective of his thinking as a polymath, one could assume his legacy (a term he greatly valued) would be diverse in form and purpose. The effects of Locke's contributions in many fields, beginning with the period shortly after his passing, are indeed notable and varied. These fields include philosophy, cultural criticism, race theory, adult education, and esthetics, among others. Locke's life and thought manifests a striking consistency, while his most outstanding contribution is usually referred to as multiculturalism or transculturalism. As with many thinkers, Locke's own terminology offers variants to this: pluralism, cultural relativism, and intercultural reciprocity are all terms he preferred. Horace Kallen revealed in his later years that Locke "insisted that he was a human being and that his color ought not to make any difference. So we had to argue out the question of how the differences did make differences, and in arguing out those questions the formulae, the phrases developed—'cultural pluralism,' the right to be different."[1] Locke was a classical pragmatist, and, although rarely appreciated as a philosopher or a pragmatist during his life, his ideas are increasingly appreciated. The consistency, depth, and range in Locke's thought have attracted any number of commentators, and Locke has become an intellectual "midwife" to yet another generation.[2]

In academic philosophy, it was at Howard, where he spent the greatest amount of time and energy, that Locke's legacy first flourished. Locke helped hire much of the early philosophy faculty at Howard, including Eugene C. Holmes, William Banner, and Winston K. McAllister. These professors formed the first department at a historically black college to offer a graduate degree in philosophy, a Master of Arts. The first master's thesis was submitted in 1932 by Frank L. Norris, and its title, "An Analysis of the Form/Quality Element in Contemporary Theories of Value," displays its Lockean concerns. Locke's own philosophy eventually emerged as a subject of study in the department of philosophy at Howard as well as at other major universities and institutions. A prominent Locke student, the pragmatist and naturalist Beth J. Singer, remembering Locke from her days at the University of Wisconsin, wrote: "We students had enormous respect for Dr. Locke, but I must admit that, in my case at least, this respect, great as it was, did not do justice to his scholarly achievement in this field [philosophy]. Part of the respect, though, was a response to his quiet dignity and personal restraint."[3]

Locke is visibly well remembered at Howard, which named the building that houses its philosophy department, Alain L. Locke Hall. Just south of Locke Hall at Howard is the Fine Arts complex, which includes approximately three hundred pieces of African sculpture and handicrafts that Locke bequeathed to Howard. Prominent among the collection are several dozen gold paperweights, an art form Locke was prescient in appreciating. (Locke also contributed his extensive collection of sheet music to Howard.) His bequest formed the basis of a teaching collection devoted to Africa's culture.

Locke enriched the Howard student body's dedication to learning and public service by acting as a faculty advisor to the Phi Beta Sigma fraternity. This fraternity, founded at Howard in 1915 with the motto "Culture for Service, Service for Humanity," has included many notables: A. Phillip Randolph, founder of the Brotherhood of Sleeping Car Porters; George Washington Carver, the wizard of science at Tuskegee Institute; and several future heads of African countries—Kwame Nkrumah of Ghana, Nnamdi Azikiwe of Nigeria, William Tolbert of Liberia, and Nelson Mandela of South Africa. Satisfying a long-held dream, Locke arranged in 1952 for the first chapter of Phi Beta Kappa at Howard. At the founding of the chapter, William Hastings, acting as the representative for the national honor fraternity, remarked on the ceremony afterwards: "And finally, I remember the very agreeable post mortem on the night of the chapter installation, in a living room of highly modernist primitivism, where in the casual conversation of the small group Alain Locke was the unobtrusive leader and enabled me, the old-fashioned Yankee, not to feel out of place."[4] Not only higher education institutions recall Locke's pedagogical dedication. In Chicago the Alain Locke Charter Academy, pre-kindergarten through the seventh grade, has as its mission, "Excellence in academics, technology, and social development and community responsibility." There are also public elementary schools named after Locke in New York, Los Angeles, West Philadelphia, and Gary, Indiana. Middle and senior high schools with similar missions are named in his honor across the country.

Locke consistently promoted the democratizing and transforming role of culture in society. When evaluating the literature of Africans, African Americans, or Afro-Caribbeans, he insisted on art's universal import combined with its particularized sense of energy and style. His sense of African art typifies his general views on artistic work: "What it is [African art] as a thing of beauty ranges it with the absolute standards of art and makes it a pure art form capable of universal appreciation and comparison; what it is as an expression of African life and thought makes it an equally precious cultural document, perhaps the ultimate key for the interpretation of the African mind" (CTAL, 131). The same approach is used for Afro-Caribbean works, as Locke comments on a specific work:

> Here we have a concrete and convincing illustration (Philippe et Pierre Thoby-Marcelin, *The Pencil of God*), of what I have been discussing. . . . [W]hen raised to the plane of formal art and universalized expression, that which was merely local and national can be made to acquire international significance and influence, and still also remain in substance racially representative. . . . [T]he significance is as intimately national and racial as it is international and human, thanks to the fact that these young writers have chosen, wisely, not to flee to an ivory tower of colorless cosmopolitanism but, on the contrary, have dug deep into the human soil.[5]

Although Locke has been criticized for being too enamored of the power of the arts to help change racial attitudes, he used his esthetic theory to encompass the art produced throughout the African diasporas. His work in this regard shows links with today's concern for the Black Atlantic and other forms of transnational cultural criticism.[6]

By communicating his social and political ideas to ever larger audiences throughout the 1940s, Locke carried his influence and his transnational cultural critique into places where the idea of a Negro intellectual was rarely entertained or embodied in a specific speaker. One such place was Sarah Lawrence College, a private women's institution that was located in a community with a restricted covenant. In Locke's time, Jews and blacks were not welcomed there as home or business owners, and the college limited the number of African American women in attendance. However, the college sponsored a series of debates unparalleled for the time: United Nationalities Roundtables. Community development representatives, lawyers, judges, and public officials attended and participated in discussion with the faculty and students on "various aspects of the problem of the relationship between different foreign born and religious and racial groups in this part of the country." In the spring of 1942, the roundtables convened for what became the scene of lively discussions. Locke participated in one such roundtable on Saturday, April 18, 1942 and was co-chairman of another session on Sunday, May 31, 1942. Among the most prominent speakers and supporters of the roundtables were Eleanor Roosevelt and Ruth Benedict. At the later roundtable, Locke and Benedict explored the importance of the demoralizing influence of prejudice, especially the "sense of difference which hurts" and the hoarding self-interested behavior of "Charter members against outsiders." The conference participants considered the social and legal standing of African Americans, other minorities, and foreign-born immigrants to be similar, so that all groups shared common problems. Locke addressed numerous themes ranging from Negro anti-Semitism, Garveyism, and Mussolini, to race war. When called on to represent his race, given his leading cultural role, he declined; instead, he chose to represent himself.[7]

Suburban college students were not the only extraterritorial audience Locke addressed in the 1940s, all as part of his effort to see that the war would end with an enriched sense of democracy throughout the world. On May 28, 1942, for a radio program titled *America's Town Meetings of the Air,* Locke discussed spirituality and democracy, a talk that was eventually published under the title "Is There a Spiritual Basis for World Unity" in the *Bahá'í World.* The Bahá'í were a marginalized sect in America, especially because of their promotion of racial amity and their approval of interracial marriage. Locke did not wear his affiliation openly nor practice as a doctrinaire Bahá'í, but he did serve on the group's National Committee on Racial Amity. Encouraging cross-racial dialogues, Locke reportedly said, prior to attending a fireside with a group of educators in New York: "How surprised they will be to know me as a Bahá'í." In the basement archives of the Bahá'í Temple in Wilmette, Illinois, just outside of Chicago, records for the National Committee on Racial Amity are assiduously maintained, and they show how Locke guided a generation of Bahá'í Committee members in encouraging cross-racial dialogue, as chronicled in the report of their annual meetings. An issue of the group's publication, *Bahá'í World,* was dedicated to Locke in 2006.[8]

In the field of the performing arts, Locke's legacy began early and his criticism showed the way for others. Looking back at a lifelong commitment to

Negro drama, Locke said: "The real beginning of serious interest in Negro drama was the short repertory season of the Hofgood Players presenting Ridgley Torrence's 'Three Plays for the Negro Theatre.' [Montgomery] Gregory and I were inspired by these performances—and the objective of the Howard Players groups took over in 1919. . . . The technical side of the Howard Player's program was inspired by Baker's 47 workshop at Harvard; the artistic side by the Hofgood Players."[9] The Hofgood Players were the first all-black cast on Broadway that was not minstrelsy. Cultural self-expression, especially in the theater, includes the creation of different perspectives, a feature of great important to Locke and the hallmark of art theater, a movement that was deeply influenced by Locke's esthetics and exertions.

Innovative in his approach to newly emergent art forms, Locke paid attention to different media. "Talkie" movies in the 1930s had added another opportunity for persons around the world to appreciate African American culture, while it simultaneously helped transform distorted images of African Americans. Paul Robeson's voice, the syncopated rhythms of Marion Anderson, the sophisticated jazz sounds of Duke Ellington, and the entertaining characters in Langston Hughes's *Simple* stories could be heard and seen. Nuanced criticism of sound films gained a tremendous addition to its corpus with Sterling Brown and Locke's jointly published review of *Hearts in Dixie* and *Hallelujah*.[10] They held that the "oversentimental" and "over-realistic" formula of the movie version of *Uncle Tom's Cabin,* with its usual stereotypes of Daddy, Uncle, and Mammy, was continued in early talkies. Nonetheless, the films made with and by blacks showed some advances. Locke and Brown's review did not offer a one-dimensional reaction; instead, they evaluated these films as valuable if they demonstrated multiple features, such as being mimetic, authentic, entertaining, and politically efficacious as well as morally enriching. The two colleagues introduced a way of seeing films, and esthetic works in general, as having a historical place in the development of race expression. They assiduously selected features of the films they considered appealing, chiefly mercurial changes of moods, expressions of individuality, and character growth, and eschewed features of slapstick comedy, "clownish leer and the minstrel's self-pity," and the stock pantomime of minstrelsy. Arguably, this is just what so many African American audience members did to garner enjoyment and sustenance from early black cinema, given the racially degrading commercialization of African American culture by white writers and producers.[11]

Locke's legacy reaches into more than elite forms of cultural expression. Communities influenced by the Renaissance approach that Locke shaped exist in more than the places delineated by the names Harlem, African American, or American. In 1926, during the year he spent away from Howard, Locke visited the Dunbar Forum, Oberlin College; the Daytona Normal Land Industrial Institute for Negro Girls, Daytona, Florida (precursor to Bethune-Cookman College); the Robert Hungerford Normal and Industrial School, Eatonville, Florida; and Wilberforce University, Wilberforce, Ohio. He also went to different art programs throughout the Midwest, in Indianapolis, Cincinnati, and Cleveland. Locke took the Renaissance to schools still located in log cabins and single family homes in rural villages as well as to major centers of intellectual sophistication and urban panache.

This sense of an expanding arena of cultural work carried over into Locke's legacy in Africa. His African consciousness was markedly heightened at Oxford, largely through his friendship with Pixley Seme. Seme, one of three founders of the African National Congress, regularly corresponded with Locke between 1911 and 1927. "There is a great chance here of organizing and directing Native Journalism along National Lines," wrote Seme, in a letter to Locke dated January 21, 1912. In 1914 Seme asked Locke to write for the South African "Native Paper," *Abantu-Batho.* The newspaper represented the beginning of efforts to create unity across ethnic and tribal lines; it became one of the precursors to modern African literary publications. Later Seme, in a letter mailed from his law office in Johannesburg in 1923, informed Locke that "your name" is known in native councils. Seme was an organizer of native tribal leaders to help support his efforts to compel the British to empower Africans, that is, empower persons understood as "African" in addition to being understood as Zulu, Tswana, Xhosa, Ndebele, Pedi, or Tshona. In July 1925, Seme expressed his confidence in Locke's ability to overcome difficulties, having received the "distressing news" regarding Locke's conflict with Howard University in 1924. *The New Negro* would soon follow the distressing news of Howard University's dismissal of Locke, and his influence would mushroom, even in South Africa.[12]

When the writer and activist H. I. E. Dhlomo described the concept of the "New African" as a detribalized, progressive Negro shaping a renaissance, he paraphrased material from Locke's introduction to *The New Negro.* In June 1934, Dhlomo helped organize performances at the Bantu Men's Social Centre in downtown Johannesburg for a group celebrating the British empire's emancipation of slaves in 1834. Included were Negro spirituals, Zulu folk songs, and speeches by Lincoln and Frederick Douglass.[13] When Peter Abrahams, before becoming a noted South African novelist, went to the Bantu Men's Social Centre in 1936, he observed: "There was *Up from*

Slavery; Along This Way by Weldon Johnson; a slim volume called *The Black Christ;* a fat volume called *The New Negro.* I turned the pages of *The New Negro.* These poems and stories were written by Negroes! The world could never again belong to white people only! Never again! I took *The New Negro* to a chair. I turned the pages."[14] Eslanda Robeson, wife of Paul Robeson, was visiting with a future President of the African National Congress, A. B. Xuma, in Sophiatown, where she had helped Abrahams to be able to use the library at the Bantu Men's Social Centre, the same library where Xuma attended the 1934 performances Dhlomo help organize.

Locke drew a distinction between "problem" literature, as direct political protest, and self-expressions that utilized folk themes and idioms. Self-expressions were also important contributions because they displayed African people as unique individuals, not stereotypes. Although not the direct political commentary favored by some, Locke added to the popular imagination regard for distinctive African traits and African American themes and idioms in the arts. His emphasis on artistic works rather than the "problem" plays, propaganda, or "apologetic" literature has been particularly controversial, often resulting in the view that Locke promoted the idea of the "New Negro" as "apolitical." The divide between art theater and political theater, considered a divide influenced by Locke's view of the "New Negro" as an "apolitical movement of the arts," assumes that "political" means a form of explicit propaganda. Locke welcomed in 1928 the increased presence in African American culture of the self-expression of "our younger generation, who have in general turned from cultural parade to self-expression."[15]

Art changes peoples' perspectives because it helps change the definition of categories. Self-expression hardly excludes protest. Rather, self-expression includes the creation of different perspectives, an insight important to Locke and arguably a hallmark of art theater, a movement that followed in Locke's footsteps not only in the arts theater movement in America but also in various venues and through activists in the Caribbean. The reshaping of categories of thought, away from provincialism and toward internationalism, often occurs through the aid of meritorious artistic presentations. Arguably, Locke's emphasis on the importance of the arts and contribution of African themes is part of his "The Colonial Literature of France" and "Internationalism: Friend or Foe of Art?"; self-expression lives in an international world. René Maran met Locke in 1924 and in 1949 wrote that he was "one of the highest and noblest illustrations of black American University life."[16] The subtlety of Locke's effort at creating new valuations through an emphasis on folk resources is reflected in authors Locke influenced in the Negritude movement in French-speaking Africa (especially authors associated with Léopold Sédar Senghor) in Brazil and Cuba (including the "poesía negra" of the Afro-Cuban author Nicolas Guillén), and in Haiti (notably the poet René Depestre and the activist and author Jacques Roumain). Roumain, along with Philippe Thoby-Marcelin, Carl Brouard, and Antonio Vieux, formed *La Revue Indigene: Les Arts et la Vie* (The Indigenous Review: Arts and Life) in 1927. Whether evoked in Port-au-Prince by the artistry of Beauford Delaney, in Paris, or in Johannesburg, South Africa, the terms "Harlem" and "New Negro" constantly connoted a "Renaissance." Locke's method of promoting the importance of esthetic evaluations of folk and native works, for the purpose of creating new cultural presentations by self-assured persons, is an approach dear to the manifold renaissance movements among African peoples.

The cultural attainment that was *The New Negro* demonstrated a strategy that was used by creators of art, poetry, short stories, and literary commentaries. Boundaries of place were transcended by creating a collage of African American short stories, poems, and art work emanating from throughout the black world, independent of interethnic or geographic origin. In *The New Negro* Africans were both dignified and attired in the clothes of the modern West. Pictures of African artifacts juxtaposed to pictures of dignified black persons affirmed the possibility of incorporating both in one culture; Africans were able to identify themselves as courageous, diligent, and studious as well as coy, sensuous, and playful. Poetry and fiction could use folk idioms to portray a diversity of characters, and these idioms need not be the self-degrading ditties of black minstrelsy or the degrading images of native Africans as inferior primitives. The "flow of phrase, accent of rhythm in prose, verse and music, color and tone of imagery, idiom and timbre of emotion and symbolism" (NN, 51) that Locke identified in black art are philosophic arguments embedded in literature and the arts that are not only subtle psychological instruments transforming stereotypes, conceptual categories, and valuations, but convincing reasons in support of new values.

In 1974 a Harvard symposium discussed and honored Locke's contributions to the struggle for racial equality and harmony.[17] Nathan Huggins, Harold Cruse, Albert Murray, and Ralph Ellison, among others, found intellectual value in Locke's work, and each of them spoke in positive terms, but the changing demands on black artists would also create a variety of perspectives into which Locke's thought would radiate. Ellison insisted on Locke's appreciation of the mingled fertility of pluralism and the way it entered into the American idiom, saying: "There is no specifically American vernacular and language which has not been touched by us and our style. Locke sensed this." Murray stressed Locke's role as an educator: "[T]o the extent that we recognize, appreciate, and celebrate the intentions of people like Alain Locke, I think we are most likely to dedicate ourselves to the real purposes of education in the broadest sense—and find some answers to the old folks' prayers." Cruse considered the way Locke's insistence on creating universally appreciated cultural goods meant ignoring or allowing less sophisticated features of black culture to wane. Yet, Cruse took up the notion of the tradition that Locke fostered, though he recognized how easily traditions could be weakened or lost: because of "the gaps which have come down through the '20s, '30s, '40s, '50s, and '60s, . . . it [is] almost impossible at this moment for anyone following Locke's path to establish an aesthetic critique of any kind." Huggins urged the audience to put Locke into the context of his time, "because you cannot demand that he have a program when he was not a program man, you cannot demand that he have a political slogan." These several voices together captured Locke in his prismatic and polymathic achievements. A strong memory of Locke persists at Harvard, where his studies carried him into the widest ranges of learning: the Department of African American Studies has an Alain L. Locke Room, offers an Alain L. Locke award for high achievement, and hosts an annual Locke lecture.

———————

Though his legacy extends outside of America, Locke was often quite pleased to take note of his hometown identity. In a sense he lived everywhere he went as a Philadelphian, conscious of the social need for unquestioned propriety even as he slowly but certainly developed an aversion to all absolutisms. Thoroughly conscious of the racial divide that defined his sense of American identity, Locke imagined gaps and abysses being bridged by esthetic strengths, value transformations, and philosophical nuances. Locke's childhood home was four blocks from Rittenhouse Square, one of the most fashionable residential areas of Philadelphia, yet itself close to the honkytonks in Carver and Minister alleys. From these alleys the "battered bodies of black males came to the crammed halls of Philadelphia Hospital on Pine street" after a week of backbreaking construction labor, police beatings, or self-inflicted alcohol abuse. This was the Seventh Ward W. E. B. Du Bois described in his innovative sociological study, *The Philadelphia Negro;* the ward sustained Carver and Minister alleys as well as its own aristocracy, more Methodist than the Episcopalianism of the Locke family. Locke saw all the aspects of this community, but he eventually developed an esthetic that bridged the gaps between the literature of racial uplift, the "problem" plays and novels, and the fiction that engages imagination. The persuasive power of literature and the persuasive powers of discursive arguments were, for Locke, equally efficacious; both are valuable tools in arsenals of strategies to transform images. Locke helped transform the world of letters by bridging distances, including the distance between the competing ways of appreciating creative productions and methods of persuasion.

Locke achieved a level of social and professional respect, despite all the indignities and refusals to accord his ideas high regard as a result of his race. The City of Philadelphia inaugurated the first annual "Alain Locke Day" on April 16, 1999. Locke's former high school, Central High School, hosted the opening dedication of the event in its auditorium. Legacies live only as vividly as the collective memory that sustains and reinvigorates them. Because Locke's cultural legacy of transforming race, culture, and value remains alive, it is still a promise; as he said: "May art in time give us a philosophy of creative interpretation and understanding" (CTAL, 213).

NOTES

INTRODUCTION

1. This sobriquet was passed along orally for decades after Locke's lifetime, but we have been unable to discover its origin.

CHAPTER ONE

1. Quotations from Locke's correspondence and manuscripts (of published and unpublished items) in the Locke archive in the Moorland-Spingarn Research Center at Howard University are given by reference to series, box, and folder numbers; e.g. ALPHU 164-32/15.

The information about Locke's name comes from a letter from Mary Locke to Locke dated April 9, 1907, ALPHU 164-54/1. He refers to changing his name to "Alain" in a letter he wrote his mother from Harvard: "why Alain might make me famous one day, who knows? I hardly think Leroy will" (164-50/17).

2. The genealogy is in ALPHU 164-3/13. It is not clear when Locke drew it up or for what purpose. For information on Ishmael Locke listed with the Coloured School Association of Friends, see the Salem County Historical Society *Newsletter*, September 2004, no 5, Treasurer's Report of 1843.

3. Pliny Locke's career is recorded in various documents, ALPHU 164-5/1-31.

4. Information about Mary Locke is in ALPHU 164-5/31-39 and 6/1-8.

5. Du Bois's *The Philadelphia Negro: A Social Study* was originally published in 1899. For further details, see "Where Negroes Live in Philadelphia," *Opportunity* 1, no. 5 (May, 1923): 10–14.

6. Mary Locke's teaching records are in ALPHU 164-5/1-8.

7. The Emancipation Proclamation essay is in ALPHU 164-5/28.

8. The incident with the horse is recounted in an undated letter Locke wrote his mother from Oxford, in ALPHU 164-47/10.

9. "Even when he couldn't recognize anything," ALPHU 164-99/10. The story of the visit to Apprentices' Library is from a letter Locke wrote to his mother in 1906, in 164-51/9. The visit informed Locke's idea of ancestry, which he relied on in later years.

10. The 1942 essay is in *Twentieth Century Authors,* ed. Stanley Kunitz and Howard Haycraft.

11. The incident is recounted in a letter in ALPHU 164-46/49.

12. The undated autobiographical essay is in ALPHU 164-1/2. The notes are in 164-143/5.

13. John Lukacs, *Philadelphia* (New York: Farrar, Straus & Giroux, 1981), 9.

14. The records of Locke at Charles Close School are in ALPHU 164-48/15-17.

15. The Central High School records are in ALPHU 164-148/18-27. Though he used the spelling of "Alain" early, he made the change more official later on at Harvard.

16. The essays are in ALPHU 164-150/15-24, 151/1-47, and 152/1-33. The Haverford College exam is in 164-150/4, and a run of issues of the *Mirror* is in 164-149/26-29 and 150/1-3.

17. The essay from the *Teacher* is in ALPHU 164-17/11.

18. The Brandt letter is in ALPHU 164-16/10.

19. "If I could get a nice bunk," ALPHU 164-47/30.

CHAPTER TWO

1. For Greener, see Allison Blakely, "Richard Greener and the 'Talented Tenth' Dilemma," *Journal of Negro History* 59, no. 4 (October, 1974): 305–21.

2. The essay on "Self Culture . . . " is in ALPHU 164-46/5.

3. "I am going to be choice," ALPHU 164-47/28; "homeopathic doses," 164-81/46. For details about Van Wyck Brooks, see James Hoopes, *Van Wyck Brooks: In Search of American Culture* (Amherst: University of Massachusetts Press, 1977), esp. 27–51. Brooks seems never to have mentioned Locke in any of his writings.

4. "he is peculiarly mine," ALPHU 164-52/21; Locke often observed his teachers and classmates with a keen and critical eye. He described one as a "shattered idol" whose lectures were full of second hand phrases, 164-51/1.

5. "a funny looking lot," ALPHU 164-47/25.

6. "cake walk," ALPHU 164-48/3, 5; "coarse" students, 164-47/36.

7. "same old mistake," ALPHU 164-47/2.

8. "ragtime one hears," ALPHU 164-47/17.

9. Dickerman's correspondence, which spans several decades, is in ALPHU 164-24/36-37 and 164-25/1-4.

10. "A Critique of Utilitarianism" is in ALPHU 164-154/19; "Free Will . . . " is in 154/21. The Philosophy exam in 1907 is in 164-154/15.

11. "hurried over to hear," ALPHU 164-47/4.

12. "literary flourishes," ALPHU 164-46/57; only black in the audience, 164-45/1.

13. "diplomacy or something equally deceitful," ALPHU 164-49/2; "fatherly . . . financial matters," 164-46/47. When considerable debts mounted later, Locke continued to advise his mother on how to handle them.

14. "perfectly wonderful," ALPHU 164-49/41; "wouldn't it be funny," 164-50/17. Dickerman would later publish a limited amount of poetry, but never apparently a volume of poems.

15. The incident is related in a letter to Mary Locke, ALPHU 164-46/47.

16. "taken liberties with my name," ALPHU 164-47/6. Locke also told his mother he was digging into the French symboliste poets but would not recommend them to her, 164-53/52.

17. "in spite of the grudge . . . a good mark," ALPHU 164-51/14.

18. "remarkable piece of work" and the meeting with Wendell are in ALPHU 164-47/7.

19. The evening at Copeland's, which Locke referred to as a "soiree," is described in ALPHU 164-46/49. Locke characterized the room itself as one that "Emerson himself the Pope of American culture made famous by living in it 2 years."

20. The Traubel visit is recounted in ALPHU 164-47/6. Locke observed that Copeland took Traubel's book—his account of his days with Whitman—and dusted it off and cut the pages before Traubel arrived.

21. Harley, a West Indian, impressed Locke considerably; he is vividly described in letters to Mary Locke in ALPHU 164-46/49 and 164-51/36; "by selecting the ministry" 164-51/46. The opinion of Du Bois's "Litany" is in 164-52/15.

22. The incident with Harley on the bus is in ALPHU 164-54/50.

23. The Dunbar lecture is mentioned in ALPHU 164-53/17 (where Locke says he used it to gain admission to Copeland's advanced writing class), 164-47/5, and 164-46/49. The lecture was given to the Cambridge Lyceum at the local AME church, 164-46/54. An essay on Dunbar, presumably the one written at Harvard, is in 164-123/18.

24. The Prometheus essay is discussed in ALPHU 164-46/49 and 46/53, where Locke mentions it is ten thousand words. The text is in 164-156/1.

25. T. S. Eliot was a year behind Locke at Harvard, but neither man took notice of the other in print, though they shared several concerns—formalism, modernism, and the role of culture in reviving group purpose and solidarity, for example.

26. The Tennyson essay is in ALPHU 164-56/12, and the "Romantic Movement" is in 164-56/7.

27. "The Rain" is in ALPHU 164-156/5-6, and "The Ebb Tide" is in 164-154/20. Locke sent copies of these to his mother and asked her to submit them to magazines, though none apparently were ever accepted.

28. "The House of Death" is in ALPHU 164-154/23. Locke remarked to his mother that he was "not yet infected with the conceit that I am a born poet" (164-46/49), but he continued to write poetry, especially while in Berlin, and later would circulate it privately among close friends.

29. "gruesome specimens," ALPHU 164-47/4. All the records related to Locke's winning the Rhodes Scholarship are in 164-161/15-35 and 162/1-2.

30. This passage is quoted in Thomas Gosset, *Race: The History of An Idea in America* (Dallas, 1963), 285–86.

31. See Josiah Royce, *Race Relations, Provincialism, and Other American Problems* (New York: Macmillan, 1908), 29, 35. For an essay on Royce, see Jacquelyn Ann K. Kegley, "Is a Coherent Racial Identity Essential to Genuine Individuals and Communities? Josiah on Race," *Journal of Speculative Philosophy* 19, no. 3 (2005): 216–28.

32. "a crank on the race problem," ALPHU 164-53/28; "I am not a race problem," 164-53/42.

33. "I wouldn't give people clippings," ALPHU 164-54/6; "I have some privacy," 164-53/52.

34. "a typical Harvard attitude" and "when I sail," ALPHU 164-96/22.

35. "I am not going to England," ALPHU 164-54/6; the Shipman episode is in 54/9.

36. "more popularity," ALPHU 164-54/27.

37. "am on board," ALPHU 164-54/52.

CHAPTER THREE

1. "good locations," ALPHU 164-55/2.

2. "penniless as Columbus," ALPHU 164-55/9; "a brilliant Boston Ghetto Jew," 164-55/18.

3. "I have almost forgotten," ALPHU 164-55/18.

4. All these quotations are in ALPHU 164-55/37.

5. The "Wa Wa people" and other details are in ALPHU 164-55/43; "Oxford superficiality and insincerity," 164-55/51.

6. In ALPHU 164-55/29 Locke tells of his vacation at St. Malo in January 1908, and later in the summer Mary Locke would sail to England to see her son and meet his friends, among them Seme and De Fonseka.

7. "Oxford Contrasts" is in ALPHU 164-160/3-4. A detailed account of Locke's days at Oxford can be found in Jeffrey Stewart, "A Black Aesthete at Oxford," *Massachusetts Review* 34, no. 3 (Autumn 1993): 411–29.

8. Although he does not mention Locke, some of these issues and attitudes are treated in contemporary terms in the recent book by Anthony Appiah, *Cosmopolitanism: Ethics in a World of Strangers* (New York: W. W. Norton, 2006).

9. Francis Wylie, Rhodes Trust File 1122, Rhodes House, Oxford (Mar. 23, 1907). Jack C. Zoeller, "Alain Locke at Oxford: Race and the Rhodes Scholarships," *American Oxonian* 94, no. 2 (Spring 2007): 183–224. See also Francis Wylie in *The First Fifty Yeas of the Rhodes Trust and the Rhodes Scholarships, 1903–1953,* ed. Lord Elton (Oxford: Blackwell, 1955), 99–100.

10. On Scholes, see Jeffrey Green, "A Black Edwardian Scholar," *Oxford: The Journal of the Oxford Society* 11, no. 2 (December 1988): 71–76, from which a number of details are drawn.

11. On Seme, details are taken from Christopher Saunders, "Pixley Seme: Towards a Biography," *South Africa Historical Journal* 25 (1991): 196–217. He would later be an important force in the founding of the African National Congress.

12. A full account, from which details and quotations have been drawn, of Kallen and Wendell and their discussion of Locke is given in Werner Sollors, "A Critique of Pure Pluralism," in *Reconstructing American Literary History* (Cambridge, Mass.: Harvard University Press, 1986), 250–79.

13. "I should have had to complain," ALPHU 164-141/3. Locke's records at Rhodes House in Oxford indicate his lack of high competence in Latin and Greek was partly the reason he was granted a third year at Oxford only on the condition he not be in residence at Hertford College. The principal of Hertford also took note of the fact Locke was "far into debt & appeared in Vice Chancellor's Court." These records were made available to us through the kindness of Sir Colin Lucas, the Warden of Rhodes House.

14. "premeditatedly" and other details, ALPHU 164-57/2.

15. "Bachelor of Civil Law," ALPHU 164-57/28. Documents related to the Cosmopolitan Club are in 164-161/5-11. The club was in part created as part of a broad-based movement, which also had many adherents in America, among college students; it flourished in the early years of the twentieth century. In recent years cosmopolitanism has emerged as an important topic in political theory, generating a massive bibliography; however, virtually all of such work makes no mention of Locke.

16. The texts of several drafts of "Cosmopolitanism and Culture" and "Cosmopolitanism" are in ALPHU 164-159/8-15. The first issue of the *Oxford Cosmopolitan* is in 164-161/8.

17. A partial copy of the speech is in ALPHU 164-160/6.

18. Philip's letters to Locke are in ALPHU 164-77/26. In 164-57/11, Locke mentions the "crowd of extremists."

19. "you cannot write without experience" and the Newdigate Prize, ALPHU 164-55/51; "proverb of the rocket," 164-57/26.

20. "The African mind," ALPHU 164-56/40.

21. De Fonseka was one of Locke's friends from the Cosmopolitan Club. De Fonseka would later write a book on esthetics called *On the Truth of Decorative Art* (London: A. C. Fifield, 1913); born in Ceylon, he returned there and began to use his family name, Varnasuriya, and later published a book on Fatima and the miracles that allegedly occurred there (*Les eaux de lumiere*, 1953). See http://www.defonseka.com/pe0012.htm.

22. "I shall know how to live" and the travel details are in ALPHU 164-57/14, 21.

23. "They will play dice for his toga," ALPHU 164-57/24; "I admit I was fairly staggered," 164-58/17. The "colossal" scheme would remain in Locke's mind for some time, and it reflects the scale of his early vocational notions about race leadership.

24. "There seems to be a great rivalry," ALPHU 164-58/52; founding of *Crisis*, 164-59/8; famous incident, 164-59/26-7.

25. Mary Locke's encounter with the student is related in ALPHU 164-57/29.

26. "The Miraculous Draught" is in ALPHU 164-159/16, and "The Pardon of the Sea" is in 164-123/16.

27. Kallen's note to Locke, ALPHU 164-42/15. Locke's note to Schiller, 164-75/15; Shiller's note to Locke, 164-75/12.

28. Undated, written on or soon after Monday, May 18, 1908, ALPHU 164-76/12.

29. Undated, apparently written before James received the honorary D.Sc., ALPHU 164-42/15.

30. Locke to Mary Locke, ALPHU 164-55, Dec 1, 1907; also see lecture and tutorial assignments, Michaelmas Term 1907, 164-160/19.

31. "I pray that you may be saved," ALPHU 164-84/35, Seme to Locke, November 26, 1909, Amsterdam.

32. Report regarding Locke's removal from Hertford College, Hertford College, *Minutes of the Governing Body*, 1874–1929, 362.

33. "was not regarded . . .," Rhodes Trust Archives, Harvard Class of 1908, Second Report, p. 207.

34. "blame of being largely responsible," ALPHU 161-141/3; also Locke to Mary Locke: "I don't think there will be a [Negro] Rhodes Scholar soon again though, do you?" 164-57 (April 29, 1909).

35. "One must pay the fiddler," ALPHU 164-59/29.

36. Many of the details about the university, and Simmel, are drawn from Fritz Ringer, *The Decline of the German Mandarins: The German Academic Community, 1890–1933* (Cambridge, Mass.: Harvard University Press, 1969.) Simmel's writings are available in many editions; the best one volume edition is *On Individuality and Social Form*, (Chicago: University of Chicago Press, 1971.) Also still of interest,

especially for the section on contemporary views of Simmel, is Lewis Coser, ed., *Georg Simmel* (New Jersey: Prentice Hall, 1965).

37. The biographical details on Münsterberg are taken from http://www .earlham.edu/%7Edominel/professionalbiography.htm.

38. The records for Locke as a student at the University of Berlin are in ALPHU 164-162/3-9.

39. "sometimes I almost wish," ALPHU 164-59/12; "I think your plans may all miscarry," 164-59/29.

40. The various scraps are in ALPHU 164-162/3. Locke saved many things, but seldom scraps or jottings, so one can assume these Berlin mementos meant a great deal to him.

41. The letters from his mother to Locke in Berlin are in ALPHU 164-59/1-49.

42. "I don't acknowledge," ALPHU 164-190/32.

43. On the First Universal Races Congress, see Ulysses G. Weatherly, "The First Universal Races Congress," *American Journal of Sociology* 17, no. 3 (November 1911): 315–28; Elliott M. Rudwick, "W. E. B. Du Bois and the Universal Races Congress of 1911," *Phylon Quarterly* 20, no. 4 (Winter 1959): 372-78; Robert Holton, "Cosmopolitanism or Cosmopolitanisms? The Universal Races Congress in 1911," *Global Networks* 2, no. 2 (2002): 170.

44. "I'm awfully glad about Phillip," ALPHU 164-25/2; the undated letter is in 164-24/36.

45. "The American Temperament" went through several drafts; they are in ALPHU 164-157/21-2. It appeared in the *North American Review* 19 (August 1911): 261–70. The quotations are taken from CTAL, 399–406. A fuller treatment of the essay can be found in Charles Molesworth, "Alain Locke and Walt Whitman: Manifestos and National Identity," in *The Critical Pragmatism of Alain Locke*, ed. Leonard Harris (Lanham, Md.: Rowman & Littlefield, 1999), 175–90.

46. "I do not want you at Howard," ALPHU 164-59/31; "Now if you can make Egypt go," 164-59/48.

CHAPTER FOUR

1. Locke's portraits of himself from the Harvard Class Reports are in ALPHU 164-153/3.

2. Du Bois's reflection is in his *Autobiography of W. E. B. Du Bois: A Soliloquy on Viewing My Life from the Last Decade of the First Century* (New York: International Publishers, 1968), 263.

3. "bullseye with Washington," ALPHU 164-60/4; "As I write this," 164-60/7. The letters from Locke's southern trip are in 164-60/7-14. "I have seen a lot," 164-60/16.

4. Crummell's works are available in J. R. Oldfield, ed., *Civilization and Black Progress: Selected Writings of Alexander Crummell on the South* (Charlottesville: Published for the Southern Texts Society by the University of Virginia Press, 1995). Also see Wilson J. Moses, ed., *Classical Black Nationalism: From the American Revolution to Marcus Garvey* (New York: New York University Press, 1996).

5. Biographical details for Kelly Miller are taken from the *Dictionary of American Negro Biography,* ed. Rayford Logan and Michael Winston (New York: Norton and Co., 1982), 435–39.

6. Biographical details for Carter Woodson taken from the *Dictionary of American Negro Biography,* 665–67.

7. "looked at the dome of the Capitol," Langston Hughes, *The Big Sea* (New York: Hill and Wang, 1964). In this volume of his autobiography, Hughes's chapter, "Washington Society," gives a tangy account of Seventh Street and life among the capital's blacks in the 1920s. A dense and useful study of Toomer's reaction to, and fictional use of, the Seventh Street milieu is Barbara Foley's "Jean Toomer's Washington and the Politics of Class: From 'Blue Veins' to Seventh-Street Rebels," at http://newark.rutgers.edu/~bfoley/jean_toomers_washington.html. Also of interest is Wilson J. Moses, "The Lost World of the Negro, 1895–1919: Black Literary and Intellectual Life before the 'Renaissance,'" *Black American Literature Forum* 21, nos. 1–2 (Spring–Summer 1967): 61–84.

8. Phi Beta Kappa ceremony, ALPHU 164-60/45. The council that lobbied Congress, 164-60/38. "It is a great satisfaction," 164-60/62; "sybarite," 164-61/15; question of his salary, 164-60/57. The salary issue was raised by Locke in November 1913, and a number of years later it would be one of the pretexts on which he would be dismissed from his position at Howard. Locke insisted that black faculty be paid at the same scale as white faculty.

9. "I almost bankrupt myself," ALPHU 164-161/60.

10. "It is disgusting," ALPHU 164-60/63.

11. Biographical details on Bruce are taken from the *Dictionary of American Negro Biography,* ed. Rayford Logan and Michael Winston (New York: Norton and Co., 1982), 132–33. His correspondence with Locke is in ALPHU 164-17/38-42. Locke also addressed the American Negro Historical Society in Philadelphia on 24 October 1911, on the subject "The Negro and a Race Tradition."

12. Alain L. Locke, *Race Contacts and Interracial Relations,* ed. Jeffrey Stewart (Washington, D.C.: Howard University Press, 1992).

13. The Yonkers lecture is in an appendix of RCIR, 105–10. Locke wrote his mother supporting Germany as late as October 1914, ALPHU 164-60/59.

14. "I had an interview with Miss Lerney," ALPHU 164-63/7; "I don't go in for," 164-65/15; "teaching is really dragging work," 164-62/9.

15. "Young William James," ALPHU 164-62/23; "She is really talented," 164-63/50.

16. "wasn't it sad," ALPHU 164-63/49.

17. The essay, titled "Booker T. Washington as a Writer," is in ALPHU 164-107/4; the "Strategies" essay is in 164-107/5.

18. By March 1917, Locke had formed his dissertation committee: Profs. Perry, Hoernle, and Sheffer. After he submitted it to Perry in September 1917, the thesis was accepted, with a call for some stylistic revision, in March 1918. The records of Locke's registration at Harvard for his graduate work are in ALPHU 164-152/43.

The dissertation, "The Problem of Classification in the Theory of Value," is in ALPHU 164-157/23-24, 158/1-24, and 159/1-7. The dissertation, however, makes no substantive use of plays, poetry, drama, novels or art work. Yet, Locke had spent his early Howard University years appreciating the drama community in Washington, D.C., and thinking of the literary arts as capable of representing how massive conceptual and paradigm shifts are possible.

19. "As a result aesthetic values have become" is from Locke's dissertation, p. 201; "Art could never successfully carry," dissertation, 205.

20. "it is the development," Wilbur Urban in *Fundamentals of Ethics* (New York: Holt & Co., 1930), 118. The Austrian school (not to be confused with the Austrian School of Values that concentrates on economic issues) is explored in two books: David F. Lindenfeld, *The Transformation of Positivism: Alexius Meinong and European Thought, 1880–1920* (Berkeley and Los Angeles: University of California Press, 1980), and Howard O. Eaton, *The Austrian Philosophy of Values* (Norman: University of Oklahoma Press, 1930). Locke used the latter title in courses he taught at Howard; see ALPHU 164-162/13.

21. The review of Bosanquet is in ALPHU 164-155/5. See Bosanquet, *Logic, or the Morphology of Knowledge,* 2 vols. (London and New York: Macmillan, 1888). The outline of the thesis is in 164-55/12, with some largely illegible marginalia in Locke's hand. A memo in the same folder shows that Locke wrote two seminar papers with Perry, called "The Genesis of the Normative Categories" and "The Types of Classification in the Theory of Values," in the Fall 1906 and Spring 1907 semesters, respectively. His paper for Professor Hoernle's seminar was entitled "The Metaphysical Implications of the Value Categories."

22. Ralph B. Perry, "Dewey and Urban on Value Judgments," *Journal of Philosophy, Psychology and Scientific Methods* 14, no. 7. (March 29, 1917): 169–81.

The arguments in which Dewey gives the impression that he favors a system of values appear in: "The Logic of Judgments in Practice. I. Their nature, and II. Judgments of value," *Journal of Philosophy* 12 (1915): 505–23; "The Logic of Judgments in Practice. III. Sense-Perception as Knowledge," *Journal of Philosophy* 12 (1915): 533–43. There is also an article that shows Locke's work on the philosophical questions of categories and their roles in human judgment: "On Kant's Deduction of the Categories." It was written while Locke was at Harvard and is in ALPHU 164-155.

Examples of critical discussions by Perry, Dewey, Schiller, and Urban on valuation: Dewey, "Philosophy's Search for a Satisfying Vision of Reality" (1927), review of Alfred Hoernlé, *Idealism as a Philosophy,* and Bernard Bosanquet, *Science and Philosophy and Other Essays,* in *The Later Works of John Dewey,* vol. 3, 1925–1953 (Hoernlé, at the University of Witwaterstrand, South Africa, would receive Locke's *The New Negro*); Dewey, "Tribute to F. C. S. Schiller," *Journal of Philosophy* 34 (October 28, 1937): 616 (address to memorial meeting for F. C. S. Schiller at Second Conference of Methods in Philosophy and the Sciences, New School for Social Research, New York); Ralph Barton Perry, review of F. C. S. Schiller, *Riddles of the Sphinx: A Study in the Philosophy of Humanism,* in *Philosophical Review* 21, no. 1 (Jan. 1912): 112–13; Wilbur M. Urban, review of Ralph Barton Perry, *General Theory of Value: Its Meaning and Basic Principles Construed in Terms of Interest,* in *Journal of Philosophy* 24, no. 4 (February 1927): 104–10; F. C. S. Schiller, *Studies in Humanism* (London and New York: Macmillan, 1907).

23. The correspondence with Pfromm is in ALPHU 164-77/19-21; Dickerman's letters are in 164-24/36-7 and 25/1-4.

24. The poem is in ALPHU 164-24/36.

25. Dickerman on being almost blackmailed and "The Park is a sort of Gomorrah," ALPHU 164-25/3; "the urge is far less," 164-25/4. Locke is referred to briefly, though largely without documentation, in George Chauncey, *Gay New York: Gender, Urban Culture and the Making of the Gay Male World 1890–1940* (New York: Basic Books, 1994).

26. Locke's last letter to Dickerman, ALPHU 164-25/4.

27. "The students have been very manly," ALPHU 164-65/7.

28. Biographical details for Gregory are taken from http://www.dclibrary .org/blkren/bios/gregorytm.html. His correspondence with Locke is in ALPHU 164-32/51-3. Locke and Gregory shared an elevated view of the aims of black theater. Locke referred, in "Steps Towards The Negro Theatre," in *Crisis* 25, no. 2 (December 1922), to the Memorial Theatre at Howard as "at one and the same time a Gibraltar of national pride and self-respect and a Mecca of human civilization and culture." When he and Gregory resigned from the NAACP Committee on the Drama, Locke wrote in his resignation letter that there was "an utter incompatibility of point of view—something more than a mere difference of opinion." He wanted the NAACP to sponsor plays other than what were referred to as "problem plays," a sort of didactic social analysis rather than an artistically conceived dramatic expression. ALPHU 164-33/7.

29. The article is in ALPHU 164-115/27; the other two faculty members were Profs. Lightfoot and MacLear. The writing style suggests it was chiefly authored by Locke.

30. These documents, along with other personal papers of Locke, are in ALPHU 164-1/7. The material relating directly to the Army is in 164-1/19-20.

CHAPTER FIVE

1. "I miss you so much," ALPHU 164-65/48. Mary Locke also chose to sit at her son's place at the table when he was traveling, as she did not like to stare at his empty chair across the table.

2. Mary Locke's notes on her European trips are in ALPHU 164-5/44.

3. The incidents in Berlin in 1914 are recounted by Locke in two letters to Charlotte Osgood Mason, July 29, 1931 and August 8, 1931, ALPHU 164-69/8.

4. The details of Mary Locke's wake are told by Helen Irvin in ALPHU 164-39/4. Irvin later offered to help Locke edit his correspondence to his mother, but the plan came to naught, ALPHU 164-1/5; she continued to correspond with Locke after Mary's death.

5. This early version of Locke's will, dated June 30, 1922, is in ALPHU 164-1/6.

6. The "Impressions of Luxor" is in the *Howard Alumnus* 2 (May 1924): 74–78 and in ALPHU 164-115/33.

7. The meeting with Belata Heroui and other notes are in ALPHU 164-105/2. Du Bois's letter asking Locke to write an account of his visit with Ras Tafari is in 164-26/7. Locke's news article on Egypt and Turkey is in 164-126/33, "Roosevelt Agitated Anti-British Factions: Egyptian Speech Recalls Myriad Grievances of Nationalism Based on England's Negligence of Education."

8. Locke was drawn to the Bahá'í with the encouragement of his mother. "Mother's feeling toward the [Bahá'í] cause, and the friends who exemplify it, was unusually receptive and cordial for one who had reached her conservative years,—it was her wish that I identify myself more closely with it," wrote Locke to Agnes Parsons, June 28, 1922. (The letter to Parsons is in the Agnes Parsons Papers, Biographical Information Collection, National Bahá'í Archives, Illinois.) The Bahá'í offered a wide array of spiritual comfort, such as a belief in the co-fraternity of humanity across lines. Their acceptance of all racial groups, their consideration of racism as a religious sin, their integration of cultures as 'reciprocal' sources of value, and their democratic governance all were a welcome reprieve from the racially segregated world of black–white Christianity and its accompanying chauvinism and bigotry. Throughout the last three decades of his life, Locke would attend Bahá'í firesides, meeting members of the faith and friends, to discuss their experiences and promote the faith. He also participated in lectures, traveled to its center in Haifa, and communicated with Shogi Effendi, grandson of Abdull Baha, founder of the Bahá'í. Twice two brief essays of his appeared in the *Bahá'í World*. At the January 1927 National Spiritual Assembly, Locke, along with Agnes Parsons, Louis Gregory, and others, were appointed to the membership committee; he published annual reports of this committee in the *Bahá'í News Letter* until late in his life. Gregory himself published *The Advancement of Racial Unity in America* (Wilmette, Illinois: Baha'i Publishing Trust, 1982). Although not a doctrinaire believer, he considered himself

a fellow spirit among the Bahá'í. One way Locke differed from other pragmatists was in his inclination toward this cultural and religious influence—it provided a lived experience of other than narrow American racial religious and cultural sensibilities and ideas. Locke consistently considered it an example of metaphysical absolutism to think there is only "one way" to religious peace, rather than the Bahá'í sense that all religions have a contribution to make to the appreciation of spirituality. For a full account of Locke's relations with the Bahá'í, see Christopher Buck, *Alain Locke: Faith and Philosophy* (California: Kalimat Press, 2005).

9. The documents related to the Sanhedrin conference are in ALPHU 164-127/20.

10. "The Black Watch on the Rhine" is in ALPHU 164-107/2; 164-114/13 contains the exchange between Maran and Locke. The review of René Maran's novel is in 164-110/15. In it Locke argues that "the non-moralistic and purely aesthetic approach" will triumph over humanitarianism and sentimental romanticism. Also, art for art's sake must be combined with "that stark cult of veracity—the truth, whether it hurts or not." This goal, paradoxically combining what some would call estheticism and realism, was one Locke held to for many years; it would later determine much of the commentary and judgment of the African American fiction he would review.

A convoluted discussion of Locke's relationship with Maran, and their exchange in *Opportunity*, is set out in Brent Hayes Edwards, *The Practice of Diaspora: Literature, Translation and the Rise of Black Nationalism* (Cambridge, Mass.: Harvard University Press, 2003), 105–108. Edwards echoes the attitudes of commentators on Locke by referring to how he "scrambl[ed] mightily" to "admit . . . his narrow motives," and how he "hedg[ed] his bets," in part because of his "strategic misrecognition of French colonialism." Of Locke's writing, Edwards uses such descriptors as "sly," "gushing," "flippant," and "fawning." Recent theorized studies of the African diaspora seldom take account of Locke's pioneering work on this subject—such as his Haiti lecture series—except to criticize his not fully enlightened views.

The relations between French intellectuals and African Americans is discussed in Michel Fabre, *From Harlem to Paris: Black American Writers in France, 1840–1980* (Urbana and Chicago: University of Illinois Press, 1993).

11. Biographical details of Charles S. Johnson are taken from Steven Watson, *The Harlem Renaissance: Hub of African-American Culture, 1920–1930* (New York: Pantheon, 1995), 24–26, and from George Hutchinson, *The Harlem Renaissance in Black and White* (Cambridge, Mass.: Harvard University Press, 1995), 50–61. The latter treats Johnson's relationship to Robert Park. See also, Patrick Gilpin, "Charles S. Johnson: Entrepreneur of the Harlem Renaissance," in Arna Bontemps, *The Harlem Renaissance Remembered* (New York: Dodd Mead, 1972), 215–46. This gives a thorough account of the Opportunity Awards dinners. A later study is Ralph L. Pearson, "Combatting Racism With Art: Charles S. Johnson and the Harlem Renaissance," *American Studies* 18, no. 1:123–34.

12. Details are taken from the biographical essay by Gerald Early, which serves as an introduction to *My Soul's High Song: The Collected Writings of Countee Cullen* (New York: Doubleday, 1991), 3–73.

13. Rudolf Dressler is mentioned in letters of June 1923 in ALPHU 164-22/36; Yolande Du Bois is mentioned in a letter dated August 23, 1923.

14. Hughes's correspondence with Locke is in two places (which has sometimes led to their relationship being presented in a one-sided way). Hughes's letters to Locke are in ALPHU 164-38/3-6; Locke's letters to Hughes are in the Beinecke Library at Yale University, as part of the James Weldon Johnson collection. See JWJ MSS Langston Hughes Papers, Series 1, Personal Correspondence, Box 104, Folder 1975-76, "Locke, Alain." Quotations from Hughes's biography are taken from *The Big Sea* (New York: Hill & Wang, 1993).

The story of the relationship between Locke and Hughes has been told before, most notably in Arnold Rampersad, *The Life of Langston Hughes,* vol. 1, *1902-41* (Oxford and New York: Oxford University Press, 1968), passim, and David Levering Lewis, *When Harlem Was in Vogue* (Oxford and New York: Oxford University Press, 1981), 81–88.

15. The letters from Rudolf Dressler are in ALPHU 164-26/3. We are grateful to the services of Marc-Oliver Schach for translating and annotating this correspondence.

16. Biographical details taken from Cynthia Earl Kerman and Richard Eldridge, *The Lives of Jean Toomer: A Hunger for Wholeness* (Baton Rouge: Louisiana State University Press, 1987). Letters of Toomer were graciously made available by Dr. Mark Whalan, Lecturer in American Literature and Culture at the University of Exeter.

17. The documents related to Locke's dismissal are in ALPHU 164-2/20. There is also a long undated letter from Locke to Du Bois spelling out various incidents in connection with the dismissal in 164-26/6.

18. For a full account of Du Bois's role in protesting the dismissal, see David Levering Lewis, *W. E. B. Du Bois: The Fight for Equality and the American Century, 1919-1963* (New York: Henry Holt, 2000), 144–45 and 161–65. In the space of two pages, 161-63, Lewis uses the following adjectives in connection with Locke: "epicene," "mauve," and "flaccid"; he also speaks of Locke as "infused" with snobbery, decadence, and misogyny. Du Bois's letter to the *Nation* appeared in volume 122 (March 3, 1926), 228–30. A strong letter urging Locke's reinstatement was sent by Du Bois to Jesse Moorland, one of Howard's trustees; it is in *The Correspondence of W. E. B. Du Bois,* vol. 1, *Selections 1877-1934,* ed. Herbert Aptheker (Amherst: University of Massachusetts Press), 352–53.

19. Details about Mordecai Johnson can be found in Richard I. McKinley, "Mordecai Johnson: An Early Pillar of African-American Higher Education," *Journal of Blacks in Higher Education* 27 (Spring 2000): 99–104.

CHAPTER SIX

1. Langston Hughes, *The Big Sea* (New York: Hill & Wang, 1993), 81; Rudolph Fisher, "City of Refuge," NN, 57–74; Douglas, quoted in Amy Helene Kirschke, *Aaron Douglas: Art, Race, and the Harlem Renaissance* (Jackson: University of Mississippi Press, 1995), 12.

2. "we have concentrated," NN, xxv.

3. For Harlem facts, see James Weldon Johnson, *Black Manhattan* (New York: De Capo Press, 1991); this is a reprint of the original 1930 edition.

4. "During the time" in Arthur P. Davis, "Growing Up in the Harlem Renaissance: 1920–1935," *Negro American Literature Forum* 2, no. 3 (Autumn 1968): 53–59 at 57; the entire article is of interest. A contemporary account of Harlem in general is Arna Bontemps, "The Awakening: A Memoir," in *The Harlem Renaissance Remembered,* ed. Arna Bontemps (New York: Dodd & Mead, 1972), 11–26.

5. Arguments over the starting and concluding dates of the Renaissance are too numerous—and inconclusive—to list completely. See Nathan Irvin Huggins, *Harlem Renaissance* (New York: Oxford University Press, 1971), for a comprehensive and sometimes skeptical view. Remarks on Locke and the "metaphor" of the New Negro are on 55–65. Skepticism also dominates the views in Henry Louis Gates Jr, "The Trope of a New Negro and the Reconstruction of the Image of the Black," *Representations* 24 (Autumn 1988): 129–55. An article that combines an analysis of the renaissance metaphor and some interesting sociological statistics is Gregory Holmes Singleton, "Birth, Rebirth, and the New Negro of the 1920s," *Phylon* 43, no. 1 (1982): 29–45. See "The old Uncle Tom" in *Negro World,* July 16, 1921.

6. The tangle of political issues here is searchingly addressed by Barbara Foley, *Specters of 1919: Class and Nation in the Making of the New Negro* (Urbana and Chicago: University of Illinois Press, 2003).

7. "Internationalism: Friend or Foe?" is in ALPHU 164-116/4-5.

8. A facsimile of the *Survey Graphic* Harlem issue is accessible at http://etext .lib.virginia.edu/harlem/index.html. The original idea of the dinner and its main purpose have occasioned some debate. Nine years after the event (and when relations between Fauset and Locke were strained), Jessie Fauset claimed it was meant to celebrate her novel, *There Is Confusion,* and that it had sprung from a discussion among Fauset's friends associated with Georgia Douglas Johnson's salon in Washington. But Johnson's letter to Locke, which is much closer to the event, makes it clear that the dinner had more than one purpose, namely the much broader goal of creating opportunities by enlisting the services of white publishers and black cultural leaders. See especially Ronald M. Johnson, "Those Who Stayed: Washington Black Writers of the 1920s," *Records of the Columbia Historical Society* 50 (1980): 484–99, and Jeffrey C. Stewart, "Alain Locke and Georgia Douglas Johnson, Washington Patrons of Afro-American Modernism," *Washington Studies* 12 (1986): 37–44.

9. For an account of the history of *Survey Graphic,* see Cara Finnegan, "Social Welfare and Visual Politics: The Story of Survey Graphic," at http://newdeal.feri .org/sg/essay.htm.

10. The changes in the contents between the journal and the book are explored by Barbara Foley, *Specters of 1919,* though her conclusions are different from ours. The details behind the journal and the book versions are also discussed in Richard A. Long, "The Genesis of Locke's *The New Negro,*" *Black World* (February 1976): 14–21.

11. Kellogg's correspondence with Locke is in ALPHU 164-42/30 and, on the matters related to the *Survey Graphic,* 164-88/4-16. These folders contain many of the reviews of the Harlem issue as well as Locke's detailed negotiations with contributors and with Kellogg, many of which are cited herein. In addition to Barbara Foley's detailed discussion of the changes between the journal issue and the book version in her *Specters of 1919,* the account of the politics of the gestation and appearance of *The New Negro* is covered in great detail in George Hutchinson, *The Harlem Renaissance in Black and White* (Cambridge, Mass.: Harvard University Press, 1995), 389 et seq.

12. A good discussion of Reiss's impact, and his background, is in Sieglinde Lemke's *Primitivist Modernism: Black Culture and the Origins of Transatlantic Modernism* (New York: Oxford University Press, 1998). A study of visual culture in the Renaissance is Ann Elizabeth Carroll, *Word, Image, and the New Negro: Representation and Identity in the Harlem Renaissance* (Bloomington: Indiana University Press, 2005).

13. See Amy Helene Kirschke, *Aaron Douglas: Art, Race, and the Harlem Renaissance* (Jackson: University of Mississippi Press, 1995).

14. For more on the background of Fauset's relationship with Du Bois, see David Levering Lewis, *W. E. B. Du Bois: The Fight for Equality and the American Century, 1919–1963* (New York: Henry Holt, 2000), 49–50, 188–90, and passim. Locke's correspondence with Fauset is in ALPHU 164-28/40-1. The earliest item is a postcard dated November 1912, about their having taken a walk together.

15. The correspondence between Locke and McKay is in ALPHU 164-67/8-9 and at the Beinecke, JWJ MSS, Claude McKay Collection, Series I Correspondence, Box 5, Folder 138, "Locke, Alain."

16. For biographical background on McKay, see his autobiography, *A Long Way from Home* (San Diego: Harcourt, Brace, 1970); this is a reprint of the original 1937 edition. Also we have consulted Tyrone Tillery, *Claude McKay: A Black Poet's Struggle for Identity* (Amherst: University of Massachusetts Press, 1992).

17. McKay and Ras Tafari in ALPHU 164-26/7; "a nasty attitude towards The Crisis" in David Levering Lewis, *Du Bois,* 162; "While I have known Mr. Locke" in Du Bois, *Correspondence of W. E. B. Du Bois,* vol. 1, *Selections 1877–1934,* ed. Herbert Aptheker (Amherst: University of Massachusetts Press), 352.

18. At least one person has heard in Locke's language echoes of Hegelian dia-

lectic (Molesworth), while others disagree (Harris), seeing most importantly a broad assimilation of African American self-historicizing and Locke's ethics of self-realization.

19. Du Bois's "Criteria of Negro Art" has been reprinted often; see *The Portable Renaissance Reader*, ed. David Levering Lewis (New York: Viking, 1994), 100–106.

20. "Beauty Instead of Ashes" is in CTAL, 23–6; "Art or Propaganda" is in CTAL, 27–8. Some aspects of Locke's approach to esthetics, and his relationship with Dewey in this regard, are discussed in George Hutchinson, *The Harlem Renaissance in Black and White* (Cambridge, Mass.: Harvard University Press, 1995), 39–50.

CHAPTER SEVEN

1. Details in this and following paragraphs are taken from Charles W. Scruggs, "Alain Locke and Walter White: Their Struggle for Control of the Harlem Renaissance," *Black American Literature Forum* 14, no. 3 (Autumn 1980): 91–99.

2. Barnes is discussed in George Hutchinson, *Harlem Renaissance in Black and White* (Cambridge, Mass.: Harvard University Press, 1995), 44–46 and 425–26, and by William Schack, *Art and Argyrol: The Life and Career of Albert C. Barnes* (New York: T. Yoseloff, 1960).

3. For Locke's work as a critic of the visual arts in the context of twentieth-century American art, see Mary Ann Calo, "Alain Locke and American Art Criticism," *American Art* 18, no. 1 (Spring 2004): 88–95.

4. "Locke argued optatively": Before quoting the passage about the forefathers from Locke's essay, James A. Porter says this about Locke's attitude toward African art: "As a constructive critic, Locke was interested in the sobriety, homogeneity, unique stylism, and disciplined craftsmanship of the African forms. He did not seek to impose these forms directly through imitation or by recourse to the academic whiplash of repetitious recital. I refocus his perfectly calm and reasonable viewpoint by the following quotation from his essay, 'Legacy of the Ancestral Arts.'" In *The New Negro Thirty Years Afterward* (Washington, D.C.: Howard University Press, 1955), 51.

Hutchinson, in *Harlem Renaissance in Black and White*, 425–27, shows clearly how Garry Wills has misread Locke's argument. Others have shared Wills's misreading. Wills (*New York Review of Books* 41, no. 14 [August 11, 1994]: 11) claimed Locke located African American "authenticity" in African culture, and Hutchinson rightly points out that Locke contrasts African and African American culture.

5. Locke's writings on African art are in ALPHU 1105/10-27, and the "statement of purpose" and other papers related to the Harlem Museum are in 164-179/23. The introduction by Locke to the Blondiau-Theatre Arts Collection is in 164-179/27. Also of interest is an article that connects Locke's interest in African anthropol-

ogy with the work of a famous German anthropologist who was instrumental in saving the Benin bronzes: Malgorzata Irek, "From Berlin to Harlem: Felix von Luschan, Alain Locke, and the New Negro," in *Black Columbiad: Defining Moments in African American Literature and Culture,* ed. Werner Sollors and Maria Diedrich (Cambridge, Mass.: Harvard University Press, 1994), 174–84. James B. Barnes, "Alain Locke and the Sense of the African Legacy," in *Alain Locke: Reflections on a Modern Renaissance Man,* ed. Russell J. Linneman (Baton Rouge: Louisiana State University Press, 1982), 100–108, discusses Locke's idea of "ancestry."

6. "The Negro and the American Stage" is in ALPHU 164-26/7. Later this essay would be reprinted in the *Theatre Arts Anthology,* ed. Rosamond Gilder (New York: Theatre Arts Books, 1950).

7. The documents related to Locke's work on the African Mandates are in various places: the memos and correspondence with the Foreign Policy Association are in ALPHU 164-105/16-22; minutes from the Foreign Policy Association are in 179/11; and the typescript of Locke's report is in 116/26. Locke's correspondence with Buell is in 164-18/2. Locke's typescript report is rather detached, though his Howard colleague, Rayford Logan, published a sardonic article on the Mandates, "The Operation of the Mandate System in Africa," *Journal of Negro History* 13, no. 4 (October 1928): 423–77.

Susan Pederson generously made available to us two of her essays, soon to be published, on the Mandates: " 'Sacred Trust of Civilization': A New Look at the Mandates System of the League of Nations" and "Settler Colonialism at the Bar of the League of Nations."

8. A thorough account of the issues raised by Van Vechten's novel is Robert F. Worth, "*Nigger Heaven* and the Harlem Renaissance," *African American Review* 29, no. 3 (Fall 1995): 461–73. This article explores the reactions of Du Bois, Hughes, and others. Du Bois's review of the novel is in *Crisis* 32, no. 7 (December 1926): 81. Many rumors circulated about the reception of this novel, some of them persistently. One claimed Van Vechten was hanged in effigy from a lamppost in Harlem. We have been unable to confirm this.

9. For details about Harlem life at this time, a collection of the correspondence of Van Vechten and Hughes is helpful; see *Remember Me To Harlem: The Letters of Langston Hughes and Carl Van Vechten, 1925–1964,* ed. Emily Bernard (New York: Alfred Knopf, 2001).

10. Details about Van Vechten's life are in Bruce Kellner, *Carl Van Vechten and the Irreverent Decades* (Norman: University of Oklahoma Press, 1968), and Edward Lueders, *Carl Van Vechten and the Twenties* (Albuquerque: University of New Mexico Press, 1955).

11. A readily available edition of the novel is *Infants of the Spring,* intro. E. Lynn Harris, Northeastern Library of Black Literature (Boston: Northeastern University Press, 1992). Thurman is the subject of Granville Gantner, "Decadence, Sexuality

and the Bohemian Vision of Wallace Thurman," *MELUS* (Summer 2003). For an exploration of homosexuality in *Infants of the Spring,* see Michael L. Cobb, "Insolent Racing, Rough Narrative: The Harlem Renaissance's Polite Queers," *Callaloo* 23, no. 1 (2000): 328–51. Cobb sees Locke as the exemplar of a conservative esthetic attitude that does not allow for the representation of queer sexuality. However, he makes the claim in a footnote that "[i]t is interesting to remember that Locke, himself, was most likely [*sic*] queer." A volume of Thurman's work is available as *The Collected Writings of Wallace Thurman: A Harlem Renaissance Reader,* ed. Amritjit Singh and Daniel M. Scott III (New Brunswick, N.J.: Rutgers University Press, 2003).

12. For an extended analysis of coded language as used by various African American writers, mostly poets, in dealing with homosexuality, see A. B. Christa Schwartz, *Gay Voices of the Harlem Renaissance* (Bloomington: University of Indiana Press, 2003).

13. Carrington's correspondence with Locke is in ALPHU 164-19/45 and in the Carrington archive, also at the Moorland-Spingarn Research Center.

14. Hughes's essay, "The Negro Artist and the Racial Mountain," is reprinted in *The Portable Renaissance Reader,* ed. David Levering Lewis (New York: Viking, 1994), 91–95.

15. As early as 1920 Locke drafted a six-page essay called "Georgia Douglas Johnson: An Appreciation," in ALPHU 164-114/23, which dealt with *The Heart of a Woman and Other Poems.* Some of this he reworked for the foreword to *An Autumn Love Cycle,* in 164-114/5.

16. The extensive correspondence with Mason is in ALPHU 164-68/16 to 164-72/1-7. A number of documents related to Mason, such as her death certificate, the signed agreement between her and Hurston, as well as detailed expense accounts, are in 164-199/5-9. There are also Mason's notebooks and correspondence with people other than Locke, in 164-99/2-23 and 164-100/1-9, which contain many contemporaneous observations and drafts of letters. A M.A. thesis submitted to George Washington University by Ardie Sue Myers in 1981 is called "Relations of a Godmother: Patronage during the Harlem Renaissance." R. Osgood Mason's entry in the *National Cyclopedia of American Biography* is in vol. 27. Two studies of patronage in the Renaissance touch on Mason: Bruce Kellner, " 'Refined Racism': White Patronage in the Harlem Renaissance," in *The Harlem Renaissance Re-examined,* ed. Victor Kramer (New York: AMS Press, 1987), 93–106, and Ralph D. Story, "Patronage and the Harlem Renaissance: You Get What You Pay For," *CLA Journal* 32, no. 3 (1988): 284–95.

17. Natalie Curtis's *The Indians' Book: Authentic Native American Legends, Lore & Music,* is available in a reprint (Avenel, N.J.: Gramercy Books, 1994), with a foreword by Robert J. Schwendinger.

18. Hurston's correspondence, with letters to Locke and Mason and others,

has been edited and glossed by Carla Kaplan, *Zora Neale Hurston: A Life in Letters* (New York: Doubleday, 2002). For her biography see Robert Hemenway, *Zora Neale Hurston: A Literary Biography* (Urbana: University of Illinois Press, 1977).

CHAPTER EIGHT

1. An account of the ballet is given in Charles Molesworth, "In Search of *Sahdji: Alain Locke and the Making of an African American Ballet," Berlin Journal* 12 (Spring 2006): 56–59. The festival in Rochester is discussed in *Musical America* 13 (June 1931): 30. The ballet was staged again at the Rochester Festival in 1934 and 1950. Our thanks to David Peter Coppen, Special Collections Librarian and Archivist at the Eastman School, for making programs of these performances available. In Jon Michael Spencer, *The New Negroes and Their Music: The Success of the Harlem Renaissance* (Knoxville: University of Tennessee Press, 1997), 81–83, one can find a full account of the ballet, which came to our attention only after the article above appeared.

2. Nugent's letter and Locke's story of the background of the ballet, as he related it to Van Vechten, are in the Van Vechten archive at the Beinecke Library, Yale University. A selection of Bruce Nugent's writing, with a useful introduction, is *Gay Rebel of the Harlem Renaissance,* ed. Thomas H. Wirth (Durham: Duke University Press, 2002).

3. Van Vechten's interest in the original manuscript was sparked by his preparing his archive for donation to the Beinecke Library at Yale University. Locke, though at this time distant from Van Vechten, wanted the record to be accurate

4. Still's correspondence with Locke—which stretches over two decades—is in ALPHU 164-87/20-21 and at the William Grant Still Foundation, Arkansas. See also, Catherine Parsons Smith, *William Grant Still: A Study in Contradictions* (Berkeley and Los Angeles: University of California Press, 2000).

5. Programs "Cenacle presents Three Negro Plays," Saturday, March 24, 1934, and "Sahdji-An African Dream by Richard Bruce and Directed by Miss Ione Johnson and Mr. Wesley Swanson," The University Archives, Student Organization Publications, Record Series 41/6/840, Box 7, University of Illinois at Urbana-Champaign. *Daily Illini,* Saturday, March 24, 1934.

6. Locke's correspondence with Mary Beattie Brady, which deals with the Harmon Foundation, is in ALPHU 164-15/30-36. For a study of the Harmon Foundation, see Gary A. Reynolds, Beryl J. Wright, and David C. Driskell, *Against the Odds: African-American Artists and the Harmon Foundation* (Newark, N.J.: Newark Museum, 1990). For the visual arts generally, also see *Harlem Renaissance: Art of Black America,* intro. Mary Schmidt Campbell (New York: Abradale Press/ Harry N. Abrams, 1987).

7. In ALPHU 164-106/1; "The American Negro as Artist," *American Magazine of Art* 23 (September 1931): 211–20. Locke would later draw on this for his Bronze Booklet, *Negro Art: Past and Present.*

8. See Rayford Logan, *Howard University: The First Hundred Years* (New York: New York University Press, 1969). Locke's correspondence with Ralph Bunche, who became a close friend, is in ALPHU 164-18/7.

9. The story of the will and Locke's possible legacy is in ALPHU 164-69/5.

10. The story of the *Mule Bone* controversy is told in great detail, using letters from all the parties and accounts from some commentators, in Langston Hughes and Zora Neale Hurston, *Mule Bone: A Comedy of Negro Life,* ed. with intros. George Houston Bass and Henry Louis Gates Jr (New York: Harper, 1991). One of the commentators, after detailing bad faith on the part of all concerned, says: "Only Locke's behavior was almost entirely reprehensible."

11. The story of sailing with Hughes and his Russia-bound party is told in letters Locke wrote to Mason in ALPHU 164-69/17 and 70/1.

12. This letter, the last one extant from Fauset, is in ALPHU 164-28/41.

13. The first autobiographical note—"the strategy of covering up"—is in ALPHU 164-141/3; the "race problem" is in 143/5.

14. All the year-end reviews are reprinted in CTAL.

15. For a full account of Schomburg's life, see Elinor DesVerney Sinnette, *Arthur Alfonso Schomburg: Black Bibliophile & Collector* (Detroit: Wayne State University Press, 1989).

16. A thoughtful account of Locke's work in the field of adult education is Rudolph Alexander Kofi Cain, *Alain Leroy Locke: Race, Culture, and the Education of African American Adults* (Amsterdam and New York: Rodopi, 2003).

17. "The task of adult educationists . . . " quoted in ibid., 40.

CHAPTER NINE

1. "Spiritual Truancy" is reprinted in *Voices from the Harlem Renaissance,* ed. Nathan Irvin Huggins (New York and Oxford: Oxford University Press, 1976), 404–406.

2. Details are taken from Tyrone Tillery, *Claude McKay: A Black Poet's Struggle for Identity* (Amherst: University of Massachusetts Press, 1992).

3. "lunch at the most expensive . . . " This and other details are from Claude McKay, *A Long Way from Home* (1937; rpt. San Diego: Harcourt, Brace., 1970), 313–15.

4. Dorothy West's correspondence with Locke is in ALPHU 164-74/48.

5. Richard Wright's correspondence with Locke is at the Beinecke Library, JWJ MSS, Richard Wright Papers, Series II Correspondence, Box 100, Folder 1452, "Locke, Alain," and in ALPHU 164-96/3.

6. "the elder statesman gave the commencement address": for a full and even-

handed account of the relation between Du Bois and Locke as regards education, see Manning Marable, "Alain Locke, W. E. B. Du Bois and the Crisis of Black Education During the Great Depression," in *Alain Locke: Reflections on a Modern Renaissance Man,* ed. Russell J. Linnemann (Baton Rouge: Louisiana State University Press, 1982), 63–76. For the speech itself, see Du Bois, "Education and Work," in *The Education of Black People,* ed. Herbert Aptheker (Amherst: University of Massachusetts Press, 1973).

7. Some of the details of the Du Bois contribution to the pamphlet series are drawn from Du Bois's letters in *The Correspondence of W. E. B. Du Bois,* ed. Herbert Aptheker (Amherst: University of Massachusetts Press, 1976), 2:77–85. The typescript of "The Negro and Social Reconstruction" is in ALPHU 164-110/3. The entire episode of the rejection of Du Bois's manuscript is recounted in David Levering Lewis, *W. E. B. Du Bois: The Fight for Equality and the American Century, 1919–1963* (New York: Henry Holt, 2000), 423–26. Lewis characteristically paints Locke in negative terms. Besides mentioning Du Bois's mistrust of Locke's intellectual integrity, Lewis refers to Locke's actions as "wheedling" and says Locke "dithered and demurred until Du Bois sailed" for Europe, to avoid rejecting the manuscript while the senior leader was still in the country.

Two other articles investigate the relations between Du Bois and Locke on different issues: M. Anthony Fitchue, "Locke and Du Bois: Two Major Black Voices Muzzled by Philanthropic Organizations," *Journal of Blacks in Higher Education* 14 (Winter 1996–97): 111–16, and Tommy Lott, "Du Bois and Locke on the Scientific Study of the Negro," *Boundary 2* 27, no. 3 (2000): 135–52. Locke's typescript of "The Negro Vote and the New Deal" is in ALPHU 164-120/27. It is also available at http://www.huarchivesnet.howard.edu/9911huarnet/locke1.htm.

8. "How the logic of justice works!" Locke's letter to Mason, ALPHU 164-71/9.

9. Smith's correspondence with Locke is in ALPHU 164-86/15.

10. Documents related to "Harlem: Dark Weather Vane" are in ALPHU 164-114/31-36.

11. Documents related to the two booklets are in ALPHU 164-108/3-17 and 109/1-3 (Music), and 164-109/4-11 (Art). Russell J. Linnemann, "Alain Locke's Theory of the Origins and Nature of Jazz," in *Alain Locke: Reflections on a Modern Renaissance Man,* ed. Linnemann, 109–21, discusses the arguments in *The Negro and His Music.*

12. For a study of music during the Renaissance, see Jon Michael Spencer, *The New Negroes and Their Music: The Success of the Harlem Renaissance* (Knoxville: University of Tennessee Press, 1997), which argues that the centrality of music to the Renaissance accounts for the "success" of the movement. See also the collection of essays edited by Samuel A. Floyd Jr, *Black Music in the Harlem Renaissance* (Knoxville: University of Tennessee Press, 1993). A full and important study is available in Paul Allen Anderson, *Deep River: Music and Memory in Harlem Renaissance Thought* (Durham, N.C.: Duke University Press, 2001).

13. It is worth recalling a passage in J. A. Rogers's essay on jazz from *The New Negro:* "Musically jazz has a great future. It is rapidly being sublimated. In the more famous jazz orchestras like those of Will Marion Cook, Paul Whiteman, Sissle and Blake, Sam Stewart, Fletcher Henderson, Vincent Lopez and the Clef Club units, there are none of the vulgarities and crudities of the lowly origin or the only too prevalent cheap imitations. The pioneer work in the artistic development of jazz was done by Negro artists; it was the lead of the so-called 'syncopated orchestras' of Tyers and Will Marion Cook, the former playing for the Castles of dancing fame, and the latter touring as a concertizing orchestra in the great American centers and abroad. Because of the difficulties of financial backing, these expert combinations have had to yield ground to white orchestras of the type of the Paul Whiteman and Vincent Lopez, organizations that are now demonstrating the finer possibilities of jazz music." Locke thought of Cook as one of the originators of the jazz orchestra. Unfortunately, his place in the standard histories of jazz is clouded.

14. Arthur Fauset, who was Jessie's stepbrother, had a voluminous correspondence with Locke, much of it taken up with real estate details. See ALPHU 164-28/27-38. Biographical information is available at http://www.mnsu.edu/ emuseum/information/biography/fghij/fauset_arthur.html. His book is *Black Gods of the Metropolis: Negro Religious Cults in the Urban North* (Philadelphia: University of Pennsylvania Press, 1971).

15. The details here are drawn from an article by Wayne D. Shirley, "William Grant Still's choral ballad 'And They Lynched Him on a Tree,'" *American Music* 12, no. 14 (Winter 1944): 425-61.

16. The two typescripts on Freud are in ALPHU 164-114/14, 15.

CHAPTER TEN

1. C. B. Macpherson, *Democratic Theory: Essays in Retrieval* (Oxford, 1973), 4.

2. The archives of the Joseph and Miriam Ratner Center for the Study of Conservative Judaism at the Jewish Theological Seminary hold the records of the Conference on Science, Philosophy, and Religion. A brief history of the conference is available at http://www.jtsa.edu/x4754.xml.

3. The text of Mortimer Adler's "God and the Professors" is available at http:// www.ditext.com/adler/gp.html. A perceptive account of this debate can be found in David Hollinger, *Science, Jews, and Secular Culture* (Princeton: Princeton University Press, 1996), specifically chap. 5, "The Defense of Democracy and Robert K. Merton's Formulation of the Scientific Ethos," 80-96.

4. The selection from Myrdal is taken from *The American Intellectual Tradition,* vol. 2, *1865 to the Present,* ed. David Hollinger and Charles Capper (New York: Oxford University Press, 2001), 256-57.

5. The Douglass material is in ALPHU 164-114/11-12.

6. The materials related to *When Peoples Meet* are in ALPHU 164-129/10-27, 130/1-14, and 131/1-8. Citations are taken from the 1946 edition.

7. The materials related to "Color" are in ALPHU 164-110/16-36 and 111/1-12.

8. The typescripts for "Democracy Faces a World Order" are in ALPHU 164-113/5-6. The printed version is in *Harvard Educational Review* 12, no. 2 (March 1942): 121–28. With something like supreme irony, Locke's address figured into part of a racial protest. The preceding December the Ohio State chapter of PDK had inducted a Chinese and a Negro as members, and the national organization threatened the chapter with expulsion unless it honored the "whites only" clause of the fraternity's constitution, which the Ohio State chapter refused to do. The Harvard chapter of Phi Delta Kappa had therefore deliberately invited Locke in order to protest against the national fraternity and make clear Harvard's opposition to racial prejudice. This involved more than college politics. Members of PDK at Harvard told reporters that the fraternity was "sufficiently influential in some parts of the country to control professional appointments, and in many cases it is impossible for non-members of the society to acquire teaching positions." See *Harvard Crimson,* February 11, 1942.

9. The materials related to the trip to Haiti are in ALPHU 164-126/24 and in 164-126/4-30; these include the typescripts in English and in French, as well as a printed copy of "The Negro in the Three Americas" from the *Journal of Negro Education* 13 (Winter 1944): 7–18.

10. The correspondence with Arthur Wright is in ALPHU 164-95/10-23.

11. The correspondence with Maurice Victor Russell is in ALPHU 164-82/23 and 163-83/1-2.

12. A typescript of a summary of the talk is in ALPHU 164-125/15, and the printed version of its appearance in *Town Hall* 6 (August 7, 1944) is in 164-125/16. "A Philosophy of Human Brotherhood" does not survive, at least with that title.

CHAPTER ELEVEN

1. The correspondence between Kallen and Locke is in the American Jewish Archives in Cincinnati, Ohio, Box 19, folder 2, and ALPHU 164-42/15.

2. The three essays are in PAL.

3. The biography of Dodson is James V. Hatch, *Sorrow Is the Only Faithful One: The Life of Owen Dodson* (Urbana: University of Illinois Press, 1995). Prof. Hatch generously shared with us his transcript of his interview with Dodson. Dodson also supplied Hatch with a memoir that, among other things, described Locke as "a dandy little man, light taffy colored skin, small bones, large searchlight eyes—grey hat over his hair—grey." Dodson's account received added circulation when Hilton Als, theater critic for the *New Yorker,* wrote about it in his memoir, *The Women* (New York: Farrar, Straus and Giroux, 1996).

4. The correspondence with Jimmy Daniels is in ALPHU 164-23/13-15.

5. For the background on Kenneth Clark and his path-breaking study, see Richard Kluger, *Simple Justice: The History of Brown v. Board of Education and Black America's Struggle for Equality* (New York: Vintage, 2004), 318, passim.

6. The versions are as follows: "The Negro's Contribution to American Art and Literature," *Annals of the American Academy of Political and Social Science* 140 (November 1928): 234-47; "The Negro in American Culture," in *Anthology of American Literature*, ed. Sylvestre C. Watkins (New York: Modern Library, 1944), 155-73 (this is a reprint of an article that first appeared in *Carolina Magazine*); and "The Negro in American Literature," in *New World Writing* (New York: New American Library, 1952), 18-33.

7. The acceptance speech is in ALPHU 164-2/16.

8. Du Bois's remarkable tribute is in *Phylon* 15 no. 3 (1954), along with the comments by Ralph Bunche, and others by Y. H. Krikorian, William Stuart Nelson, William Stanley Braithwaite, and Benjamin Karpman. Any final accounting of the complex relationship between Du Bois and Locke should take this eulogy into account.

CHAPTER TWELVE

1. Sarah Schmidt, "A Conversation with Horace M. Kallen," *Reconstructionist* 41, no. 8 (Nov. 1975): 28-33.

2. Some of the more pertinent examinations of Locke's philosophy include the following. Chielozona Eze, *Dilemma of Ethnic Identity: Alain Locke's Vision of Transcultural Society* (New York: Mellen Press, 2005) considers Locke's views of cosmopolitanism as a form of transculturalism. Richard Shusterman, *Surface & Depth: Dialectics of Criticism and Culture* (Ithaca: Cornell University Press, 2003) includes his interpretation of Locke's pragmatist esthetics and race. Talmadge C. Guy, "Alain Locke and the AAAE Movement: Cultural Pluralism and Negro Adult Education," *Adult Education Quarterly* 46, no. 4 (Summer 1996): 209-23 and Rudolph A. K. Cain, *Alain LeRoy Locke: Race, Culture, and the Education of African American Adults* (New York: Rodopi, 2003), offer considerations of Locke's role in shaping adult education in relationship to his pluralism. Jane Duran, *Worlds of Knowing* (New York: Routledge 2001), explores the esthetic assumptions and principles that make for a defensible epistemology and esthetic sensibility in Locke's approach to culture. Judith M. Green, *Deep Democracy: Community, Diversity, and Transformation* (New York: Rowman & Littlefield, 1999), offers an account of Locke's theorizing of democracy. Tommy L. Lott is notable for exploring the differences between Locke and Du Bois, in "Du Bois and Locke on the Scientific Study of Race," *Boundary* 2 27, no. 3 (Fall 2000): 135-52, and on the same subject, see Leonard Harris, "The Great Debate: Alain L. Locke vs. W. E. B. Du Bois," *Philosophia Africana* 7, no. 1 (March 2004): 13-37. Two earlier studies of

Locke's axiology are by Ernest D. Mason, "Alain Locke's Philosophy of Value," in *Alain Locke,* ed. Russell J. Linnemann (Baton Rouge: Louisiana State University Press, 1982), 1–16, and "Deconstruction in the Philosophy of Alain Locke," *Transactions of the Charles S. Pierce Society* 34, no 1 (1988): 86–105. The Linnemann volume has several useful essays on various aspects of Locke's work and thought. More recent studies are Terrance MacMullan, "Challenges to Cultural Diversity: Absolutism, Democracy, and Alain Locke's Value Relativism," *Journal of Speculative Philosophy* 19, no. 2 (2005): 129–39 and Jacquelyn Ann Kegley, "Is a Coherent Racial Identity Essential to Genuine Individuals and Communities? Josiah Royce on Race," *Journal of Speculative Philosophy* 19, no. 3 (2005): 216–28.

3. Beth J. Singer, Professor Emerita, Brooklyn College, interviewed by Leonard Harris, Oct. 17, 1997 at the conference "Philosophy Born of Struggle IV," New School for Social Research, New York. Singer was a student of Locke in Philosophy 53, Philosophy of Art, University of Wisconsin; see her "Alain Locke Remembered," in *The Critical Pragmatism of Alain Locke,* ed. Leonard Harris (Lanham, Md.: Rowman and Littlefield, Inc., 1999), 327–33. Within this remembrance, especially see the interview of Locke on democracy by Cedric Parker for the *Madison Capital Times,* January 26, 1946.

4. "And finally, I remember": William T. Hastings, "A Memory of Alain Locke," in *The New Negro Thirty Years Afterward* (Washington, D.C.: Howard University Press, 1955), 13–16.

5. "The Negro's Contribution to the Culture of the Americas," Inaugural Lecture: "The Negro in the Three Americas," first in *A Series of Public Lectures given under the auspices of the Haitian Ministry of Public Instruction,* delivered when Locke was an Exchange-Professor for the Committee for Inter-American Artistic and Intellectual Relations, 1944, p. 10. The materials related to the trip to Haiti are in ALPHU 164-126/24 and in 164-126/4-30.

6. The book that coined the term "Black Atlantic" is Paul Gilroy, *The Black Atlantic: Modernity and Double Consciousness* (Cambridge, Mass.: Harvard University Press, 1993). Gilroy does not mention Locke's efforts to treat of the cultural ramifications of the diaspora.

7. The proceedings of the United Nationalities Roundtables at Sarah Lawrence College were recorded, and the transcriptions of the Saturday, April 18 and Sunday, May 31, 1942 sessions are in the Sarah Lawrence College Archives, Bronxville, New York. Also see "United Nations Start on Main Street," *Sarah Lawrence Alumnae Magazine,* October 1942; "Speaker Emphasizes Straight Thinking Straight Attitudes: Prejudice Hinders War Effort," *Campus,* June 4, 1942; "Airing of Discrimination in the U.S. Only Way Toward United War Effort, United Nationalities Forum Agrees," *Campus,* April 22, 1942.

8. "How surprised they will be . . . ": Louise Boyle, undated letter (late 1925) to Mrs. El Fleda Spaulding, Chairman, Teaching Committee, Office of the Secretary

Records, National Teaching Committee Files, National Bahá'í Archives, Wilmette, Illinois.

9. Beinecke Library, Yale University, Van Vechten papers, C-CT 1942-64. Locke's note to Van Vechten on the front flyleaf of *Plays of Negro Life*, dated July 29, 1941.

10. Locke and Sterling A. Brown, "Folk Values in a New Medium," in *Folk-Say: A Regional Miscellany*, ed. B. A. Botkin (Norman: University of Oklahoma Press, 1930), 340–45.

11. "clownish leer and the minstrel's self-pity" in Locke and Sterling A. Brown, "Folk Values in a New Medium," in Botkin, *Folk-Say*, 341. Also see Locke, "Sterling Brown: The New Negro Folk Poet," *Negro Anthology*, ed. Nancy Cunard (1934; New York: Ungar, 1970), 88–92, and John Edgar Tidwell, "'Steady and Unaccusing': An Interview with Sterling A. Brown," *Callaloo* 21, no. 4 (Fall 1998): 811–21, for Brown's critical view of Locke's role in promoting folk art.

12. "There is a great chance," ALPHU 164-84/36; "Native Paper," 164-84/36; "distressing news," 164-84/38.

13. *The Democrat*, November 17, 1945, 19–24; December 1, 1945, 21–24. Dhlomo, "Because I'm black" *Ilanga Lase Natal*, January 22, 1949. The relationship of Dhlomo to Locke is explored in Tim Couzens, *The New African: A Study of the Life and Work of H. I. E. Dhlomo* (Johannesburg: Ravan Press, 1985); see also Loren Kruger, "Placing 'New Africans' in the 'Old' South Africa: Drama, Modernity, and Racial Identities in Johannesburg, circa 1935," *Modernism/Modernity* 1, no. 2 (1994): 113–31.

14. Peter Abrahams, *Tell Freedom* (New York: Alfred A. Knopf, 1954), 194. Locke wrote a dedication on the front pages of *The New Negro* to Professor R. F. Alfred Hoernlé of South Africa; the book is held by Wartenweiler Library, University of Witwatersrand, South Africa; see Couzens, *New African*, 123. Hoernlé was an assistant professor in the philosophy department at Harvard.

15. "apolitical," Henry Louis Gates Jr., "The Trope of a New Negro and the Reconstruction of the Image of the Black," *Representations* 24 (Autumn 1988): 129–55; "our younger generation," "Preface," *A Decade of Negro Self Expression: Occasional Paper*, no. 26, Charlottesville, Va.: Trustees of the John F. Slater Fund, 1928, 7–8.

16. "The Colonial Literature of France," *Opportunity* 1 (November 1923): 331; "Internationalism: Friend or Foe of Art?" *The World Tomorrow*, March 1925: 75–76; "one of the highest" René Maran, "Le Professeur Alain LeRoy Locke," *Présence africaine*, no. 6 (1st trimester 1949): 135–38. Also see an early account of the influence of African Americans on African and Caribbean authors: Léon-Gontran Damas, "Nouvelle somme de poésie; présentation afro-americaine," *Présence africaine*, no. 57 (December 15, 1965): 353–56, and Thomas A. Hale, "From Afro-America to Afro-France: The Literary Triangle Trade," *French Review* 49, no. 6, (Bicentennial issue: "Historical and Literary Relations between France and the United States"; May 1976): 1089–96.

17. Contributions to the symposium were published as a special issue of the *Harvard Advocate* 107, no. 4 (1973). A committee to preserve the legacy of Locke was founded by William Stanley Braithwaite as a result of the symposium, and there were plans for a biography, but they did not come to fruition. Documents related to this—including a letter by Braithwaite to Ralph Barton Perry—are in the Schomburg Center for Research in Black Culture. See also Eugene C. Holmes, "The Legacy of Alain Locke," *Freedomways,* Summer 1963, 293–306.

INDEX

The abbreviation AL is used throughout the index for Alain L. Locke. References to the anthology The New Negro (1925) are abbreviated as NN. Italicized page numbers indicate photographs.